Rise & Dine

Savory Secrets from
America's Bed & Breakfast Inns

MARCY CLAMAN

Callawind
Publications Inc.

MONTREAL, CANADA

Rise & Dine: Savory Secrets from America's Bed & Breakfast Inns

Copyright © 1995, 1996, by Callawind Publications Inc.

Cataloguing in Publication Data

Claman, Marcy, 1963–
    Rise & dine : savory secrets from America's bed & breakfast inns

ISBN 1-896511-05-8

    1. Cookery.   2. Bed and breakfast accommodations—United States—Directories.
I. Title.   II. Title: Rise and dine.

TX715.C53 1995   641.5   C95-900431-9

Cover illustration and design by Shari Blaukopf
Book design by Marcy Claman

10 9 8 7 6 5 4 3 2 1

Printed in Canada

Callawind Publications Inc.
    3383 Sources Boulevard, Suite 205, Dollard-des-Ormeaux, Quebec, Canada H9B 1Z8
    2083 Hempstead Turnpike, Suite 355, East Meadow, New York, USA 11554-1730
    E-mail: callawind@accent.net

This book is dedicated to my parents
(after all — you made me!).

$\mathcal{A}$cknowledgments

A *heartfelt thank you goes out to all the bed & breakfast inns described in this book for allowing me to publish their recipes, and especially for their encouragement and unfailing interest throughout the project.*

Thank you to Tracy Fairchild for all her wise editorial guidance, epicurean knowledge, and inspiring enthusiasm.

Many thanks to Shari Blaukopf for designing and illustrating the cover of my dreams and providing artistic guidance.

My family and friends have been a constant source of inspiration from the beginning and I thank them for giving me the feedback I needed to make this book the best it could be.

To Lenny, all I can say is you're the best breakfast partner a girl could ever hope for.

Contents

Introduction

I've always loved breakfast, and I believe there's no better way to enjoy it than at a charming and intimate bed & breakfast inn (or B&B, for short). Whether you're sitting down to a multi-course, candle-lit breakfast on antique china, or enjoying a continental breakfast on a sunny porch or in front of a roaring fire, the combination of home-made food, warm ambience, hospitable innkeepers, and the company of other guests is sure to add an unforgettable chapter to your travels.

The purpose of this cookbook is to bring those savory B&B recipes for breakfast, brunch, and teatime to your kitchen. What's more, since innkeepers don't have much time to fuss, you'll find the recipes easy to prepare yet mouth-wateringly delicious!

If this book whets your appetite for exploring America's bed & breakfasts, use it to guide you in your travels. Beside each recipe is a description of the contributing B&B, along with innkeeper name(s), address, telephone number, season of operation, and accommodations.

Here's to many memorable breakfasts and adventures!

Measurement Equivalents

Margarine/butter:

¼ stick = ⅛ cup
½ stick = ¼ cup
1 stick = ½ cup
2 sticks = 1 cup
3 sticks = 1½ cups
4 sticks = 2 cups

Miscellaneous:

3 tsps. = 1 tbsp.
4 tbsps. = ¼ cup
5⅓ tbsps. = ⅓ cup
1 cup = ½ pint
2 cups = 1 pint
4 cups = 1 quart
2 pints = 1 quart
4 quarts = 1 gallon

Liquid (fluid) ounces versus weight ounces:

1 liquid oz. = 2 tbsps. or ⅛ cup
2 liquid ozs. = 4 tbsps. or ¼ cup
3 liquid ozs. = 6 tbsps.
4 liquid ozs. = 8 tbsps. or ½ cup
5 liquid ozs. = 10 tbsps.
6 liquid ozs. = 12 tbsps. or ¾ cup
7 liquid ozs. = 14 tbsps.
8 liquid ozs. = 16 tbsps. or 1 cup

Index of Inns

Beverages
Cereals

Bircher Muesli

"In 1895, Swiss physician Dr. Bircher-Benner concocted this combination of fruit and cereal and, to demonstrate its nutritional value, fed it to children with rickets three times a day. Our own data confirms its value, because we haven't had a single case of rickets break out amongst our guests since we've been serving it!" — Suzanne Huston

1 cup whole oats
⅓ cup golden raisins
Milk
1 cored and grated apple
Juice of ½ lemon
Chopped fruit of the season
2 large spoonfuls whipped cream or vanilla yogurt
⅛ cup toasted almonds

Soak oats and raisins overnight in just enough milk to cover them. In the morning, add the grated apple, lemon juice, and fruit of the season. Fold in the whipped cream or vanilla yogurt and top with toasted almonds. *Serves 4.*

Thornrose House at Gypsy Hill

Suzanne and Otis Huston
531 Thornrose Avenue
Staunton, Virginia 24401
Tel: (800) 861-4338 or
(703) 885-7026

ABOUT THE B&B

Thornrose House is a turn-of-the-century Georgian Revival with a wraparound veranda and nearly one acre of gardens with Greek colonnades. It is adjacent to the 300-acre Gypsy Hill Park with facilities for tennis, golf, swimming, and summer band concerts. Breakfast begins with the house specialty of Bircher muesli, a Swiss concoction of oats, fruit, nuts, and whipped cream. This is followed by an ever changing menu of hot entrées and fresh baked muffins and breads. Fireplaces in the sitting room and dining room warm you on chilly mornings and winter evenings, while a baby grand piano invites you to share your musical talents. Thornrose House is conveniently located in the heart of the Shenandoah Valley, which offers hiking, biking, antique hunting, historical museums, summer theater, and numerous fine restaurants.

SEASON

all year

ACCOMMODATIONS

five rooms with private baths

The Blushing Rosé B&B

Ellen and Bucky Laufersweiler
11 William Street
Hammondsport, New York
14840
Tel: (607) 569-3402

ABOUT THE B&B

In the heart of the wine country, The Blushing Rosé has served as a pleasant hideaway for honeymooners, anniversary couples, and romantic trysters alike. Whether you spend your day driving, hiking, biking, or just plain relaxing, The Blushing Rosé is the ideal haven in which to end your day. Arise to the wonderful aroma of fresh baked granola and whole grain bread, and begin your day with a special breakfast. The inn itself has an ambience of warm, cozy, 19th-century America. There are four spacious guest rooms each with a sitting area and private bath. Air conditioning and ceiling fans are among some of the amenities offered. Located on the southern tip of Keuka Lake, one of New York's famous Finger Lakes.

SEASON

March through November

ACCOMMODATIONS

four rooms with private baths

Breakfast Granola

4 cups old-fashioned oatmeal
1 cup powdered non-fat milk
1 cup wheat germ
½ cup chopped almonds or peanuts
1 tablespoon ground cinnamon
1¼ cups packed brown sugar
¼ cup warm water
¾ cup vegetable oil
2 teaspoons vanilla
½ cup raisins

Preheat oven to 200°F. Combine first 5 ingredients. In a separate bowl, mix sugar, water, oil, and vanilla together. Combine with oat mixture and mix well. Bake on a large cookie sheet, stirring every ½ hour or until dry (about 2 hours). Cool and mix in raisins if you like — or leave plain. *Tips:* There are 281 calories per ½ cup serving. Store in a tight container. *Makes 8 cups.*

Cape Colada

Pulp of 1 pineapple
5 ozs. coconut cream
1 small ripe banana
6 ice cubes

Purée all ingredients in a blender. Pour into a wine glass and garnish with a few halved cranberries. *Tips:* You can buy coconut cream at a liquor store. This drink is nice with a French toast breakfast. *Serves 6.*

Captain Ezra Nye House
Sandwich, MA

Captain Ezra Nye House

Elaine and Harry Dickson
152 Main Street
Sandwich, Massachusetts 02563
Tel: (800) 388-CAPT
in US or Canada,
or (508) 888-6142

ABOUT THE B&B

A sense of history and romance fills this 1829 Federal home, built by the distinguished sea captain, Ezra Nye. Located in the heart of historical Sandwich Village, Captain Ezra Nye House is within walking distance of Sandwich Glass and Doll museums, Thornton Burgess Museum, Shawme Lake, fine dining, and antique shops. Heritage Plantation, the marina, an auction house, as well as Cape Cod Bay and Canal are nearby. Activities also include whale watching or a day at the beach. The inn was chosen one of the top 50 inns in America, one of the five best on the Cape, and was Cape Cod Life magazine's readers' choice as best bed and breakfast on the upper Cape. It has been featured in Glamour, Toronto Life, and Innsider magazines. A full breakfast is served each morning, and specialties include walnut goat cheese soufflé, peach kuchen, or baked French toast. Harry's interests include golfing and collecting Chinese export porcelain, while Elaine is an avid cyclist and enjoys yoga.

SEASON

all year

ACCOMMODATIONS

seven rooms with private baths

Natural
Bed & Breakfast

L. Marc Haberman
3150 East Presidio Road
Tucson, Arizona 85716
Tel: (520) 881-4582

ABOUT THE B&B

*A*s much a private spa as a B&B, the Natural B&B offers visitors natural, whole foods served in a non-toxic, non-allergenic environment, professional therapeutic massages, and health consultation services. Wake to a full vegetarian breakfast and spend your day horseback riding in the beautiful Tucson desert or visiting the Sonora museum (only 10 miles away). You can opt for a swim in the nearby pool or relax on the patio or your own private sun deck. In-room telephones and laundry service are other amenities. Your host invites you to share his large, homey living room with a fireplace, and enjoy a complimentary cocktail, tea, or juice. If arriving from the airport, your host can arrange for your pick-up or you can hop on an airport shuttle bus. In addition to English, other languages spoken are Greek, Spanish, and German. (Please be advised that nudity is permitted.)

SEASON

open all year
(season January to April)

ACCOMMODATIONS

one room with private bath;
two rooms with shared bath

Granola Supreme

14 cups rolled oats (not quick)
¾ cup raw sunflower seeds
3 cups raw chopped or roasted nuts
4 cups fresh wheat germ (not toasted)
3 cups grated fresh coconut
¾ cup sesame seeds
2 cups brown sugar
1½ cups cold water
1 tablespoon vanilla
1½ cups vegetable oil
1½ teaspoons salt

Preheat oven to 275°F. Mix first 7 ingredients. In a separate bowl, mix remaining ingredients. Combine both mixtures, stirring thoroughly. Add more water if necessary. Bake 45 – 60 minutes, stirring as needed. Don't brown too much. Serve with yogurt, milk, or soy milk. *Makes 20 – 25 servings.*

Hearty Granola

"This recipe was given to me by the wife of one of the original Jordannaires singers (who later started the Foggy River Boy of Branson, Missouri)." — Pat Cameron

½ cup oleo (or margarine or butter)
1 cup brown sugar
2 tablespoons water
4½ cups old-fashioned rolled oats
1 cup sunflower seeds (unsalted)
1 cup nuts (pecans, walnuts, almonds, or mixture of these)
1 cup whole wheat flour or graham flour
1 teaspoon ground cinnamon
1 cup raisins
1 cup flaked unsweetened coconut

Preheat oven to 350°F. Melt first 3 ingredients together in a 13 x 9" pan. Stir in remaining ingredients and bake for 45 minutes, stirring every 10 minutes. After you remove from the oven, add raisins and flaked coconut, if wished. Serve with fresh bananas and milk. *Serves 15 – 20.*

Freeman House

Pat and Bob Cameron
1825 Lakeshore Drive
Branson, Missouri 65616
Tel: (800) 727-0723 or
(417) 334-8564

ABOUT THE B&B

A quiet, little resort town nestled in the beautiful Ozark mountains, Branson is home to a variety of music shows and to three of the finest fishing lakes in the country. It is also home to Freeman House, situated in a park-like setting along Lake Taneycomo (renowned nationwide for some of the finest trout fishing anywhere). This B&B offers fishermen all the amenities you could want: Cast your line by the nearby dock or by boat, catch up to five trout, bring your bounty home, warm up in the spa after your brisk morning on the lake, then sit down to a fresh trout breakfast. Or, if you prefer, you can cook your own catch on the lakefront grill. For the non-fishermen, you can enjoy a relaxing day in one of Freeman House's three distinctive guest rooms or around the pool, or browse through the quaint shops in Branson. In the evening, you can treat your ears to one of the many music shows in town — just minutes away.

SEASON

all year

ACCOMMODATIONS

three rooms (including two suites) with private baths

Natural
Bed & Breakfast

L. Marc Haberman
3150 East Presidio Road
Tucson, Arizona 85716
Tel: (520) 881-4582

ABOUT THE B&B

*A*s much a private spa as a B&B, the Natural B&B offers visitors natural, whole foods served in a non-toxic, non-allergenic environment, professional therapeutic massages, and health consultation services. Wake to a full vegetarian breakfast and spend your day horseback riding in the beautiful Tucson desert or visiting the Sonora museum (only 10 miles away). You can opt for a swim in the nearby pool or relax on the patio or your own private sun deck. In-room telephones and laundry service are other amenities. Your host invites you to share his large, homey living room with a fireplace, and enjoy a complimentary cocktail, tea, or juice. If arriving from the airport, your host can arrange for your pick-up or you can hop on an airport shuttle bus. In addition to English, other languages spoken are Greek, Spanish, and German. (Please be advised that nudity is permitted.)

SEASON

open all year
(season January to April)

ACCOMMODATIONS

one room with private bath;
two rooms with shared bath

Hot Carob Cereal Drink

⅓ cup non-fat powdered milk
1 cup granola cereal
1 tablespoon carob powder
¼ teaspoon vanilla or 1 teaspoon instant coffee
1 cup hot water
1 tablespoon honey or sugar to taste
Whipped cream (optional)
Granola (optional)

In a blender, combine powdered milk, cereal, carob powder, and vanilla or coffee. Add hot water and honey, and blend until liquefied. Pour into cups. Top with whipped cream sprinkled with granola, if desired. *Serves 2.*

Instant Spiced Tea

(Recipe from Favorites from the Lazy Bee.)

"We like this spiced tea when the winds are whistling outside and we've just come in from cross-country skiing. This is a 'good ole' Iowa recipe from a state where folks really know what cold weather is all about!" — Jo Ann Bender

1½ cups lemon-flavored tea, artificially sweetened
18-oz. jar Tang beverage
1 teaspoon ground cinnamon
½ teaspoon ground cloves
¼ teaspoon ground ginger

Mix ingredients and store in an airtight container. Put 1 – 2 teaspoons of this mix in a mug and add boiling water. *Serves 24.*

Hillside House Bed & Breakfast

Jo Ann, Bud, and Sue
1729 East 18th Street
Spokane, Washington 99203
Tel: (509) 534-1426 during the day or (509) 535-1893 during nights and weekends

ABOUT THE B&B

*S*ituated on the South Hill of Spokane, Hillside House offers exquisite hospitality in a country setting that's only three miles from downtown. Overlooking city and mountains, this cozy and tastefully decorated house features antiques, including linens and dishes, and rooms with views. Your hosts Bud, Jo Ann, and Sue are third generation B&B innkeepers — Jo Ann's mother helped her mother host guests in 1916 in Rush City, Minnesota. Bud owns an engineering firm and lectures nationally to the construction/ engineering industry, while Jo Ann operates a marketing firm. They enjoy cooking (having published a cookbook of their own), entertaining, and guiding guests to the area's most exciting places and events. Bud and Jo Ann also operate the Lazy Bee, a remote getaway near the Canadian border where they lead jeep safaris in the mountains.

SEASON

all year

ACCOMMODATIONS

two rooms with shared bath

Down the Shore B&B

Annette and Al Bergins
201 Seventh Avenue
Belmar, New Jersey 07719
Tel: (908) 681-9023

ABOUT THE B&B

Down the Shore Bed & Breakfast is unique. The house was built specifically to be used as a residence and as a bed and breakfast. There are two guest rooms with a shared guest parlor and a shaded 40-foot front porch. Down the Shore Bed & Breakfast is located one block from the beach and boardwalk. The house may be new but the proprietors are not new to innkeeping. Before moving to Belmar, they operated another bed and breakfast in their lakeside home in Denville, New Jersey. As you can see from this recipe, healthful food is the mainstay of the breakfasts here.

SEASON

summer

ACCOMMODATIONS

two rooms with private baths

Many-Grain Hot Cereal

Note: Some of the ingredients are available in regular supermarkets, while the rest are available in many health food stores.

Cereal mix (prepared in bulk):
22-oz. box Cream of Rye
½ box Wheatena cereal
1 cup wheat germ
18-oz. carton rolled oats
16-oz. box Quick and Creamy Brown Rice
14-oz. box Maypo
24-oz. box Cream of the West

For single serving (*serves 1*):
⅓ cup cereal mix (recipe above)
1 cup water
Raisins, chopped walnuts, or chopped apples (optional)
Brown sugar

Combine cereal ingredients and keep a small amount in the pantry and the balance in the freezer. To cook: Heat batter ingredients to boiling (optionally adding raisins, chopped walnuts, or chopped apples beforehand). Cook 5 minutes, then sprinkle with a small amount of brown sugar before serving.

Orange-Banana Smoothie

The Parsonage Inn
Elizabeth and Ian Browne
202 Main Street, PO Box 1501
East Orleans, Massachusetts
02643
Tel: (508) 255-8217

"This is a great, healthy breakfast beverage that's high in potassium and vitamin C and whips up like a rich and frothy milkshake." — Elizabeth Browne

1 cup orange juice
½ sliced banana
Orange slice
Mint leaf

In a blender, whip orange juice and banana. Serve in a tall glass, garnished with an orange slice and mint leaf. *Tip:* This drink tastes best when made to order. *Serves 1.*

ABOUT THE B&B

Dating back to around 1770, The Parsonage Inn was a vicarage in the 1880s and is now a romantic inn. Despite having been remodeled over the years, the house still retains the feeling of historic old Cape Cod. Each of the eight guest rooms (with its own private bath) is uniquely decorated with country antiques, quilts, stenciling, and fresh flowers. A delicious breakfast of waffles, French toast, crepes, scones, muffins, and fresh fruit is served in the dining room or on the brick patio (a popular gathering place for guests). The Parsonage Inn is conveniently located close to Cape Cod's main attractions — Nauset Beach, the National Seashore, and the many bike paths that crisscross the Cape — and is within walking distance of fine restaurants and antique stores. Both born in England, Elizabeth was raised in Kenya and is a pianist and piano teacher, while Ian is an accountant and former medical group executive.

SEASON

all year

ACCOMMODATIONS

eight rooms with private baths

Turtleback Farm Inn

Susan and William Fletcher
Route 1, Box 650
Eastsound, Orcas Island,
Washington 98245
Tel: (206) 376-4914

ABOUT THE B&B

Located on the loveliest of the San Juan Islands, Turtleback Farm Inn is noted for its detail-perfect restoration, elegantly comfortable and spotless rooms, glorious setting, and award-winning breakfasts. A perfect spot for a memorable getaway, you'll feel welcome and pampered by the warm hospitality of Susan and Bill Fletcher and their staff. A short ferry ride from Anacortes, Washington, Orcas Island is a haven for anyone who covets spectacular scenery, varied outdoor activities, unique shopping, and superb food. As spring turns into summer, the warm days encourage you to enjoy nature and island life at their best: Flowers are in full bloom, birds flutter, and whales, seals, and porpoise lazily coast through the shimmering waters of the Sound. After a day of hiking, fishing, bicycling, kayaking, sailing, windsurfing or just reading by the inn's pond, enjoy a relaxing soak in your private bath or a sherry on the deck overlooking the valley below. After a tasty dinner at one of the Island's many fine restaurants, snuggle down under one of the inn's custom-made woolen comforters and peacefully doze off — with visions of the delicious breakfast awaiting you in the morning.

SEASON

all year

ACCOMMODATIONS

seven rooms with private baths

Spiced Cider with Apple Brandy

2 broken cinnamon sticks
1 tablespoon allspice berries
3 cloves
1 quart apple cider or apple juice
¾ cup apple brandy (Calvados) or applejack
6 cinnamon sticks (for serving)

Tie the spices in a cheesecloth bag. Place in a 2-quart pot and add the cider. Heat slowly until hot but not boiling. Put 1 cinnamon stick and 1 oz. brandy in each of 6 mugs. Pour in the hot cider and stir with the cinnamon stick to blend. Serve immediately. *Serves 6.*

Strawberry Frappe

"This recipe is one of our guests' favorites. It's like having a milkshake for breakfast." — Leicha Welton

2 cups orange juice
1 cup whipping cream
2 cups frozen strawberries
4 ripe bananas

Place all ingredients into a blender. Whip at high speed until smooth. Pour into tall, clear glasses and enjoy. *Serves 8.*

7 Gables Inn

Leicha and Paul Welton
PO Box 80488
Fairbanks, Alaska 99708
Tel: (907) 479-0751

ABOUT THE B&B

This 10,000 square foot Tudor-style house is located within walking distance of the University of Alaska Fairbanks campus, which is probably why 7 Gables began as a fraternity house. Its convenient location (between the airport and train station) is further enhanced by being right in the middle of a number of major attractions in the area: Riverboat Discovery, Pump House Restaurant, Cripple Creek Resort, University Museum, and Alaskaland. You enter the B&B through a floral solarium into a foyer with antique stained glass and indoor waterfall. Other features include cathedral ceilings, wine cellar, and wedding chapel. Some additional amenities include laundry facilities, Jacuzzis, cable TV and in-room phones, canoes, bikes, gourmet breakfasts, luggage or game storage, and library collection. Leicha enjoys cooking, music, hosting parties, and learning foreign languages, while Paul collects books and manages the inn's marketing and maintenance.

SEASON

all year

ACCOMMODATIONS

eight rooms with private baths; one room with shared bath

Down the Shore B&B

Annette and Al Bergins
201 Seventh Avenue
Belmar, New Jersey 07719
Tel: (908) 681-9023

ABOUT THE B&B

Down the Shore Bed & Breakfast is unique. The house was built specifically to be used as a residence and as a bed and breakfast. There are two guest rooms with a shared guest parlor and a shaded 40-foot front porch. Down the Shore Bed & Breakfast is located one block from the beach and boardwalk. The house may be new but the proprietors are not new to innkeeping. Before moving to Belmar, they operated another bed and breakfast in their lakeside home in Denville, New Jersey. As you can see from this recipe, healthful food is the mainstay of the breakfasts here.

SEASON

summer

ACCOMMODATIONS

two rooms with private baths

Walnut Granola

"We serve this granola not by itself as a cereal, but as a topping for vanilla yogurt, fresh fruit, and other cereals."
— Annette Bergins

4 cups uncooked rolled oats
1 cup chopped walnuts
1 cup water
¾ cup raisins
2 teaspoons ground cinnamon
1 teaspoon ground nutmeg
½ teaspoon salt
½ teaspoon orange extract
3 tablespoons maple syrup
¼ cup orange juice
2 tablespoons canola oil

Preheat oven to 350°F. Combine oatmeal and walnuts; set aside. Boil water, remove from heat, and add raisins; set aside. Combine all the other ingredients. Mix well and pour over the oatmeal-walnut mixture. Spread mixture on an ungreased baking pan or cookie sheet. Bake for 15 minutes, stir it around, then bake another 15 minutes. Allow mixture to cool, then dry the raisins and add to mixture. Store in airtight containers.
Makes approx. 6 cups.

West Hill House Granola

4 cups oats (not quick oats)
1 cup wheat germ
1 cup grated unsweetened coconut
¾ cup chopped walnuts
½ cup sesame seeds
¾ cup brown sugar
½ cup hot water
¼ cup honey
¼ cup vegetable oil
1 cup chopped dates
¾ cup golden raisins

Preheat oven to 250°F. Mix all dry ingredients (except dates and raisins) together in a large bowl. Mix water, honey, and oil together and pour over dry ingredients. Mix until moistened. Spread in large flat pans. Bake for 3 hours or until dry. Stir every ½ hour. Add dates about ½ hour before done. Add raisins after baking is done. Store in an airtight container to maintain freshness. Use as a cereal (serves 16 – 24) or as a topping for fruit, yogurt, or ice cream. *Makes 8 cups.*

West Hill House

Dotty Kyle and Eric Brattstrom
RR1, Box 292
Warren, Vermont 05674
Tel: (802) 496-7162

ABOUT THE B&B

Up a quiet country lane on nine peaceful acres, this 1860s farmhouse boasts stunning mountain views, gardens, pond, and apple orchard, and is just one mile from Sugarbush Ski Resort and adjacent golf course/ cross-country ski trails. Besides having an outdoor sports paradise at its doorstep, West Hill House is also near fine restaurants, quaint villages, covered bridges, unique shops, antique hunting, arts, museums, theater, and concerts. After a busy day, guests enjoy the comfortable front porch or roaring fireplace, eclectic library of books and videos, Oriental rugs, art, antiques, and the interesting company of other guests. Bedrooms feature premium linens, down comforters, and good reading lights. There's also a common guest pantry with wet bar and fridge. Breakfast specialties include sticky buns, soufflés, baked apple pancakes, fresh fruits, and more. Dotty and Eric, veteran B&B vacationers themselves, work to create an atmosphere of warmth and hospitality in their lovely small inn. Dotty's the chef, artist, and decorator, while Eric's the creative builder, remodeler, and stained glass artisan.

SEASON

all year

ACCOMMODATIONS

six rooms with private baths

Fruits
Vegetables
Soups

Amorous Pears

29-oz. can pear halves
Ground cinnamon
1½ cups light ricotta cheese
3 tablespoons sugar
¼ teaspoon ground nutmeg
3 tablespoons orange liqueur
½ cup sliced toasted almonds

Preheat oven to 325°F. Empty pears and juice into a shallow baking dish and arrange pears cut side up. Sprinkle each pear half with cinnamon. Bake for 20 minutes. Meanwhile, in a small bowl combine ricotta cheese, sugar, nutmeg, and liqueur. Whip with a fork until smooth. Refrigerate. When pears are warmed, remove each with a slotted spoon and place a pear half in each of 8 stemmed sherbet or small saucer champagne glasses. Spoon chilled cheese mixture evenly over tops of pears. Top each with toasted almond slices. *Serves 8.*

Durham House Bed & Breakfast Inn

Marguerite and Dean Swanson
921 Heights Boulevard
Houston, Texas 77008
Tel: (713) 868-4654

ABOUT THE B&B

Located just five minutes from downtown Houston, Durham House Bed & Breakfast Inn is a fully restored Queen Anne Victorian home listed on the National Register of Historic Places. The present owners, Marguerite and Dean Swanson, acquired the home in 1985 with full intention of restoring it to its original elegance and opening it to the public as an authentic Victorian bed and breakfast inn. Today, guests are invited to experience the genuine Victorian ambiance of the inn, and can select from gracious accommodations that include upstairs bedrooms and the privacy of a spacious carriage house. Perhaps the best reason for choosing Durham House is to experience Marguerite's special brand of southern hospitality, not to mention her fantastic full breakfast. For a change of pace, this unique bed and breakfast hosts murder mystery dinner parties using original mysteries written exclusively for Durham House.

SEASON

all year

ACCOMMODATIONS

five rooms with private baths;
one room with shared bath

Brambly Hedge Cottage

Jacquelyn Smyers
HCR 31, Box 39
Jasper, Arkansas 72641
Tel: 1-800-BRAMBLY or
(501) 446-5849

ABOUT THE B&B

"**A**bsolutely charming," wrote *National Geographic Traveler* of this old Ozark mountaintop farmhouse on scenic Highway 7, four miles south of Jasper, Arkansas. A Tennessee guest commented, "The place is uniquely beautiful, the food delicious, and the view inspiring." Three guest rooms with private baths reflect country French elegance in a homestead log cabin. A full breakfast is served on the deck overlooking Buffalo River Valley or behind the screened porch in rocking chairs. You're only minutes from the "Grand Canyon of the Ozarks," challenging-to-easy hiking trails, and canoeing on Buffalo National River. If art is more your style, you'll be happy to know that discriminating collectors still find the work of true artisans in the Jasper area. For those who wish to sample a night out on the town, Eureka Springs and Branson (Missouri) are nearby. Small group special-interest tours and relaxing massages can be arranged. Hostess Jacquelyn Smyers includes her handmade tatted lace and samovar collection in the decor. She's also a designer, commercial artist, and author of *Come For Tea* and the children's book *The Cloud That Came Into The Cabin* (inspired by the clouds on Sloan Mountain where Brambly Hedge is located).

SEASON

all year

ACCOMMODATIONS

three rooms with private baths

Applesauce Sundae

"This little dish is easy, looks special, and is good for your guests." — Jacquelyn Smyers

⅔ cup applesauce
2 sprinkles of ground cinnamon
2 heaped tablespoons raisins
2 heaped tablespoons walnuts, large broken pieces
2 tablespoons plain no-fat yogurt, unsweetened

Divide the applesauce into 2 small bowls. Sprinkle generously with cinnamon, raisins, and walnuts. Top with a dollop of yogurt in the center of each dish. *Serves 2.*

Baked Apples New England

6 baking apples (Cortland or McIntosh)
6 heaping teaspoons sugar mixed with 1 teaspoon
    ground cinnamon
3 tablespoons butter
2 tablespoons water

Preheat oven to 350°F. Core apples and make a slit through the skin with a knife all the way around, about ⅓ of the way from the top (this keeps the apples from exploding). Place apples in a glass pie plate. Spoon a heaping teaspoon of sugar-cinnamon mixture into the center of each apple, followed by a dab of butter. Pour water into pie plate. Bake 1 hour, basting after 30 minutes. *Tip:* For a little different flavor, add raisins to apple centers or a tablespoon of dark rum to the water. ***Serves 6.***

Captain Ezra Nye House
Sandwich, MA

Captain Ezra Nye House

Elaine and Harry Dickson
152 Main Street
Sandwich, Massachusetts 02563
Tel: (800) 388-CAPT
in US or Canada,
or (508) 888-6142

ABOUT THE B&B

A sense of history and romance fills this 1829 Federal home, built by the distinguished sea captain, Ezra Nye. Located in the heart of historical Sandwich Village, Captain Ezra Nye House is within walking distance of Sandwich Glass and Doll museums, Thornton Burgess Museum, Shawme Lake, fine dining, and antique shops. Heritage Plantation, the marina, an auction house, as well as Cape Cod Bay and Canal are nearby. Activities also include whale watching or a day at the beach. The inn was chosen one of the top 50 inns in America, one of the five best on the Cape, and was Cape Cod Life magazine's readers' choice as best bed and breakfast on the upper Cape. It has been featured in Glamour, Toronto Life, and Innsider magazines. A full breakfast is served each morning, and specialties include walnut goat cheese soufflé, peach kuchen, or baked French toast. Harry's interests include golfing and collecting Chinese export porcelain, while Elaine is an avid cyclist and enjoys yoga.

SEASON

all year

ACCOMMODATIONS

seven rooms with private baths

Beverley Allison and
Dorsey Allison Comer
16280 Blue Ridge Turnpike
Gordonsville, Virginia 22942
Tel: (800) 215-4804 or
(703) 832-5555

ABOUT THE B&B

Along the scenic and historic byway of Virginia Route 231, a red mailbox signals your arrival to Sleepy Hollow Farm. If you miss the mailbox, look for a green barn with a very red roof, a gazebo, a pond, and a brick house snoozing under trees in a sleepy hollow. Generations of farm families have lived here since the late 1700s, and today Sleepy Hollow Farm attracts a wide spectrum of guests, including many international sojourners. Memories to take home with you include the "Dolley Madison hospitality" of innkeepers Beverley Allison and Dorsey Allison Comer, the farm's pure spring water, and the commanding landscapes of surrounding horse, cattle, and sheep farms. And, unlike many B&Bs, this one is equipped to handle children.

SEASON

all year

ACCOMMODATIONS

four rooms (including one suite)
with private baths;
guest cottage with two suites
and private baths

Baked Tomatoes

Olive oil
3 large and firm tomatoes, cut in halves with stem and
    seeds removed
Dijon mustard
½ cup Italian-style bread crumbs
1 tablespoon sugar
¼ cup grated Parmesan cheese
3 large and fresh chopped mushrooms
Butter

Preheat oven to 400°F. Cover bottom of an oven-proof glass dish with olive oil. Place the 6 tomato halves in the dish, cut side up. Cover each tomato with some mustard. Mix bread crumbs, sugar, Parmesan cheese, and mushrooms, then sprinkle over each tomato, covering completely. Top each with a ½ pat of butter. Bake until fork-tender (approximately 20 – 25 minutes). Serve immediately. *Serves 6.*

Barbecue Green Beans

4 slices bacon
¼ cup chopped onions
½ cup tomato catsup
¼ cup brown sugar
1 tablespoon Worcestershire sauce
2 cans French-style green beans, well drained

Preheat oven to 350°F. Cook bacon until crisp. Using bacon grease, cook onions until they turn yellow. Add catsup, brown sugar, and Worcestershire sauce to the bacon grease and onions. Crumble the bacon slices into the sauce and simmer for 2 minutes. Place green beans in a casserole dish; pour sauce over top (do not stir). Bake for about 20 minutes. *Serves 6.*

Down to Earth Lifestyles Bed and Breakfast

Lola and Bill Coons
12500 North Crooked Road
Parkville, Missouri 64152
Tel: (816) 891-1018

ABOUT THE B&B

Located near downtown Kansas City, Down to Earth Lifestyles is a beautiful earth-integrated home situated on 86 acres of peaceful woods and rolling hills. Cozy, quiet rooms feature private bath, telephone, radio, color TV, and skylight or picture window. Spacious leisure areas include a guest lounge and patio where you can enjoy a cold beverage and complimentary popcorn, and an indoor, heated swimming pool where you can take a soothing dip. The "great room" is the perfect place to relax with music, games, books, and magazines, or just sit in front of the fire. Comfortable walking shoes are a must as nature and wildlife are abundant. Stroll through woods and over pastures among the cattle, horses, and geese. Fishermen will want to try their luck in the two stocked ponds. Breakfast is truly a mouth-watering experience, served where and when you'd like. Your hosts have a background in education, music, counseling, and agriculture, and invite you to commune with nature and enjoy their down-to-earth hospitality.

SEASON

all year

ACCOMMODATIONS

four rooms with private baths

Gundalow Inn

Cevia and George Rosol
6 Water Street
Kittery, Maine 03904
Tel: (207) 439-4040

ABOUT THE B&B

Gundalow Inn is a brick Victorian on the Kittery town green and on the banks of the Piscataqua River, just across the bridge from colonial Portsmouth. Six romantic guest rooms all have private baths, and many overlook the river. The friendly, hospitable innkeepers have furnished this "no-smoking" inn for your comfort and invite you to join them in the pleasures of another era. Situated halfway between Boston and Portland, the inn's a short drive away from beaches and outlet malls, and a pleasant walk from Portsmouth's harbor, museums, theaters, shops, and restaurants. Fireside breakfasts feature fresh juices, a fruit dish (such as baked apple with home-made granola), freshly baked scones, and an entrée served with meat or fish (perhaps honey-pecan pancakes and home-made sausage, or creamy scrambled eggs with George's own smoked salmon). Before opening Gundalow Inn in 1990, George was an electrical engineer and Cevia an editor. Their love of music and books is evident throughout the inn, which has been recommended by the New York Times.

SEASON

all year

ACCOMMODATIONS

six rooms with private baths

Blueberry-Lemon Soup

1 pint blueberries (preferably Maine wild)
1 cup water
½ cup sugar
1 thinly sliced lemon
1 stick cinnamon
1 cup plain low-fat yogurt
2 tablespoons freshly squeezed lemon juice
2 tablespoons confectioners' sugar
Yogurt
Ground cinnamon

Combine berries, water, sugar, lemon, and cinnamon stick in a saucepan. Bring to a boil over medium heat. Reduce heat and simmer 15 minutes. Cool. Remove cinnamon and process in blender until quite smooth. Chill overnight. Next day, combine 1 cup yogurt, lemon juice, and confectioners' sugar. Whisk into blueberry mixture. Garnish with a swirl of yogurt and sprinkle with ground cinnamon. *Serves 6.*

Blue Spruce Rellenos

"My cousin Sonny is a fantastic cook and this was his first published recipe, which appeared in his local paper many years back. I still have the original yellowed article in my recipe box." — Pat O'Brien

1 chopped medium yellow onion
1 chopped green bell pepper
3 8-oz. cans tomato sauce
2 teaspoons dry oregano
7-oz. can whole green chilies
3 cups grated Monterey Jack cheese
¼ teaspoon baking powder
¼ cup all-purpose flour
2 slightly beaten eggs
1 cup milk
1 cup salsa

Preheat oven to 375°F. In a medium saucepan, sauté onion and pepper until barely tender. Add tomato sauce and oregano, then bring to a boil. Keep warm and set aside. Split chilies, remove any seeds, and stuff with cheese. Roll up and place in a 9 x 7" greased baking pan. Combine the rest of the ingredients and pour over chilies. Sprinkle with any remaining cheese. Bake for 35 – 40 minutes. To serve, let dish set 5 minutes. Lift out each chili, top with sauce, and serve. *Serves 6.*

Blue Spruce Inn

Pat and Tom O'Brien
2815 Main Street
Soquel, California 95073
Tel: (800) 559-1137 or
(408) 464-1137

ABOUT THE B&B

The Blue Spruce Inn welcomes you with the distinct Pacific breeze that freshens the Central Coast hillsides that are golden with poppies, tempers the heat of the summer sun, and warms the sands during afternoon strolls on winter beaches. The inn is four miles south of Santa Cruz and one mile from Capitola Beach at the northern curve of Monterey Bay. Gracious personal service is the hallmark of this 1875 B&B inn, where beds are graced with Amish quilts and walls hung with original local art that blends the flavor of yesteryear with the luxury of today. There are quiet gardens in which to enjoy the sunshine of Soquel Village, delightful antique shops at the corner of the street and, a little farther, wineries, gift shops, and regional art displays. Bountiful breakfasts feature fresh fruits, homemade breads, and exceptional entrées. At the end of the day, the hot tub offers welcome respite and, when guests return to their rooms, pillows are fluffed and a special treat awaits — assuring the perfect ending to a wonderful day.

SEASON

all year

ACCOMMODATIONS

five rooms with private baths

Brambly Hedge Cottage

Jacquelyn Smyers
HCR 31, Box 39
Jasper, Arkansas 72641
Tel: 1-800-BRAMBLY or
(501) 446-5849

ABOUT THE B&B

"**A**bsolutely charming," wrote *National Geographic Traveler* of this old Ozark mountaintop farmhouse on scenic Highway 7, four miles south of Jasper, Arkansas. A Tennessee guest commented, "The place is uniquely beautiful, the food delicious, and the view inspiring." Three guest rooms with private baths reflect country French elegance in a homestead log cabin. A full breakfast is served on the deck overlooking Buffalo River Valley or behind the screened porch in rocking chairs. You're only minutes from the "Grand Canyon of the Ozarks," challenging-to-easy hiking trails, and canoeing on Buffalo National River. If art is more your style, you'll be happy to know that discriminating collectors still find the work of true artisans in the Jasper area. For those who wish to sample a night out on the town, Eureka Springs and Branson (Missouri) are nearby. Small group special-interest tours and relaxing massages can be arranged. Hostess Jacquelyn Smyers includes her hand-made tatted lace and samovar collection in the decor. She's also a designer, commercial artist, and author of Come For Tea and the children's book The Cloud That Came Into The Cabin (inspired by the clouds on Sloan Mountain where Brambly Hedge is located).

SEASON

all year

ACCOMMODATIONS

three rooms with private baths

Brambly Hedge Fruit Mix

"A nice change from the usual citrus fruits makes this simple mixture taste quite special." — Jacquelyn Smyers

1 cup purple seedless grapes
1 cup canned pineapple chunks, drained
1 cup thickly sliced and halved bananas
¼ cup or less Grand Marnier liqueur

Mix all together. Serve in pretty, small bowls. *Serves 4.*

Broiled Grapefruit

"Guests claim they've never enjoyed grapefruit so much!"
— Christopher Sellers

2 grapefruits
4 tablespoons maple syrup
Ground cinnamon

Cut grapefruit into halves. Remove seeds and loosen sections in each half. Top with 1 tablespoon maple syrup and dust with cinnamon. Broil until edges just turn brown. Serve warm.
Serves 4.

Grünberg Haus Bed & Breakfast
Waterbury, Vermont

Grünberg Haus Bed and Breakfast

Christopher Sellers and
Mark Frohman, RR2,
Box 1595RD, Route 100 South
Waterbury, Vermont 05676-9621
Tel: (800) 800-7760 (reservations)
or (802) 244-7726

ABOUT THE B&B

This picture-postcard Austrian-style B&B is tucked away on a secluded hillside in Vermont's Green Mountains, perfectly situated for visits to Stowe, Montpelier, Waterbury, and Burlington. Individually decorated guest rooms open onto the carved wood balcony, which offers wonderful views from the stucco and wood-trimmed chalet. The giant stone fireplace and wood stove in the BYOB pub are favorite gathering places. After hiking or cross-country skiing on the inn's trails, help Mark feed the chickens and enjoy a full, musical breakfast, with selections such as maple-poached pears, apple and cheddar muffins, and ricotta-stuffed French toast. The evening fire warms up the grand piano where you're likely to hear innkeeper Chris playing anything from Mozart to Phantom of the Opera. Nearby activities include spectacular autumn leaf-picking, world-class downhill skiing, golf, boating, bicycling, gliding, canoeing, antique hunting, outlet shopping, and touring Ben & Jerry's ice cream factory. And you can enjoy the Grünberg Haus's own Jacuzzi, sauna, tennis courts, cross-country ski center, and hiking trails.

SEASON

all year

ACCOMMODATIONS

six rooms with private baths; five rooms with shared baths; three cabins and one carriage house with private baths

The Inn at The Brass Lantern

Andy Aldrich
717 Maple Street
Stowe, Vermont 05672
Tel: (800) 729-2980 or
(802) 253-2229

ABOUT THE B&B

The Inn at The Brass Lantern is located at the edge of the village of Stowe, Vermont. Stowe is a full-service, four-season resort town, and boasts a vast multitude of world-class restaurants and activities, a cultural center, unique cottage industries, craftspeople, and artists. Originally built as a farmhouse and carriage barn, The Brass Lantern was restored by Andy Aldrich, the present innkeeper, to retain its original Vermont character (for which he won an award). Today, the inn carries the traditional Vermont B&B theme throughout — from its decor of period antiques, handmade quilts, and locally crafted amenities to the food and beverages reflecting local and Vermont state products. In addition, guests are treated to a unique ambience and casual, attentive service. The inn's setting provides panoramic views of Mt. Mansfield and its valley from nearly every room.

SEASON

all year

ACCOMMODATIONS

nine rooms with private baths

Butternut Squash Soup

2 lbs. butternut squash, trimmed, seeded, and cleaned
4 cups water
1 tablespoon salt
½ cup diced celery
½ cup diced onions
½ cup diced green bell peppers
¼ cup melted butter
¼ cup white wine
1 teaspoon tarragon leaves
½ teaspoon ground cinnamon
½ teaspoon ground nutmeg
¼ teaspoon ground cloves
4 cups chicken stock
¼ cup all-purpose flour
¼ cup melted butter
½ cup Vermont maple syrup
¼ cup dry sherry

Add squash to a large pot with salted water, and cook until soft (approximately 40 minutes). Strain out the squash, reserving 2 cups of liquid and discarding the rest. In the large pot, sauté the diced vegetables in ¼ cup butter and wine for 5 minutes. Add the herbs and spices. Add the chicken stock and 1 cup of reserved liquid. Bring to a boil, then thicken with a roux made by mixing the flour with ¼ cup melted butter. Purée the cooked squash in a blender or food processor with the remaining 1 cup of reserved liquid. Add to the pot and cook on low heat for 5 minutes, stirring often. Add the syrup and sherry. Mix well and serve. *Serves 12 – 16.*

Cantaloupe Mousse

2 envelopes unflavored gelatin (2 tablespoons)
¼ cup cold water
½ medium cantaloupe, seeded, pared, and pureed
2 cups heavy cream
4 egg whites at room temperature
2 cups sugar

Sprinkle gelatin over cold water to soften. Stir over a double boiler with bottom pan full of hot water to dissolve. Cool and add to the pureed melon. Beat cream until soft peaks form, then gradually add 1 cup of sugar. Beat whites until fluffy, then gradually add remaining cup of sugar. Fold together and fold into melon mixture. Chill 1 hour then serve. *Serves 8+.*

Buttonwood Inn

Liz Oehser
190 Georgia Road
Franklin, North Carolina 28734
Tel: (704) 369-8985

ABOUT THE B&B

This small mountain bed and breakfast with a cozy home atmosphere awaits your visit. Sleep in chenille- or quilt-covered antique beds surrounded by country furnishings, collectibles, and crafts. Two rooms on the first floor each have a double and twin bed with private bath, while the two rooms on the second floor each have a double bed and share a common bath. Breakfast delights include artichoke quiche, sausage apple ring filled with puffy scrambled egg, Dutch babies with raspberry sauce, stuffed French toast, blintz soufflé, muffins, and cinnamon scones with home-made lemon butter. After breakfast, enjoy gem mining, hiking, horseback riding, water rafting, golf, or tennis. Stay long enough to tour Biltmore Estate in nearby Asheville, drive through the Smokey Mountain Parkway to Cherokee Indian Reservation, or "shop till you drop" in Gatlinburg. Hospitality, comfort, and delightful breakfasts are this inn's priorities.

SEASON

April to December 15

ACCOMMODATIONS

two rooms with private baths;
two rooms with shared bath

Ferry Point House Bed & Breakfast on Lake Winnisquam

Diane and Joe Damato
100 Lower Bay Road
Sanbornton, New Hampshire
03269
Tel: (603) 524-0087

ABOUT THE B&B

This gracious, 175-year-old Country Victorian is located on picturesque Lake Winnisquam, in a spot commanding a panoramic view of lake and mountains. The gazebo on the point compliments the sandy beach and allows for quiet moments by the water. A 60-foot veranda and all of the rooms are blessed with breathtaking views. Return to the warm, friendly feeling of New England's past with antique furniture, collectibles, and fresh flowers in your room. The lake and surrounding area offer an endless variety of activities, including swimming, fishing, and boating at the inn. Horseback riding, golf, tennis, dinner cruises, scenic train and plain rides, antique shopping, and fine restaurants are all close by. Each morning, you'll be treated to a very special gourmet breakfast with delights such as stuffed French toast, cheese baked apples, poached pears, and select home-baked breads and muffins.

SEASON

Memorial Day through October

ACCOMMODATIONS

six rooms with private baths

Cheese-Baked Apples

"I wait for cool fall mornings to serve these. The aroma literally plucks my guests from their warm beds."
— *Diane Damato*

6 large Cortland apples
8 ozs. softened cream cheese
1 egg
½ cup sugar
1 teaspoon vanilla
Sprinkle of ground cinnamon

Preheat oven to 350°F. Peel away 1" of skin around the top of each apple. Remove core (being careful not to pierce the rest of the skin) and remove some of the pulp, leaving a shell about ¾" thick. Combine cream cheese, egg, sugar, and vanilla. Beat until smooth and creamy. Put ⅓ cup of filling in each apple and place apples into greased ramekins. Place ramekins in a baking pan and add about ½" of water to pan. Sprinkle tops of apples with a little cinnamon. Bake for 30 – 45 minutes. Check for consistent softness around the apples. Serve immediately. *Tip:* Apples may be split — what you want is a consistently soft apple with the cream cheese filling puffed on the top. ***Makes 6 apples.***

Cranberry-Liquered Apples

6 medium apples
2½ tablespoons butter
6 tablespoons cranberry liqueur
10 teaspoons sugar
1½ teaspoons ground cinnamon
¾ teaspoon ground nutmeg
Ground ginger
¾ cup water with 1 drop red food coloring

Preheat oven to 350°F. Core and peel each apple and place in a baking dish. Put ½ teaspoon butter in cavity of each apple. Evenly coat apples with liqueur. Sprinkle 1 teaspoon sugar over each apple and put 1 teaspoon sugar in each apple cavity. Dust each apple with cinnamon and nutmeg. Add a dash of ginger to each. Add water to dish. Bake covered for 45 minutes or until tender, basting every 10 minutes. *Tip:* Be careful not to overcook apples as they may fall apart. *Serves 6.*

Beaver Creek House

Shirley and Donald Day
20432 Beaver Creek Road
Hagerstown, Maryland 21740
Tel: (301) 797-4764

ABOUT THE B&B

*C*omfort, relaxation, and hospitality await you at this turn of the century country Victorian home, located in the historic area of Beaver Creek, Maryland. Step back to a quiet, gentler time and enjoy the family antiques and memorabilia that fill the inn. Choose from five centrally air-conditioned guest rooms, and enjoy a country breakfast served on the spacious wraparound screen porch or in the elegantly appointed dining room. Sit in the courtyard by the fountain, stroll through the country garden, or linger by the fish pond and gaze at the mountain. Nearby are the National Historic parks of Antietam, Harpers Ferry, the C&O Canal, and the Appalachian Trail. Guests may also hike, bike, golf, ski, shop at the many local antique shops, and dine at excellent restaurants in Hagerstown.

SEASON

all year

ACCOMMODATIONS

five rooms with private baths

High Meadows Inn

Peter Sushka and Jae Abbitt
High Meadows Lane,
Route 4, Box 6
Scottsville, Virginia 24590
Tel: (804) 286-2218

ABOUT THE B&B

As Virginia's only inn that is on the National Register of Historic Homes and has a renaissance farm vineyard, High Meadows offers a rare opportunity to experience 170 years of architectural history and 10 years of new viticultural growth. High Meadows is a grand, unique house, where guests are welcomed with champagne and stay in rooms furnished with period antiques and art, each with private bath. The innkeepers' many special touches and attention to detail make your visit one to be remembered. Enjoy the simplicity of nature on the 50 surrounding acres of gardens, footpaths, forests, and ponds. Owner/chef Peter Sushka ensures that dining at High Meadows is just as pleasurable as lodging there. Start with a breakfast of fresh orange juice, a variety of home-made breads, muffins, and scones, fresh fruit, gourmet egg dishes, and coffee or tea. End your day with a multi-course dinner, offering distinctive northern European and Mediterranean dishes.

SEASON

all year

ACCOMMODATIONS

11 rooms (including four suites) with private baths; two-room cottage with private bath

Creamy Breakfast Ambrosia

(Recipe from The Best of High Meadows — A Selected Recipe Collection.)

2 cups sliced peaches (or pears or apples), peeled
2 sliced bananas
10 – 12 sliced strawberries
2 peeled and sliced oranges
1 tablespoon lemon juice
1 cup shredded unsweetened coconut
1 cup miniature marshmallows
1 cup vanilla or lemon yogurt
1 tablespoon sugar (optional)

In a large bowl, combine fruit and lemon juice. Toss lightly. Stir in coconut, marshmallows, yogurt, and sugar (if desired). Chill for ½ – 1 hour and serve in stemmed, clear sherbet glasses. **Serves 8.**

Fried Apples

(Recipe from Favorites from the Lazy Bee.)

My favorite among wines — the lighthearted blush — is used for this fried apple recipe, which happens to go well with scrambled eggs or with any pork or venison dish."
— Jo Ann Bender

6 sliced red apples, unpeeled
3 tablespoons butter
1 cup blush wine
½ cup water
1 cup sugar
1½ teaspoons ground cinnamon
1 tablespoon lemon juice

Fry apples in melted butter for about 6 – 8 minutes. Boil wine, water, sugar, cinnamon, and lemon juice for 5 minutes. Pour over apples and cook uncovered until apples are tender. Serve warm or cold. *Serves 6.*

Hillside House Bed & Breakfast

Jo Ann, Bud, and Sue
1729 East 18th Street
Spokane, Washington 99203
Tel: (509) 534-1426 during the day or (509) 535-1893 during nights and weekends

ABOUT THE B&B

Situated on the South Hill of Spokane, Hillside House offers exquisite hospitality in a country setting that's only three miles from downtown. Overlooking city and mountains, this cozy and tastefully decorated house features antiques, including linens and dishes, and rooms with views. Your hosts Bud, Jo Ann, and Sue are third generation B&B innkeepers — Jo Ann's mother helped her mother host guests in 1916 in Rush City, Minnesota. Bud owns an engineering firm and lectures nationally to the construction/engineering industry, while Jo Ann operates a marketing firm. They enjoy cooking (having published a cookbook of their own), entertaining, and guiding guests to the area's most exciting places and events. Bud and Jo Ann also operate the Lazy Bee, a remote getaway near the Canadian border where they lead jeep safaris in the mountains.

SEASON

all year

ACCOMMODATIONS

two rooms with shared bath

The Duff Green Mansion

Mr. and Mrs. Harry Carter Sharp
1114 First East Street
Vicksburg, Mississippi 39188
Tel: (601) 636-6968

ABOUT THE B&B

The Duff Green Mansion is located in Vicksburg's historic district. Built in 1856, it's considered one of the finest examples of Paladian architecture in the state of Mississippi. The mansion was built by Duff Green, a prosperous merchant, for his bride Mary Lake Green (whose parents gave the land property as a wedding gift). Many parties were held here during the antebellum days but it was hastily converted to a hospital for both Confederate and Union soldiers during the siege of Vicksburg and the remainder of the Civil War. Mary Green gave birth to a son during the siege in one of the caves next to the mansion and appropriately named him Siege Green. The over 12,000 square foot mansion has been restored and features seven guest rooms, luxurious antiques, private baths, room service, southern plantation breakfasts, cocktails, and a swimming pool.

SEASON

all year

ACCOMMODATIONS

seven rooms (including two suites) with private baths

Fruit Kabobs

"A slightly modern twist on an old southern favorite."
— *Stephen Kerr, chef of Duff Green Mansion*

8 wooden skewers (12" long)
16 slices bacon
1 fresh pineapple, peeled and cored
2 Granny Smith apples
2 Rome apples
6-oz. can pineapple juice
⅓ cup firmly packed brown sugar

Soak wooden skewers in water and set aside. Cook bacon until limp but not crisp; drain and set aside. Cut pineapple in 1" pieces. Core all apples and cut into 1" pieces. Combine pineapple, apple, and pineapple juice, tossing to coat fruit. Thread end of a piece of bacon on skewer, alternate pieces of Granny Smith apple, pineapple, and Rome apple, weaving bacon around each. Add another slice of bacon to skewer when needed. Repeat with remaining skewers, bacon, and fruit. Reserve remaining fruit for other uses. Sprinkle each kabob with brown sugar. Broil 6" from heat for 6 minutes, turning once or until fruit begins to brown around edges. *Makes 8 kabobs.*

Glazed Bananas

2 teaspoons butter
2 tablespoons brown sugar
¼ teaspoon ground cinnamon
½ peeled and diced orange
2 whole bananas, peeled and sliced into 1" rounds
Orange juice, if needed
Whipped cream
Fresh mint leaves

Melt butter, brown sugar, and cinnamon in a sauté pan over low heat. Add orange and stir until well melted and syrupy. Add bananas and stir fry over medium-high heat, just until hot. If the syrup is too thick, add a little orange juice. Be careful not to overcook as bananas will become mushy. Serve in a stemmed glass and top with whipped cream and mint leaf. *Tip:* Recipe is easily expandable for larger numbers. *Serves 2.*

Inn at Blush Hill

Pamela Gosselin
RR #1, Box 1266
Waterbury, Vermont 05676
Tel: (802) 244-7529

ABOUT THE B&B

O*nce a stagecoach stop on the route between Montpelier and Stowe, this circa 1790 Cape Cod inn has become a haven for modern-day travelers seeking country comfort and hospitality. Cozy guest rooms are filled with country antiques and coordinated fabrics and wallpapers. One guest room has a fireplace, another has a queen canopy with Battenburg lace and a panoramic view of the mountains. On a chilly day, curl up with a book in front of one of the inn's roaring fireplaces. During summer, there's a large covered porch that beckons you to sit awhile and enjoy the magnificent view. The inn serves many native Vermont products, from fresh apple cider to Ben and Jerry's Ice Cream and Vermont maple syrup. The inn is adjacent to Ben and Jerry's Ice Cream Factory (the most popular tourist attraction in Vermont), within minutes of Cold Hollow Cider Mill, Green Mountain Chocolate Factory, and Cabot Creamery, and just a 10-minute drive from the village of Stowe.*

SEASON

all year

ACCOMMODATIONS

six rooms with private baths

Doelling Haus

Carol and David Doelling
4817 Towne South
St. Louis, Missouri 63128
Tel: (314) 894-6796

ABOUT THE B&B

Rediscover Old World hospitality at Doelling Haus, where you'll delight in beautiful rooms reminiscent of a European country home decorated with German antiques and collectibles, handed down from the hosts' families and gathered during their travels. Hearty full breakfasts include German and Austrian delicacies, and home-made truffles await beside your bed. Many points of interest are nearby, including the famous Arch monument, Grant's Farm, the historic settlement of Kimmswick, recreational areas, malls, and fine restaurants. Carol will direct you to wonderful shops for antique-hunting and David, who owns a sports memorabilia store, will gladly show off his old baseball card collection. Come experience "Gemutlichkeit" (a sense of well-being) at Doelling Haus.

SEASON

all year

ACCOMMODATIONS

one suite with private bath;
one room with shared bath

Isle of Jersey Orange Cups

"This is an elegant finale to a wonderful breakfast. I first tasted this recipe at a bed and breakfast on the Isle of Jersey and have since modified it to enchant guests at our own breakfast table." — Carol Doelling

6 medium oranges
½ cup sugar
2 tablespoons cornstarch
¼ cup Amaretto liqueur
Maraschino cherries or whipped cream

Cut the top quarter off of each orange. Scoop out the juice and pulp into a saucepan. Cut the top edge of each orange in a zigzag pattern. Discard any seeds or thick membrane, then set orange shells aside. Over medium heat, stir together orange juice and pulp, sugar, and cornstarch until mixture just starts to boil. Add the Amaretto liqueur and continue to cook while constantly stirring until the mixture starts to thicken. Remove from heat and pour mixture into each orange shell. Chill in the refrigerator for at least 1 hour before serving. Top each orange with a maraschino cherry or whipped cream and serve.

Tip: This recipe can be topped with vanilla ice cream and served for a dinner dessert. *Serves 6.*

Jeanne's Zucchini Fritters

"When I was growing up, my mother used to make wonderful squash pancakes. I don't recall ever seeing a recipe written down, so this is my version, developed for Gundalow Inn and using those wonderful ingredients found in today's market. I've named the recipe for my mother." — Cevia Rosol

3 lbs. grated zucchini
1 small chopped onion
1 medium chopped red bell pepper
3 extra-large eggs
1½ cups all-purpose flour
1 tablespoon baking powder
¾ teaspoon salt
¾ teaspoon Hungarian sweet paprika
Canola oil

Combine all ingredients (except oil) well. Heat griddle or large, heavy skillet and add oil. Drop batter by large spoonfuls. Fry until crispy and brown on both sides. Serve hot with maple syrup or sour cream. *Makes approx. 24 fritters.*

Gundalow Inn

Cevia and George Rosol
6 Water Street
Kittery, Maine 03904
Tel: (207) 439-4040

ABOUT THE B&B

Gundalow Inn is a brick Victorian on the Kittery town green and on the banks of the Piscataqua River, just across the bridge from colonial Portsmouth. Six romantic guest rooms all have private baths, and many overlook the river. The friendly, hospitable innkeepers have furnished this "no-smoking" inn for your comfort and invite you to join them in the pleasures of another era. Situated halfway between Boston and Portland, the inn's a short drive away from beaches and outlet malls, and a pleasant walk from Portsmouth's harbor, museums, theaters, shops, and restaurants. Fireside breakfasts feature fresh juices, a fruit dish (such as baked apple with home-made granola), freshly baked scones, and an entrée served with meat or fish (perhaps honey-pecan pancakes and home-made sausage, or creamy scrambled eggs with George's own smoked salmon). Before opening Gundalow Inn in 1990, George was an electrical engineer and Cevia an editor. Their love of music and books is evident throughout the inn, which has been recommended by the New York Times.

SEASON

all year

ACCOMMODATIONS

six rooms with private baths

The Georges

Marie and Carolyn George
RR 1, Box 50
Dixon, Nebraska 68732-9728
Tel: (402) 584-2625

ABOUT THE B&B

Look past the large grove of trees and you'll discover The Georges, a large remodeled, air-conditioned farmhouse designed to comfortably accommodate the travel needs of a large family. Your stay includes a hearty breakfast featuring home-made jellies and jams, while other meals can be arranged. Bunking at The Georges offers you the opportunity to see a modern farming operation first-hand, including the planting and harvesting of corn, soybeans, and alfalfa. You'll also hear the chickens clucking and make the acquaintance of several farm cats. During the warm season, you can hike, bird-watch, relax with a book in a quiet spot, or visit county fairs and local festivals. In the fall, pheasant hunting season is in its prime and, depending on the winter snowfall, you can choose from sledding, hiking, cross-country skiing, or ice skating on farm ponds.

SEASON

all year

ACCOMMODATIONS

five rooms with shared baths

Lefse (Potato Pancakes)

"A traditional Norwegian potato pancake recipe from a Norwegian neighbor." — Marie George

3 cups prepared mashed potatoes (not instant)
½ cup melted oleo (or margarine)
1 teaspoon salt (if mashed potatoes not already salted)
1 tablespoon sugar
½ teaspoon baking powder
1½ cups (approximate) all-purpose flour
Confectioners' sugar (optional)

Combine all ingredients except flour. Add enough flour so that dough doesn't stick to your hands. Form dough into balls about the size of a walnut, and roll thin. Fry in an ungreased skillet over medium heat until set and lightly brown on underside, then flip and brown lightly on other side. Serve with your choice of butter, ground cinnamon, and sugar; jelly or jam; maple syrup; or fresh fruits (such as strawberries, raspberries, or blueberries). Sprinkle with confectioners' sugar, if you wish. You can roll the pancakes with any of these or serve pancakes flat. *Tips:* Make these ahead and reheat in a skillet or micro-wave. An electric pancake griddle is ideal for frying 4 – 6 pancakes at a time. *Serves 4 – 8.*

Maple-Poached Pears

"A warm maple-scented pear served in a pool of creamy yogurt on a crystal plate often sends guests for their cameras before their forks!" — Christopher Sellers

6 large pears
2 quarts boiling water
¾ cup Vermont maple syrup
12 mint sprigs
12 ozs. French vanilla yogurt
Ground nutmeg

Peel, half, and core pears. Combine boiling water and syrup. Poach pears for 20 minutes in syrup/water mixture. Drain pears. To serve, create a "pool" of vanilla yogurt on a glass plate. Position warm pear, cut side down, on pool of yogurt. Garnish with mint sprig in place of stem. Dust with nutmeg. *Serves 12.*

*Grünberg Haus Bed & Breakfast
Waterbury, Vermont*

Grünberg Haus Bed and Breakfast

Christopher Sellers and Mark Frohman, RR2, Box 1595RD, Route 100 South Waterbury, Vermont 05676-9621 Tel: (800) 800-7760 (reservations) or (802) 244-7726

ABOUT THE B&B

This picture-postcard Austrian-style B&B is tucked away on a secluded hillside in Vermont's Green Mountains, perfectly situated for visits to Stowe, Montpelier, Waterbury, and Burlington. Individually decorated guest rooms open onto the carved wood balcony, which offers wonderful views from the stucco and wood-trimmed chalet. The giant stone fireplace and wood stove in the BYOB pub are favorite gathering places. After hiking or cross-country skiing on the inn's trails, help Mark feed the chickens and enjoy a full, musical breakfast, with selections such as maple-poached pears, apple and cheddar muffins, and ricotta-stuffed French toast. The evening fire warms up the grand piano where you're likely to hear innkeeper Chris playing anything from Mozart to Phantom of the Opera. Nearby activities include spectacular autumn leaf-picking, world-class downhill skiing, golf, boating, bicycling, gliding, canoeing, antique hunting, outlet shopping, and touring Ben & Jerry's ice cream factory. And you can enjoy the Grünberg Haus's own Jacuzzi, sauna, tennis courts, cross-country ski center, and hiking trails.

SEASON

all year

ACCOMMODATIONS

six rooms with private baths; five rooms with shared baths; three cabins and one carriage house with private baths

The Marlborough

Diana Smith
320 Woods Hole Road
Woods Hole, Massachusetts
02543
Tel: (508) 548-6218

ABOUT THE B&B

The Marlborough is a romantic Cape Cod cottage complete with picket fence, trellis, and garden set up on a hill among the trees. Rooms have private baths and are individually decorated with quilts, coordinated scented linens, and collectibles. Gather for conversation, read, or watch television in the large comfortable parlor. Full gourmet breakfast, including wonderfully brewed coffee and teas, is served outside by the kidney-shaped pool or inside by the fireplace, depending on the season. Informal afternoon tea is served in season, while high tea is served on Sundays in the off-season. Excellent restaurants are nearby, as is Woods Hole Oceanographic Institute, beaches, shopping, bike paths, and ferries to Martha's Vineyard. Great starting point for day trips to locations all over Cape Cod and the islands, Plymouth, Boston, and Providence. Innkeeper Diana Smith enjoys helping guests get the most out of their visit. A computer consultant before purchasing the inn, Diana enjoys bicycle touring, hand needlework (including quilting, cross-stitch, and crewel) and cooking.

SEASON

all year

ACCOMMODATIONS

five rooms with private baths

Marlborough Baked Apples

6 large baking apples (Cortland, Winesap, Rome, or Golden Delicious)
½ cup granola
½ cup chopped dates or raisins
½ cup chopped walnuts
½ teaspoon ground cinnamon
¼ teaspoon ground nutmeg
3 tablespoons lemon juice
½ cup honey
9 tablespoons butter
1 cup fruit juice (e.g., apple, nectarine)
2 cups granola
Whipped cream
Ground nutmeg
Fresh mint sprig

Preheat oven to 350°F. Core apples, making a big hole to hold as much delicious filling as possible. Combine ½ cup granola and following 5 ingredients with 4 tablespoons of the honey to make filling. Spoon filling into cored apples and place in a shallow baking pan. Combine remaining honey with butter and fruit juice and heat to boiling. Pour over apples. Cover pan with foil and bake for about 10 minutes. Remove cover and baste apples. Continue baking until apples are tender when pricked with a fork (about 20 minutes more). Put apples in individual serving bowls and top each with ¼ cup granola, apple juice from baking, and a dollop of whipped cream. Sprinkle with a little nutmeg and garnished with a sprig of fresh mint. Serve warm. *Serves 6.*

Norwegian Fruit Pizza

Crust:
¾ cup butter
½ cup confectioners' sugar
1½ cups all-purpose flour

Preheat oven to 350°F. Mix crust ingredients until crumb-like. Pat into a pizza pan and bake for about 11 – 13 minutes or until a light golden brown.

Cream filling:
8 ozs. softened cream cheese
½ cup sugar
½ teaspoon vanilla
3 fruits of your choice

Blend cream filling ingredients. Spread over cooled crust. Top with 3 kinds of fruit (such as peaches, bananas, kiwis, strawberries, or blueberries).

Glaze:
1 cup fruit juice
2 tablespoons cornstarch
1 tablespoon lemon juice
½ cup sugar
2 tablespoons kirsch or brandy

Heat together glaze ingredients in a saucepan. Cook, stirring constantly, until clear and thick. Spread on top of pizza after sliced. *Serves 10 – 12.*

The Albert Stevens Inn & Cat's Garden

Diane and Curt Diviney-Rangen
127 Myrtle Avenue
Cape May, New Jersey 08204
Tel: (800) 890-CATS or
(609) 884-4717

ABOUT THE B&B

Built in 1898 by Dr. Albert G. Stevens, this Victorian Queen-Anne classic features a unique floating staircase suspended from the third-floor turret. After enjoying a three-course Norwegian-style breakfast, you can wander off to the nearby historical shopping mall, swimming beaches, the lighthouse, bird observatory, and shops. Or, you may want to unwind in the Cat's Garden. Established in 1992 as a safe haven for the wild or forgotten cats that wander the shore, the garden is landscaped with hundreds of plants and herbs and a little pond, and enjoyed by cats and humans alike. Innkeepers Diane and Curt invite you to join them in rediscovering the soothing sights and sounds of the shore without pretentious overtones. Here, you'll find two hard-working individuals who escaped the corporate world for a life now dedicated to balancing man with nature.

SEASON

February to December

ACCOMMODATIONS

nine rooms (including two suites) with private baths

Ashling Cottage

Goodi and Jack Stewart
106 Sussex Avenue
Spring Lake, New Jersey 07762
Tel: (800) 237-1877 or
(908) 449-3553

ABOUT THE B&B

For generations, rambling Victorian homes have fronted the spring-fed lakes from which Spring Lake, New Jersey, gets its name. Tree-lined walkways surround the lakes, and wooden foot bridges connect grassy areas of park. Sun, sand, surf, and serenity in equal measure — Spring Lake offers all this and Ashling Cottage, too. Since 1877, the visiting gentry have enjoyed sumptuous breakfasts on the porches of this lovely and intimate seaside inn, overlooking both ocean and lake. Today, the tradition continues with casual hospitality and personal attention offered for your vacationing pleasure. While leisure activities abound (such as golf, tennis, biking, horseback riding, and sightseeing in nearby New York and Philadelphia), the most delightful feature of this inn and this town is the guilt-free ability to do absolutely nothing!

SEASON

May to October

ACCOMMODATIONS

eight rooms with private baths;
two rooms with shared bath

Peaches with Honey-Lime Whip

"This recipe came from the owners of a nearby 'pick your own' orchard where we pick our peaches and prepare them while still warm from the ripening sun." — Goodi Stewart

4 tablespoons honey
2 teaspoons grated lime rind
3 tablespoons lime juice
¼ teaspoon ground mace or nutmeg
9 – 10 medium peeled and sliced peaches

Combine honey, lime rind, lime juice, and mace in a small bowl, mixing well with a wire whisk. Pour over peaches, tossing gently. *Serves 9 – 12.*

Peach Melba

1 tablespoon raspberry jam
1 tablespoon currant or apple jelly
½ cup frozen raspberries
1 peeled and halved peach
Vanilla ice cream
Mint leaf

Melt jam and jelly in a small saucepan over low heat. Add the frozen raspberries and stir. Simmer over low heat until warmed through. Arrange 1 peach half in a stemmed fruit glass. Top with melon ball-sized scoop of vanilla ice cream. Top with warmed fruit sauce and garnish with a mint leaf. Repeat with other peach half. *Tip:* Recipe is easily expandable for larger numbers. *Serves 2.*

Inn at Blush Hill

Pamela Gosselin
RR #1, Box 1266
Waterbury, Vermont 05676
Tel: (802) 244-7529

ABOUT THE B&B

O*nce a stagecoach stop on the route between Montpelier and Stowe, this circa 1790 Cape Cod inn has become a haven for modern-day travelers seeking country comfort and hospitality. Cozy guest rooms are filled with country antiques and coordinated fabrics and wallpapers. One guest room has a fireplace, another has a queen canopy with Battenburg lace and a panoramic view of the mountains. On a chilly day, curl up with a book in front of one of the inn's roaring fireplaces. During summer, there's a large covered porch that beckons you to sit awhile and enjoy the magnificent view. The inn serves many native Vermont products, from fresh apple cider to Ben and Jerry's Ice Cream and Vermont maple syrup. The inn is adjacent to Ben and Jerry's Ice Cream Factory (the most popular tourist attraction in Vermont), within minutes of Cold Hollow Cider Mill, Green Mountain Chocolate Factory, and Cabot Creamery, and just a 10-minute drive from the village of Stowe.*

SEASON

all year

ACCOMMODATIONS

six rooms with private baths

Shadwick House Bed & Breakfast

Ann Epperson
411 South Main Street
Somerset, Kentucky 42501
Tel: (606) 678-4675

ABOUT THE B&B

*S*tanding in the foothills of the Cumberland Mountains, Shadwick House has been known for its southern hospitality for over 70 years. Built in 1920 by Nellie Stringer Shadwick (the great-grandmother of the present owners), the house has been carefully restored to its original stature by Nellie's descendants. The first floor has been converted into a gift shop featuring authentic Kentucky antiques and crafts. There are four upstairs guest rooms, tastefully furnished in antiques. In the days of the Roaring Twenties and the Great Depression, Shadwick House served as a boarding house for railroad workers and traveling salesmen. It's rumored that John Dillinger once stayed here while casing the Farmers Bank in town. Nearby are great attractions such as the Big South Fork National Park, Renfro Valley, Cumberland Falls State Park, General Burnside Island State Park, Tombstone Junction, Lake Cumberland, Natural Arch State Park, and Daniel Boone National Forest.

SEASON

all year

ACCOMMODATIONS

four rooms with shared baths

Pumpkin Casserole

15½-oz. can pumpkin
14-oz. can Eagle brand condensed milk
¼ cup melted butter
½ cup sugar
4 eggs
2 teaspoons ground cinnamon

Preheat oven to 325°F. Mix all ingredients together in a medium bowl and pour into a 2-quart baking dish. Bake for 45 minutes or until set. *Serves 6 – 8.*

Pumpkin Soup

"On cool mornings, this sweet harvest soup is a great start with a slice of pumpkin bread topped with cream cheese."
— *Diane Diviney-Rangen*

1 small chopped onion
¼ cup butter
4 cups fresh pumpkin, cooked and mashed
4 cups chicken broth
1 cup brown sugar
⅔ cup half-and-half cream
¼ teaspoon paprika
Pinch of ground nutmeg
Vanilla yogurt
Croutons

Cook onion in butter for 3 minutes. Combine with pumpkin, broth, and brown sugar. Bring to a boil, then simmer for 25 minutes. In a blender or food processor, purée mixture. Clean pan and pour in purée and stir in half-and-half — adding a little at a time so as not to thin soup too much. While warming mixture, stir in paprika. Top with nutmeg and a swirl of vanilla yogurt. Add 2 or 3 croutons for a little crunch! *Serves 6 – 8.*

The Albert Stevens Inn & Cat's Garden

Diane and Curt Diviney-Rangen
127 Myrtle Avenue
Cape May, New Jersey 08204
Tel: (800) 890-CATS or
(609) 884-4717

ABOUT THE B&B

Built in 1898 by Dr. Albert G. Stevens, this Victorian Queen-Anne classic features a unique floating staircase suspended from the third-floor turret. After enjoying a three-course Norwegian-style breakfast, you can wander off to the nearby historical shopping mall, swimming beaches, the lighthouse, bird observatory, and shops. Or, you may want to unwind in the Cat's Garden. Established in 1992 as a safe haven for the wild or forgotten cats that wander the shore, the garden is landscaped with hundreds of plants and herbs and a little pond, and enjoyed by cats and humans alike. Innkeepers Diane and Curt invite you to join them in rediscovering the soothing sights and sounds of the shore without pretentious overtones. Here, you'll find two hard-working individuals who escaped the corporate world for a life now dedicated to balancing man with nature.

SEASON

February to December

ACCOMMODATIONS

nine rooms (including two suites) with private baths

The Signal House

Betsy and Vic Billingsley
234 North Front Street
Ripley, Ohio 45167
Tel: (513) 392-1640

ABOUT THE B&B

Located just one hour east of Cincinnati, this stately and historic 1830s home on the Ohio River offers spectacular sunsets from three relaxing porches and elegant twin parlors, with river views from every room. Two Civil War officers lived in this house and legend has it that it was also part of the Underground Railroad. Steeped in a rich past, the village of Ripley features 55 acres that are recorded in the National Register of Historic Places. Visit antique and specialty shops, restaurants, three museums (themed on the early pioneers and the Underground Railroad), covered bridges, and lots of friendly people. The beautiful Ohio River offers boating, fishing, and water and jet skiing, with pick-up service from local marinas provided by The Signal House. Your hosts Betsy and Vic enjoy their B&B guests, family, grandchildren, river sports, and life in general! Vic is a letter carrier for the US Postal Service and Betsy is a former dental assistant and business telephone trainer. A full home-made breakfast is served at guests' preferred time.

SEASON

all year

ACCOMMODATIONS

two rooms with shared bath

Scalloped Pineapple

"I serve this dish with ham and eggs and also as a side dish for a pork or roast dinner." — Betsy Billingsley

½ cup margarine
20-oz. can crushed pineapple
¾ cup sugar
1 tablespoon all-purpose flour
2 slightly beaten eggs
5 slices bread, diced

Preheat oven to 350°F. In a skillet, brown the margarine. Remove from heat and cool. In a medium bowl, add the pineapple, sugar, and flour. Add pineapple mixture to the margarine in the skillet. Stir in eggs and mix. Place half the bread in the bottom of a 9" square pan. Cover with the pineapple mixture and top with remaining bread. Bake for 35 minutes. *Tip:* Recipe can be doubled and baked in a 13 x 9" pan. *Serves 4 – 6.*

Shrimp Gazpacho

"Looks great in stemmed glasses!" — *Pat O'Brien*

1 quart clam-flavored tomato cocktail
½ cup chopped and peeled cucumber
⅓ cup thinly sliced green onions
1 teaspoon dill weed
¼ lb. small cooked shrimp
2 tablespoons each olive oil and red wine vinegar
1 tablespoon sugar
1 minced garlic clove
3 ozs. cream cheese, cut in ¼ – ½" cubes
1 medium avocado, peeled, pitted, and diced
2 – 3 dashes hot pepper sauce (such as Tabasco)
Sour cream
Minced cilantro (also known as coriander)

In a deep bowl, combine first 10 ingredients. Stir until well blended. Season with hot pepper sauce. Cover and chill as long as 2 days. If storing longer than 6 – 8 hours, add shrimp and cream cheese just before serving. Ladle into bowls and garnish with sour cream and minced cilantro. *Serves 4 – 5.*

Blue Spruce Inn

Pat and Tom O'Brien
2815 Main Street
Soquel, California 95073
Tel: (800) 559-1137 or
(408) 464-1137

ABOUT THE B&B

The Blue Spruce Inn welcomes you with the distinct Pacific breeze that freshens the Central Coast hillsides that are golden with poppies, tempers the heat of the summer sun, and warms the sands during afternoon strolls on winter beaches. The inn is four miles south of Santa Cruz and one mile from Capitola Beach at the northern curve of Monterey Bay. Gracious personal service is the hallmark of this 1875 B&B inn, where beds are graced with Amish quilts and walls hung with original local art that blends the flavor of yesteryear with the luxury of today. There are quiet gardens in which to enjoy the sunshine of Soquel Village, delightful antique shops at the corner of the street and, a little farther, wineries, gift shops, and regional art displays. Bountiful breakfasts feature fresh fruits, home-made breads, and exceptional entrées. At the end of the day, the hot tub offers welcome respite and, when guests return to their rooms, pillows are fluffed and a special treat awaits — assuring the perfect ending to a wonderful day.

SEASON

all year

ACCOMMODATIONS

five rooms with private baths

Martha and Greg Lau
R.D. 1, Box 196
Schellsburg, Pennsylvania, 15559
Tel: (814) 733-4093

ABOUT THE B&B

*S*ituated near Exit 11 of I-76 (the Pennsylvania Turnpike), Bedford's Covered Bridge Inn borders 4000-acre Shawnee State Park, a lovely trout stream, and the Colvin covered bridge. From this idyllic location, guests can pursue hiking, biking, fishing, cross-country skiing, birding, and antique hunting right from the inn's door. Nearby swimming and boating on Shawnee Lake, visits to Old Bedford Village and Bedford's historic district, driving tours, downhill skiing at Blue Knob Resort, and tours of Bedford's 14 covered bridges round out the list of local activities. Inside the inn, the Lau's attention to detail creates an atmosphere that is comfortable and inviting. The historic farmhouse (circa 1823) boasts six guest rooms with private baths, traditional and country decor, and memorable breakfasts. "There's no doubt what everyone's favorite activity is," say Greg and Martha, "sitting on the inn's wraparound porch and wishing for a life in Bedford County, too!"

SEASON

all year

ACCOMMODATIONS

six rooms with private baths;
one cottage for couples
or families

Spiced Broiled Peaches

8 peach halves
Sprinkle of ground cinnamon
8 tablespoons brown sugar
Maple syrup

Arrange peach halves, pit side up, in a shallow baking pan. Sprinkle each with cinnamon. Press 1 tablespoon brown sugar into cavity. Pour a little syrup onto each half. Broil on top shelf of oven until brown sugar melts. *Serves 8.*

Stuffed Mushrooms

"These tasty morsels can be prepared in advance, refrigerated for a few hours, and baked just before serving." — Lily Vieyra

24 large mushrooms (1½ to 2" in diameter), washed and dried
3 – 4 small green onions (white and green part), chopped
2 sprigs chopped parsley
4 – 6 tablespoons sherry (to taste)
4 – 6 tablespoons butter
3 ozs. cream cheese (at room temperature)

Remove stems and chop them. Sauté stems, onions, and parsley in part of the butter until lightly browned. Add 3 tablespoons or so of sherry. Continue cooking until most of the liquid has evaporated. Remove from heat and add to cream cheese. Mix well, then set aside. Lightly sauté mushroom caps with remaining butter, then add about 2 tablespoons of sherry. Do not overcook. Remove mushrooms from pan. When cool enough to handle, fill caps with a generous amount of the cream cheese filling and place in a baking dish. When ready to serve, heat in a 325°F oven for 10 or 15 minutes. Serve hot with a glass of your favorite white wine. *Serves 6.*

Ferry Point House Bed & Breakfast on Lake Winnisquam

Diane and Joe Damato
100 Lower Bay Road
Sanbornton, New Hampshire
03269
Tel: (603) 524-0087

ABOUT THE B&B

This gracious, 175-year-old Country Victorian is located on picturesque Lake Winnisquam, in a spot commanding a panoramic view of lake and mountains. The gazebo on the point compliments the sandy beach and allows for quiet moments by the water. A 60-foot veranda and all of the rooms are blessed with breathtaking views. Return to the warm, friendly feeling of New England's past with antique furniture, collectibles, and fresh flowers in your room. The lake and surrounding area offer an endless variety of activities, including swimming, fishing, and boating at the inn. Horseback riding, golf, tennis, dinner cruises, scenic train and plain rides, antique shopping, and fine restaurants are all close by. Each morning, you'll be treated to a very special gourmet breakfast with delights such as stuffed French toast, cheese baked apples, poached pears, and select home-baked breads and muffins.

SEASON

Memorial Day through October

ACCOMMODATIONS

six rooms with private baths

Stuffed Orange Cups

"These orange cups have lots of eye appeal and are very refreshing on a warm summer morning." — Diane Damato

6 large navel oranges
½ cup chopped dates
½ cup shredded unsweetened coconut
½ cup chopped pecans or walnuts

Cut off tops of oranges. Remove orange segments with a paring knife and cut up into bite-size pieces, discarding membranes. Catch any juices over a bowl. In the same bowl, toss orange pieces, dates, coconut, and nuts. Put mixture in hollowed out orange shells (you may need to cut a thin slice from the bottom to prevent tipping). Serve on glass plates with a fresh mint leaf. *Tip:* Do not prepare ahead of time — these are best served immediately after preparing. *Serves 6.*

Spreads
Toppings
Jams

Apple Butter

(Recipe from What's Cooking at Carrington's Bluff.)

2 cups unsweetened applesauce
½ cup sugar
1 teaspoon ground cinnamon
¼ teaspoon ground allspice
Pinch of ground ginger
Pinch of ground cloves

In a saucepan, combine the ingredients and bring to a boil. Reduce heat and simmer for 1 hour. Cool. *Tip:* This butter is great to serve on pear bread. *Makes 2½ cups.*

Carrington's Bluff B&B

Gwen and David Fullbrook
1900 David Street
Austin, Texas 78705
Tel: (512) 479-0638

ABOUT THE B&B

The setting is Shoal Creek Bluff and an 1877 Texas farmhouse nestled in the arms of a 500-year-old oak tree. Enter innkeepers Gwen (from Texas) and David (from Britain), who transformed it into an English country B&B. Today, Carrington's Bluff B&B combines Texas hospitality with English charm to make your stay both unique and delightful. Upon arrival, you'll find yourself surrounded by rooms filled with English and American antiques, handmade quilts, and the sweet smell of potpourri. The 35-foot front porch beckons you to sit among the plants and flowers and enjoy the gentle breezes with your morning coffee and afternoon tea. The smell of fresh brewed gourmet coffee invites you to a breakfast that begins with fresh fruit and home-made granola served on fine English china. Home-made muffins or breads and a house specialty ensure you won't go away hungry. Carrington's Bluff is near the University of Texas and the State Capital grounds, and just minutes from parks, hiking and biking trails, shopping, and wonderful restaurants.

SEASON

all year

ACCOMMODATIONS

six rooms with private baths;
two rooms with shared bath

Brambly Hedge Cottage

Jacquelyn Smyers
HCR 31, Box 39
Jasper, Arkansas 72641
Tel: 1-800-BRAMBLY or
(501) 446-5849

ABOUT THE B&B

"**A**bsolutely charming," wrote National Geographic Traveler of this old Ozark mountaintop farmhouse on scenic Highway 7, four miles south of Jasper, Arkansas. A Tennessee guest commented, "The place is uniquely beautiful, the food delicious, and the view inspiring." Three guest rooms with private baths reflect country French elegance in a homestead log cabin. A full breakfast is served on the deck overlooking Buffalo River Valley or behind the screened porch in rocking chairs. You're only minutes from the "Grand Canyon of the Ozarks," challenging-to-easy hiking trails, and canoeing on Buffalo National River. If art is more your style, you'll be happy to know that discriminating collectors still find the work of true artisans in the Jasper area. For those who wish to sample a night out on the town, Eureka Springs and Branson (Missouri) are nearby. Small group special-interest tours and relaxing massages can be arranged. Hostess Jacquelyn Smyers includes her handmade tatted lace and samovar collection in the decor. She's also a designer, commercial artist, and author of Come For Tea and the children's book The Cloud That Came Into The Cabin (inspired by the clouds on Sloan Mountain where Brambly Hedge is located).

SEASON

all year

ACCOMMODATIONS

three rooms with private baths

Apricot-Date Fruit Spread

"Guests appreciate a really good sugarless spread for toast or pancakes." — Jacquelyn Smyers

1 handful dried apricots
4 – 5 pitted dates
Water to cover

Put a handful of dried apricots into a 2-cup glass measuring cup. Add dates. Add water to cover. Cook in the microwave oven until water boils and fruit is steamed and softened. Insert a small electric drink mixer into cup and purée the fruit. Add more water, if needed, to make a spreadable consistency.
Tips: Add more dates for a sweeter spread. Canned apricots that are water-packed and slightly drained work okay in a pinch and don't need to be steamed. *Makes 1+ cups.*

Blueberry-Cranberry Compote

½ cup fresh blueberries
½ cup fresh cranberries
½ cup sugar (or more if desired)
¼ cup Port
¼ cup orange juice
Grated rind of 1 orange
Cornstarch (if necessary)

In a medium saucepan, combine ingredients and simmer for ½ hour. Thicken with a little cornstarch if necessary. Serve warm with waffles. *Makes approx. 1 cup.*

The Parsonage Inn

Elizabeth and Ian Browne
202 Main Street, PO Box 1501
East Orleans, Massachusetts
02643
Tel: (508) 255-8217

ABOUT THE B&B

Dating back to around 1770, The Parsonage Inn was a vicarage in the 1880s and is now a romantic inn. Despite having been remodeled over the years, the house still retains the feeling of historic old Cape Cod. Each of the eight guest rooms (with its own private bath) is uniquely decorated with country antiques, quilts, stenciling, and fresh flowers. A delicious breakfast of waffles, French toast, crepes, scones, muffins, and fresh fruit is served in the dining room or on the brick patio (a popular gathering place for guests). The Parsonage Inn is conveniently located close to Cape Cod's main attractions — Nauset Beach, the National Seashore, and the many bike paths that crisscross the Cape — and is within walking distance of fine restaurants and antique stores. Both born in England, Elizabeth was raised in Kenya and is a pianist and piano teacher, while Ian is an accountant and former medical group executive.

SEASON

all year

ACCOMMODATIONS

eight rooms with private baths

Bedford's Covered Bridge Inn

Martha and Greg Lau
R.D. 1, Box 196
Schellsburg, Pennsylvania, 15559
Tel: (814) 733-4093

ABOUT THE B&B

*S*ituated near Exit 11 of I-76 (the Pennsylvania Turnpike), Bedford's Covered Bridge Inn borders 4000-acre Shawnee State Park, a lovely trout stream, and the Colvin covered bridge. From this idyllic location, guests can pursue hiking, biking, fishing, cross-country skiing, birding, and antique hunting right from the inn's door. Nearby swimming and boating on Shawnee Lake, visits to Old Bedford Village and Bedford's historic district, driving tours, downhill skiing at Blue Knob Resort, and tours of Bedford's 14 covered bridges round out the list of local activities. Inside the inn, the Lau's attention to detail creates an atmosphere that is comfortable and inviting. The historic farmhouse (circa 1823) boasts six guest rooms with private baths, traditional and country decor, and memorable breakfasts. "There's no doubt what everyone's favorite activity is," say Greg and Martha, "sitting on the inn's wraparound porch and wishing for a life in Bedford County, too!"

SEASON

all year

ACCOMMODATIONS

six rooms with private baths;
one cottage for couples
or families

Crimson Sauce

1¼ cups sugar
6 tablespoons cornstarch
3 cups water
12-oz. can frozen cranberry juice concentrate
16-oz. bag frozen blueberries
2 pinches ground cloves
1 teaspoon ground cinnamon

Combine sugar and cornstarch in a large saucepan. Add remaining ingredients and stir often over medium heat until thickened slightly. Serve over pancakes, waffles, or ice cream. *Serves 12.*

Devonshire Cream

(Recipe from What's Cooking at Carrington's Bluff.)

8-oz. package sour cream
½ cup confectioners' sugar
1½ teaspoons vanilla
1 cup whipping cream

Whip together all ingredients and refrigerate. Serve on fresh fruit or breakfast breads. ***Makes 2 cups.***

Carrington's Bluff B&B

Gwen and David Fullbrook
1900 David Street
Austin, Texas 78705
Tel: (512) 479-0638

ABOUT THE B&B

The setting is Shoal Creek Bluff and an 1877 Texas farmhouse nestled in the arms of a 500-year-old oak tree. Enter innkeepers Gwen (from Texas) and David (from Britain), who transformed it into an English country B&B. Today, Carrington's Bluff B&B combines Texas hospitality with English charm to make your stay both unique and delightful. Upon arrival, you'll find yourself surrounded by rooms filled with English and American antiques, handmade quilts, and the sweet smell of potpourri. The 35-foot front porch beckons you to sit among the plants and flowers and enjoy the gentle breezes with your morning coffee and afternoon tea. The smell of fresh brewed gourmet coffee invites you to a breakfast that begins with fresh fruit and home-made granola served on fine English china. Home-made muffins or breads and a house specialty ensure you won't go away hungry. Carrington's Bluff is near the University of Texas and the State Capital grounds, and just minutes from parks, hiking and biking trails, shopping, and wonderful restaurants.

SEASON

all year

ACCOMMODATIONS

six rooms with private baths; two rooms with shared bath

Deer Run Ranch
Bed and Breakfast

Muffy and David Vhay
5440 Eastlake Boulevard
Carson City,
Washoe Valley, Nevada 89704
Tel: (702) 882-3643

ABOUT THE B&B

Relax and unwind on 200 of the most beautiful acres in western Nevada. This working alfalfa ranch is located just eight miles north of Carson City and 22 miles south of Reno, Nevada. Watch the deer in the fields, enjoy the smell of western sage, and listen for the night cry of coyotes. The unique architect-designed and built western ranch house, shaded by tall cottonwood trees, overlooks a pond, Washoe Valley, and the Sierra Nevada Mountains to the west. Two comfortable guest rooms have queen-size beds, private baths, window seats, spectacular views, and lots of privacy. Both guest rooms share the sitting room with wood burning stove, dining area, guest refrigerator, TV/VCR, and other amenities. The owners' pottery studio and woodshop are also on the premises. Full ranch breakfasts include house specialties and fresh fruits and vegetables from the garden. Recreation at the ranch includes swimming, horseshoes, hiking, biking, and ice skating on the pond in winter. Deer Run is conveniently located near golf, skiing, casinos and show theaters, and many excellent restaurants.

SEASON

all year

ACCOMMODATIONS

two rooms with private baths

Fresh Berry Syrup

"We often serve this with French toast that's stuffed with the same fruit or fruit jam as the syrup." — Muffy Vhay

1¼ cups juice from your choice of strawberries, blueberries, blackberries, elderberries, or raspberries
1½ cups sugar
¼ cup white corn syrup
1 tablespoon lemon juice

Note: Adapt basic recipe to the amount of juice you have. Don't make more than you can fit in a water-bath canner in 1 load.

Extract the juice (as for jelly making) from fruit. Combine juice with remaining ingredients in a large, heavy kettle. Bring to a rolling boil and boil for 1 minute. Remove from heat, skim off any foam, and pour into hot, sterile canning jars. Seal with 2-piece canning lids, and process in a boiling water bath for 10 minutes (add 10 minutes more if you're over 5,000 feet altitude). Store in a cool, dark place. No refrigeration necessary. *5 cups of juice will make about 5 pints of syrup.*

Honey-Orange Sauce

(Recipe from Breakfast Inn Bed, Easy and Elegant Recipes from Garth Woodside Mansion.)

2 cups honey
4 teaspoons grated orange rind
½ cup orange juice
4 teaspoons Grand Marnier or Triple Sec

Warm in a saucepan and serve over sliced oranges or apples.

Garth Woodside Mansion

Diane and Irv Feinberg
RR #1, Box 304
Hannibal, Missouri 63401
Tel: (314) 221-2789

ABOUT THE B&B

Experience affordable elegance in this 1871 Victorian country estate on 39 magnificent acres of meadows and woodlands. On the National Register of Historic Places, Garth Woodside Mansion has remained unchanged outside, while graceful arched doors, handsomely decorated rooms featuring original furnishings spanning over 150 years, and magnificent three-story spiral "Flying Staircase" await you inside. You'll enjoy marble fireplaces, canopy beds, your own nightshirt, an exceptional full breakfast, an afternoon beverage, and more. All rooms are air conditioned and have a private bath. The location is ideal for seeing Mark Twain Country. Come for a romantic and magical stay — your experience will be something out of the ordinary.

SEASON

all year

ACCOMMODATIONS

eight rooms with private baths

Pilialoha
Bed & Breakfast
Cottage

Machiko and Bill Heyde
2512 Kaupakulua Road
Haiku, Maui, Hawaii 96708
Tel: (808) 572-1440

ABOUT THE B&B

Located in cool upcountry Maui, this quiet cottage sits on lush pasture land, surrounded by a rose and flower garden and overlooking a eucalyptus grove. Only 20 minutes from Kahului Airport and less than five minutes from Makawao town, Pilialoha is also convenient to Haleakala National Park, the drive to the quaint town of Hana, and other points of interest. This private cottage is fully furnished with a full kitchen (stocked with gourmet coffees and teas), cable TV/VCR, phone, washer/dryer, picnic coolers, beach chairs, mats and towels, snorkel gear, as well as informative books and videos. It's most comfortable for two people but will accommodate up to five people. Freshly baked bread or muffins, fruits, and juice are brought to the cottage daily. Your hosts Machiko (an artist) and Bill (self-employed) reside on the same property and are available to provide visitor information during your stay.

SEASON

all year

ACCOMMODATIONS

one fully furnished cottage
with private bath

Macadamia-Cranberry Conserve

"This conserve makes a special gift for Christmas. It's also great with toasted Pilialoha Grain Bread (see recipe in Breads section)." — Machiko Heyde

2 oranges
2 cups water
12-oz. package cranberries
5½ cups sugar
3-oz. package liquid fruit pectin
1 cup unsalted chopped macadamia nuts (or walnuts)

Peel oranges, trim away inner white part (pith) from peels, and cut peels into very thin strips. Mix peels and water in a Dutch oven. Bring to boiling; reduce heat. Cover and simmer 10 minutes. Chop orange fruit and add it, along with cranberries and sugar, to the peel and water mixture. Bring to a full rolling boil over high heat, stirring constantly. Add fruit pectin and stir well into fruit mixture. Boil 1 minute, stirring constantly. Remove from heat. Add chopped macadamia nuts. Ladle into hot, sterilized jars, filling to within ⅛" of tops. Wipe rims and seal completely. Cool the jars in an upright position and store in a cool, dark place. *Makes 6 8-oz. jars.*

Muskmelon Jam

"This recipe has been a family favorite since my mother whipped up the first batch over 50 years ago. It's wonderful served on toast, biscuits, yogurt, or ice cream."
— Marie George

1 quart ripe (but not prime) muskmelons, peeled, seeded, and
    chopped into ½" or smaller cubes (don't substitute honeydew
    for muskmelon)
2 tablespoons lemon juice
⅛ teaspoon ground cinnamon
1 cup sugar

Place fruit in a heavy kettle, then let stand a few minutes until it begins to form its own juice. Add lemon juice and heat carefully to avoid scorching. Simmer until soft and juicy, then add cinnamon mixed with sugar. Continue simmering until no longer runny, stirring occasionally to prevent scorching. Seal in pint jars or refrigerate until used. *Tips:* Since jam has a low sugar content, it won't keep more than a few days — even with refrigeration. If multiplying recipe, don't cook more than 3 quarts fruit at a time. *Makes almost 4 cups.*

The Georges

Marie and Carolyn George
RR 1, Box 50
Dixon, Nebraska 68732-9728
Tel: (402) 584-2625

ABOUT THE B&B

Look past the large grove of trees and you'll discover The Georges, a large remodeled, air-conditioned farmhouse designed to comfortably accommodate the travel needs of a large family. Your stay includes a hearty breakfast featuring home-made jellies and jams, while other meals can be arranged. Bunking at The Georges offers you the opportunity to see a modern farming operation first-hand, including the planting and harvesting of corn, soybeans, and alfalfa. You'll also hear the chickens clucking and make the acquaintance of several farm cats. During the warm season, you can hike, bird-watch, relax with a book in a quiet spot, or visit county fairs and local festivals. In the fall, pheasant hunting season is in its prime and, depending on the winter snowfall, you can choose from sledding, hiking, cross-country skiing, or ice skating on farm ponds.

SEASON

all year

ACCOMMODATIONS

five rooms with shared baths

Singleton House

Barbara Gavron
11 Singleton
Eureka Springs, Arkansas 72632
Tel: (800) 833-3394 or
(501) 253-9111

ABOUT THE B&B

Singleton House is an old-fashioned place with a touch of magic. Sheltering a hidden enchanted garden on a hillside in Eureka Spring's historic district, this 1890s Victorian home is whimsically decorated with an eclectic collection of cherished antiques and unexpected treasures. Light and airy guest rooms are uniquely furnished with romantic touches and homey comforts. Enjoy a full breakfast served on the balcony overlooking the fantasy wildflower garden, winding stone paths, and a lily-filled goldfish pond. Browse through the small nature library and identify the feathered inhabitants of some 50 birdhouses scattered over the grounds. A short stroll down a scenic wooded footpath leads to shops and cafes. For would-be B&Bers, your host offers an apprenticeship program with hands-on training for anyone wanting to try on the innkeeper's hat before taking the plunge!

SEASON

all year

ACCOMMODATIONS

four rooms with private baths; two rooms with shared bath

No-Cholesterol Tofu Whipped Cream

"This recipe is excellent for people watching their sugar intake." — Barbara Gavron

1 cup tofu
6 tablespoons rice syrup
1 tablespoon vegetable oil or nut butter
Pinch of sea salt
3 tablespoons agar-agar* flakes
½ cup apple juice
1 teaspoon vanilla

Drop tofu into boiling, salted water. Remove from heat and let sit 2 – 3 minutes. Drain. Squeeze out liquid. Blend tofu, rice syrup, oil or nut butter, and sea salt together until creamy. Set aside. Combine agar-agar with apple juice and bring to a boil. Lower heat and simmer until agar-agar dissolves. Remove from heat. Add vanilla and tofu cream mixture. Beat with a wire whisk or electric mixer until smooth and creamy. Set aside to gel. When the mixture has almost set, beat again. Set aside for a few hours to mellow. Chill if not using immediately. To freshen, beat again before using. *Makes 1¼ cups.*

* Agar-agar is an unflavored, gelatinous product made from Eastern seaweed that's high in protein. You can find it in health food stores.

Raspberry-Rhubarb Compote

1 lb. fresh rhubarb
10-oz. package frozen raspberries
½ cup sugar

Combine and cook on low heat until tender. Use as a topping on waffles, biscuits, etc. Refrigerate covered or freeze for later use. *Makes 4 cups.*

The Blushing Rosé B&B

Ellen and Bucky Laufersweiler
11 William Street
Hammondsport, New York
14840
Tel: (607) 569-3402

ABOUT THE B&B

*I*n the heart of the wine country, The Blushing Rosé has served as a pleasant hideaway for honeymooners, anniversary couples, and romantic trysters alike. Whether you spend your day driving, hiking, biking, or just plain relaxing, The Blushing Rosé is the ideal haven in which to end your day. Arise to the wonderful aroma of fresh baked granola and whole grain bread, and begin your day with a special breakfast. The inn itself has an ambience of warm, cozy, 19th-century America. There are four spacious guest rooms each with a sitting area and private bath. Air conditioning and ceiling fans are among some of the amenities offered. Located on the southern tip of Keuka Lake, one of New York's famous Finger Lakes.

SEASON

March through November

ACCOMMODATIONS

four rooms with private baths

The Inn On Golden Pond

Bonnie and Bill Webb
PO Box 680, Route 3
Holderness, New Hampshire
03245
Tel: (603) 968-7269

ABOUT THE B&B

*I*n 1984, Bonnie and Bill Webb *left their desk jobs in southern California to establish The Inn On Golden Pond, an 1879 colonial home located near Squam Lake, setting for the classic film On Golden Pond. Ideal in all seasons, this central area of beautiful New Hampshire offers hiking, bicycling, golfing, water activities, skiing, and skating. The inn is known for its refreshingly friendly yet professional atmosphere. Rooms are individually decorated in traditional country style, featuring hardwood floors, braided rugs, country curtains, and bedspreads. There are seven spacious guest rooms and one extra-large suite, all with private baths. Morning is a treat as Bonnie makes all the breads, muffins, coffee cakes, and her special rhubarb jam. A full breakfast is offered each day featuring regional favorites like baked French toast and apple pancakes.*

SEASON

all year

ACCOMMODATIONS

eight rooms (including one suite) with private baths

Rhubarb Jam

"This jam makes its appearance every morning on the breakfast tables. Guests enjoy it particularly with my home-made white bread. The rhubarb is grown in the inn's backyard." — Bonnie Webb

6 cups chopped rhubarb
5 cups sugar
20-oz. can crushed pineapple
6-oz. box strawberry Jell-O

In a large pot, bring rhubarb, sugar, and pineapple to a boil. Boil 2 minutes. Add Jell-O and stir well. Pour into sterilized jars and top with paraffin. *Makes 8 8-oz. jars.*

Rhubarb Sauce

4 cups chopped rhubarb
¼ cup water
1 cup sugar

Cook rhubarb in water until tender. Add sugar until dissolved. Use as a topping on waffles, biscuits, etc. Refrigerate. *Serves 8.*

The Blushing Rosé B&B

Ellen and Bucky Laufersweiler
11 William Street
Hammondsport, New York
14840
Tel: (607) 569-3402

ABOUT THE B&B

*I*n the heart of the wine country, The Blushing Rosé has served as a pleasant hideaway for honeymooners, anniversary couples, and romantic trysters alike. Whether you spend your day driving, hiking, biking, or just plain relaxing, The Blushing Rosé is the ideal haven in which to end your day. Arise to the wonderful aroma of fresh baked granola and whole grain bread, and begin your day with a special breakfast. The inn itself has an ambience of warm, cozy, 19th-century America. There are four spacious guest rooms each with a sitting area and private bath. Air conditioning and ceiling fans are among some of the amenities offered. Located on the southern tip of Keuka Lake, one of New York's famous Finger Lakes.

SEASON

March through November

ACCOMMODATIONS

four rooms with private baths

The Mainstay Inn

Sue and Tom Carrol
635 Columbia Avenue
Cape May, New Jersey 08204
Tel: (609) 884-8690

ABOUT THE B&B

According to the Washington Post, "The jewel of them all has got to be the Mainstay." Built by a pair of wealthy gamblers in 1872, this elegant, exclusive clubhouse is now among the premier B&B inns in the country. The Mainstay now comprises three historic buildings on one of the most beautiful streets of the historic Cape May district. Guests enjoy 16 antique-filled rooms and suites (some with fireplaces and whirlpool baths), three parlors, spacious gardens, and rocker-filled verandas. Breakfast and afternoon tea served daily. Beautiful beaches, historic attractions, biking, birding, golf, and tennis are all available in Cape May, a National Historic Landmark community.

SEASON

all year

ACCOMMODATIONS

16 rooms (including seven suites) with private baths

Spicy Apple Syrup

(Recipe from Breakfast at Nine, Tea at Four: Favorite Recipes From The Mainstay Inn.)

1 cup apple sauce
10-oz. jar apple jelly
½ teaspoon ground cinnamon
⅛ teaspoon ground cloves
Dash of salt

Combine all ingredients in a small saucepan. Cook over medium heat, stirring constantly until jelly melts and syrup is hot. Serve with pancakes or French toast. *Makes 2 cups.*

Strawberry Butter

½ cup butter
8-oz. package cream cheese
¼ cup honey
½ cup mashed strawberries (or try blueberries)

Combine all ingredients. Best served with muffins, waffles, pancakes, or whole grain bread. Store in a covered container in the refrigerator. *Makes 2 cups.*

The Blushing Rosé B&B

Ellen and Bucky Laufersweiler
11 William Street
Hammondsport, New York
14840
Tel: (607) 569-3402

ABOUT THE B&B

*I*n the heart of the wine country, The Blushing Rosé has served as a pleasant hideaway for honeymooners, anniversary couples, and romantic trysters alike. Whether you spend your day driving, hiking, biking, or just plain relaxing, The Blushing Rosé is the ideal haven in which to end your day. Arise to the wonderful aroma of fresh baked granola and whole grain bread, and begin your day with a special breakfast. The inn itself has an ambience of warm, cozy, 19th-century America. There are four spacious guest rooms each with a sitting area and private bath. Air conditioning and ceiling fans are among some of the amenities offered. Located on the southern tip of Keuka Lake, one of New York's famous Finger Lakes.

SEASON

March through November

ACCOMMODATIONS

four rooms with private baths

New Berne House Inn

Marcia Drum and
Howard Bronson
709 Broad Street
New Bern, North Carolina 28560
Tel: (800) 842-7688 or
(919) 636-2250

ABOUT THE B&B

New Berne House Inn is centrally located in the Colonial town of New Bern and within comfortable walking distance of numerous historic sights, highlighted by Tryon Palace and its formal gardens, only one block away. Quaint shops, fine restaurants, and historic buildings are all in the neighborhood. New Berne House's seven guest rooms feature queen- and king-size beds, antiques and collectibles, private baths, and telephones and clock radios, along with other amenities to pamper guests. A full breakfast is served in the dining room from 8:00 to 9:00 a.m., but coffee is available as early as 6:30 a.m. Throughout the day, guests are invited to join the innkeepers in the library or parlor for light refreshments, television, and good conversation. Two weekends each month are reserved for a "juicy" who-done-it Mystery Package, which blends in nicely with the Inn's two haunted rooms (where "odd occurrences" have been reported over the years!).

SEASON

all year

ACCOMMODATIONS

seven rooms with private baths

Whipped Fruit Butter

"We used to call this Strawberry Butter . . . that was before we tried blueberries, peaches, apple sauce, maple syrup, jams, and orange marmalade!" — Marcia Drum

1 cup butter
1 cup washed and hulled fresh strawberries

Let butter stand at room temperature until it is soft enough to spread. Put butter in a bowl with berries and beat at medium-high speed until the berries are absorbed and the mixture is fluffy. Heap into a serving bowl and serve at room temperature with pancakes, waffles, French toast, toasted muffins, scones, etc.

Cakes

Apple Annie Coffee Cake

2 cups all-purpose flour
½ cup sugar
2 teaspoons baking powder
½ teaspoon salt
¼ cup shortening
1 beaten egg
½ cup milk
1 teaspoon vanilla
2 cups apples, peeled, cored, and thinly sliced
½ cup firmly packed brown sugar
½ teaspoon ground cinnamon
¼ teaspoon ground nutmeg
⅓ cup melted butter

Preheat oven to 400°F. Sift first 4 dry ingredients together, then cut in shortening. Combine egg, milk, and vanilla. Add to dry ingredients and mix only until moistened (batter will be stiff). Spread batter into a well-greased 8" square pan. Arrange sliced apples evenly over the top of the batter. Combine spices and brown sugar. Sprinkle over sliced apples. Drizzle melted butter over sugar and spices. Bake for 25 minutes. Serve warm. *Serves 6.*

Durham House Bed & Breakfast Inn

Marguerite and Dean Swanson
921 Heights Boulevard
Houston, Texas 77008
Tel: (713) 868-4654

ABOUT THE B&B

Located just five minutes from downtown Houston, Durham House Bed & Breakfast Inn is a fully restored Queen Anne Victorian home listed on the National Register of Historic Places. The present owners, Marguerite and Dean Swanson, acquired the home in 1985 with full intention of restoring it to its original elegance and opening it to the public as an authentic Victorian bed and breakfast inn. Today, guests are invited to experience the genuine Victorian ambiance of the inn, and can select from gracious accommodations that include upstairs bedrooms and the privacy of a spacious carriage house. Perhaps the best reason for choosing Durham House is to experience Marguerite's special brand of southern hospitality, not to mention her fantastic full breakfast. For a change of pace, this unique bed and breakfast hosts murder mystery dinner parties using original mysteries written exclusively for Durham House.

SEASON

all year

ACCOMMODATIONS

five rooms with private baths; one room with shared bath

The Inn at The Brass Lantern

Andy Aldrich
717 Maple Street
Stowe, Vermont 05672
Tel: (800) 729-2980 or
(802) 253-2229

ABOUT THE B&B

The Inn at The Brass Lantern is located at the edge of the village of Stowe, Vermont. Stowe is a full-service, four-season resort town, and boasts a vast multitude of world-class restaurants and activities, a cultural center, unique cottage industries, craftspeople, and artists. Originally built as a farmhouse and carriage barn, The Brass Lantern was restored by Andy Aldrich, the present innkeeper, to retain its original Vermont character (for which he won an award). Today, the inn carries the traditional Vermont B&B theme throughout — from its decor of period antiques, handmade quilts, and locally crafted amenities to the food and beverages reflecting local and Vermont state products. In addition, guests are treated to a unique ambience and casual, attentive service. The inn's setting provides panoramic views of Mt. Mansfield and its valley from nearly every room.

SEASON

all year

ACCOMMODATIONS

nine rooms with private baths

Apple Crumb Cake

"A special favorite for the Brass Lantern's afternoon tea."
— Andy Aldrich

Crumb topping:
¼ cup sugar
3 tablespoons all-purpose flour
½ teaspoon ground cinnamon
2 tablespoons butter

Cake ingredients:
2 cups all-purpose flour
1¼ cups sugar
1 tablespoon baking powder
1¼ teaspoons ground cinnamon
1 teaspoon salt
½ teaspoon baking soda
½ teaspoon ground allspice
¼ teaspoon ground cloves
½ cup melted butter
1¼ cups sour cream
2 large eggs
1½ cups finely diced apples

Preheat oven to 350°F. Butter a 9" tube pan. In a small bowl, mix together ingredients for topping. In a large bowl, mix cake ingredients. Spread cake batter into pan and sprinkle on crumb topping. Bake for approximately 60 minutes, then let cool and serve. *Serves 10 – 12.*

Applesauce Cake

"Our family never liked fruit cake so at Christmas my mother baked an applesauce cake to which she added glazed fruits and nuts. This particular recipe, which was given to me by one of the inn's first guests, reminds me of my childhood Christmas traditions." — Pat O'Brien

¾ cup raisins
⅓ cup cream sherry or apple juice
½ cup vegetable oil
1½ cups brown sugar
1 teaspoon salt
½ teaspoon ground cinnamon
½ teaspoon ground allspice
¼ teaspoon ground cloves
¼ teaspoon ground nutmeg
2 unbeaten eggs
1½ cups applesauce
2½ cups all-purpose flour
¾ cup chopped walnuts (optional)
2 teaspoons baking soda

Preheat oven to 350°F. Grease and flour a 12-cup bundt pan (or 9 x 5" loaf pan or 12-cup muffin pan). In a medium saucepan, combine raisins and sherry and heat to boiling; set aside. In a mixing bowl, beat oil, sugar, salt, spices, and eggs until smooth and creamy (scrape bowl often). Blend in applesauce, then flour and walnuts. Stir baking soda into raisin-sherry mixture and add to applesauce batter. Mix well, then pour into bundt pan. Bake 45 minutes or until tester comes out clean. *Serves 12 – 16.*

Blue Spruce Inn

Pat and Tom O'Brien
2815 Main Street
Soquel, California 95073
Tel: (800) 559-1137 or
(408) 464-1137

ABOUT THE B&B

The Blue Spruce Inn welcomes you with the distinct Pacific breeze that freshens the Central Coast hillsides that are golden with poppies, tempers the heat of the summer sun, and warms the sands during afternoon strolls on winter beaches. The inn is four miles south of Santa Cruz and one mile from Capitola Beach at the northern curve of Monterey Bay. Gracious personal service is the hallmark of this 1875 B&B inn, where beds are graced with Amish quilts and walls hung with original local art that blends the flavor of yesteryear with the luxury of today. There are quiet gardens in which to enjoy the sunshine of Soquel Village, delightful antique shops at the corner of the street and, a little farther, wineries, gift shops, and regional art displays. Bountiful breakfasts feature fresh fruits, home-made breads, and exceptional entrées. At the end of the day, the hot tub offers welcome respite and, when guests return to their rooms, pillows are fluffed and a special treat awaits — assuring the perfect ending to a wonderful day.

SEASON

all year

ACCOMMODATIONS

five rooms with private baths

Robin and Rupert Sommerauer
PO Box 769, 244 Forest Trail
Winter Park, Colorado 80482
Tel: (303) 726-5039

ABOUT THE B&B

Hidden in the forest just *minutes from downtown Winter Park, the Alpen Rose is a bed and breakfast with Austrian warmth and hospitality. Share Robin and Rupert's love of the mountains by taking in the breathtaking view from the "common room," enhanced by aspens, wildflowers, and lofty pines. At Alpen Rose, you'll feel right at home whatever the season — from the spare cozy slippers and lushly quilted beds with down pillows to the steaming outdoor hot tub. What's more, each of the five bedrooms is decorated with treasures brought over from Austria, including traditional featherbeds. A full breakfast featuring home-made yogurt, granola, fresh fruit, freshly baked coffee cake or bread, an egg dish, and a meat dish awaits guests each morning in the sunny common room. Rupert was born in Salzburg, Austria. His wife, an American, met him in Germany after a stint there with Outward Bound. The superb natural beauty of Winter Park makes a great place to visit year-round.*

SEASON

all year

ACCOMMODATIONS

five rooms with private baths

Austrian Breakfast Cake

1 teaspoon vanilla
2 eggs
1 cup milk
2½ cups all-purpose flour
1½ cups sugar
¾ cup cold butter
½ cup finely chopped nuts

Preheat oven to 375°F. Whisk together the vanilla, eggs, and milk. In a separate bowl, blend together the rest of the ingredients to make coarse meal. Reserve ½ of this dry mixture. Stir liquid egg mixture into dry mixture, and pour into a greased 12"-diameter bundt pan. Sprinkle remaining dry mixture over batter. Bake for 25 – 30 minutes. *Serves 12.*

Blueberry Buckle

¾ cup sugar
¼ cup vegetable oil
1 egg
½ cup milk
2 cups all-purpose flour
2 teaspoons baking powder
½ teaspoon salt
2 cups well-drained blueberries (fresh, canned, or frozen)

Crumb topping:
½ cup sugar
⅓ cup all-purpose flour
½ teaspoon ground cinnamon
¼ cup softened butter

Preheat oven to 375°F. Cream sugar, oil, and egg. Add milk. Sift together dry ingredients. Stir into creamed mixture (do not beat). Carefully fold in blueberries. Spread batter in a greased 9" square pan. Mix ingredients for crumb topping and sprinkle over batter. Bake for 45 – 50 minutes if using fresh blueberries and approximately 30 – 35 minutes if using canned blueberries. Insert a toothpick in cake's center to test for doneness. *Serves 9.*

Custer Mansion B&B

Carole and Mill Seaman
35 Centennial Drive
Custer, South Dakota 57730
Tel: (605) 673-3333

ABOUT THE B&B

This unusual 1891 Victorian Gothic home, which has quite a historic past in Custer, is now on the National Register of Historic Places. Antique light fixtures, ceiling fans, door transoms, stained glass windows, and "gingerbread" accents help preserve Custer Mansion's turn-of-the-century mood. Six lovely bedrooms are individually decorated in country and Victorian flavor and are named for songs. Delicious home-cooked breakfasts are served in the spacious dining room, with adjacent butler pantry used for serving juice, coffee, and tea. The one-acre yard offers plenty of room for outdoor relaxing and features a shaded patio near a natural rocky hillside. Custer Mansion is located near Mt. Rushmore, town of Crazy Horse, Custer State Park, and many other attractions. Nearby activities include swimming, hiking, fishing, golfing, and hiking in the beautiful Black Hills. Mill, a retired school administrator, and Carole, mother of six and grandmother of twelve, specialize in western hospitality and delicious food.

SEASON

all year

ACCOMMODATIONS

two rooms with private baths; four rooms with shared baths

Bed & Breakfast at Edie's

Edie Senalik
233 East Harpole
Williamsville, Illinois 62693
Tel: (217) 566-2538

ABOUT THE B&B

*S*tep back in time to an era when life was more leisurely. Bed & Breakfast at Edie's is located in the peaceful and charming village of Williamsville, Illinois, just 10 minutes north of Springfield. The 1915 mission-style house is large and gracious. Edie serves a delicious and bountiful continental breakfast, with home-made bagels being her specialty. Sleep in queen-size beds with down pillows. Relax in the large living room, TV room, or enjoy the wide wraparound veranda or rear patio. The nearby state capitol offers plays, symphonies, Abraham Lincoln's tomb and home, and many other interesting attractions. Lincoln's New Salem village is just 20 minutes to the east.

SEASON

all year

ACCOMMODATIONS

four rooms with shared baths

Blueberry-Oat Coffee Cake

1 cup blueberries
2 tablespoons sugar
⅓ cup margarine at room temperature
½ cup sugar
1 egg
¾ cup all-purpose flour
1 teaspoon baking powder
⅓ cup uncooked quick or old-fashioned oats
½ teaspoon grated lemon rind
½ teaspoon ground cinnamon
½ cup plain low-fat yogurt

Preheat oven to 350°F. Grease bottom and sides of a 9"-diameter round layer pan. Line bottom with parchment or waxed paper. In a small bowl, combine blueberries and 2 tablespoons sugar. Spoon into pan. In a large bowl, cream margarine with ½ cup sugar. Add egg and beat until light and fluffy. Combine flour, baking powder, oats, lemon rind, and cinnamon. Stir into egg mixture, alternating with yogurt. Spoon over berries. Bake for 30 – 40 minutes. *Serves 8.*

Bourbon Street Fudge Cake

(Recipe from The Best of High Meadows — A Selected Recipe Collection.)

"This is the best chocolate cake ever! It tastes delicious with cream cheese frosting or with fresh raspberries or strawberries." — *Peter Sushka*

Dusting of unsweetened cocoa
1¾ cups water
2 teaspoons instant coffee
¼ cup bourbon liquor
5 ozs. unsweetened chocolate
1 cup butter
2 cups sugar
2 cups all-purpose flour
1 teaspoon baking soda
2 large eggs
1 teaspoon vanilla

Grease a bundt pan and dust with unsweetened cocoa. Preheat oven to 275°F (no higher!). Simmer water, coffee, and bourbon together for 3 minutes. Add chocolate and butter and stir gently over medium heat until melted and smooth. Remove from heat, stir in sugar until blended, and cool 3 minutes. Transfer chocolate to a large bowl of an electric mixer. Separately, stir together flour and baking soda. At medium speed, add flour ½ cup at a time to chocolate batter, then mix another minute. Add eggs 1 at a time, then add vanilla (batter will be thin). Pour into pan and bake for 1 hour and 20 minutes or until cake tests done. Cool on a rack 20 minutes. *Tips:* This cake is best if not refrigerated. It may be difficult to remove cake from pan, which is why the dusting of cocoa is recommended — it works better than flour. *Serves 12 – 14.*

High Meadows Inn

Peter Sushka and Jae Abbitt
High Meadows Lane,
Route 4, Box 6
Scottsville, Virginia 24590
Tel: (804) 286-2218

ABOUT THE B&B

A s Virginia's only inn that is on the National Register of Historic Homes and has a renaissance farm vineyard, High Meadows offers a rare opportunity to experience 170 years of architectural history and 10 years of new viticultural growth. High Meadows is a grand, unique house, where guests are welcomed with champagne and stay in rooms furnished with period antiques and art, each with private bath. The innkeepers' many special touches and attention to detail make your visit one to be remembered. Enjoy the simplicity of nature on the 50 surrounding acres of gardens, footpaths, forests, and ponds. Owner/chef Peter Sushka ensures that dining at High Meadows is just as pleasurable as lodging there. Start with a breakfast of fresh orange juice, a variety of homemade breads, muffins, and scones, fresh fruit, gourmet egg dishes, and coffee or tea. End your day with a multi-course dinner, offering distinctive northern European and Mediterranean dishes.

SEASON

all year

ACCOMMODATIONS

11 rooms (including four suites) with private baths; two-room cottage with private bath

Bed & Breakfast at Sills Inn

Tony Sills
270 Montgomery Avenue
Versailles, Kentucky 40383
Tel (800) 526-9801

ABOUT THE B&B

Guests are treated to true southern hospitality as soon as they step into this restored 1911, three-story Victorian inn in downtown Versailles — the center of bluegrass horse country and just seven minutes west of Lexington Airport/Keeneland Racetrack and 10 minutes from the Lexington area. Each of the 11 accommodations is distinctively decorated and has its own private bath, including six suites with double Jacuzzis. A full gourmet breakfast is served on the sun porch on china, crystal, and linen. Guests are also treated to freshly baked chocolate chip cookies, a refrigerator stocked with soft drinks, hot drinks, and popcorn anytime they're in need of a snack. The pampering continues as guests choose from the inn's restaurant menu book, have dinner reservations made for them, and are given a map highlighting their way to the restaurant. Guests fall asleep reading previous comments from the guest diary and dream about those wonderful blueberry muffins and eggs Benedict waiting for them in the morning.

SEASON

all year

ACCOMMODATIONS

11 rooms (including six suites) with private baths

Brown Sugar Pound Cake

1 cup butter (no substitutes)
1 cup brown sugar
2 cups white sugar
6 eggs
1 heaping cup sour cream
2 teaspoons almond extract
¼ teaspoon baking soda
3 cups all-purpose flour
2 cups chopped pecans

Preheat oven to 300°F. Melt butter; cream with sugars. Add eggs, sour cream, and almond extract. Add baking soda and flour. Add pecans. Spray 18 mini bundt pans well with non-stick cooking spray. Pour in batter and bake for 30 – 35 minutes. *Makes 18 mini bundt cakes.*

Carrot Spice Cake

1⅓ cups butter
1¾ cups sugar
4 eggs
2 cups all-purpose flour
2 teaspoons baking soda
1 teaspoon ground cinnamon
½ teaspoon ground allspice
¼ teaspoon ground nutmeg
¼ teaspoon ground cloves
3 cups grated carrots
1¼ cups chopped walnuts
¼ cup golden raisins
¼ cup walnuts (for decoration)

Cream cheese frosting:
¼ cup softened butter
6 ozs. softened cream cheese
2¾ cups confectioners' sugar
2 teaspoons lemon juice

Preheat oven to 325°F. Grease and flour 2 cake pans (9 or 10"). Cream butter and sugar until light and fluffy, then add eggs one at a time. Sift flour and spices together, add to butter mixture, and blend well. Stir in carrots, walnuts, and raisins. Spread into pans and bake 45 – 55 minutes, then cool. To make frosting, cream butter and cream cheese, then add sugar and juice. Beat until smooth. Frost cakes when cool and decorate with walnuts. *Serves 12 – 16.*

The Inn at The Brass Lantern

Andy Aldrich
717 Maple Street
Stowe, Vermont 05672
Tel: (800) 729-2980 or
(802) 253-2229

ABOUT THE B&B

*T*he Inn at The Brass Lantern is located at the edge of the village of Stowe, Vermont. Stowe is a full-service, four-season resort town, and boasts a vast multitude of world-class restaurants and activities, a cultural center, unique cottage industries, craftspeople, and artists. Originally built as a farmhouse and carriage barn, The Brass Lantern was restored by Andy Aldrich, the present innkeeper, to retain its original Vermont character (for which he won an award). Today, the inn carries the traditional Vermont B&B theme throughout — from its decor of period antiques, handmade quilts, and locally crafted amenities to the food and beverages reflecting local and Vermont state products. In addition, guests are treated to a unique ambience and casual, attentive service. The inn's setting provides panoramic views of Mt. Mansfield and its valley from nearly every room.

SEASON

all year

ACCOMMODATIONS

nine rooms with private baths

Middle Plantation Inn

Shirley and Dwight Mullican
9549 Liberty Road
Frederick, Maryland 21701-3246
Tel: (301) 898-7128

ABOUT THE B&B

Middle Plantation Inn is a rustic bed and breakfast nestled on 26 acres, several miles east of Frederick in Mt. Pleasant (known for its beautiful horse farms). This charming stone and log home offers guests a peaceful setting, which includes Addison's Run (a nearby brook) and a 10-acre woods. You'll wake each morning to the sound of birds (and an occasional rooster) and see nature in all its glory. Your hosts take great pleasure in sharing their antique furnishings. Each guest room offers a delightful 19th century ambience combined with the modern conveniences of private bath, air conditioning, and TV. A massive stone fireplace, stained glass windows, and skylights highlight the public Keeping Room (a Colonial term for gathering place). A deluxe continental breakfast of seasonal fruit, fresh baked bread, cheese, and cereal are served each morning. Visit 33 historic blocks of downtown Frederick, with its unique mix of specialty and antique shops, dining establishments, museum, and art galleries. Nearby is New Market — antique capitol of Maryland. The inn is located near Baltimore, (Maryland), the Antietam Battlefield in Sharpesburg (Maryland), Washington (DC), Gettysburg (Pennsylvania), and Harpers Ferry (West Virginia).

SEASON

all year

ACCOMMODATIONS

four rooms with private baths

Cherry Coffee Cake

18¼-oz. package yellow cake mix
1 cup all-purpose flour
1 package active dry yeast (1 tablespoon)
⅔ cup warm water (120°F)
2 large eggs
21-oz. can cherry pie filling
⅓ cup butter or margarine

Glaze:
1 cup sifted confectioners' sugar
1 tablespoon light corn syrup
1 tablespoon water

Preheat oven to 350°F. Combine 1½ cups cake mix, flour, and yeast in a bowl; add lukewarm water, stirring until smooth. Stir in eggs. Spoon batter into a greased 13 x 9 x 2" pan. Spoon pie filling evenly over batter; set aside. Cut butter into remaining cake mix with a pastry blender or fork until mixture is crumbled. Sprinkle over pie filling. Bake for 25 – 30 minutes. While cake is cooling in pan on a wire rack, prepare glaze by combining all ingredients. Drizzle glaze over cake and cut into squares. *Tip:* You can substitute any 21-oz. can of fruit pie filling for the cherry filling. *Serves 15 – 18.*

Cinnamon Coffee Cake

Batter:
½ cup oleo (or margarine)
2 beaten eggs
2 cups all-purpose flour
1 teaspoon baking powder
1 teaspoon baking soda
1 teaspoon vanilla
¾ cup sugar
Dash of salt
1 cup buttermilk

Topping:
1 tablespoon ground cinnamon
¾ cup brown sugar
3 tablespoons melted oleo (or margarine)
1 cup chopped nuts of your choice

Glaze:
1 cup sugar
2 teaspoons vanilla
½ cup milk
½ cup butter

Preheat oven to 340°F. Mix all batter ingredients together. Pour half the dough into a 13 x 9" baking pan. Mix all topping ingredients and sprinkle dough in pan with half of topping. Add rest of dough to pan, followed by remaining topping. Bake for 45 minutes. While cake is warm, prepare glaze by boiling all ingredients together (do not beat) for 1 minute. Pour hot glaze over cake. *Serves 12.*

Down to Earth Lifestyles Bed and Breakfast

Lola and Bill Coons
12500 North Crooked Road
Parkville, Missouri 64152
Tel: (816) 891-1018

ABOUT THE B&B

Located near downtown Kansas City, Down to Earth Lifestyles is a beautiful earth-integrated home situated on 86 acres of peaceful woods and rolling hills. Cozy, quiet rooms feature private bath, telephone, radio, color TV, and skylight or picture window. Spacious leisure areas include a guest lounge and patio where you can enjoy a cold beverage and complimentary popcorn, and an indoor, heated swimming pool where you can take a soothing dip. The "great room" is the perfect place to relax with music, games, books, and magazines, or just sit in front of the fire. Comfortable walking shoes are a must as nature and wildlife are abundant. Stroll through woods and over pastures among the cattle, horses, and geese. Fishermen will want to try their luck in the two stocked ponds. Breakfast is truly a mouth-watering experience, served where and when you'd like. Your hosts have a background in education, music, counseling, and agriculture, and invite you to commune with nature and enjoy their down-to-earth hospitality.

SEASON

all year

ACCOMMODATIONS

four rooms with private baths

Singleton House

Barbara Gavron
11 Singleton
Eureka Springs, Arkansas 72632
Tel: (800) 833-3394 or
(501) 253-9111

ABOUT THE B&B

Singleton House is an old-fashioned place with a touch of magic. Sheltering a hidden enchanted garden on a hillside in Eureka Spring's historic district, this 1890s Victorian home is whimsically decorated with an eclectic collection of cherished antiques and unexpected treasures. Light and airy guest rooms are uniquely furnished with romantic touches and homey comforts. Enjoy a full breakfast served on the balcony overlooking the fantasy wildflower garden, winding stone paths, and a lily-filled goldfish pond. Browse through the small nature library and identify the feathered inhabitants of some 50 birdhouses scattered over the grounds. A short stroll down a scenic wooded footpath leads to shops and cafes. For would-be B&Bers, your host offers an apprenticeship program with hands-on training for anyone wanting to try on the innkeeper's hat before taking the plunge!

SEASON

all year

ACCOMMODATIONS

four rooms with private baths; two rooms with shared bath

Couscous Cake with Apricot Glaze

"This recipe is excellent for people watching their sugar intake." — Barbara Gavron

5 cups apple juice
Pinch of sea salt
Grated rind and juice from 1 lemon
5 – 8 tablespoons agar-agar flakes*
2 cups couscous
1 cup soaked and cooked apricots

Bring apple juice and salt to boil in a saucepan. Add lemon rind and juice. Add agar-agar and cook until flakes dissolve. Add couscous, lower heat, and stir until almost thick. Remove from stove and stir in cooked apricots. Oil a mold and pour mixture into it (you may also use a cake pan). If using a mold, allow to cool, unmold, then spoon glaze (see below) over cake and serve with toasted, slivered almonds.

(continued on next page)

Apricot glaze:

3 cups apple juice
3 tablespoons kuzu or arrowroot
Pinch of sea salt
1 – 2 tablespoons rice syrup or barley malt (optional, for
    extra sweetness)
2 cups cooked apricots

Bring 2½ cups apple juice to simmer. Add kuzu or arrowroot to
½ cup remaining apple juice and dissolve, then add to simmering apple juice and stir until thickened. Add pinch of salt and
rice syrup or barley malt, if desired. Stir in cooked apricots. Pour
over couscous cake. *Serves 8 – 10.*

* *Agar-agar is an unflavored, gelatinous product made from Eastern seaweed
that's high in protein. You can find it in health food stores.*

The Shaw House Bed and Breakfast

Mary and Joe Shaw
613 Cypress Court
Georgetown, South Carolina
29440
Tel: (803) 546-9663

ABOUT THE B&B

The Shaw House Bed and Breakfast is a spacious two-story home in a serene, natural setting. From the glass-walled den, enjoy bird-watching and a beautiful view overlooking miles of marshland formed by four rivers, which converge and flow into the Intercoastal Waterway. Outlined by tall white columns, the wide front porch extends the width of the home and features old-fashioned rockers — ready and waiting for guests who are welcomed as family. All rooms are air conditioned, with private baths and a smattering of antiques. Enjoy a full southern breakfast come morning and bed turn-backs and chocolate come bed-time — plus some loving extras.

SEASON

all year

ACCOMMODATIONS

three rooms with private baths

Delicious Apple Cake

1½ cups vegetable oil
3 eggs
2¼ cups sugar
3 cups all-purpose flour
2 teaspoons vanilla
1 teaspoon baking soda
1 teaspoon salt
1½ cups chopped pecans
3 cups apple slices

Glaze:
1 cup light-brown sugar
¼ cup cream
½ cup butter

Preheat oven to 300°F. Mix oil, eggs, sugar, and vanilla. In a separate bowl, sift together flour, baking soda, and salt. Combine mixtures and blend well. Fold in pecans and apple slices. Pour batter into a greased tube pan and bake for 1 hour and 45 minutes. To make glaze, combine ingredients in a saucepan and bring to a boil for 3 minutes. Pour over hot cake and let set in pan 2 hours before serving. *Serves 20+.*

Graham-Streusel Coffee Cake

"Our guests often seem embarrassed to have eaten a whole basket of this coffee cake." — Christopher Sellers

Streusel:
1½ cups graham cracker crumbs
¾ cup chopped walnuts
¾ cup packed brown sugar
1½ teaspoons ground cinnamon
⅔ cup melted butter

Batter:
Yellow cake mix
1 cup water
¼ cup vegetable oil
3 eggs

Maple icing:
1 cup confectioners' sugar
Maple syrup

Preheat oven to 350°F. For streusel, combine graham cracker crumbs, walnuts, brown sugar, and cinnamon. Stir in the melted butter. Set aside. Combine cake mix, water, vegetable oil, and eggs. Beat on low speed until moistened, then on high speed for 2 minutes. Pour half the batter into a greased 13 x 9" pan. Bake for 7 minutes, then top with remaining batter and half the streusel topping. Bake 7 minutes longer, then top with remaining streusel topping. Continue baking 35 – 40 minutes. Cool. Drizzle with maple sugar icing (combine 1 cup confectioners' sugar with maple syrup until of drizzling consistency.) *Serves 12 – 14.*

Grünberg Haus Bed & Breakfast
Waterbury, Vermont

Grünberg Haus Bed and Breakfast

Christopher Sellers and Mark Frohman, RR2, Box 1595RD, Route 100 South Waterbury, Vermont 05676-9621 Tel: (800) 800-7760 (reservations) or (802) 244-7726

ABOUT THE B&B

This picture-postcard Austrian-style B&B is tucked away on a secluded hillside in Vermont's Green Mountains, perfectly situated for visits to Stowe, Montpelier, Waterbury, and Burlington. Individually decorated guest rooms open onto the carved wood balcony, which offers wonderful views from the stucco and wood-trimmed chalet. The giant stone fireplace and wood stove in the BYOB pub are favorite gathering places. After hiking or cross-country skiing on the inn's trails, help Mark feed the chickens and enjoy a full, musical breakfast, with selections such as maple-poached pears, apple and cheddar muffins, and ricotta-stuffed French toast. The evening fire warms up the grand piano where you're likely to hear innkeeper Chris playing anything from Mozart to Phantom of the Opera. Nearby activities include spectacular autumn leaf-picking, world-class downhill skiing, golf, boating, bicycling, gliding, canoeing, antique hunting, outlet shopping, and touring Ben & Jerry's ice cream factory. And you can enjoy the Grünberg Haus's own Jacuzzi, sauna, tennis courts, cross-country ski center, and hiking trails.

SEASON

all year

ACCOMMODATIONS

six rooms with private baths; five rooms with shared baths; three cabins and one carriage house with private baths

Garth Woodside Mansion

Diane and Irv Feinberg
RR #1, Box 304
Hannibal, Missouri 63401
Tel: (314) 221-2789

ABOUT THE B&B

Experience affordable elegance in this 1871 Victorian country estate on 39 magnificent acres of meadows and woodlands. On the National Register of Historic Places, Garth Woodside Mansion has remained unchanged outside, while graceful arched doors, handsomely decorated rooms featuring original furnishings spanning over 150 years, and magnificent three-story spiral "Flying Staircase" await you inside. You'll enjoy marble fireplaces, canopy beds, your own nightshirt, an exceptional full breakfast, an afternoon beverage, and more. All rooms are air conditioned and have a private bath. The location is ideal for seeing Mark Twain Country. Come for a romantic and magical stay — your experience will be something out of the ordinary.

SEASON

all year

ACCOMMODATIONS

eight rooms with private baths

Ladyfinger Cake

(Recipe from Breakfast Inn Bed, Easy and Elegant Recipes from Garth Woodside Mansion.)

8 ozs. cream cheese
1 cup sugar
1 teaspoon vanilla
2 cups heavy cream
3 packages unfilled Ladyfingers
21-oz. can fruit topping (cherry, blueberry, or strawberry)

Mix cream cheese, sugar, and vanilla. In a separate bowl, beat cream until stiff. Add to cheese mixture. Line a 9" springform pan with Ladyfingers, both bottom and sides, putting brown side of Ladyfingers toward pan. Layer cheese mixture and remaining Ladyfingers, ending with cheese mixture. Refrigerate overnight. Release springform pan and top with fruit topping of your choice. Keep refrigerated until ready to serve. *Serves 10 – 12.*

Lemon-Walnut Breakfast Cake

"My all-time favorite!" — Lily Vieyra

⅓ cup butter
¾ cup sugar
2 eggs
1⅛ cups all-purpose flour
⅛ teaspoon baking soda
⅛ teaspoon salt
⅜ cup buttermilk (or ⅜ cup regular milk with 1 teaspoon
    lemon juice)
Grated rind of ½ lemon
Scant ½ cup chopped walnuts

Glaze:
Juice of ½ lemon
⅜ cup sugar

Preheat oven to 350°F. Cream butter with sugar, and add
eggs one at a time. Mix well between additions. Combine dry
ingredients and add to butter mixture. Add buttermilk and mix
well. Add lemon rind and nuts, and mix well. Place in a 9 x 5"
greased loaf pan. Bake for 30 – 35 minutes. Test with toothpick
and remove from pan, if ready. Prepare glaze by combining
lemon juice and sugar, then spreading over top of cake while
still warm. Cool cake completely and wrap. Will keep 2 – 3 days.
Serves 8.

"An Elegant Victorian Mansion" Bed & Breakfast Inn

Lily and Doug Vieyra
1406 'C' Street
Eureka, California 95501
Tel: (800) 386-1888 or
(707) 442-5594

ABOUT THE B&B

Featured in many newspapers
and magazines — not to
mention on television and
radio — this restored national
historic landmark offers Eureka's
most prestigious and luxurious
accommodations. Spirited and
eclectic innkeepers provide lavish
hospitality in the splendor of a
meticulously restored 1888
Victorian masterpiece, complete
with original family antique furnishings. The inviting guest rooms
offer both graceful refinement and
modern-day comfort, individually
decorated with Victorian elegance.
Guests enjoy gourmet breakfasts
and a heavenly night's sleep on
top-quality mattresses, as well as
secured parking and laundry
service. Located in a quiet, historic
residential neighborhood overlooking the city and Humboldt Bay, the
non-smoking inn is near carriage
rides, bay cruises, restaurants, and
the theater, and is just minutes
from giant Redwood parks, coastal
beaches, ocean charters, and
horseback riding.

SEASON

all year

ACCOMMODATIONS

one suite with private bath;
three rooms with shared baths

Ruth and John Hanrahan
344 North 2nd Street
Raton, New Mexico 87740
Tel: (800) 624-9778 or
(505) 445-9778

ABOUT THE B&B

Follow the Sante Fe Trail and step back into the past at this appealing 1902 red brick Victorian home, three blocks from Raton's historic downtown. Guests have use of the parlor, dining room, porches, and flower-filled yard, and are invited to enjoy the classical music during the social hour from 5:30 – 6:30 p.m. Full breakfast is served in the formal dining room, accompanied by friendly conversation. A theater and gallery are within a few blocks, hiking and fishing facilities (at Surarite State Park) are just 10 miles away, and Capulin Volcano National Monument is less than 30 minutes away. Other area attractions include a golf course, several antique shops, and a museum. Red Violet is a non-smoking inn.

SEASON

all year

ACCOMMODATIONS

two rooms with private baths; two rooms with shared bath

New York Cheesecake

16 ozs. cream cheese
⅔ cup sugar
3 large eggs
1 teaspoon vanilla (preferably clear)

Topping:
½ teaspoon vanilla
3 tablespoons sugar
8 ozs. sour cream

Raspberry sauce:
10 ozs. fresh frozen raspberries in heavy syrup
1 tablespoon Kirsch liqueur

Preheat oven to 350°F. Beat first 4 ingredients until smooth (preferably in a food processor). Pour into a buttered 9" glass pie pan. Bake for 25 – 30 minutes or until puffy (top should spring back when pressed lightly with your fingertips). Let cake stand 20 minutes on a wire rack. Hand mix topping ingredients together until smooth. Spread across cake and bake again at same temperature for another 20 minutes. To make raspberry sauce: Defrost raspberries, and swirl in a blender until they become a soft purée. Strain out seeds. Add Kirsch. Put a tablespoon of a sauce in the center of a plate, then swirl to cover bottom. Place a piece of cheesecake on plate, and serve. *Serves 16.*

(continued on next page)

To make mini cheesecakes: Preheat oven to 350°F. Put mini vanilla wafers in bottom of mini muffin pans. Pour in cheesecake mixture and bake for about 10 minutes or until puffy (tops should spring back when pressed lightly with your fingertips). Let cool 10 minutes, spoon topping on top, and bake again at same temperature for another 10 minutes. Cool, then top with jam or jelly of your choice. *Tips:* Baking times may vary depending on your oven so take notes the first time around and adjust times as needed. Line mini muffin pans with mini paper cups.

The Rosewood Mansion Inn

Lynn and David Hausner
54 North Hood Street
Peru, Indiana 46970
Tel: (317) 472-7051

ABOUT THE B&B

Built by Elbert Shirk in 1872, The Rosewood Mansion Inn is a lovely Victorian home situated near the downtown area of Peru, Indiana. The mansion has 19 rooms, including eight bedrooms, each with private bath. As a welcome change from impersonal hotel or motel accommodations, the inn offers the warmth and friendliness of home, coupled with the privacy and elegance of a fine hotel — a combination that makes for a truly unique experience. Enjoy the warmth of the oak panel library, the splendor of the three-story staircase with stained glass windows, the elegance of the Victorian parlor, or the comfort and charm of your room. Consider Rosewood Mansion for your next romantic getaway, anniversary, party, business meeting, or corporate retreat. Nearby points of interest include Mississinewa Reservoir (featuring boating, fishing, hiking, picnicking, and water skiing), Miami County Museum, International Circus Hall of Fame, Cole Porter's home and burial site, tennis, golf, and antique shops.

SEASON

all year

ACCOMMODATIONS

eight rooms with private baths

Oatmeal Coffee Cake

1¼ cups boiling water
1 cup oatmeal
½ cup butter
1 cup white sugar
1 cup brown sugar
1½ cups all-purpose flour
1 teaspoon ground cinnamon
1 teaspoon baking powder
1 teaspoon baking soda
½ teaspoon salt
½ cup walnuts
1 teaspoon vanilla
2 eggs

Topping:
6 tablespoons butter
¼ cup evaporated milk
½ cup sugar
¼ cup chopped walnuts
½ cup shredded unsweetened coconut
½ teaspoon vanilla

Preheat oven to 350°F. Mix boiling water, oatmeal, and butter. Let stand until butter melts. Combine dry ingredients. Mix and add to oatmeal mix along with vanilla and eggs. Mix well. Pour into a greased 13 x 9" pan. Bake for 35 minutes. Prepare topping; melt butter then stir all ingredients together and pour over hot cake. *Serves 12 – 15.*

Overnight Coffee Cake

¾ cup softened margarine
1 cup sugar
2 eggs
8 ozs. sour cream
2 cups all-purpose flour
1 teaspoon baking powder
1 teaspoon baking soda
½ teaspoon salt
1 teaspoon ground nutmeg

Topping:
¾ cup firmly packed brown sugar
½ cup chopped pecans
1 teaspoon ground cinnamon

Combine margarine and sugar, and cream until light and fluffy. Add eggs and sour cream, mixing well. Combine next 5 ingredients; add to batter and mix well. Pour into a greased and floured 13 x 9 x 2" baking pan. To prepare topping, combine ingredients and mix well. Sprinkle evenly over batter. Cover pan with aluminum foil and chill in refrigerator overnight. Remove from fridge ¾ hour before baking. Uncover and bake in a preheated 350°F oven for 35 – 40 minutes. *Serves 16.*

Anchuca

May Burns
1010 First East Street
Vicksburg, Mississippi 39180
Tel: (800) 469-2597 or
(601) 631-6800

ABOUT THE B&B

"*A*nchuca," *which means "my happy home" in the Amerindian language of Choctaw, is an opulent, gas-lighted Greek Revival mansion that has been lovingly restored to its original elegance. Listed on the National Register of Historic Places, Anchuca houses magnificent period antiques and artifacts and recreates the grandeur of yesterday in all its splendor. Beautifully landscaped gardens and brick courtyards surround the mansion, swimming pool, and covered Jacuzzi hot tub. All six rooms and suites have private baths, cable TV with HBO, and private telephones. Children of all ages and small pets are welcome. Anchuca is located in historic Vicksburg, Mississippi — site of one of the most important battles of the Civil War and home of the Vicksburg National Military Park. The mansion is close to the Military Park, Mississippi River boating, and new gambling casinos.*

SEASON

all year

ACCOMMODATIONS

six rooms (including one suite)
with private baths

The Red Violet Inn

Ruth and John Hanrahan
344 North 2nd Street
Raton, New Mexico 87740
Tel: (800) 624-9778 or
(505) 445-9778

ABOUT THE B&B

Follow the Sante Fe Trail and step back into the past at this appealing 1902 red brick Victorian home, three blocks from Raton's historic downtown. Guests have use of the parlor, dining room, porches, and flower-filled yard, and are invited to enjoy the classical music during the social hour from 5:30 – 6:30 p.m. Full breakfast is served in the formal dining room, accompanied by friendly conversation. A theater and gallery are within a few blocks, hiking and fishing facilities (at Surarite State Park) are just 10 miles away, and Capulin Volcano National Monument is less than 30 minutes away. Other area attractions include a golf course, several antique shops, and a museum. Red Violet is a non-smoking inn.

SEASON

all year

ACCOMMODATIONS

two rooms with private baths; two rooms with shared bath

Poppy Seed Cake

18½-oz. package yellow cake mix with pudding in the mix
4 large eggs
1 cup sour cream
½ cup melted butter
½ cup champagne or cream sherry
½ cup poppy seeds

Preheat oven to 350°F. Combine all ingredients in a large bowl and beat for 5 minutes. Place mixture in a prepared 12-cup bundt pan or a 10" tube pan. Bake for 50 minutes to 1 hour (at 50 minutes, check with a toothpick inserted into cake's center — toothpick should come out clean). Cool in pan completely. *Tip:* Try slicing the cake in half lengthwise (creating a layer), then fill with fresh sliced strawberries (or fruit of your choice) and whipped cream. Put the top layer back on, add more whipped cream, and garnish with whole strawberries. *Serves 16.*

Quick Coffee Cake

¼ cup butter
½ cup sugar
½ cup brown sugar
2 well-beaten eggs
1½ cups all-purpose flour
½ teaspoon salt
2 teaspoons baking powder
1 cup milk
½ cup chopped nutmeats
1 teaspoon ground cinnamon
1 tablespoon butter
1 tablespoon all-purpose flour

Preheat oven to 350°F. Cream butter and sugar. Add eggs. Add sifted dry ingredients alternately with milk. Put half of dough in a buttered 8 x 8" pan. Combine remaining ingredients. Put half of this nut mixture on top of the dough in pan. Cover with remaining dough. Sprinkle with remaining nut mixture. Bake for 30 – 35 minutes. *Serves 6.*

Dreams of Yesteryear Bed and Breakfast

Bonnie and Bill Maher
1100 Brawley Street
Stevens Point, Wisconsin 54481
Tel: (715) 341-4525

ABOUT THE B&B

*T*his elegant, turn-of-the-century Victorian Queen Anne was home to three generations of the Jensen family before being purchased in 1987 and restored by current owners Bonnie and Bill Maher. An article Bonnie wrote about the restoration was featured in the Winter 1991 issue of Victorian Homes magazine. In 1990, after giving many tours, the Mahers opened their home as the Dreams of Yesteryear Bed and Breakfast. Listed on the National Register of Historic Places, Dreams of Yesteryear is located three blocks from historic downtown Stevens Point, two blocks from the Wisconsin River and Green Circle jogging/hiking/biking trails, a half mile from the University of Wisconsin, and near wonderful restaurants, theaters, and antique shops. Your visit includes a gourmet breakfast, warm hospitality, and wonderful memories.

SEASON

all year

ACCOMMODATIONS

two rooms with private baths;
two rooms with shared bath

Campbell Ranch Inn

Mary Jane and Jerry Campbell
1475 Canyon Road
Geyserville, California 95441
Tel: (800) 959-3878 or
(707) 857-3476

ABOUT THE B&B

*W*hether swimming in the pool, relaxing in the hot tub spa, or playing tennis, you're always surrounded by the Campbell Ranch Inn's spectacular valley and mountain views and beautiful flower gardens. In warm weather, breakfast is served on the terrace where you overlook rolling hills and vineyards. Only 80 miles north of San Francisco, the inn has five spacious rooms with king-size beds, fresh flowers, and fruit. You may choose to read or visit by the living room fireplace, play tennis, horseshoes, or Ping-Pong, hike the trails at Lake Sonoma, or use the available bikes to tour the neighboring wine country. The surrounding area has many wineries and excellent restaurants, but remember to save some room for Campbell Ranch's home-made pie and coffee served every evening.*

SEASON

all year

ACCOMMODATIONS

four rooms with private baths;
one private cottage with
private bath

Raspberry Cream Cheese Coffee Cake

Coffee cake:
2½ cups all-purpose flour
¾ cup sugar
¾ cup butter
½ teaspoon baking powder
½ teaspoon baking soda
¼ teaspoon salt
¾ cup dairy sour cream
1 egg
1 teaspoon almond extract

Filling:
8-oz. package cream cheese
¼ cup sugar
1 egg
½ cup raspberry jam

Topping:
½ cup sliced almonds

(continued on next page)

Preheat oven to 350°F. In a large bowl, combine flour and sugar; cut in the butter using a pastry blender until mixture resembles coarse crumbs. Reserve 1 cup of crumbs for topping. To remaining crumb mixture, add baking powder, baking soda, salt, sour cream, egg, and almond extract. Blend well. Spread batter over bottom and 2" up sides of a greased and floured 9" springform pan. Batter should be ¼" thick on sides. In a small bowl, combine cream cheese, sugar, and egg and blend well. Pour over batter in pan. Spoon jam evenly over the cheese filling. In a small bowl, combine 1 cup of reserved crumbs and almonds and sprinkle over top. Bake for 55 – 60 minutes or until cream cheese is set and crust is a deep golden brown. Cool 15 minutes, remove sides, and cool completely. *Tip:* Best served at room temperature. *Serves 8.*

New Berne House Inn

Marcia Drum and
Howard Bronson
709 Broad Street
New Bern, North Carolina
28560
Tel: (800) 842-7688 or
(919) 636-2250

ABOUT THE B&B

New Berne House Inn is centrally located in the Colonial town of New Bern and within comfortable walking distance of numerous historic sights, highlighted by Tryon Palace and its formal gardens, only one block away. Quaint shops, fine restaurants, and historic buildings are all in the neighborhood. New Berne House's seven guest rooms feature queen- and king-size beds, antiques and collectibles, private baths, and tele- phones and clock radios, along with other amenities to pamper guests. A full breakfast is served in the dining room from 8:00 to 9:00 a.m., but coffee is available as early as 6:30 a.m. Throughout the day, guests are invited to join the innkeepers in the library or parlor for light refresh- ments, television, and good conversation. Two weekends each month are reserved for a "juicy" who-done-it Mystery Package, which blends in nicely with the Inn's two haunted rooms (where "odd occurrences" have been reported over the years!).

SEASON

all year

ACCOMMODATIONS

seven rooms with private baths

Ricotta Cake

White cake mix
2 lbs. ricotta cheese
4 eggs
1 cup sugar
1 teaspoon vanilla
1 teaspoon lemon juice
Confectioners' sugar, or whipped cream and berries, or ground
    cinnamon and sugar

Preheat oven to 350°F. Prepare white cake mix according to package directions and pour into a well-greased 13 x 9" pan. Mix cheese, eggs, sugar, vanilla, and lemon juice together. Pour over white cake. Bake for 50 – 60 minutes, until brown on top and toothpick inserted in the center comes out clean. Sprinkle with confectioners' sugar, top with whipped cream and berries for dessert, or top with cinnamon and sugar and serve as a breakfast pastry. Freezes well. *Serves approx. 24.*

Always Ready Bran Muffins

"This batter will keep for up to a month in a plastic-covered container in the refrigerator — which means you're always ready to serve them fresh from the oven." — Ruth Hanrahan

3 cups bran
1½ cups sugar
2½ cups all-purpose flour
1 teaspoon salt
2½ teaspoons baking soda
1 cup boiling water
½ cup vegetable oil
2 large beaten eggs
2 cups buttermilk
1½ cups raisins

Preheat oven to 350°F. In a large mixing bowl, combine first 5 ingredients. Stir to mix. Add remainder of ingredients, mixing by hand. Bake for 13 minutes in 2 mini muffin pans or (20 minutes in 2 regular muffin pans). *Tips:* Muffins freeze well after baking. If taking batter out of refrigerator, take from off the top and don't stir. *Makes 50 mini muffins.*

The Red Violet Inn

Ruth and John Hanrahan
344 North 2nd Street
Raton, New Mexico 87740
Tel: (800) 624-9778 or
(505) 445-9778

ABOUT THE B&B

Follow the Sante Fe Trail and step back into the past at this appealing 1902 red brick Victorian home, three blocks from Raton's historic downtown. Guests have use of the parlor, dining room, porches, and flower-filled yard, and are invited to enjoy the classical music during the social hour from 5:30 – 6:30 p.m. Full breakfast is served in the formal dining room, accompanied by friendly conversation. A theater and gallery are within a few blocks, hiking and fishing facilities (at Surarite State Park) are just 10 miles away, and Capulin Volcano National Monument is less than 30 minutes away. Other area attractions include a golf course, several antique shops, and a museum. Red Violet is a non-smoking inn.

SEASON

all year

ACCOMMODATIONS

two rooms with private baths; two rooms with shared bath

Grünberg Haus Bed and Breakfast

Christopher Sellers and Mark Frohman, RR2, Box 1595RD, Route 100 South Waterbury, Vermont 05676-9621 Tel: (800) 800-7760 (reservations) or (802) 244-7726

ABOUT THE B&B

This picture-postcard Austrian-style B&B is tucked away on a secluded hillside in Vermont's Green Mountains, perfectly situated for visits to Stowe, Montpelier, Waterbury, and Burlington. Individually decorated guest rooms open onto the carved wood balcony, which offers wonderful views from the stucco and wood-trimmed chalet. The giant stone fireplace and wood stove in the BYOB pub are favorite gathering places. After hiking or cross-country skiing on the inn's trails, help Mark feed the chickens and enjoy a full, musical breakfast, with selections such as maple-poached pears, apple and cheddar muffins, and ricotta-stuffed French toast. The evening fire warms up the grand piano where you're likely to hear innkeeper Chris playing anything from Mozart to Phantom of the Opera. Nearby activities include spectacular autumn leaf-picking, world-class downhill skiing, golf, boating, bicycling, gliding, canoeing, antique hunting, outlet shopping, and touring Ben & Jerry's ice cream factory. And you can enjoy the Grünberg Haus's own Jacuzzi, sauna, tennis courts, cross-country ski center, and hiking trails.

SEASON

all year

ACCOMMODATIONS

six rooms with private baths; five rooms with shared baths; three cabins and one carriage house with private baths

Apple-Cheddar Muffins

"Apple muffins without cheese are like a kiss without a squeeze. Naturally, we use Vermont cheddar in these."
— Christopher Sellers

¼ cup margarine
¾ cup sugar
½ teaspoon vanilla
1 beaten egg
1½ cups all-purpose flour
1 teaspoon baking powder
½ teaspoon baking soda
½ teaspoon ground cinnamon
¼ teaspoon salt
¼ teaspoon ground nutmeg
1 tablespoon cream
1½ cups chopped apples
1 cup shredded Vermont cheddar cheese

Preheat oven to 350°F. Cream margarine and sugar. Add vanilla and beaten egg. In a separate bowl, stir together dry ingredients and add to batter, stirring just to moisten. Add apples, cheese, and cream, stirring gently. Bake for 20 – 25 minutes. ***Makes 12 muffins.***

Grünberg Haus Bed & Breakfast
Waterbury, Vermont

Bacon-Cheddar Muffins

Cornmeal
1¾ cups all-purpose flour
½ cup shredded sharp cheese
¼ cup sugar
2 teaspoons baking powder
¼ teaspoon salt
¼ teaspoon ground red pepper (cayenne)
1 beaten egg
¾ cup milk
⅓ cup vegetable oil
6 strips crispy-cooked bacon, drained, and crumbled

Preheat oven to 400°F. Grease muffin cups and top of pan. Sprinkle with cornmeal. In a bowl, stir together flour, cheese, sugar, baking powder, salt, and pepper. Make a well in the center. In a small bowl, combine egg, milk, and oil. Add egg mixture all at once to flour mixture, stirring just until moistened (batter should be lumpy). Fold in crumbled bacon. Fill prepared cups even with top. Bake for 20 – 25 minutes or until golden. Remove muffins from pan and serve warm. *Makes 8 muffins.*

Middle Plantation Inn

Shirley and Dwight Mullican
9549 Liberty Road
Frederick, Maryland 21701-3246
Tel: (301) 898-7128

ABOUT THE B&B

Middle Plantation Inn is a rustic bed and breakfast nestled on 26 acres, several miles east of Frederick in Mt. Pleasant (known for its beautiful horse farms). This charming stone and log home offers guests a peaceful setting, which includes Addison's Run (a nearby brook) and a 10-acre woods. You'll wake each morning to the sound of birds (and an occasional rooster) and see nature in all its glory. Your hosts take great pleasure in sharing their antique furnishings. Each guest room offers a delightful 19th century ambience combined with the modern conveniences of private bath, air conditioning, and TV. A massive stone fireplace, stained glass windows, and skylights highlight the public Keeping Room (a Colonial term for gathering place). A deluxe continental breakfast of seasonal fruit, fresh baked bread, cheese, and cereal are served each morning. Visit 33 historic blocks of downtown Frederick, with its unique mix of specialty and antique shops, dining establishments, museum, and art galleries. Nearby is New Market — antique capitol of Maryland. The inn is located near Baltimore, (Maryland), the Antietam Battlefield in Sharpesburg (Maryland), Washington (DC), Gettysburg (Pennsylvania), and Harpers Ferry (West Virginia).

SEASON

all year

ACCOMMODATIONS

four rooms with private baths

The Hen-Apple
Bed and Breakfast

Flo and Harold Eckert
409 South Lingle Avenue
Palmyra, Pennsylvania 17078
Tel: (717) 838-8282

ABOUT THE B&B

Built around 1825, the Hen-Apple is an intimate and fully restored bed and breakfast filled to the brim with everything country and old-fashioned. It offers a relaxed atmosphere with six air-conditioned guest rooms (each with private bath), a porch filled with rockers, a screened porch for warm weather dining, a herb garden, lots of flowers, and a shady retreat in the orchard. The Hen-Apple's well-rounded breakfasts are something to remember — especially the cinnamon French toast — with tea served in the afternoon. Just two miles from Hershey, Pennsylvania, Palmyra is an antique lover's dream. In addition, wineries, shopping outlets, Hershey attractions, the riverboat, and horse racing are nearby. Your hosts, Flo and Harold Eckert, love going to flea markets and auctions, and enjoy reading, gardening, and music. Flo is also a Christmas enthusiast so, come the merry season, the B&B sports a tree in just about every room and an impressive Santa collection.

SEASON

all year

ACCOMMODATIONS

six rooms with private baths

Banana Crumb Muffins

3 large mashed bananas
¾ cup sugar
1 slightly beaten egg
⅓ cup melted butter or margarine
1 teaspoon baking soda
1 teaspoon baking powder
½ teaspoon salt
1½ cups all-purpose flour

Crumb topping:
¼ cup all-purpose flour
¼ cup brown sugar
¼ cup rolled oats
2 tablespoons butter or shortening

Preheat oven to 375°F. Add sugar and beaten egg to mashed bananas, and mix. Add melted butter, and mix. Add dry ingredients and stir until moistened. Fill muffin cups ⅓ full. Blend crumb topping ingredients with a fork until moist crumbs form. Top muffins with crumbs. Bake for 20 minutes or until slightly brown on top. *Tips:* These muffins are just as good without the crumbs. They also freeze very well — just pop in your microwave oven for 1 minute to reheat. **Makes 12 regular-size muffins or 36 mini muffins.**

Banana-White Chocolate Muffins

1 egg
¼ cup vegetable oil
1 cup (4) pureed bananas
½ cup milk
2 cups all-purpose flour
¼ cup sugar
2 tablespoons baking powder
⅓ cup grated white chocolate
⅓ cup ground pecans

Preheat oven to 400°F. In a bowl, blend eggs, oil, bananas, and milk. In a separate bowl, mix together flour, sugar, baking powder, white chocolate, and pecans. Make a well in center of dry ingredients, and pour in milk mixture. Stir until moistened (do not overmix). Fill muffin cups ¾ full. Bake for 15 – 20 minutes until tops are golden brown. *Makes 16 muffins.*

Glynn House Victorian Inn

Betsy and Karol Paterman
43 Highland Street, PO Box 719
Ashland, New Hampshire 03217
Tel: (603) 968-3775

ABOUT THE B&B

Come enjoy the gracious elegance of this beautifully restored 1890 Queen Anne home — from the cupola of the inn's tower and gingerbread wrap-around veranda to the carved oak foyer and pocket doors. Each of the beautifully appointed bedrooms has its own distinctive mood, distinguished by unique interior design, period furniture, the fragrance of fresh flowers, and soft, fluffy robes. A memorable full breakfast is served in the dining room, consisting perhaps of eggs Benedict or eggs Neptune, Belgian waffles, thick French toast, ambrosia, juice, and the specialty of the house — strudel. After breakfast, take a walk or boat ride around famous Squam Lake (where the movie On Golden Pond was filmed) just a few minutes away, and enjoy all that the Lakes Region and White Mountains have to offer. Allow Betsy and Karol to provide hospitality with a warm smile and make you feel as though you're part of their family.

SEASON

all year

ACCOMMODATIONS

five rooms with private baths; two rooms with shared bath

The Signal House

Betsy and Vic Billingsley
234 North Front Street
Ripley, Ohio 45167
Tel: (513) 392-1640

ABOUT THE B&B

Located just one hour east of Cincinnati, this stately and historic 1830s home on the Ohio River offers spectacular sunsets from three relaxing porches and elegant twin parlors, with river views from every room. Two Civil War officers lived in this house and legend has it that it was also part of the Underground Railroad. Steeped in a rich past, the village of Ripley features 55 acres that are recorded in the National Register of Historic Places. Visit antique and specialty shops, restaurants, three museums (themed on the early pioneers and the Underground Railroad), covered bridges, and lots of friendly people. The beautiful Ohio River offers boating, fishing, and water and jet skiing, with pick-up service from local marinas provided by The Signal House. Your hosts Betsy and Vic enjoy their B&B guests, family, grandchildren, river sports, and life in general! Vic is a letter carrier for the US Postal Service and Betsy is a former dental assistant and business telephone trainer. A full home-made breakfast is served at guests' preferred time.

SEASON

all year

ACCOMMODATIONS

two rooms with shared bath

Best Ever Chocolate Chip-Banana Muffins

3 large ripe bananas
¾ cup sugar
1 slightly beaten egg
⅓ cup melted butter
1 teaspoon baking soda
1 teaspoon baking powder
½ teaspoon salt
1½ cups all-purpose flour
6 ozs. chocolate chips

Preheat oven to 375°F. Mash bananas. Add sugar and egg. Add the melted butter, then add the dry ingredients. Stir in chocolate chips. Pour batter into lined 12- or 6-cup muffin pan and bake for 20 minutes. *Makes 12 muffins.*

Blueberry-Banana Muffins

"I dreamed up this recipe one day after finding some bananas that were getting too ripe. It makes very moist and tasty muffins." — Anna Belle Schock

1 egg
½ cup buttermilk
½ cup vegetable oil
1 ripe banana
2 cups all-purpose flour
2 teaspoons baking powder
1 teaspoon baking soda
1 teaspoon salt
⅓ cup sugar
1½ cups frozen blueberries

Preheat oven to 400°F. Grease 12 medium muffin cups. In a blender, mix egg, buttermilk, vegetable oil, and banana until banana is pureed. Sift dry ingredients into a medium bowl. Add frozen blueberries and blended ingredients and mix just until flour is moistened (batter will be lumpy). Fill muffin cups about ¾ full. Bake for 20 minutes until golden brown. Immediately remove muffins from pan. *Makes 12 muffins.*

The Blue Door

Anna Belle and Bob Schock
13707 Durango Drive
Del Mar, California 92014
Tel: (619) 755-3819

ABOUT THE B&B

Enjoy New England charm in a quiet southern California setting overlooking Torrey Pines State Reserve. A garden level two-room suite, with wicker accessories, king-size or twin beds, and adjoining private bath, is yours. The sitting room with couch, desk, chairs, and color TV opens onto your private patio. Breakfast is served in the spacious country kitchen-dining room warmed by a fire on chilly days. Anna Belle prides herself on creative breakfast menus featuring home-baked goods. Breakfast specialties include blueberry-banana muffins, Swedish oatmeal pancakes, and Blue Door orange French toast. Bob is a retired Navy Commander now designing and building custom furniture. Your hosts will gladly direct you to the nearby racetrack, beach, zoo, or University of California at San Diego.

SEASON

all year

ACCOMMODATIONS

two-room suite with private bath

The Summer House

Kay and David Merrell
158 Main Street
Sandwich, Massachusetts 02563
Tel: (508) 888-4991

ABOUT THE B&B

The Summer House is an elegant circa 1835 Greek Revival twice featured in Country Living magazine. It was owned by Hiram Dillaway, a prominent mold-maker and colorist at the Boston & Sandwich Glass Factory. Large, sunny bedchambers feature antiques, hand-stitched quilts, and working fireplaces. Stroll to dining, shops, museums, galleries, pond and gristmill, and boardwalk to beach. Bountiful breakfasts change daily and include freshly ground coffee, tea, fruit juice, and fresh fruit served in stemware. Entrées of frittata, stuffed French toast, quiche, or omelets are accompanied by scones, puff pastry, muffins, or fruit cobblers. Dishes are enhanced with vegetables, berries, and herbs from the inn's garden. English-style afternoon tea is served at an umbrella table in the garden. Boston, Newport, Providence, Martha's Vineyard, and Nantucket make pleasant day trips. Innkeepers Kay and David Merrell (former executive secretary and aerospace engineer respectively) enjoy woodworking, gardening, quilting, jogging, backpacking, and the tranquility of Cape Cod.

SEASON

all year

ACCOMMODATIONS

one room with private bath;
four rooms with shared baths

Carrot-Zucchini Muffins

1¾ cups all-purpose flour
2½ teaspoons baking powder
¾ teaspoon salt
3 tablespoons sugar
½ teaspoon ground cinnamon
1 cup coarsely grated carrots
1 cup coarsely grated zucchini
2 eggs
¼ cup canola oil
¼ cup orange juice
Sprinkle of ground cinnamon
Sprinkle of sugar

Preheat oven to 400°F. In a large bowl, combine first 7 ingredients. In a small bowl, combine eggs, oil, and juice. Make a well in center of dry ingredients, pour in liquid mixture, and combine until dry ingredients are just moistened (don't overmix). Spoon into a 12-cup Teflon muffin pan and sprinkle tops with a mixture of cinnamon and sugar. Bake 15 – 18 minutes or until tops spring back when gently touched.
Makes 1 dozen muffins.

Chocolate Cheesecake Muffins

3-oz. package cream cheese
2 tablespoons sugar
1 cup all-purpose flour
½ cup sugar
3 tablespoons unsweetened cocoa powder
2 teaspoons baking powder
½ teaspoon salt
1 beaten egg
¾ cup milk
⅓ cup vegetable oil
Confectioners' sugar

Preheat oven to 375°F. In a small bowl, beat cream cheese and 2 tablespoons sugar until light and fluffy; set aside. In a large bowl, stir together flour, ½ cup sugar, cocoa, baking powder, and salt. Make a well in center of dry ingredients. Combine egg, milk, and oil. Add all at once to dry ingredients, stirring just until moistened (batter should be lumpy). Spoon about 2 tablespoons of batter into greased muffins cups. Drop 1 teaspoon of cream cheese mixture on top and cover with more chocolate batter. Bake for 20 minutes. Dust with confectioners' sugar when cool. *Makes 12 muffins.*

The Hen-Apple Bed and Breakfast

Flo and Harold Eckert
409 South Lingle Avenue
Palmyra, Pennsylvania 17078
Tel: (717) 838-8282

ABOUT THE B&B

Built around 1825, the Hen-Apple is an intimate and fully restored bed and breakfast filled to the brim with everything country and old-fashioned. It offers a relaxed atmosphere with six air-conditioned guest rooms (each with private bath), a porch filled with rockers, a screened porch for warm weather dining, a herb garden, lots of flowers, and a shady retreat in the orchard. The Hen-Apple's well-rounded breakfasts are something to remember — especially the cinnamon French toast — with tea served in the afternoon. Just two miles from Hershey, Pennsylvania, Palmyra is an antique lover's dream. In addition, wineries, shopping outlets, Hershey attractions, the riverboat, and horse racing are nearby. Your hosts, Flo and Harold Eckert, love going to flea markets and auctions, and enjoy reading, gardening, and music. Flo is also a Christmas enthusiast so, come the merry season, the B&B sports a tree in just about every room and an impressive Santa collection.

SEASON

all year

ACCOMMODATIONS

six rooms with private baths

Victoria Place

Edee Seymour
3459 Lawai Loa Lane
Koloa, Kauai, Hawaii 96756
(Mailing address:
PO Box 930, Lawai, HI 96765)
Tel: (808) 332-9300

ABOUT THE B&B

Perched high in the lush hills of southern Kauai, overlooking thick jungle, whispering cane fields, and the beckoning Pacific, Victoria Place offers an oasis of pampered comfort and privacy to travelers from around the world. Three bedrooms in one wing of this spacious, skylit home open directly through glass doors onto a pool surrounded by flowering walls of hibiscus, gardenia, ginger, and bougainvillea. By day, guests can relax by the poolside or explore the island. By evening, they may retreat to the "lanai" (a long, second-story deck) and watch plumeria, coconut, banana, and avocado trees become silhouettes under the stars. Enjoy waking up each morning to the aroma of Hawaiian coffee, hot home-made bread and muffins, plus an assortment of fresh fruits adorned with gardenias and hibiscus, served at poolside. Victoria Place is nestled in a quiet cul-de-sac, about two minutes from Highway 50, Kauai's main route. Tracing the island shoreline, it links all major towns and attractions, from the rugged hiking trails and cliffs of the Waimea Canyon to the galleries and boutiques of Princeville and Hanalei.

SEASON

all year

ACCOMMODATIONS

three rooms with private baths; one studio apartment with private bath

Coconut Muffins

"This recipe was sent to me by a physician and his wife from Michigan who have stayed at Victoria Place twice already."
— Edee Seymour

1 egg
1¾ cups all-purpose flour
½ cup sugar
3 teaspoons baking powder
1 cup shredded unsweetened coconut
1 cup milk
¼ cup vegetable oil

Preheat oven to 400°F. Beat egg. Stir in other ingredients and place in greased muffin pans. Bake for 20 minutes. *Makes 12 muffins.*

Cranberry-Almond Muffins

(Recipe from The Best of High Meadows — A Selected Recipe Collection.)

1½ cups all-purpose flour
½ cup sugar
1 teaspoon baking powder
¼ teaspoon baking soda
¼ teaspoon salt
2 large eggs
¼ cup melted butter
½ cup sour cream
½ teaspoon almond extract
¾ cup sliced almonds
½ cup whole cranberry sauce

Preheat oven to 375°F. Mix flour, sugar, baking powder, and baking soda, and salt in a large bowl. Break eggs into another bowl and whisk in butter, sour cream, and almond extract. When blended, stir in ½ cup almonds. Pour egg mixture over dry ingredients and fold in until dry ingredients are moistened. Spoon 2 tablespoons of batter into each greased muffin cup and top with a tablespoon of cranberry sauce. Sprinkle remaining almonds over batter. Bake 30 – 35 minutes and cool 15 minutes before serving. *Makes 10 muffins.*

High Meadows Inn

Peter Sushka and Jae Abbitt
High Meadows Lane,
Route 4, Box 6
Scottsville, Virginia 24590
Tel: (804) 286-2218

ABOUT THE B&B

As Virginia's only inn that is on the National Register of Historic Homes and has a renaissance farm vineyard, High Meadows offers a rare opportunity to experience 170 years of architectural history and 10 years of new viticultural growth. High Meadows is a grand, unique house, where guests are welcomed with champagne and stay in rooms furnished with period antiques and art, each with private bath. The innkeepers' many special touches and attention to detail make your visit one to be remembered. Enjoy the simplicity of nature on the 50 surrounding acres of gardens, footpaths, forests, and ponds. Owner/chef Peter Sushka ensures that dining at High Meadows is just as pleasurable as lodging there. Start with a breakfast of fresh orange juice, a variety of home-made breads, muffins, and scones, fresh fruit, gourmet egg dishes, and coffee or tea. End your day with a multi-course dinner, offering distinctive northern European and Mediterranean dishes.

SEASON

all year

ACCOMMODATIONS

11 rooms (including four suites)
with private baths;
two-room cottage with
private bath

The Mainstay Inn

Sue and Tom Carroll
635 Columbia Avenue
Cape May, New Jersey 08204
Tel: (609) 884-8690

ABOUT THE B&B

According to the Washington Post, "The jewel of them all has got to be the Mainstay." Built by a pair of wealthy gamblers in 1872, this elegant, exclusive clubhouse is now among the premier B&B inns in the country. The Mainstay now comprises three historic buildings on one of the most beautiful streets of the historic Cape May district. Guests enjoy 16 antique-filled rooms and suites (some with fireplaces and whirlpool baths), three parlors, spacious gardens, and rocker-filled verandas. Breakfast and afternoon tea served daily. Beautiful beaches, historic attractions, biking, birding, golf, and tennis are all available in Cape May, a National Historic Landmark community.

SEASON

all year

ACCOMMODATIONS

16 rooms (including seven suites) with private baths

Gingerbread-Date Muffins

(Recipe from Breakfast at Nine, Tea at Four: Favorite Recipes From The Mainstay Inn.)

2 cups all-purpose flour
1½ teaspoons baking powder
½ teaspoon baking soda
1½ teaspoons ground ginger
1 teaspoon ground cinnamon
½ teaspoon ground nutmeg
¼ teaspoon ground cloves
¼ teaspoon salt
1 large egg
¾ cup milk
¼ cup molasses
¼ cup maple syrup
2 tablespoons sugar
½ cup chopped dates
4 tablespoons melted butter

Preheat oven to 350°F. Grease 12 muffin cups. Put flour, baking powder, baking soda, spices, and salt into a large bowl and stir to mix thoroughly. Beat egg and add milk, molasses, maple syrup, sugar, dates, and butter. Mix well and pour over dry ingredients. Stir just until dry ingredients are well mixed in. Scoop batter into muffin cups. Bake for 20 minutes.
Makes 12 muffins.

Hazelnut Muffins

¾ cup shortening
2¼ cups all-purpose flour
1 cup sugar
1 teaspoon baking powder
1 teaspoon salt
¾ teaspoon baking soda
¾ teaspoon ground cinnamon
¾ cup brown sugar
¾ cup milk
¼ cup hazelnut liqueur
3 eggs
¾ cup walnuts

Preheat oven to 350°F. Stir shortening just to soften. Sift in dry ingredients except brown sugar. Add brown sugar, milk, liqueur; mix well until all flour is dampened. Beat vigorously for 2 minutes. Add eggs; beat 2 minutes more. Add walnuts. Bake in a paper-lined 12-cup muffin pan for 30 – 35 minutes. *Serves 12.*

La Corsette Maison Inn

Kay Owen
629 1st Avenue East
Newton, Iowa 50208
Tel: (515) 792-6833

ABOUT THE B&B

To spend the night at the Maison Inn is to be the personal house guest of Kay Owen, and to enjoy charming French bed chambers, down-filled pillows, and beckoning hearths. Kay lives in this opulent, mission-style mansion built in 1909 by early Iowa state senator August Bergman. Here amid the charm of the original mission oak woodwork, art nouveau stained glass windows, brass light fixtures, and even some of the original furnishings, Kay operates the highly acclaimed La Corsette restaurant, considered a unique dining experience by gourmets nationwide. The Maison Inn is a delightful extension of that experience. Choose from seven distinctive accommodations (some with double whirlpools and fireplaces), including the penthouse, where you'll be nudged awake in the morning by a rainbow of sunlight coming through the mass of beveled glass windows. In the morning, be prepared for a delectable breakfast served in the gracious tradition of La Corsette.

SEASON

all year

ACCOMMODATIONS

seven rooms (including two suites) with private baths

The Heirloom

Melisande Hubbs and
Patricia Cross
214 Shakeley Lane
Ione, California 95640
Tel: (209) 274-4468

ABOUT THE B&B

Down a country lane to an expansive English romantic garden is a touch of the old south. The Heirloom is a brick, two-story southern antebellum home, circa 1863, located in the heart of California gold country. It was built by Virginians who came to California during the Gold Rush to be merchants in Ione, the supply center to the mining camps of Amador County. Sweet magnolias, wisteria, hammocks, croquet, verandas, cozy fireplaces, and heirloom antiques (including a historic piano) await you, not to mention a royal breakfast and gracious hospitality. Near the inn are over 20 wineries, Gold Rush historical points, museums, and nature walks, and opportunities for gourmet dining, gold panning, gliding, and hiking.

SEASON

all year

ACCOMMODATIONS

four rooms with private baths;
two rooms with shared bath

Healthy Hot Corn Bread Muffins

"This corn recipe reflects the combined influence of the south, the gold miners, and the American Indians on our county"
— *Melisande Hubbs*

1 cup yellow cornmeal
1 cup all-purpose flour
4 teaspoons baking powder
1 tablespoon sugar
½ teaspoon salt
1½ cups milk
4 tablespoons salad oil
3 egg whites

Preheat oven to 375°F. Mix first 5 ingredients well. Add milk and salad oil, mixing well. Beat egg whites to soft peaks. Fold into batter. Spoon into 12-cup muffin pan and bake for 20 minutes. *Makes 12 muffins.*

Heart-Healthy Golden Rosemary Muffins

¾ cup 1% or skimmed milk
½ cup golden raisins
1 teaspoon dried rosemary
¼ cup Promise light margarine
1½ cups all-purpose flour
½ cup sugar
2 teaspoons baking powder
¼ teaspoon salt (optional)
2 ozs. egg beaters or egg substitute

Preheat oven to 350°F. Simmer milk, raisins, and rosemary for 2 minutes in a small saucepan. Remove from heat, add margarine, and stir until melted. Let cool. Grease muffin cups or use liners. Mix flour, sugar, baking powder, and salt in a large bowl. Whisk egg beaters into milk mixture, pour over dry ingredients, and fold just until moistened. Place batter into muffin pans and bake 20 minutes or until lightly browned. *Tip:* These muffins are best when served warm, and can also be served as a bread with dinner. *Makes 12 muffins.*

Henry Ludlam Inn

Ann and Marty Thurlow
Cape May County
1336 Route 47
Woodbine, New Jersey 08270
Tel: (609) 861-5847

ABOUT THE B&B

*I*n a quiet corner of southern New Jersey, by the bank of the spring-fed freshwater lake, a wealthy 18th century family of landowners and merchants built a quaint country homestead. Today that homestead is the Henry Ludlam Inn, offering traveling guests the good life — colonial style. Centrally located in historic colonial Dennisville in Cape May County (voted one of the 10 best bird-watching areas in the US), the inn is minutes away from the colorful gingerbread homes of Victorian Cape May, the beautiful dunes of Avalon and Stone Harbor, and the sparkle of Atlantic City. Innkeepers Ann and Marty offer full B&B services, including heart-healthy food, fishing, canoeing, beach entrance tags to local beaches, or simply the chance to get away from the world. With fireplaces in many rooms and a big swing at the shore of the freshwater lake, the Henry Ludlam Inn is the ideal getaway.*

SEASON

all year

ACCOMMODATIONS

five rooms with private baths

Durham House
Bed & Breakfast Inn

Marguerite and Dean Swanson
921 Heights Boulevard
Houston, Texas 77008
Tel: (713) 868-4654

ABOUT THE B&B

Located just five minutes from downtown Houston, Durham House Bed & Breakfast Inn is a fully restored Queen Anne Victorian home listed on the National Register of Historic Places. The present owners, Marguerite and Dean Swanson, acquired the home in 1985 with full intention of restoring it to its original elegance and opening it to the public as an authentic Victorian bed and breakfast inn. Today, guests are invited to experience the genuine Victorian ambiance of the inn, and can select from gracious accommodations that include upstairs bedrooms and the privacy of a spacious carriage house. Perhaps the best reason for choosing Durham House is to experience Marguerite's special brand of southern hospitality, not to mention her fantastic full breakfast. For a change of pace, this unique bed and breakfast hosts murder mystery dinner parties using original mysteries written exclusively for Durham House.

SEASON

all year

ACCOMMODATIONS

five rooms with private baths;
one room with shared bath

Lemon-Zucchini Muffins

2 cups all-purpose flour
¾ cup sugar
1 tablespoon baking powder
½ teaspoon salt
Grated rind of 1 lemon
½ teaspoon ground nutmeg
½ cup chopped pecans or walnuts
2 large eggs
½ cup milk
⅓ cup vegetable oil
1 teaspoon lemon extract
1½ cups shredded zucchini

Preheat oven to 400°F. In a large bowl, mix flour, sugar, baking powder, salt, lemon rind, and nutmeg. Stir in the nuts. In a small bowl, beat the eggs slightly. Beat in milk, oil, and lemon extract. Add to flour mixture and stir in the shredded zucchini just until blended. Fill a greased 12-cup muffin pan with the mixture. Bake for 20 minutes or until a wooden pick inserted in a muffin center comes out clean. *Makes 12 muffins.*

Mexican Muffins

1 cup yellow cornmeal
2 cups all-purpose flour
2 teaspoons sugar
1½ teaspoons baking powder
½ teaspoon baking soda
Dash of salt
½ cup shredded cheddar cheese
½ cup taco sauce
½ cup sour cream
1 lightly beaten egg
3 tablespoons corn oil
3 – 4 oz. can chopped green chilies, drained

Preheat oven to 400°F. Grease or paper-line 9 muffin cups. In a large bowl, combine cornmeal, flour, sugar, baking powder, baking soda, and salt; stir in cheese. In another bowl, stir together taco sauce, sour cream, egg, oil, and chilies to combine. Make a well in the center of dry ingredients; add liquid mixture and stir to combine. Spoon batter into prepared muffin cups and bake for 15 – 20 minutes. Cool 5 minutes before removing from pan. *Tip:* These muffins freeze well. *Makes 9 muffins.*

Blue Spruce Inn

Pat and Tom O'Brien
2815 Main Street
Soquel, California 95073
Tel: (800) 559-1137 or
(408) 464-1137

ABOUT THE B&B

*T*he Blue Spruce Inn welcomes you with the distinct Pacific breeze that freshens the Central Coast hillsides that are golden with poppies, tempers the heat of the summer sun, and warms the sands during afternoon strolls on winter beaches. The inn is four miles south of Santa Cruz and one mile from Capitola Beach at the northern curve of Monterey Bay. Gracious personal service is the hallmark of this 1875 B&B inn, where beds are graced with Amish quilts and walls hung with original local art that blends the flavor of yesteryear with the luxury of today. There are quiet gardens in which to enjoy the sunshine of Soquel Village, delightful antique shops at the corner of the street and, a little farther, wineries, gift shops, and regional art displays. Bountiful breakfasts feature fresh fruits, home-made breads, and exceptional entrées. At the end of the day, the hot tub offers welcome respite and, when guests return to their rooms, pillows are fluffed and a special treat awaits — assuring the perfect ending to a wonderful day.

SEASON

all year

ACCOMMODATIONS

five rooms with private baths

Victoria Place

Edee Seymour
3459 Lawai Loa Lane
Koloa, Kauai, Hawaii 96756
(Mailing address:
PO Box 930, Lawai, HI 96765)
Tel: (808) 332-9300

ABOUT THE B&B

Perched high in the lush hills of southern Kauai, overlooking thick jungle, whispering cane fields, and the beckoning Pacific, Victoria Place offers an oasis of pampered comfort and privacy to travelers from around the world. Three bedrooms in one wing of this spacious, skylit home open directly through glass doors onto a pool surrounded by flowering walls of hibiscus, gardenia, ginger, and bougainvillea. By day, guests can relax by the poolside or explore the island. By evening, they may retreat to the "lanai" (a long, second-story deck) and watch plumeria, coconut, banana, and avocado trees become silhouettes under the stars. Enjoy waking up each morning to the aroma of Hawaiian coffee, hot home-made bread and muffins, plus an assortment of fresh fruits adorned with gardenias and hibiscus, served at poolside. Victoria Place is nestled in a quiet cul-de-sac, about two minutes from Highway 50, Kauai's main route. Tracing the island shoreline, it links all major towns and attractions, from the rugged hiking trails and cliffs of the Waimea Canyon to the galleries and boutiques of Princeville and Hanalei.

SEASON

all year

ACCOMMODATIONS

three rooms with private baths; one studio apartment with private bath

Mini Fruit Muffins

"While watching me bake one day, one of my guests (a retired executive secretary) jotted down this recipe for me to try. I'm glad she did because my guests simply love it."
— Edee Seymour

3 beaten eggs
¼ cup brown sugar
¾ cup each chopped walnuts, white raisins, shredded unsweetened coconut, chopped dried apricots

Preheat oven to 325°F. Mix together all ingredients and place in foil or paper-lined mini muffin pans. Bake for approximately 30 minutes. *Tip:* Flour is not used in this recipe. As a result, if mini muffin pans are not used, muffins may fall apart. **Makes 24 – 32 *mini muffins*.**

Mixed Berry Muffins with Pecan-Streusel Topping

Streusel topping:
½ cup dark-brown sugar, firmly packed
¼ cup all-purpose flour
1½ teaspoons grated lemon rind
¾ cup chopped toasted pecans, cooled completely
2 tablespoons unsalted butter, melted and cooled

Batter:
1½ cups all-purpose flour
½ cup firmly packed dark-brown sugar
¼ cup sugar
2 teaspoons baking powder
1½ teaspoons grated lemon rind
1 teaspoon ground cinnamon
¼ teaspoon salt

½ cup milk
½ cup melted and cooled butter
2 beaten eggs
¾ cup frozen blueberries, defrosted
¾ cup frozen raspberries, defrosted
¼ cup all-purpose flour

(continued on next page)

The Voss Inn

Frankee and Bruce Muller
319 South Willson
Bozeman, Montana 59715
Tel: (406) 587-0982

ABOUT THE B&B

Built in 1883 by a prominent journalist and mining engineer named Mat Alderson, The Voss Inn is an elegant brick Victorian with a spacious front porch overlooking an English cottage perennial garden. The six guest rooms (each with private bath) and the guest parlor are furnished in Victorian antiques. Guests eat a full gourmet breakfast in the privacy of their rooms. The antique radiator bun warmer is a star attraction of the upstairs buffet area where guests help themselves to an elegant fruit plate, freshly baked muffins or cinnamon rolls, and their choice of an egg/meat dish served in individual ramekins or hot or cold cereal. Owners Frankee and Bruce Muller previously operated a photographic safari camp in the African country of Botswana. Bruce now guides customized trips into Yellowstone National Park and the surrounding areas. Their special interests include wildlife, fly fishing, skiing, golf, and, of course, gourmet cooking — all of which can be enjoyed to the utmost in Bozeman.

SEASON

all year

ACCOMMODATIONS

six rooms with private baths

To prepare streusel: Mix brown sugar, flour, and lemon rind in a bowl. Stir in pecans and melted butter. Set aside (streusel should be dry and crumbly).

To prepare batter: Preheat oven to 375°F. Grease a 12-cup muffin pan and line with 2½" paper baking cups. Combine flour, sugars, baking powder, lemon rind, cinnamon, and salt in a large bowl. Make a well in center. Mix milk, butter, and eggs together and pour into well. Mix until smooth. Combine defrosted berries and ¼ cup flour and toss well. Fold berries into batter and spoon into prepared tins, filling cups. Top each with 1 heaping tablespoon of streusel. Bake muffins until tester inserted in middle comes out clean (about 25 – 30 minutes). Cool 10 – 15 minutes in tin on rack. Remove muffins from tin and serve warm. *Makes 12 muffins.*

Plantation Muffins

1 cup chopped pecans
2 cups all-purpose flour
1 teaspoon baking soda
1 teaspoon salt
3 ozs. softened cream cheese
1 cup sugar
2 teaspoons vanilla
1 beaten egg
½ cup sour cream
20-oz. can crushed pineapple, drained

Preheat oven to 400°F. Heavily grease a 12-cup muffin pan and sprinkle with pecans; set aside. Sift together flour, baking soda, and salt and set aside. In a separate bowl, beat cream cheese, sugar, and vanilla, then add egg. Mix in flour mixture alternately with sour cream. Fold in drained pineapple. Bake for 20 – 25 minutes. *Makes 12 muffins.*

Middle Plantation Inn

Shirley and Dwight Mullican
9549 Liberty Road
Frederick, Maryland 21701-3246
Tel: (301) 898-7128

ABOUT THE B&B

Middle Plantation Inn is a rustic bed and breakfast nestled on 26 acres, several miles east of Frederick in Mt. Pleasant (known for its beautiful horse farms). This charming stone and log home offers guests a peaceful setting, which includes Addison's Run (a nearby brook) and a 10-acre woods. You'll wake each morning to the sound of birds (and an occasional rooster) and see nature in all its glory. Your hosts take great pleasure in sharing their antique furnishings. Each guest room offers a delightful 19th century ambience combined with the modern conveniences of private bath, air conditioning, and TV. A massive stone fireplace, stained glass windows, and skylights highlight the public Keeping Room (a Colonial term for gathering place). A deluxe continental breakfast of seasonal fruit, fresh baked bread, cheese, and cereal are served each morning. Visit 33 historic blocks of downtown Frederick, with its unique mix of specialty and antique shops, dining establishments, museum, and art galleries. Nearby is New Market — antique capitol of Maryland. The inn is located near Baltimore, (Maryland), the Antietam Battlefield in Sharpesburg (Maryland), Washington (DC), Gettysburg (Pennsylvania), and Harpers Ferry (West Virginia).

SEASON

all year

ACCOMMODATIONS

four rooms with private baths

The Hen-Apple
Bed and Breakfast

Flo and Harold Eckert
409 South Lingle Avenue
Palmyra, Pennsylvania 17078
Tel: (717) 838-8282

ABOUT THE B&B

Built around 1825, the Hen-Apple is an intimate and fully restored bed and breakfast filled to the brim with everything country and old-fashioned. It offers a relaxed atmosphere with six air-conditioned guest rooms (each with private bath), a porch filled with rockers, a screened porch for warm weather dining, a herb garden, lots of flowers, and a shady retreat in the orchard. The Hen-Apple's well-rounded breakfasts are something to remember — especially the cinnamon French toast — with tea served in the afternoon. Just two miles from Hershey, Pennsylvania, Palmyra is an antique lover's dream. In addition, wineries, shopping outlets, Hershey attractions, the riverboat, and horse racing are nearby. Your hosts, Flo and Harold Eckert, love going to flea markets and auctions, and enjoy reading, gardening, and music. Flo is also a Christmas enthusiast so, come the merry season, the B&B sports a tree in just about every room and an impressive Santa collection.

SEASON

all year

ACCOMMODATIONS

six rooms with private baths

Potluck Muffins

1 cup all-purpose flour
2 tablespoons baking powder
½ teaspoon salt
½ cup sugar
¼ cup melted butter or margarine
1 beaten egg
½ cup milk
Potluck (anything you have in your cupboard, such as chocolate or peanut butter chips, creamy peanut butter, nuts, fruits, or shredded unsweetened coconut), to taste

Preheat oven to 375°F. Stir together dry ingredients. Add the melted butter and beaten egg to milk. Add liquid ingredients to dry mixture. Stir only enough to moisten. Add potluck ingredients (or add nothing and serve with home-made jam). Bake for 15 – 20 minutes. *Makes 8 muffins.*

Pumpkin-Chocolate Chip Muffins

3⅓ cups all-purpose flour
1½ cups sugar
2 tablespoons pumpkin pie spice
2 teaspoons baking soda
1 teaspoon baking powder
½ teaspoon salt
4 large eggs, lightly beaten
2 cups plain canned pumpkin
1 cup melted butter
1½ cups chocolate chips

Preheat oven to 350°F. Thoroughly mix together the flour, sugar, pie spice, baking soda, baking powder, and salt in a large bowl. In a smaller bowl, mix together the eggs, pumpkin, and butter and blend well. Stir in the chocolate chips. Pour the pumpkin mixture into the dry ingredients and fold in with a spatula until dry ingredients are just moistened. Spoon into 2 greased 6-cup muffin pans and bake for about 25 minutes. *Makes 12 large muffins.*

The Melville House

Vince De Rico and David Horan
39 Clarke Street
Newport, Rhode Island 02840
Tel: (401) 847-0640

ABOUT THE B&B

Built circa 1750 and on the National Register of Historic Places, The Melville House is located in the heart of Newport's historic Hill District on a quiet gas-lit street. One of the few inns in Newport dedicated to the Colonial style, it's just one block up from Thames Street with its Brick Market and the harborfront where many of the city's finest restaurants, luxurious sailboats, antique shops, and galleries can be found. The Melville House is also close to the Tennis Hall of Fame, lavish Vanderbilt, Astor, and Belmont family mansions, the Naval War College, and Newport's finest ocean beaches. The Melville House breakfast menu features home-made granola, muffins, breads, buttermilk biscuits, scones, Yankee cornbread, stuffed French toast, fresh fruit sourdough pancakes, and Rhode Island johnny-cakes. An afternoon tea is served every day, featuring refreshments, home-made biscotti, and soup (on cold days), over which innkeepers Vince and David share their Newport experiences.

SEASON

all year

ACCOMMODATIONS

five rooms with private baths;
two rooms with shared bath;
winter fireplace suite

Hidden Pond
Bed & Breakfast

Priscilla and Larry Fuerst
PO Box 461
Fennville, Michigan 49408
Tel: (616) 561-2491

ABOUT THE B&B

Hidden Pond Bed & Breakfast is set on 28 acres of woods, perfect for bird-watching, hiking, cross-country skiing, or just relaxing in a rowboat on the pond. Guests can enjoy seven entry-level rooms, including bedrooms and baths, living room with fireplace, dining room, library, kitchen, and breakfast porch. Priscilla and Larry, who work for rival airlines, understand the importance of a soothing, calm, and slow-paced overnight stay. They enjoy pleasing guests and creating an atmosphere of quiet elegance. Unwind and take in the sun on the outdoor deck or patio. Turndown service, complimentary soft drinks, tea, hot chocolate, or an evening sherry is offered. Full hot breakfast is served in the sunwashed garden room at your leisure, and features fresh fruits, breads, muffins, and a hot entrée. This lovely retreat is near the beaches of Lake Michigan, the boutiques of Saugatuck, and the winery and cider mill in Fennville.

SEASON

all year

ACCOMMODATIONS

two rooms with private baths

Pumpkin Muffins

2 cups all-purpose flour
2 teaspoons baking powder
½ teaspoon baking soda
1 teaspoon ground cinnamon
½ teaspoon ground nutmeg
½ teaspoon ground allspice
½ teaspoon ground ginger
½ teaspoon salt
1 cup fresh (preferable) or canned pumpkin
¾ cup sugar
½ cup milk
2 eggs
2 tablespoons vegetable oil
2 tablespoons applesauce
¼ cup whole wheat flour

Preheat oven to 400°F. Sift all-purpose flour, baking powder, baking soda, spices, and salt. Set aside. Combine pumpkin, sugar, milk, eggs, oil, and applesauce and add to dry ingredients. Beat until blended. Add whole wheat flour until blended. Bake for 20 – 25 minutes. *Serves 8 – 10.*

Rhubarb Muffins

"This recipe comes from my friend, Ruth Roemer, who has a huge part of her garden devoted to rhubarb that she shares with her friends. Often, we'll pack up a few of these muffins for our departing guests to munch on as they continue their travels." — Erma Rummel

½ cup buttermilk
½ cup vegetable oil
1 egg
2 teaspoons vanilla
1¼ cups brown sugar
2½ cups all-purpose flour
1 teaspoon salt
1 teaspoon baking soda
1 teaspoon baking powder
½ cup chopped pecans
1½ cups diced rhubarb

Topping:
1¼ teaspoons melted butter or margarine
⅓ cup white sugar
1 (generous) tablespoon all-purpose flour
1 teaspoon ground cinnamon

Preheat oven to 400°F. Beat together all ingredients except rhubarb and pecans. Add rhubarb and pecans. Mix well. Fill 2 greased (or paper-lined) muffin pans ⅔ full. Sprinkle with topping and bake for 18 – 20 minutes. These muffins freeze well. *Makes 24 muffins.*

Rummel's Tree Haven Bed & Breakfast

Erma and Carl Rummel
41 North Beck Street (M-25)
Sebewaing, Michigan 48759
Tel: (517) 883-2450

ABOUT THE B&B

Located in the village of Sebewaing, Michigan, in the hollow of the thumb on Saginaw Bay, Rummel's Tree Haven was originally built as the farm home of Barbara and Frederick Beck in 1878. Today, Erma and Carl Rummel call it home and offer comfort and convenience to all travelers. The B&B is surrounded by many trees, which gives it an air of privacy — one tree even grows right through the porch roof! Saginaw Bay offers fine fishing, hunting, boating, bird-watching, or just relaxing. The Rummels love having company and will make you feel welcome.

SEASON

all year

ACCOMMODATIONS

two rooms with private baths

Brambly Hedge Cottage

Jacquelyn Smyers
HCR 31, Box 39
Jasper, Arkansas 72641
Tel: 1-800-BRAMBLY or
(501) 446-5849

ABOUT THE B&B

"**A**bsolutely charming," wrote National Geographic Traveler of this old Ozark mountaintop farmhouse on scenic Highway 7, four miles south of Jasper, Arkansas. A Tennessee guest commented, "The place is uniquely beautiful, the food delicious, and the view inspiring." Three guest rooms with private baths reflect country French elegance in a homestead log cabin. A full breakfast is served on the deck overlooking Buffalo River Valley or behind the screened porch in rocking chairs. You're only minutes from the "Grand Canyon of the Ozarks," challenging-to-easy hiking trails, and canoeing on Buffalo National River. If art is more your style, you'll be happy to know that discriminating collectors still find the work of true artisans in the Jasper area. For those who wish to sample a night out on the town, Eureka Springs and Branson (Missouri) are nearby. Small group special-interest tours and relaxing massages can be arranged. Hostess Jacquelyn Smyers includes her handmade tatted lace and samovar collection in the decor. She's also a designer, commercial artist, and author of Come For Tea and the children's book The Cloud That Came Into The Cabin (inspired by the clouds on Sloan Mountain where Brambly Hedge is located).

SEASON

all year

ACCOMMODATIONS

three rooms with private baths

Six Week Muffins

"People LOVE these hot or cold. They freeze well, too."
— Jacquelyn Smyers

15-oz. box Raisin Bran cereal
3 cups sugar
5 cups all-purpose flour
5 teaspoons baking soda
2 teaspoons salt
1 cup vegetable oil
4 beaten eggs
1 quart buttermilk

Preheat oven to 375 – 400°F. Mix dry ingredients in a large bowl. Add wet ingredients and mix well. Store in a covered container in the refrigerator and use as needed — batter will keep for 6 weeks. Fill greased muffin cups ⅔ full and bake for 15 – 20 minutes. *Makes 5 dozen muffins.*

Sour Cream-Peach Muffins

1½ cups brown sugar
⅔ cup vegetable oil
1 egg
1 teaspoon vanilla
1 cup sour cream
1 teaspoon baking soda
1 teaspoon salt
2¼ cups all-purpose flour
1½ cups chopped peaches (fresh or canned)
½ cup chopped nuts

Preheat oven to 325°F. Mix brown sugar, oil, egg, vanilla, and sour cream. Beat well. Combine dry ingredients in a bowl. Slowly stir into creamed mixture (do not beat or overmix). Fold in peaches and nuts. Bake for 25 minutes or until done. *Tip:* Try fresh raspberries instead of peaches, and always remember to drain fruit first. *Makes 2 dozen muffins.*

Custer Mansion B&B

Carole and Mill Seaman
35 Centennial Drive
Custer, South Dakota 57730
Tel: (605) 673-3333

ABOUT THE B&B

This unusual 1891 Victorian Gothic home, which has quite a historic past in Custer, is now on the National Register of Historic Places. Antique light fixtures, ceiling fans, door transoms, stained glass windows, and "gingerbread" accents help preserve Custer Mansion's turn-of-the-century mood. Six lovely bedrooms are individually decorated in country and Victorian flavor and are named for songs. Delicious home-cooked breakfasts are served in the spacious dining room, with adjacent butler pantry used for serving juice, coffee, and tea. The one-acre yard offers plenty of room for outdoor relaxing and features a shaded patio near a natural rocky hillside. Custer Mansion is located near Mt. Rushmore, town of Crazy Horse, Custer State Park, and many other attractions. Nearby activities include swimming, hiking, fishing, golfing, and hiking in the beautiful Black Hills. Mill, a retired school administrator, and Carole, mother of six and grand-mother of twelve, specialize in western hospitality and delicious food.

SEASON

all year

ACCOMMODATIONS

two rooms with private baths;
four rooms with shared baths

Lindgren's Bed & Breakfast

Shirley Lindgren
County Road 35, PO Box 56
Lutsen, Minnesota 55612-0056
Tel: (218) 663-7450

ABOUT THE B&B

*L**ess than two hours from Duluth, Minnesota, and Thunder Bay, Ontario, this 1920s rustic log home with manicured grounds and walkable shoreline resides on Lake Superior in Superior National Forest. The living room features an 18-foot beamed ceiling, massive stone fireplace, and hunting trophies. Guest rooms are cozily designed in either knotty cedar, pine, or rustic paneling. Scenic points of interest include Split Rock Lighthouse, Gooseberry Falls, and Tettegouche State Park. Depending on the season, you can choose from hiking trails, skyride and alpine slide, mountain biking, horseback riding, golf, tennis, fishing, snowmobiling, and cross-country and downhill skiing. Any number of fine restaurants are nearby, and you're within walking distance of Lutsen Resort, the oldest in the state. Your hosts are retired after 35 years of owning and operating a successful garden center, landscaping, nursery, and floral business in Minneapolis, and enjoy fishing, hunting and, most of all, people, which is why they opened their home as a bed and breakfast!*

SEASON

all year

ACCOMMODATIONS

four rooms with private baths

Wild Raspberry Muffins

1¼ cups sugar
½ cup margarine
2 eggs
1 cup sour cream
1 teaspoon vanilla
2 cups all-purpose flour
1 teaspoon baking powder
½ teaspoon baking soda
¼ teaspoon salt
1 cup fresh or frozen wild raspberries

Topping:
2 tablespoons sugar
¼ teaspoon ground cinnamon
¼ teaspoon ground nutmeg

Preheat oven to 375°F. Cream sugar and shortening. Add eggs, sour cream, and vanilla. Add sifted dry ingredients and mix until just moist. Fold in berries. Place batter in 2 prepared muffin pans. Mix topping ingredients and sprinkle ¼ teaspoon on each muffin. Bake for 25 – 30 minutes. ***Makes 24 muffins.***

Breads

Anadama Bread

3½ cups water
¾ cup molasses
½ cup margarine
1 cup cornmeal
2 packages active dry yeast (2 tablespoons)
1 tablespoon salt
10 cups (approx.) all-purpose flour

In a medium pot, heat water, molasses, and margarine to boiling. Stir in cornmeal with a wire whisk and cook for 2 minutes, stirring constantly. Set aside and cool for approximately 45 minutes. In a large bowl, combine yeast, salt, and 2 cups flour. Beat in cornmeal mixture for several minutes. Add 1½ cups flour and beat for several more minutes. Add 5 cups flour to form a soft dough. Knead for 5 – 10 minutes, adding more flour if needed. Shape into a ball and place into a greased bowl. Cover with a damp cloth and let rise for 1½ hours. Punch down center with fist and let rest 15 minutes. Grease 2 large bread pans and roll out dough and place into pans. Let rise for 45 minutes. Bake in a preheated 350°F oven for 30 – 35 minutes. Remove immediately from pans and cool. *Makes 1 loaf.*

The Inn at The Brass Lantern

Andy Aldrich
717 Maple Street
Stowe, Vermont 05672
Tel: (800) 729-2980 or
(802) 253-2229

ABOUT THE B&B

The Inn at The Brass Lantern is located at the edge of the village of Stowe, Vermont. Stowe is a full-service, four-season resort town, and boasts a vast multitude of world-class restaurants and activities, a cultural center, unique cottage industries, craftspeople, and artists. Originally built as a farmhouse and carriage barn, The Brass Lantern was restored by Andy Aldrich, the present innkeeper, to retain its original Vermont character (for which he won an award). Today, the inn carries the traditional Vermont B&B theme throughout — from its decor of period antiques, handmade quilts, and locally crafted amenities to the food and beverages reflecting local and Vermont state products. In addition, guests are treated to a unique ambience and casual, attentive service. The inn's setting provides panoramic views of Mt. Mansfield and its valley from nearly every room.

SEASON

all year

ACCOMMODATIONS

nine rooms with private baths

Phil Irwin
47 Dearing Road
Flint Hill, Virginia 22627
Tel: (800) BNB-1812 or
(703) 675-3693

ABOUT THE B&B

With Virginia's Blue Ridge Mountains as a backdrop, Caledonia Farm offers its guests a beautiful setting amid scenic pasturelands surrounded by stone fences. The farm's federal-style house and companion summer kitchen were completed in 1812. Restoration was completed in 1965, with the original two-foot-thick stone walls and 32-foot-long beams remaining intact along with the original mantels, paneled windows, and wide pine floors. The winter kitchen's huge fireplace provides a delightful atmosphere during cool seasons while three porches offer a variety of views in the warmer months. Guest rooms are air conditioned, and have working fireplaces, individual heat control, and fine double beds. The B&B is called Caledonia (the mythological name for Scotland) to honor the original immigrants to this magnificent area.

SEASON

all year

ACCOMMODATIONS

two suites with private baths; two rooms with shared bath

Apple-Nut Bread

2 cups all-purpose flour
¾ cup sugar
1 tablespoon baking powder
½ tablespoon baking soda
½ tablespoon ground cinnamon
1 egg
1 cup applesauce
2 tablespoons vegetable oil
1 cup chopped nuts

Preheat oven to 350°F. In a mixing bowl, combine first 5 dry ingredients. Add egg, applesauce, and oil, then blend. Add nuts. Pour batter into a greased 9 x 5" loaf pan (or 12-cup muffin pan). Bake for 45 minutes. Test center with a toothpick. Cool and serve. *Makes 1 loaf.*

Aunt Marie's Spoon Bread

"This corn recipe reflects the combined influence of the south, the gold miners, and the American Indians on our county."
— *Melisande Hubbs*

2 cups milk
¾ cup white cornmeal or ½ cup yellow cornmeal
1 tablespoon butter
¼ teaspoon salt
1 tablespoon sugar
2 separated eggs

Preheat oven to 350°F. In a medium saucepan, scald milk. Stir in the cornmeal, butter, salt, and sugar. Remove from heat. Beat egg yolks and add to saucepan. Cool, then fold in stiffly beaten egg whites. Pour into a covered 1 quart baking dish and set in a pan of warm water. Bake for 1 hour. Just before serving, uncover dish and brown top until golden. Serve with butter as a side dish or breakfast entrée. *Serves 4.*

The Heirloom

Melisande Hubbs and
Patricia Cross
214 Shakeley Lane
Ione, California 95640
Tel: (209) 274-4468

ABOUT THE B&B

Down a country lane to an expansive English romantic garden is a touch of the old south. The Heirloom is a brick, two-story southern antebellum home, circa 1863, located in the heart of California gold country. It was built by Virginians who came to California during the Gold Rush to be merchants in Ione, the supply center to the mining camps of Amador County. Sweet magnolias, wisteria, hammocks, croquet, verandas, cozy fireplaces, and heirloom antiques (including a historic piano) await you, not to mention a royal breakfast and gracious hospitality. Near the inn are over 20 wineries, Gold Rush historical points, museums, and nature walks, and opportunities for gourmet dining, gold panning, gliding, and hiking.

SEASON

all year

ACCOMMODATIONS

four rooms with private baths;
two rooms with shared bath

The Ancient Pines B&B

Genevieve Simmens
2015 Parley Street
Nauvoo, Illinois 62354
Tel: (217) 453-2767

ABOUT THE B&B

Surrounded by 140-year-old evergreens, this turn-of-the century home features exquisite exterior brick detailing, stained glass windows, and etched glass front door — all part of the original construction. Pressed tin ceilings, carved woodwork, an open staircase, claw-foot tubs, and lovingly decorated bedrooms grace the interior. You can relax on the front veranda and watch the workers at the nearby winery or find seclusion on the side porch. There are herb and flower gardens to wander in, a lawn for croquet, and a library for playing chess or music. When day is done, you'll drift off in clean, comfortable beds, lulled to sleep by the whispering pines, then awake to the smell of baking bread. A heart-healthy menu can be provided upon request.

SEASON

all year

ACCOMMODATIONS

three rooms with shared baths

B&B Mini Loaves

2 packages active dry yeast (2 tablespoons)
2 cups lukewarm water
2 tablespoons sugar
1 tablespoon salt
¼ cup salad oil
½ cup potato flour
4 – 6 cups all-purpose flour

In a large bowl, dissolve yeast in lukewarm water. Let rest until foam rises to top (about 5 minutes). Add sugar, salt, salad oil, potato flour, and 2½ cups of the all-purpose flour. Beat until smooth. Add enough additional all-purpose flour, stirring, until dough is ready to knead. Knead 10 minutes by hand. Put in a warm place in a lightly greased bowl. Let rise until size has doubled (about 45 minutes). Punch down, then let rest 10 minutes. Preheat oven to 400°F. Shape into 10 mini loaves and place on baking sheets. Let rise and bake 20 minutes on bottom shelf of oven. *Makes 10 mini loaves.*

The

Ancient Pines

Beer Bread

3½ cups all-purpose flour
¼ cup sugar
1 teaspoon salt
1 teaspoon baking soda
1 teaspoon baking powder
1 can warm (but not flat) beer
1 egg

Preheat oven to 350°F. Mix dry ingredients. Add beer and egg. Spread in either a greased standard loaf pan and bake at 350°F for approximately 50 minutes, or spread in 3 greased mini-sized loaf pans and bake for approximately 35 minutes. *Makes 1 loaf.*

Hutton House

Loretta Murray and Dean Ahren
PO Box 88, Route 250/219
Huttonsville, West Virginia
26273
Tel: (304) 335-6701

ABOUT THE B&B

Majestically situated above the tiny town of Huttonsville, this meticulously restored turn-of-the-century Queen Anne Victorian commands a broad view of the Tygart River Valley and the Laurel Mountains. Hutton House, which is listed in the National Register of Historic Places, features original oak woodwork, ornate windows, a three-story turret, arched pocket doors, wraparound porch, and a winding staircase. Antiques abound, and each of the guest rooms is furnished in its own individual style. Breakfast is a time to get to know your hosts and the other guests, while enjoying a variety of pancakes, French toast, and egg dishes along with fresh fruit, crème brulée, sorbet, or even porridge. Guests can then relax on the porch, play games on the lawn, or take a leisurely hike on the trail behind the house. Nearby attractions include Cass Railroad, National Radio Observatory, underground caverns, and rock climbing.

SEASON

all year

ACCOMMODATIONS

six rooms with private baths

High Meadows Inn

Peter Sushka and Jae Abbitt
High Meadows Lane,
Route 4, Box 6
Scottsville, Virginia 24590
Tel: (804) 286-2218

ABOUT THE B&B

As Virginia's only inn that is on the National Register of Historic Homes and has a renaissance farm vineyard, High Meadows offers a rare opportunity to experience 170 years of architectural history and 10 years of new viticultural growth. High Meadows is a grand, unique house, where guests are welcomed with champagne and stay in rooms furnished with period antiques and art, each with private bath. The innkeepers' many special touches and attention to detail make your visit one to be remembered. Enjoy the simplicity of nature on the 50 surrounding acres of gardens, footpaths, forests, and ponds. Owner/chef Peter Sushka ensures that dining at High Meadows is just as pleasurable as lodging there. Start with a breakfast of fresh orange juice, a variety of homemade breads, muffins, and scones, fresh fruit, gourmet egg dishes, and coffee or tea. End your day with a multi-course dinner, offering distinctive northern European and Mediterranean dishes.

SEASON

all year

ACCOMMODATIONS

11 rooms (including four suites) with private baths; two-room cottage with private bath

Blackberry-Orange Tea Bread

(Recipe from The Best of High Meadows — A Selected Recipe Collection.)

5 cups all-purpose flour
1 cup sugar
1 cup brown sugar
2 tablespoons and 1 teaspoon baking powder
2 teaspoons salt
2 cups fresh blackberries
2 teaspoons grated orange rind
2 eggs
2½ cups milk
2 teaspoons vanilla
6 tablespoons vegetable oil

Preheat oven to 350°F. Mix dry ingredients. Add remaining ingredients and mix gently. Pour into 2 greased loaf pans and bake for 1 hour. *Makes 2 loaves.*

Brass Lantern Banana-Nut Bread

"Served hot at breakfast." — Andy Aldrich

3 ripe mashed bananas
2 eggs
2 cups all-purpose flour
¾ cup sugar
½ teaspoon salt
1 teaspoon baking soda
½ cup chopped walnuts
Splash of your favorite brandy

Preheat oven to 350°F. Grease and flour a 9 x 5" loaf pan. Mix ingredients in a bowl. Pour batter into pan and bake for 1 hour. Enjoy hot or cold. ***Makes 1 loaf.***

The Inn at The Brass Lantern

Andy Aldrich
717 Maple Street
Stowe, Vermont 05672
Tel: (800) 729-2980 or
(802) 253-2229

ABOUT THE B&B

The Inn at The Brass Lantern is located at the edge of the village of Stowe, Vermont. Stowe is a full-service, four-season resort town, and boasts a vast multitude of world-class restaurants and activities, a cultural center, unique cottage industries, craftspeople, and artists. Originally built as a farmhouse and carriage barn, The Brass Lantern was restored by Andy Aldrich, the present innkeeper, to retain its original Vermont character (for which he won an award). Today, the inn carries the traditional Vermont B&B theme throughout — from its decor of period antiques, handmade quilts, and locally crafted amenities to the food and beverages reflecting local and Vermont state products. In addition, guests are treated to a unique ambience and casual, attentive service. The inn's setting provides panoramic views of Mt. Mansfield and its valley from nearly every room.

SEASON

all year

ACCOMMODATIONS

nine rooms with private baths

New Berne House Inn

Marcia Drum and
Howard Bronson
709 Broad Street
New Bern, North Carolina 28560
Tel: (800) 842-7688 or
(919) 636-2250

ABOUT THE B&B

New Berne House Inn is centrally located in the Colonial town of New Bern and within comfortable walking distance of numerous historic sights, highlighted by Tryon Palace and its formal gardens, only one block away. Quaint shops, fine restaurants, and historic buildings are all in the neighborhood. New Berne House's seven guest rooms feature queen- and king-size beds, antiques and collectibles, private baths, and telephones and clock radios, along with other amenities to pamper guests. A full breakfast is served in the dining room from 8:00 to 9:00 a.m., but coffee is available as early as 6:30 a.m. Throughout the day, guests are invited to join the innkeepers in the library or parlor for light refreshments, television, and good conversation. Two weekends each month are reserved for a "juicy" who-done-it Mystery Package, which blends in nicely with the Inn's two haunted rooms (where "odd occurrences" have been reported over the years!).

SEASON

all year

ACCOMMODATIONS

seven rooms with private baths

Breakfast Bread

"We serve tea sandwiches on very thin white and whole wheat bread and remove and freeze the crusts, which we then use to make our Breakfast Bread." — Marcia Drum

4 cups cubed white or whole wheat bread
4 eggs
2 cups half-and-half cream
1 teaspoon vanilla
1 teaspoon ground cinnamon
⅛ teaspoon ground ginger
⅛ teaspoon ground nutmeg
⅛ teaspoon ground cloves

Preheat oven to 350°F. Beat eggs and cream until well blended. Add vanilla and spices. Pour over bread and let stand 20 minutes. Pour into a lightly oiled 9 x 5 x 2" loaf pan. Bake for 40 – 45 minutes or until a knife blade inserted in the center comes out clean. Slice and serve with syrup as French toast or spoon into cereal bowls and serve with berries and cream as bread pudding. *Tip:* Egg substitute and skimmed milk turns this into a dieter's delight. *Makes 1 loaf.*

Cheddar-Date Nut Bread

(Recipe from Breakfast at Nine, Tea at Four: Favorite Recipes From The Mainstay Inn.)

1 cup all-purpose flour
1 cup whole wheat flour
3 teaspoons baking powder
1 cup sugar
½ teaspoon salt
1 beaten egg
¼ cup vegetable oil
1 cup milk
1 cup grated cheddar cheese
½ cup chopped dates
½ cup chopped walnuts

Preheat oven to 350°F. Grease a 9 x 5" loaf pan. Stir the dry ingredients together. In a separate bowl, beat egg, oil, and milk. Add to dry ingredients. Stir in cheese, dates, and walnuts. Bake for about 45 minutes. *Makes 1 loaf.*

The Mainstay Inn

Sue and Tom Carroll
635 Columbia Avenue
Cape May, New Jersey 08204
Tel: (609) 884-8690

ABOUT THE B&B

Accrding to the Washington Post, "The jewel of them all has got to be the Mainstay." Built by a pair of wealthy gamblers in 1872, this elegant, exclusive clubhouse is now among the premier B&B inns in the country. The Mainstay now comprises three historic buildings on one of the most beautiful streets of the historic Cape May district. Guests enjoy 16 antique-filled rooms and suites (some with fireplaces and whirlpool baths), three parlors, spacious gardens, and rocker-filled verandas. Breakfast and afternoon tea served daily. Beautiful beaches, historic attractions, biking, birding, golf, and tennis are all available in Cape May, a National Historic Landmark community.

SEASON

all year

ACCOMMODATIONS

16 rooms (including seven suites) with private baths

Ghent House
Bed & Breakfast

Diane and Wayne Young
411 Main, PO Box 478 (US 42)
Ghent, Kentucky 41045
Tel: (502) 347-5807

ABOUT THE B&B

*H*alfway between Cincin- *nati and Louisville, Ghent House is a gracious reminder of the antebellum days of the old South. It was built in 1833 in the usual style of the day — a central hall with rooms on either side of the kitchen and a dining room in back. A beautiful fantail window and two English coach lights enhance the front entrance, while a rose garden and gazebo grace the rear of the home. There are crystal chandeliers, fireplaces, and Jacuzzis in the guest rooms. Ghent House has a spectacular view of the Ohio River, and one can almost imagine the time when steamboats regularly traveled up and down its waters. Awake mornings to the aroma of coffee or tea, then have your breakfast in either the formal dining room or the breakfast room overlooking the river. At Ghent House, you'll enjoy and appreciate the charming blend of yesteryear with modern convenience and relaxation.*

SEASON

all year

ACCOMMODATIONS

three suites with private baths

Cinnamon Crunch Walnut Bread

1½ cups coarsely chopped walnuts
1 tablespoon melted margarine
1 cup sugar
2 teaspoons ground cinnamon
1½ teaspoons salt
3 cups all-purpose flour
4½ teaspoons baking powder
¼ cup margarine
1 egg
1¼ cups milk

Preheat oven to 350°F. Toss walnuts with melted margarine, then add ¼ cup sugar and cinnamon, mixing until coated. Reserve ¼ cup and set aside. Mix salt, flour, baking powder, remaining sugar, and ¼ cup margarine. Beat egg lightly and add milk. Stir into flour mixture. Add bulk of walnut mixture to batter and mix. Spoon into 2 greased loaf pans. Sprinkle with reserved ¼ cup nut mixture and let stand 15 minutes. Bake for approximately 1 hour or until done. Let stand 10 minutes before turning out of pans. **Makes 2 loaves.**

Cranberry-Orange Nut Bread

Isaiah Hall B&B Inn

Marie Brophy
PO Box 1007, 152 Whig Street
Dennis, Massachusetts 02638
Tel: (800) 736-0160 or
(508) 385-9928

"The inn is located in front of the oldest, cultivated cranberry bog in America. Isaiah Hall's brother Henry cultivated the first cranberries here in 1816, while Isaiah patented and produced the first cranberry barrels for transport."
— Marie Brophy

ABOUT THE B&B

Enjoy country ambience and hospitality in the heart of Cape Cod. Located on a quiet historic street, this lovely 1857 farmhouse is a leisurely walk to the beach or village with its restaurants, shops, theater, and fine arts museum. Close by, enjoy bike trails, tennis, golf, and whale watching. The inn offers an ideal home base for day trips to other points of interest — from Province-town to Plymouth — as well as to the Islands (including Nantucket and Martha's Vineyard). Or, you can choose to simply relax in the inn's beautiful gardens or parlor surrounded by antiques and Oriental rugs, or cozy up in the carriage house "great room" with its white wicker furniture and knotty pine walls. Guest rooms are decorated with charming country antiques with most having private baths and queen beds, a few having two beds or balconies, and one having a fireplace.

¾ cup orange juice
1 beaten egg
2 tablespoons vegetable oil
2 cups all-purpose flour
¾ cup sugar
1½ teaspoons baking powder
1 teaspoon salt
½ teaspoon baking soda
1 cup chopped fresh or frozen cranberries
½ cup chopped walnuts

Preheat oven to 350°F. Combine first 3 ingredients; set aside. Stir together flour, sugar, baking powder, salt, and baking soda. Add orange juice mixture and stir until moistened. Fold in cranberries and walnuts. Turn into a lightly greased and floured loaf pan. Bake for 50 – 60 minutes. Cool 10 minutes, remove from pan, and cool on a rack. Freezes well.
Makes 1 loaf.

SEASON

April to October

ACCOMMODATIONS

10 rooms with private baths; one room with shared bath

The Summer House

Kay and David Merrell
158 Main Street
Sandwich, Massachusetts 02563
Tel: (508) 888-4991

ABOUT THE B&B

The Summer House is an elegant circa 1835 Greek Revival twice featured in Country Living magazine. It was owned by Hiram Dillaway, a prominent mold-maker and colorist at the Boston & Sandwich Glass Factory. Large, sunny bedchambers feature antiques, hand-stitched quilts, and working fireplaces. Stroll to dining, shops, museums, galleries, pond and gristmill, and boardwalk to beach. Bountiful breakfasts change daily and include freshly ground coffee, tea, fruit juice, and fresh fruit served in stemware. Entrées of frittata, stuffed French toast, quiche, or omelets are accompanied by scones, puff pastry, muffins, or fruit cobblers. Dishes are enhanced with vegetables, berries, and herbs from the inn's garden. English-style afternoon tea is served at an umbrella table in the garden. Boston, Newport, Providence, Martha's Vineyard, and Nantucket make pleasant day trips. Innkeepers Kay and David Merrell (former executive secretary and aerospace engineer respectively) enjoy woodworking, gardening, quilting, jogging, backpacking, and the tranquility of Cape Cod.

SEASON

all year

ACCOMMODATIONS

one room with private bath; four rooms with shared baths

Cranberry-Pumpkin Bread

2 lightly beaten eggs
1 cup sugar
½ cup canola oil
1 cup canned pumpkin
2¼ cups all-purpose flour
1 tablespoon pumpkin pie spice
1 teaspoon baking soda
½ teaspoon salt
1 cup chopped cranberries

Preheat oven to 350°F. Combine eggs, sugar, oil, and pumpkin, and mix well. Combine flour, pie spice, baking soda, and salt in a large bowl, making a well in center. Pour pumpkin mixture into well, and stir just until dry ingredients are moistened. Stir in cranberries. Spoon batter into 2 greased and floured loaf pans. Bake for about 1 hour or until toothpick inserted in center comes out clean. *Makes 2 loaves.*

Crispies

"This easy, quick, and different breakfast "bread" was taught to us by our Mexican exchange student, Ricardo, and has been a favorite in our house for many years." — Muffy Vhay

White or wheat flour tortilla
Vegetable oil
½ cup sugar
1 teaspoon ground cinnamon

Cut tortilla into 4 quarters. Heat ½" oil in a heavy fry pan until smoking hot (which ensures the tortilla won't absorb the oil). Fry the tortilla (not overlapping) until crisp and puffed. Turn and brown the other side. Make sure the tortilla is totally crisped (about a minute). Drain on a paper towel. While still warm, shake tortilla in a paper bag filled with the sugar and cinnamon. Keep warm in the oven until serving time (for up to 1 hour). Adapt basic recipe for amount of servings needed. *Serves 1.*

Deer Run Ranch Bed and Breakfast

Muffy and David Vhay
5440 Eastlake Boulevard
Carson City, Washoe Valley,
Nevada 89704
Tel: (702) 882-3643

ABOUT THE B&B

R*elax and unwind on 200 of the most beautiful acres in western Nevada. This working alfalfa ranch is located just eight miles north of Carson City and 22 miles south of Reno, Nevada. Watch the deer in the fields, enjoy the smell of western sage, and listen for the night cry of coyotes. The unique architect-designed and built western ranch house, shaded by tall cottonwood trees, overlooks a pond, Washoe Valley, and the Sierra Nevada Mountains to the west. Two comfortable guest rooms have queen-size beds, private baths, window seats, spectacular views, and lots of privacy. Both guest rooms share the sitting room with wood burning stove, dining area, guest refrigerator, TV/VCR, and other amenities. The owners' pottery studio and woodshop are also on the premises. Full ranch breakfasts include house specialties and fresh fruits and vegetables from the garden. Recreation at the ranch includes swimming, horseshoes, hiking, biking, and ice skating on the pond in winter. Deer Run is conveniently located near golf, skiing, casinos and show theaters, and many excellent restaurants.*

SEASON

all year

ACCOMMODATIONS

two rooms with private baths

Middle Plantation Inn

Shirley and Dwight Mullican
9549 Liberty Road
Frederick, Maryland 21701-3246
Tel: (301) 898-7128

ABOUT THE B&B

Middle Plantation Inn is a rustic bed and breakfast nestled on 26 acres, several miles east of Frederick in Mt. Pleasant (known for its beautiful horse farms). This charming stone and log home offers guests a peaceful setting, which includes Addison's Run (a nearby brook) and a 10-acre woods. You'll wake each morning to the sound of birds (and an occasional rooster) and see nature in all its glory. Your hosts take great pleasure in sharing their antique furnishings. Each guest room offers a delightful 19th century ambience combined with the modern conveniences of private bath, air conditioning, and TV. A massive stone fireplace, stained glass windows, and skylights highlight the public Keeping Room (a Colonial term for gathering place). A deluxe continental breakfast of seasonal fruit, fresh baked bread, cheese, and cereal are served each morning. Visit 33 historic blocks of downtown Frederick, with its unique mix of specialty and antique shops, dining establishments, museum, and art galleries. Nearby is New Market — antique capitol of Maryland. The inn is located near Baltimore, (Maryland), the Antietam Battlefield in Sharpesburg (Maryland), Washington (DC), Gettysburg (Pennsylvania), and Harpers Ferry (West Virginia).

SEASON

all year

ACCOMMODATIONS

four rooms with private baths

Easy Apple Bread

4 eggs
2 cups sugar
1 cup vegetable oil
1 teaspoon salt
1 teaspoon vanilla
1 teaspoon baking soda
3 cups all-purpose flour
3 cups sliced apples

Preheat oven to 300°F. Combine all and mix with electric mixer. Pour batter into 2 greased and floured loaf pans. Bake for 1½ hours. *Tip:* Freezes well. *Makes 2 loaves.*

French Bread

(Recipe from Favorites from the Lazy Bee.)

"My granddaughter Anna and I began baking this bread together when she was just three years old. This recipe conjures up memories of a little girl peeking under a moist towel to see if the bread has risen." — Jo Ann Bender

2 tablespoons active dry yeast (2 packages)
5 cups lukewarm water
4 tablespoons sugar
2 tablespoons salt
14 cups all-purpose flour
Margarine
2 fork-beaten egg whites

Put yeast in a large bowl. Add warm water and stir until dissolved. Add sugar, salt, and enough flour to make a ball and then knead, adding flour, for about 10 minutes (or count 200 kneading actions). Put in a margarine-coated bowl and cover with a towel wrung out in hot water. Place to rise in as warm a spot as you can find (a closed oven preheated to 200°F and then turned off works fine). Let rise until doubled. Punch down and knead 3 – 4 times to remove air. Divide into 6 parts. Shape into long, thin loaves and put on 2 well-greased cookie sheets. Slash tops with a sharp knife. Brush with 2 egg whites. Let rise again. Bake 15 minutes in a preheated 450°F oven, then for 30 minutes at 350°F. Remove from pans and cool on racks. Wrap in foil if freezing. To serve after the bread comes from freezer, warm in foil for 20 minutes. *Makes 6 loaves.*

Hillside House Bed & Breakfast

Jo Ann, Bud, and Sue
1729 East 18th Street
Spokane, Washington 99203
Tel: (509) 534-1426 during the day or (509) 535-1893 during nights and weekends

ABOUT THE B&B

Situated on the South Hill of Spokane, Hillside House offers exquisite hospitality in a country setting that's only three miles from downtown. Overlooking city and mountains, this cozy and tastefully decorated house features antiques, including linens and dishes, and rooms with views. Your hosts Bud, Jo Ann, and Sue are third generation B&B innkeepers — Jo Ann's mother helped her mother host guests in 1916 in Rush City, Minnesota. Bud owns an engineering firm and lectures nationally to the construction/engineering industry, while Jo Ann operates a marketing firm. They enjoy cooking (having published a cookbook of their own), entertaining, and guiding guests to the area's most exciting places and events. Bud and Jo Ann also operate the Lazy Bee, a remote getaway near the Canadian border where they lead jeep safaris in the mountains.

SEASON

all year

ACCOMMODATIONS

two rooms with shared bath

Henry Ludlam Inn

Ann and Marty Thurlow
Cape May County
1336 Route 47
Woodbine, New Jersey 08270
Tel: (609) 861-5847

ABOUT THE B&B

*I*n a quiet corner of southern New Jersey, by the bank of the spring-fed freshwater lake, a wealthy 18th century family of landowners and merchants built a quaint country homestead. Today that homestead is the Henry Ludlam Inn, offering traveling guests the good life — colonial style. Centrally located in historic colonial Dennisville in Cape May County (voted one of the 10 best bird-watching areas in the US), the inn is minutes away from the colorful gingerbread homes of Victorian Cape May, the beautiful dunes of Avalon and Stone Harbor, and the sparkle of Atlantic City. Innkeepers Ann and Marty offer full B&B services, including heart-healthy food, fishing, canoeing, beach entrance tags to local beaches, or simply the chance to get away from the world. With fireplaces in many rooms and a big swing at the shore of the freshwater lake, the Henry Ludlam Inn is the ideal getaway.

SEASON

all year

ACCOMMODATIONS

five rooms with private baths

Heart-Healthy Strawberry-Blueberry Bread

1 pint blueberries and strawberries combined
1 tablespoon sugar
1½ cups all-purpose flour
1 cup packed brown sugar
1½ teaspoons ground cinnamon
½ teaspoon salt
1 teaspoon baking soda
¾ cup canola oil
4 ozs. egg beaters or egg substitute
¾ cup chopped pecans

Preheat oven to 350°F. Grease and flour a 9 x 5" loaf pan. Wash, hull, and slice strawberries. Mix with blueberries and sugar and set aside. Combine flour, brown sugar, cinnamon, salt, and baking soda in a large bowl. Stir oil and egg beaters into berry mixture, mixing well. Pour wet into dry ingredients. Stir briefly, add pecans, and blend just until moistened. Smooth into a prepared pan and bake about 45 minutes or until tested done. Cool in pan 10 minutes, then turn onto a rack to cool completely. *Tips:* For better flavor, bake a day before serving. They can also be prepared and frozen for up to 1 month. *Makes 1 loaf.*

Honey Wheat Bread

(Recipe from The Campbell Ranch Inn Cookbook.)

"I serve these individual honey wheat loaves piping hot on bread boards for each guest. Even though I make them ahead and freeze them, they smell and taste like they're freshly baked." — Mary Jane Campbell

1½ cups boiling water
1 cup rolled oats
¾ cup honey
3 tablespoons softened butter
2 teaspoons salt
1 package active dry yeast (1 tablespoon)
2 cups lukewarm water
1 cup 7-grain cereal
3 cups whole wheat flour
4 cups all-purpose flour
Melted butter

Pour boiling water over the oats and let stand 30 minutes. Add honey, butter, and salt. Dissolve the yeast in the lukewarm water and add to the oat mixture. Stir in the 7-grain cereal and whole wheat flour. Add the all-purpose flour to make a medium-soft dough. Turn onto a floured board, and knead 10 minutes until smooth and elastic. Place dough in a greased bowl. Grease top of dough and cover with a towel. Let rise until double in bulk. Knead again 4 – 5 minutes. Divide the dough

(continued on next page)

Campbell Ranch Inn

Mary Jane and Jerry Campbell
1475 Canyon Road
Geyserville, California 95441
Tel: (800) 959-3878 or
(707) 857-3476

ABOUT THE B&B

Whether swimming in the pool, relaxing in the hot tub spa, or playing tennis, you're always surrounded by the Campbell Ranch Inn's spectacular valley and mountain views and beautiful flower gardens. In warm weather, breakfast is served on the terrace where you overlook rolling hills and vineyards. Only 80 miles north of San Francisco, the inn has five spacious rooms with king-size beds, fresh flowers, and fruit. You may choose to read or visit by the living room fireplace. Play tennis, horseshoes, or Ping-Pong, hike the trails at Lake Sonoma, or use the available bikes to tour the neighboring wine country. The surrounding area has many wineries and excellent restaurants, but remember to save some room for Campbell Ranch's home-made pie and coffee served every evening.

SEASON

all year

ACCOMMODATIONS

four rooms with private baths;
one private cottage with
private bath

into 6 equal portions. Shape into small loaves and place in 6 greased 5 x 3 x 2" loaf pans. Place the pans on a large cookie sheet, cover with a towel, and let rise until doubled in size. Preheat oven to 400°F and bake 5 minutes. Lower heat to 350°F and bake 25 – 30 minutes longer (until loaves sound hollow when tapped). Remove from pans onto wire cooling racks and brush tops with butter. Serve warm or wrap in foil when completely cold and freeze (reheat to serve). *Makes 6 loaves.*

Irish Soda Bread

"An Irish specialty I learned during (of all things!) a Spanish course taught by Joyce McNamara. I brought it to The Quail's Nest and found it to be a hit. Thanks, Joyce!"
— *Nancy Diaz*

2 cups whole wheat flour
2 cups all-purpose flour
1 tablespoon sugar
3 teaspoons baking powder
1 teaspoon baking soda
1 teaspoon salt
¼ teaspoon shortening
1½ cups buttermilk
1 egg

Preheat oven to 350°F. Place both flours, sugar, baking powder, baking soda, and salt in a mixing bowl. Cut in shortening. In a separate bowl, mix the milk and egg together, then add to dry ingredients. Mix just until blended (do not overmix). Knead just until smooth (do not overknead). Divide into 2 rounds. Make 2 ¼" cross-shaped cuts in the top of each loaf. Bake on a lightly greased cookie sheet for 40 minutes or until golden brown. *Makes 2 loaves.*

The Quail's Nest Bed and Breakfast

Nancy and Gregory Diaz
PO Box 221, Main Street
Danby, Vermont 05739
Tel: (802) 293-5099

ABOUT THE B&B

A circa 1835 country inn, The Quail's Nest is located just off Route 7 in Danby, Vermont — a quiet and picturesque town reminiscent of the last century. The inn's six rooms are wrapped in the warmth of handmade quilts, and a delightful home-cooked breakfast will tempt you out of those quilts each morning! To the east of the inn is the magnificent Green Mountains National Forest, which boasts some of the finest swimming, hiking, fishing, hunting, and skiing in Vermont. Located 13 miles to the south, Manchester, Vermont, features factory outlet shopping, while crafts and antiques can be purchased right in the heart of Danby. A wide variety of restaurants to satisfy every palate are either a short drive or walk away.

SEASON

all year

ACCOMMODATIONS

four rooms with private baths; two rooms with shared bath

Grünberg Haus
Bed and Breakfast

Christopher Sellers and
Mark Frohman, RR2,
Box 1595RD, Route 100 South
Waterbury, Vermont 05676-9621
Tel: (800) 800-7760 (reservations)
or (802) 244-7726

ABOUT THE B&B

This picture-postcard Austrian-style B&B is tucked away on a secluded hillside in Vermont's Green Mountains, perfectly situated for visits to Stowe, Montpelier, Waterbury, and Burlington. Individually decorated guest rooms open onto the carved wood balcony, which offers wonderful views from the stucco and wood-trimmed chalet. The giant stone fireplace and wood stove in the BYOB pub are favorite gathering places. After hiking or cross-country skiing on the inn's trails, help Mark feed the chickens and enjoy a full, musical breakfast, with selections such as maple-poached pears, apple and cheddar muffins, and ricotta-stuffed French toast. The evening fire warms up the grand piano where you're likely to hear innkeeper Chris playing anything from Mozart to Phantom of the Opera. Nearby activities include spectacular autumn leaf-picking, world-class downhill skiing, golf, boating, bicycling, gliding, canoeing, antique hunting, outlet shopping, and touring Ben & Jerry's ice cream factory. And you can enjoy the Grünberg Haus's own Jacuzzi, sauna, tennis courts, cross-country ski center, and hiking trails.

SEASON

all year

ACCOMMODATIONS

six rooms with private baths;
five rooms with shared baths;
three cabins and one carriage
house with private baths

Lemon Bread

1½ cups all-purpose flour
1 cup sugar
1 teaspoon baking powder
½ teaspoon salt
2 eggs
½ cup milk
½ cup salad oil
Grated rind of 1 lemon

Lemon glaze:
Juice of 1 lemon
⅓ cup sugar

Preheat oven to 350°F. Stir together flour, sugar, baking powder, and salt. In a separate bowl, beat together eggs, milk, oil, and lemon rind, and add to flour mixture, stirring just until blended. Pour batter into a greased loaf pan and bake for 45 minutes. Prepare lemon glaze by combining juice of 1 lemon with ⅓ cup sugar over heat, stirring until sugar dissolves. When bread finishes baking, use an ice pick or long skewer to poke numerous holes all the way to bottom of loaf. Drizzle hot glaze over top so that it slowly soaks into bread. Cool in pan for 15 minutes, then turn out onto rack to cool. *Makes 1 loaf.*

Grünberg Haus Bed & Breakfast
Waterbury, Vermont

Ono Banana-Nut Bread

"This bread is very 'ono' — the Hawaiian word for good!"
— *Susan Kauai*

½ cup sugar
½ cup brown sugar
½ cup butter
2 eggs
2 cups all-purpose flour
½ teaspoon baking powder
½ teaspoon salt (optional)
3 tablespoons buttermilk
1 teaspoon baking soda
3 – 4 mashed bananas
1 cup chopped macadamia nuts (or pecans, or walnuts)
1 teaspoon vanilla

Preheat oven to 350°F. Grease a 1-lb. loaf pan, bundt pan, or muffin pans. Cream sugars and butter. Blend in eggs. Sift dry ingredients and add to the batter. Combine buttermilk and baking soda and stir into batter. Add mashed bananas, nuts, and vanilla. Pour into a prepared pan. Bake 45 minutes if using pans or 30 minutes if using muffin pans. *Makes 1 loaf or 24 muffins.*

Kula View Bed and Breakfast

Susan Kauai
PO Box 322, 140 Holopuni Road
Kula, Hawaii 96790
Tel: (808) 878-6736

ABOUT THE B&B

Singing birds, blossoming flowers, glorious sunrises and sunsets, and sweeping panoramic views of the ocean from every window make your stay in "up-country" Maui pure magic. Nestled in Kula at the 2,000-foot level on the slopes of Haleakala (the dormant volcano), Kula View offers you an upper-level suite featuring a private entrance, private deck overlooking the flower and herb garden, queen-size bed, reading area, wicker breakfast nook, mini fridge, and private shower. Awake to a morning meal of exotic island fruits and juice, home-baked breads and muffins, and a pot of freshly brewed Kona coffee or tea. Kula View is located in a rural setting just 20 minutes from the Kahului Airport, close to shopping centers, restaurants, points of interest, Haleakala National Park, and beaches. Your host Susan, who's an avid hiker, gardener, and cyclist, is descended from a Kamaaina (old-time) Hawaii family. She has lived on Maui for over 19 years and will guide you to those special parts of the island as only a native resident can.

SEASON

all year

ACCOMMODATIONS

one suite with private bath

Natural
Bed & Breakfast

L. Marc Haberman
3150 East Presidio Road
Tucson, Arizona 85716
Tel: (520) 881-4582

ABOUT THE B&B

As much a private spa as a B&B, the Natural B&B offers visitors natural, whole foods served in a non-toxic, non-allergenic environment, professional therapeutic massages, and health consultation services. Wake to a full vegetarian breakfast and spend your day horseback riding in the beautiful Tucson desert or visiting the Sonora museum (only 10 miles away). You can opt for a swim in the nearby pool or relax on the patio or your own private sun deck. In-room telephones and laundry service are other amenities. Your host invites you to share his large, homey living room with a fireplace, and enjoy a complimentary cocktail, tea, or juice. If arriving from the airport, your host can arrange for your pick-up or you can hop on an airport shuttle bus. In addition to English, other languages spoken are Greek, Spanish, and German. (Please be advised that nudity is permitted.)

SEASON

open all year
(season January to April)

ACCOMMODATIONS

one room with private bath;
two rooms with shared bath

Orange-Glazed Pear-Nut Bread

16-oz. can pear halves
1½ cups all-purpose flour
¾ cup sugar
1 tablespoon baking powder
1 teaspoon salt
¼ teaspoon ground allspice
1 cup whole wheat flour
¼ cup vegetable oil
1 beaten egg
1 tablespoon grated orange rind
1 cup chopped walnuts
2 – 3 tablespoons orange juice
1 cup confectioners' sugar

Preheat oven to 350°F. Drain pears, reserving syrup. Reserve 1 pear half for garnish. Purée remaining pears. Add reserved syrup to pureed pears to measure 1 cup. Mix pureed pears with oil, egg, and orange rind. Sift together all-purpose flour, sugar, baking powder, salt, and allspice. Stir in whole wheat flour. Stir pear mixture into flour mixture. Blend in nuts. Pour into a greased 9 x 5" loaf pan. Cut reserved pear half into 6 slices. Place slices on batter. Bake for 50 – 55 minutes. Blend orange juice into confectioners' sugar to make thin glaze. Remove warm bread from pan and spoon glaze over top. Store bread overnight before slicing. *Makes 1 loaf.*

Paradise Pear Bread

3 cups all-purpose flour
1 teaspoon baking soda
1 teaspoon baking powder
1 teaspoon salt
1 tablespoon ground cinnamon
1 cup chopped pecans
¾ cup vegetable oil
3 slightly beaten eggs
2 cups sugar
2 cups extra-ripe pears, peeled and diced
1 tablespoon vanilla

Preheat oven to 350°F. Combine first 6 ingredients in a large bowl, then make a well in center of the mixture. Combine oil, eggs, sugar, pears, and vanilla. Add to dry ingredients, stirring just until moistened. Spoon mixture into 2 well-greased and floured 9 x 5 x 3" loaf pans. Bake for 30 minutes, then reduce heat to 325°F until bread tests done. Cool 10 minutes before removing from pans. *Makes 2 loaves.*

Durham House Bed & Breakfast Inn

Marguerite and Dean Swanson
921 Heights Boulevard
Houston, Texas 77008
Tel: (713) 868-4654

ABOUT THE B&B

Located just five minutes from downtown Houston, Durham House Bed & Breakfast Inn is a fully restored Queen Anne Victorian home listed on the National Register of Historic Places. The present owners, Marguerite and Dean Swanson, acquired the home in 1985 with full intention of restoring it to its original elegance and opening it to the public as an authentic Victorian bed and breakfast inn. Today, guests are invited to experience the genuine Victorian ambiance of the inn, and can select from gracious accommodations that include upstairs bedrooms and the privacy of a spacious carriage house. Perhaps the best reason for choosing Durham House is to experience Marguerite's special brand of southern hospitality, not to mention her fantastic full breakfast. For a change of pace, this unique bed and breakfast hosts murder mystery dinner parties using original mysteries written exclusively for Durham House.

SEASON

all year

ACCOMMODATIONS

five rooms with private baths;
one room with shared bath

The Babbling Brook Inn

Helen King
1025 Laurel Street
Santa Cruz, California 95060
Tel: (800) 866-1131 or
(408) 427-2437

ABOUT THE B&B

Cascading waterfalls, a meandering creek, and a romantic gazebo grace an acre of gardens, pines, and red-woods surrounding this secluded inn. Built in 1909 on the foundation of an 1870 tannery, a 1790 grist mill, and a 2000-year old Indian fishing village, the Babbling Brook features rooms in country French decor, all with private bath, telephone, and television, and most with cozy fireplace, private deck, and outside entrance. Included in your stay is a large, country breakfast and afternoon wine and cheese, where Helen's prize-winning cookies await you on the tea cart in front of a roaring fireplace. Two blocks off Highway 1, the Babbling Brook is within walking distance to the beach, wharf, boardwalk, shops, tennis, running paths, and historic homes. Three golf courses and 200 restaurants are within 15 minutes' drive. A world-record holding angler, Mrs. Pacific Palisades 1955, one-time international tour organizer, and mother of six, Helen King has happily found her niche as a gourmet cook and owner/ innkeeper of this award-winning B&B.

SEASON

all year

ACCOMMODATIONS

12 rooms with private baths

Persimmon Bread

"Wonderful sliced with cream cheese for tea." — Helen King

2 eggs
2 cups brown sugar
3 tablespoons butter
2 cups fresh persimmon pulp
2 cups chopped walnuts
1 cup seedless raisins
1 cup chopped dates
1 tablespoon grated orange rind

Dry ingredients:
4 cups all-purpose flour
4 teaspoons baking soda
3 teaspoons baking powder
2 teaspoons ground cinnamon
½ teaspoon ground cloves
½ teaspoon ground allspice
½ teaspoon ground nutmeg

1 cup buttermilk
2 teaspoons vanilla

Preheat oven to 325°F. In a large bowl, beat together first 4 ingredients. Stir in walnuts, raisins, dates, and orange rind. Sift together dry ingredients and add alternately with buttermilk and vanilla. Turn batter into 2 well-greased 9 x 5 x 3" loaf pans. Bake for 1 hour and 15 minutes or until done. Cool and serve. *Makes 2 loaves .*

Pilialoha Grain Bread

"I've been baking bread for over 25 years. When we opened our B&B, I created some healthy bread and muffin recipes and this one has proved to be the most popular."
— *Machiko Heyde*

Step 1:

1 cup scalded milk (cooled to lukewarm)
⅓ cup honey
3 teaspoons active dry yeast
1 cup warm (not hot, but hotter than lukewarm) water
1¾ cups all-purpose flour

In a large bowl, put milk and honey. In a small bowl, dissolve dry yeast in warm water; stir well. Add to the milk and honey in the bowl. Add flour. With whisk or wooden spoon, whip for 100 strokes. Cover the bowl with a towel and let dough rest 45 minutes to 1 hour.

Step 2:

2½ teaspoons salt
¼ cup vegetable oil
1 cup grain (Stone-buhr brand "4 Grain Cereal Mates" recommended)
Approximately 3 cups all-purpose flour

(continued on next page)

Pilialoha Bed & Breakfast Cottage

Machiko and Bill Heyde
2512 Kaupakulua Road
Haiku, Maui, Hawaii 96708
Tel: (808) 572-1440

ABOUT THE B&B

Located in cool upcountry Maui, this quiet cottage sits on lush pasture land, surrounded by a rose and flower garden and overlooking a eucalyptus grove. Only 20 minutes from Kahului Airport and less than five minutes from Makawao town, Pilialoha is also convenient to Haleakala National Park, the drive to the quaint town of Hana, and other points of interest. This private cottage is fully furnished with a full kitchen (stocked with gourmet coffees and teas), cable TV/VCR, phone, washer/dryer, picnic coolers, beach chairs, mats and towels, snorkel gear, as well as informative books and videos. It's most comfortable for two people but will accommodate up to five people. Freshly baked bread or muffins, fruits, and juice are brought to the cottage daily. Your hosts Machiko (an artist) and Bill (self-employed) reside on the same property and are available to provide visitor information during your stay.

SEASON

all year

ACCOMMODATIONS

one fully furnished cottage with private bath

Add salt, oil, grain, and 2½ cups flour to dough in bowl. Mix with a wooden spoon. By hand, gradually fold in until the dough holds together and begins to come cleanly off the sides of the bowl. Flour your hands and begin kneading on a lightly floured board or countertop until the dough feels springy (the consistency of your ear lobe). You may add more flour a little at a time, if necessary, and only enough to prevent the dough from sticking to your hands (it's better to be a little on the sticky side than too dry with too much flour).

In a clean and large oiled bowl, place the kneaded dough. Cover with a towel, and let the dough rest until it has doubled in size (it depends on the environment, however, 2 hours is about average).

Punch down the dough, knead, then place back in the bowl. Cover and let it rise again (it will take less time to double in size this time around).

Step 3:
Punch down and knead again. Divide the dough into 4 equal portions and shape into buns (if dough gets too sticky, flour your hands). Place 2 buns onto each of 2 greased cookie sheets, allowing about 4" space between them. Let them rise until they are almost doubled in size. Preheat oven to 375°F and bake for 35 minutes. *Tips:* This bread is good sliced and toasted, or for sandwiches. Place in a plastic bag as soon as it becomes cool. Store the portion you don't plan to use within the next 2 days in your freezer. *Makes 4 large buns.*

Rhubarb Bread

"This bread can be served with a meal or, as I enjoy it, as a mid-morning coffee cake." — Andy Aldrich

1½ cups brown sugar
¾ cup vegetable oil
1 egg
2½ cups all-purpose flour
1 cup buttermilk (or add 1 tablespoon of vinegar to fresh milk)
1 teaspoon salt
1 teaspoon baking soda
1 teaspoon ground cinnamon
1 teaspoon vanilla
2½ cups chopped rhubarb
½ cup walnuts or pecans (optional)
½ cup sugar
1 tablespoon butter

Preheat oven to 325°F. In a medium bowl, mix brown sugar, oil, and egg together, then add flour, milk, salt, baking soda, cinnamon, and vanilla. Fold in rhubarb (and nuts, if wished). Place in 2 greased 9 x 5" loaf pans. Combine sugar and butter and glaze over top of loaves. Bake for 1 hour. *Makes 2 loaves.*

The Inn at The Brass Lantern

Andy Aldrich
717 Maple Street
Stowe, Vermont 05672
Tel: (800) 729-2980 or
(802) 253-2229

ABOUT THE B&B

The Inn at The Brass Lantern is located at the edge of the village of Stowe, Vermont. Stowe is a full-service, four-season resort town, and boasts a vast multitude of world-class restaurants and activities, a cultural center, unique cottage industries, craftspeople, and artists. Originally built as a farmhouse and carriage barn, The Brass Lantern was restored by Andy Aldrich, the present innkeeper, to retain its original Vermont character (for which he won an award). Today, the inn carries the traditional Vermont B&B theme throughout — from its decor of period antiques, handmade quilts, and locally crafted amenities to the food and beverages reflecting local and Vermont state products. In addition, guests are treated to a unique ambience and casual, attentive service. The inn's setting provides panoramic views of Mt. Mansfield and its valley from nearly every room.

SEASON

all year

ACCOMMODATIONS

nine rooms with private baths

Isaiah Hall B&B Inn

Marie Brophy
PO Box 1007, 152 Whig Street
Dennis, Massachusetts 02638
Tel: (800) 736-0160 or
(508) 385-9928

ABOUT THE B&B

Enjoy country ambience and hospitality in the heart of Cape Cod. Located on a quiet historic street, this lovely 1857 farmhouse is a leisurely walk to the beach or village with its restaurants, shops, theater, and fine arts museum. Close by, enjoy bike trails, tennis, golf, and whale watching. The inn offers an ideal home base for day trips to other points of interest — from Provincetown to Plymouth — as well as to the Islands (including Nantucket and Martha's Vineyard). Or, you can choose to simply relax in the inn's beautiful gardens or parlor surrounded by antiques and Oriental rugs, or cozy up in the carriage house "great room" with its white wicker furniture and knotty pine walls. Guest rooms are decorated with charming country antiques with most having private baths and queen beds, a few having two beds or balconies, and one having a fireplace.

SEASON

April to October

ACCOMMODATIONS

10 rooms with private baths;
one room with shared bath

Spicy Pumpkin Bread

"A great fall recipe when there's an abundance of pumpkin."
— Marie Brophy

1 cup packed brown sugar
⅓ cup shortening
2 eggs
1 cup canned pumpkin
¼ cup milk
2 cups all-purpose flour
2 teaspoons baking powder
¼ teaspoon baking soda
½ teaspoon salt
1 teaspoon ground cloves
½ cup chopped walnuts and/or ½ cup raisins

Preheat oven to 350°F. Cream together the sugar and shortening. Beat in eggs. Add pumpkin and milk and mix together well. In a separate bowl, stir together the flour, baking powder, baking soda, salt, and cloves. Add flour mixture to pumpkin mixture. Stir in walnuts and/or raisins. Bake for 55 – 60 minutes in a greased loaf pan. Cool 10 minutes, remove from pan, and cool on a rack. May be frozen. *Makes 1 loaf.*

Stir Bread

¼ cup lukewarm water
1 package active dry yeast (1 tablespoon)
1 tablespoon brown sugar
2 cups warm water
3 tablespoons vegetable oil or butter
4 tablespoons honey or molasses
5 cups flour (any combination of oat, wheat, rye, etc.)
½ cup powdered milk
2 teaspoons salt

Preheat oven to 400°F. In a small bowl, mix first 3 ingredients. Let stand for 10 minutes. In a medium bowl, mix water, oil or butter, and honey or molasses. In a large bowl, mix remaining ingredients. Mix yeast mixture into flour mixture. Add liquid mixture and beat hard for 5 minutes. Batter should be slippery (add more flour if batter is too sticky, or add more water if batter is too dry). Place in a greased loaf pan and bake 10 minutes at 400°F and 35 minutes at 350°F. *Makes 1 loaf.*

Chatsworth Bed & Breakfast

Donna and Earl Gustafson
984 Ashland Avenue
St. Paul, Minnesota 55104
Tel: (612) 227-4288

ABOUT THE B&B

Whether an international traveler or a visitor from Minnesota, you can consider this spacious 1902 Victorian home on a large corner lot with maple and basswood trees as your home. Choose a room with a four-poster bed and private double whirlpool bath, one with African-Asian decor and an adjoining porch, or one with Victorian, Oriental, or antique Scandinavian decor. Enjoy a leisurely breakfast in a beautifully paneled dining room and take time to read or relax by the fireplace in the lace-curtained living room. Chatsworth B&B is just two blocks from the Governor's Mansion on historic Summit Avenue and three blocks from the many excellent restaurants and unique shops on Grand Avenue. Also in the near vicinity are numerous colleges and churches. Only minutes away from this quiet family neighborhood is the Twin Cities International Airport, the Mall of America, and the downtown areas of both Saint Paul and Minneapolis.

SEASON

all year

ACCOMMODATIONS

three rooms with private baths; two rooms with shared bath

The Melville House

Vince De Rico and David Horan
39 Clarke Street
Newport, Rhode Island 02840
Tel: (401) 847-0640

ABOUT THE B&B

Built circa 1750 and on the National Register of Historic Places, The Melville House is located in the heart of Newport's historic Hill District on a quiet gas-lit street. One of the few inns in Newport dedicated to the Colonial style, it's just one block up from Thames Street with its Brick Market and the harborfront where many of the city's finest restaurants, luxurious sailboats, antique shops, and galleries can be found. The Melville House is also close to the Tennis Hall of Fame, lavish Vanderbilt, Astor, and Belmont family mansions, the Naval War College, and Newport's finest ocean beaches. The Melville House breakfast menu features home-made granola, muffins, breads, buttermilk biscuits, scones, Yankee cornbread, stuffed French toast, fresh fruit sourdough pancakes, and Rhode Island johnnycakes. An afternoon tea is served every day, featuring refreshments, home-made biscotti, and soup (on cold days), over which innkeepers Vince and David share their Newport experiences.

SEASON

all year

ACCOMMODATIONS

five rooms with private baths;
two rooms with shared bath;
winter fireplace suite

Vince's Five-Day Sourdough Bread

"Having a sourdough starter is popular out west but not here in the east. So, after months of testing, I developed this five-day starter recipe for those easterners who wanted to try their hand at a sourdough bread but didn't want to tend a starter forever. The Melville House has a starter going all the time, which is fed every day or two to keep it active."
— Vince De Rico

Starter:
3 cups warm water
4 cups all-purpose flour
2 tablespoons honey
1 package active dry yeast (1 tablespoon)

In a large bowl, mix all ingredients together and leave uncovered in a warm place for 1 day, stirring down several times. Cover with a towel for another 2 – 4 days, stirring down twice a day for the remaining time.

(continued on next page)

Variations:

- For a better sour flavor, add 3 tablespoons of any or all of the following: buttermilk, plain yogurt, sour cream.

- Vary 2 cups of all-purpose flour and change to rye and/or stone ground wheat.

If you already have a good starter and don't want to wait 5 days, add 3½ cups starter (if it's thin) or 4 cups starter (if it's thick) to the bread recipe below.

Bread:
1 package active dry yeast (1 tablespoon)
½ cup lukewarm water
3 tablespoons non-fat powdered milk
4 tablespoons melted butter
4 tablespoons sugar
3 teaspoons salt
5 – 7 cups all-purpose flour

Put the starter in a large bowl. Add the yeast (softened for 5 minutes in the lukewarm water), powdered milk, butter, sugar, salt, and 3 cups flour. Beat the mixture until smooth, then cover with a cloth and let stand approximately 1 hour in a warm place until bubbly and doubled in size. Stir in enough flour to make a workable dough and turn out on a floured board. Knead for 10 minutes until smooth, adding additional flour if needed. Cut into 2 pieces and let rest while you grease 2 large bread pans. Form into loaves, place in pans, and brush the tops with oil (this keeps the crust soft and chewy). Cover with a cloth and let rise approximately 1½ hours until doubled in size. Bake in a preheated 375°F oven for 45 – 55 minutes until golden brown. Remove from pan and place on racks to cool. *Tip:* The bread's taste is enhanced when toasted. ***Makes 2 loaves.***

Lindgren's Bed & Breakfast

Shirley Lindgren
County Road 35, PO Box 56
Lutsen, Minnesota 55612-0056
Tel: (218) 663-7450

ABOUT THE B&B

*L*ess than two hours from Duluth, Minnesota, and Thunder Bay, Ontario, this 1920s rustic log home with manicured grounds and walkable shoreline resides on Lake Superior in Superior National Forest. The living room features an 18-foot beamed ceiling, massive stone fireplace, and hunting trophies. Guest rooms are cozily designed in either knotty cedar, pine, or rustic paneling. Scenic points of interest include Split Rock Lighthouse, Gooseberry Falls, and Tettegouche State Park. Depending on the season, you can choose from hiking trails, skyride and alpine slide, mountain biking, horseback riding, golf, tennis, fishing, snowmobiling, and cross-country and downhill skiing. Any number of fine restaurants are nearby, and you're within walking distance of Lutsen Resort, the oldest in the state. Your hosts are retired after 35 years of owning and operating a successful garden center, landscaping, nursery, and floral business in Minneapolis, and enjoy fishing, hunting and, most of all, people, which is why they opened their home as a bed and breakfast!

SEASON

all year

ACCOMMODATIONS

four rooms with private baths

Wild Blueberry-Banana Bread

⅔ cup sugar
1½ cups all-purpose flour
¼ teaspoon salt
2 teaspoons baking powder
¾ cup quick-cooking rolled oats
⅓ cup vegetable oil
2 lightly beaten eggs
2 large mashed bananas
¾ cup fresh or frozen wild blueberries

Preheat oven to 350°F. Sift together sugar, flour, salt, and baking powder in a mixing bowl. Stir in oats. Add oil, eggs, bananas, and blueberries, and stir just until ingredients are mixed and moist. Pour into a greased and floured 9 x 5" loaf pan. Bake 60 – 65 minutes. Cool in a pan 10 minutes, remove, and let cool on a wire rack. Wrap and store in the refrigerator for several hours before slicing. *Tip:* Substitute ¾ cup wild raspberries or strawberries for blueberries. *Makes 1 loaf.*

Zucchini Bread

(Recipe from The Campbell Ranch Inn Cookbook.)

3 extra-large eggs
1 cup vegetable oil
2 cups sugar
1 teaspoon salt
1 teaspoon baking soda
1 teaspoon baking powder
3 teaspoons ground cinnamon
1 tablespoon vanilla
2 cups all-purpose flour
1 cup whole wheat flour
3 cups grated zucchini

Preheat oven to 350°F. Cream together eggs, oil, and sugar. Add rest of ingredients in order listed. Grease 2 large loaf pans (or 6 small loaf pans) and divide dough evenly between them. Bake for 1 hour for large loaves or 35 – 40 minutes for small loaves. Be careful not to overbake! Freezes well. *Makes 2 loaves.*

Campbell Ranch Inn

Mary Jane and Jerry Campbell
1475 Canyon Road
Geyserville, California 95441
Tel: (800) 959-3878 or
(707) 857-3476

ABOUT THE B&B

Whether swimming in the pool, relaxing in the hot tub spa, or playing tennis, you're always surrounded by the Campbell Ranch Inn's spectacular valley and mountain views and beautiful flower gardens. In warm weather, breakfast is served on the terrace where you overlook rolling hills and vineyards. Only 80 miles north of San Francisco, the inn has five spacious rooms with king-size beds, fresh flowers, and fruit. You may choose to read or visit by the living room fireplace. play tennis, horseshoes, or Ping-Pong, hike the trails at Lake Sonoma, or use the available bikes to tour the neighboring wine country. The surrounding area has many wineries and excellent restaurants, but remember to save some room for Campbell Ranch's home-made pie and coffee served every evening.

SEASON

all year

ACCOMMODATIONS

four rooms with private baths;
one private cottage with
private bath

Isaiah Hall B&B Inn

Marie Brophy
PO Box 1007, 152 Whig Street
Dennis, Massachusetts 02638
Tel: (800) 736-0160 or
(508) 385-9928

ABOUT THE B&B

Enjoy country ambience and hospitality in the heart of Cape Cod. Located on a quiet historic street, this lovely 1857 farmhouse is a leisurely walk to the beach or village with its restaurants, shops, theater, and fine arts museum. Close by, enjoy bike trails, tennis, golf, and whale watching. The inn offers an ideal home base for day trips to other points of interest — from Provincetown to Plymouth — as well as to the Islands (including Nantucket and Martha's Vineyard). Or, you can choose to simply relax in the inn's beautiful gardens or parlor surrounded by antiques and Oriental rugs, or cozy up in the carriage house "great room" with its white wicker furniture and knotty pine walls. Guest rooms are decorated with charming country antiques with most having private baths and queen beds, a few having two beds or balconies, and one having a fireplace.

SEASON

April to October

ACCOMMODATIONS

10 rooms with private baths;
one room with shared bath

Zucchini-Nut Loaf

1½ cups all-purpose flour
1 teaspoon ground cinnamon
½ teaspoon baking soda
½ teaspoon ground nutmeg
¼ teaspoon baking powder
½ teaspoon salt
1 cup sugar
1 cup shredded zucchini (unpeeled)
1 egg
½ cup vegetable oil
¼ teaspoon grated lemon rind
½ cup chopped walnuts

Preheat oven to 350°F. Mix together first 6 ingredients; set aside. In a separate mixing bowl, beat together the sugar, zucchini, and egg. To this mixture, mix the oil and lemon rind in well. Stir flour mixture into zucchini mixture. Fold in walnuts. Turn batter into a greased loaf pan and bake for 55 – 60 minutes. Cool in pan for 10 minutes, then remove and cool on a rack. Freezes well. *Makes 1 loaf.*

Assorted
Baked
Goods

Angel Biscuits

1 package active dry yeast (1 tablespoon)
2 tablespoons lukewarm water
5 cups all-purpose flour
1 teaspoon baking soda
1 tablespoon baking powder
4 tablespoons sugar
1 teaspoon salt
1 cup shortening
2 cups buttermilk

Preheat oven to 400°F. Dissolve yeast in water. Sift flour and dry ingredients together in a bowl. Cut in shortening. Add buttermilk, then yeast. Stir until all flour is moistened. Knead on floured board for a minute. Roll out and cut with biscuit cutter. Bake on greased cookie sheets for about 12 minutes or until golden brown. *Tips:* Dough can be divided and part of it stored tightly covered in your refrigerator for 3 – 4 days. Leftovers are great split and toasted. *Makes 3 – 4 dozen biscuits.*

Historic Oakwood Bed and Breakfast

Naomi and Al Kline
715 East North Street
Talladega, Alabama 35160
Tel: (205) 362-0662

ABOUT THE B&B

Built in 1847, this antebellum home is listed on the National Register of Historic Places and furnished with many heirloom antiques. The house was commissioned by Andrew Bowie, the first mayor of Talladega. Enjoy browsing through the antique stores in the area, visiting the International Motorsports Hall of Fame, or exploring the lovely DeSoto Caverns. A public golf course and tennis courts and beautiful Cheaha Mountain State Park are nearby. The hearty breakfast your hosts serve features home-made biscuits and southern grits. Al and Naomi are musicians; Al is a retired operatic tenor and Naomi a pianist and organist. Traveling businesspeople and vacationers alike will enjoy this retreat into the quiet elegance of a bygone era.

SEASON

all year

ACCOMMODATIONS

one room with private bath;
two rooms with shared bath

Annie's
Bed and Breakfast

Anne and Larry Stuart
2117 Sheridan Drive
Madison, Wisconsin 53704
Tel: (608) 244-2224

ABOUT THE B&B

Opened April 1985 as Madison's first bed and breakfast inn, Annie's is a rustic cedar shake and stucco house in a quiet neighborhood overlooking the beautiful valley of Warner Park, a block away from Lake Mendota's eastern shore. Tall green spruces, shaggy birch trees, and extensive gardens surround the house, gazebo, and lily pond to frame views of meadows, water, and woods. Luxury, getaway accommodations include two comfortable two-bedroom suites filled with antiques and little surprises and a sumptuous whirlpool for two in a room by itself, surrounded by lush plants, mirrors, and music. Awake to Annie's famous home-made full country breakfast, then visit museums, art galleries, theaters, shopping malls, State Street, the University of Wisconsin campus, Olbrich Botanical Gardens, Farmer's Market, and more. Warner Park nature trails, bicycle-jogging path, tennis courts, swimming beach, and boat docks are just outside the back door. Innkeepers Anne (an artist) and Larry (a financial planner) enjoy nature, art, architecture, literature, music, and people.

SEASON

all year

ACCOMMODATIONS

two suites with private baths

Annie's Breakfast Cookies

"For the teenagers in the crowd, add chocolate chips to the recipe instead of fruit to knock their socks off!"
— Anne Stuart

5 cups skim milk
8 beaten eggs
½ cup light salad oil
12-oz. box golden seedless raisins
4 tablespoons brown sugar
5½ cups old-fashioned oats
2 heaping cups whole wheat flour
2 tablespoons baking powder
1 teaspoon salt
4 large sliced bananas or 1 quart fresh blueberries (or fruit of your choice)
1½ cups chopped nuts (pecans, cashews, walnuts, or almonds)
Maple syrup
Sweetened sour cream

In a large bowl, add first 6 ingredients. Let this mixture soak for 10 minutes before proceeding. Add flour, baking powder, and salt, mixing well. Add fruit of your choice and fold in carefully so as not to break the fruit. Add nuts. Oil your grill well and set at no more than 300°F (pancake cookies need to cook slowly so they don't burn). Using a ¼ cup scoop, spread batter on your grill, watching carefully. Turn once. Cookie will be nice and thick, no more than 4" in diameter. Serve 2 to a plate, and top with maple syrup and a spoonful of sweetened sour cream. *Tip:* These pancake cookies freeze very well and are easy to serve at a later date. Just spread them lightly with soft butter as you would a piece of toast and heat them on high in your microwave oven until hot — when the butter begins to melt, they are ready. **Makes 14 dozen cookies.**

Apple Brownies

"This recipe was given to me by a dear friend, Terry Farr, and is served for our afternoon tea. It's great in the fall and winter with fresh apples." — Andy Aldrich

12 tablespoons butter
1½ cups sugar
2 cups all-purpose flour
2 eggs
1 teaspoon baking powder
1 teaspoon baking soda
1 teaspoon salt
1 teaspoon ground cinnamon
2 cups peeled and chopped apples

Preheat oven to 350°F. Mix all ingredients together and place in a 13 x 9" greased pan. Bake for 35 minutes. **Makes 30 brownies.**

The Inn at The Brass Lantern

Andy Aldrich
717 Maple Street
Stowe, Vermont 05672
Tel: (800) 729-2980 or
(802) 253-2229

ABOUT THE B&B

The Inn at The Brass Lantern is located at the edge of the village of Stowe, Vermont. Stowe is a full-service, four-season resort town, and boasts a vast multitude of world-class restaurants and activities, a cultural center, unique cottage industries, craftspeople, and artists. Originally built as a farmhouse and carriage barn, The Brass Lantern was restored by Andy Aldrich, the present innkeeper, to retain its original Vermont character (for which he won an award). Today, the inn carries the traditional Vermont B&B theme throughout — from its decor of period antiques, handmade quilts, and locally crafted amenities to the food and beverages reflecting local and Vermont state products. In addition, guests are treated to a unique ambience and casual, attentive service. The inn's setting provides panoramic views of Mt. Mansfield and its valley from nearly every room.

SEASON

all year

ACCOMMODATIONS

nine rooms with private baths

Annie's
Bed and Breakfast

Anne and Larry Stuart
2117 Sheridan Drive
Madison, Wisconsin 53704
Tel: (608) 244-2224

ABOUT THE B&B

Opened April 1985 as Madison's first bed and breakfast inn, Annie's is a rustic cedar shake and stucco house in a quiet neighborhood overlooking the beautiful valley of Warner Park, a block away from Lake Mendota's eastern shore. Tall green spruces, shaggy birch trees, and extensive gardens surround the house, gazebo, and lily pond to frame views of meadows, water, and woods. Luxury, getaway accommodations include two comfortable two-bedroom suites filled with antiques and little surprises and a sumptuous whirlpool for two in a room by itself, surrounded by lush plants, mirrors, and music. Awake to Annie's famous home-made full country breakfast, then visit museums, art galleries, theaters, shopping malls, State Street, the University of Wisconsin campus, Olbrich Botanical Gardens, Farmer's Market, and more. Warner Park nature trails, bicycle-jogging path, tennis courts, swimming beach, and boat docks are just outside the back door. Innkeepers Anne (an artist) and Larry (a financial planner) enjoy nature, art, architecture, literature, music, and people.

SEASON

all year

ACCOMMODATIONS

two suites with private baths

Apple-Cranberry Breakfast Pudding

"This recipe is my own creation and one of my guests' favorites. I've even had requests for it from as far away as Germany and Australia. After I spoon a healthy dollop of sour cream topping over the steaming pudding, it looks like a breakfast sundae!" — Anne Stuart

4 cups skim milk
½ cup packed brown sugar
½ teaspoon salt
½ box (6 ozs.) golden seedless raisins
2 cups uncooked old-fashioned oatmeal
4 – 5 red delicious apples, cored, sliced thin, but not peeled
1 cup fresh halved cranberries
¼ cup brown sugar
1 cup chopped nuts (pecans, walnuts, or sliced almonds)
Non-fat sour cream
Cinnamon sugar

Preheat oven to 350°F. Add milk, sugar, and salt to a microwave-safe large bowl. Heat in the microwave oven until very hot but not boiling (about 6 – 8 minutes on high). To this mixture, add raisins, oatmeal, apples, cranberries coated with brown sugar (by shaking both in a plastic bag), and nuts. Mix well. Put into a stoneware serving/cooking bowl and bake for 30 minutes. Stir before putting into oven-proof bowls of your choice. Top with a dollop of sweetened non-fat sour cream sweetened with cinnamon sugar. *Serves 8 – 12.*

Austrian Apple Strudel

"I like to prepare the strudel in advance and freeze until baking time. It's a favorite at the inn's breakfast table, and is also wonderful in the afternoon with tea or coffee."
— *Lily Vieyra*

1 large green apple (such as Granny Smith)
2 – 3 tablespoons butter
⅓ – ½ cup golden raisins
8 – 10 dried apricot halves, cut in quarters
¼ cup water
¼ cup light-brown sugar
½ teaspoon ground cinnamon
¼ teaspoon ground nutmeg
1 sheet puff pastry (Pepperidge Farm recommended)
1 egg yolk beaten with 1 tablespoon water

Thaw puff pastry if frozen. Cut and core apple and chop into small pieces (½" size). Over medium heat, melt butter in a large skillet. Add apple, raisins, and apricots. Mix well and sauté a few minutes. Add water, sugar, cinnamon, and nutmeg. Cover and simmer for about 10 minutes, until apple is tender but not overcooked. Add sugar or seasoning to taste. If the apple appears too dry, add a little water or, if too moist, cook a few minutes without cover. Remove from skillet and cool.

(continued on next page)

"An Elegant Victorian Mansion" Bed & Breakfast Inn

Lily and Doug Vieyra
1406 'C' Street
Eureka, California 95501
Tel: (800) 386-1888 or
(707) 442-5594

ABOUT THE B&B

Featured in many newspapers and magazines — not to mention on television and radio — this restored national historic landmark offers Eureka's most prestigious and luxurious accommodations. Spirited and eclectic innkeepers provide lavish hospitality in the splendor of a meticulously restored 1888 Victorian masterpiece, complete with original family antique furnishings. The inviting guest rooms offer both graceful refinement and modern-day comfort, individually decorated with Victorian elegance. Guests enjoy gourmet breakfasts and a heavenly night's sleep on top-quality mattresses, as well as secured parking and laundry service. Located in a quiet, historic residential neighborhood overlooking the city and Humboldt Bay, the non-smoking inn is near carriage rides, bay cruises, restaurants, and the theater, and is just minutes from giant Redwood parks, coastal beaches, ocean charters, and horseback riding.

SEASON

all year

ACCOMMODATIONS

one suite with private bath; three rooms with shared baths

Place puff pastry on a flat surface and distribute apple mixture down the middle of pastry sheet. Make 2½" long cuts diagonally along both sides of exposed pastry at 1½" intervals. Fold strips over apples alternating from left to right. Press dough together where ends overlap. With fork tongs, seal top and bottom edge of dough. At this point, refrigerate for 30 minutes or wrap and freeze. At time of baking, brush with egg wash and bake in a preheated oven at 425°F for 25 minutes or until strudel is light golden brown and pastry is puffed. *Tip:* Use a cookie sheet covered with parchment paper to prevent burning on the bottom. *Serves 4 – 6.*

Betty's Apricot Kugel

1 lb. dried apricots
½ cup apricot preserves
½ cup butter
12-oz. package wide egg noodles
¼ cup sugar
2 cups sour cream
5 eggs

Preheat oven to 375°F. Simmer apricots in water to cover until soft. Drain any remaining water. Mix in apricot jam; set aside. Cut butter into 8 pieces and place in a large bowl. Add hot, cooked noodles and stir until melted. Add sugar and sour cream; let cool. Beat eggs and add to mixture. Place in a buttered 13 x 9" glass dish. Spread apricot mixture on top. Bake for 1 hour. *Serves 8.*

The Oval Door

Judith McLane and Dianne Feist
988 Lawrence Street
Eugene, Oregon 97401
Tel: (503) 683-3160

ABOUT THE B&B

This early 20th-century farmhouse-style home with a two-sided wraparound porch is actually newly built, yet its vintage 1920s design fits into the neighborhood so well that people are surprised to learn it was built circa 1990! Each of the four spacious guest rooms feature a private bath. In addition, guests can enjoy the Tub Room — a whirlpool bath for two, with bubbles, candles, and music. Newly decorated and inviting, the common living room has a fireplace and the library offers comfortable chairs to watch TV or VCR or browse through the travel books. Located just two blocks from the city's center, it's an easy walk to the Hult Center for the Performing Arts, many of Eugene's fine restaurants and shops, and a short drive to the University of Oregon. Guests enjoy a full breakfast served in the dining room. Extra touches include a terry robe, Perrier, and candies.

SEASON

all year

ACCOMMODATIONS

four rooms with private baths

The Oval Door
Bed & Breakfast Inn

Hidden Pond
Bed & Breakfast

Priscilla and Larry Fuerst
PO Box 461
Fennville, Michigan 49408
Tel: (616) 561-2491

ABOUT THE B&B

Hidden Pond Bed & Breakfast is set on 28 acres of woods, perfect for bird-watching, hiking, cross-country skiing, or just relaxing in a rowboat on the pond. Guests can enjoy seven entry-level rooms, including bedrooms and baths, living room with fireplace, dining room, library, kitchen, and breakfast porch. Priscilla and Larry, who work for rival airlines, understand the importance of a soothing, calm, and slow-paced overnight stay. They enjoy pleasing guests and creating an atmosphere of quiet elegance. Unwind and take in the sun on the outdoor deck or patio. Turndown service, complimentary soft drinks, tea, hot chocolate, or an evening sherry is offered. Full hot breakfast is served in the sunwashed garden room at your leisure, and features fresh fruits, breads, muffins, and a hot entrée. This lovely retreat is near the beaches of Lake Michigan, the boutiques of Saugatuck, and the winery and cider mill in Fennville.

SEASON

all year

ACCOMMODATIONS

two rooms with private baths

Biscuit Mold

"A favorite at Hidden Pond since the beginning!"
— Larry Fuerst

7 tablespoons melted butter
½ cup brown sugar
1 tablespoon maple syrup
¾ – 1 cup pecan halves or pieces
1 package refrigerator biscuits

Preheat oven to 375°F. Melt butter, sugar, and syrup on the bottom of a 5-cup mold. Sprinkle nuts on melted mixture. Stand biscuits up in mold. Bake for 25 – 30 minutes. *Serves 4.*

Buttermilk Scone for Two

1 cup all-purpose flour
1½ tablespoons sugar
1 teaspoon baking powder
⅛ teaspoon baking soda
¼ cup cold butter or margarine, cut into small pieces
3 tablespoons currants
¼ teaspoon grated orange rind
¼ – ⅓ cup buttermilk (depending on how well dough holds together)
⅛ teaspoon ground cinnamon mixed with ½ teaspoon sugar

Preheat oven to 375°F. In a bowl, combine flour, 1½ tablespoons sugar, baking powder, and baking soda. Add butter; rub with your fingers to form fine crumbs. Stir in currants and orange rind. Make a well in the center and pour in the buttermilk. Stir with a fork until dough holds together. Pat dough into a ball; knead lightly on a lightly floured board for 5 – 6 turns. Shape dough into a smooth ball and place in a greased 8 or 9" cake or pie pan. Sprinkle with cinnamon sugar mixture. Bake for 10 minutes then, with a sharp knife, quickly cut a cross ½" deep across the top of scone. Bake approximately 20 minutes more until golden brown. Serve warm. *Serves 2.*

Kula View Bed and Breakfast

Susan Kauai
PO Box 322, 140 Holopuni Road
Kula, Hawaii 96790
Tel: (808) 878-6736

ABOUT THE B&B

*S*inging birds, blossoming flowers, glorious sunrises and sunsets, and sweeping panoramic views of the ocean from every window make your stay in "up-country" Maui pure magic. Nestled in Kula at the 2,000-foot level on the slopes of Haleakala (the dormant volcano), Kula View offers you an upper-level suite featuring a private entrance, private deck overlooking the flower and herb garden, queen-size bed, reading area, wicker breakfast nook, mini fridge, and private shower. Awake to a morning meal of exotic island fruits and juice, home-baked breads and muffins, and a pot of freshly brewed Kona coffee or tea. Kula View is located in a rural setting just 20 minutes from the Kahului Airport, close to shopping centers, restaurants, points of interest, Haleakala National Park, and beaches. Your host Susan, who's an avid hiker, gardener, and cyclist, is descended from a Kamaaina (old-time) Hawaii family. She has lived on Maui for over 19 years and will guide you to those special parts of the island as only a native resident can.

SEASON

all year

ACCOMMODATIONS

one suite with private bath

Shadwick House
Bed & Breakfast

Ann Epperson
411 South Main Street
Somerset, Kentucky 42501
Tel: (606) 678-4675

ABOUT THE B&B

S tanding in the foothills of the Cumberland Mountains, Shadwick House has been known for its southern hospitality for over 70 years. Built in 1920 by Nellie Stringer Shadwick (the great-grandmother of the present owners), the house has been carefully restored to its original stature by Nellie's descendants. The first floor has been converted into a gift shop featuring authentic Kentucky antiques and crafts. There are four upstairs guest rooms, tastefully furnished in antiques. In the days of the Roaring Twenties and the Great Depression, Shadwick House served as a boarding house for railroad workers and traveling salesmen. It's rumored that John Dillinger once stayed here while casing the Farmers Bank in town. Nearby are great attractions such as the Big South Fork National Park, Renfro Valley, Cumberland Falls State Park, General Burnside Island State Park, Tombstone Junction, Lake Cumberland, Natural Arch State Park, and Daniel Boone National Forest.

SEASON

all year

ACCOMMODATIONS

four rooms with shared baths

Caramel Rolls

2 cups biscuit mix
½ cup milk
2 tablespoons margarine
1 teaspoon ground cinnamon
½ cup packed brown sugar (divided into ¼ cups)
¼ cup melted margarine
½ cup chopped pecans

Preheat oven to 350°F. Combine biscuit mix and milk, stirring with a fork until blended. Turn dough onto a lightly floured surface. Knead 4 – 5 times. Roll into a 15 x 9" rectangle, and spread with 2 tablespoons margarine. Combine cinnamon and ¼ cup brown sugar. Sprinkle over dough. Starting with long side, roll dough up jelly roll fashion, and pinch seam to seal (do not seal ends). Cut into 12 slices. Combine remaining ¼ cup brown sugar, melted margarine, and pecans and divide equally into 12 well-greased muffin cups. Place slices, cut side down, in pans. Bake for 20 – 22 minutes or until lightly browned. Remove immediately from pans. *Makes 12 rolls.*

Carrington's Gwenske Rolls

(Recipe from What's Cooking at Carrington's Bluff.)

⅔ cup finely chopped pecans
⅓ cup brown sugar
⅓ cup confectioners' sugar
1 teaspoon ground cinnamon
¼ cup melted butter
2 loaves frozen bread dough, thawed

Topping:
1 cup confectioners' sugar
1 tablespoon melted butter
2 – 3 tablespoons milk

Preheat oven to 375°F. In a small bowl, combine first 5 ingredients. Roll out 1 loaf of dough into a rectangle. Spread with half the nut mixture. Roll the dough starting with the long side. Cut into 1" slices and place into 2 prepared round pans. Repeat with second loaf. Bake for 15 minutes or until golden brown. Combine topping ingredients and drizzle over warm rolls. *Makes 12 – 15 rolls.*

Carrington's Bluff B&B

Gwen and David Fullbrook
1900 David Street
Austin, Texas 78705
Tel: (512) 479-0638

ABOUT THE B&B

The setting is Shoal Creek Bluff and an 1877 Texas farmhouse nestled in the arms of a 500-year-old oak tree. Enter innkeepers Gwen (from Texas) and David (from Britain), who transformed it into an English country B&B. Today, Carrington's Bluff B&B combines Texas hospitality with English charm to make your stay both unique and delightful. Upon arrival, you'll find yourself surrounded by rooms filled with English and American antiques, handmade quilts, and the sweet smell of potpourri. The 35-foot front porch beckons you to sit among the plants and flowers and enjoy the gentle breezes with your morning coffee and afternoon tea. The smell of fresh brewed gourmet coffee invites you to a breakfast that begins with fresh fruit and home-made granola served on fine English china. Home-made muffins or breads and a house specialty ensure you won't go away hungry. Carrington's Bluff is near the University of Texas and the State Capital grounds, and just minutes from parks, hiking and biking trails, shopping, and wonderful restaurants.

SEASON

all year

ACCOMMODATIONS

six rooms with private baths;
two rooms with shared bath

Durbin Street Inn B&B

Sherry and Don Frigon
843 South Durbin Street
Casper, Wyoming 82601
Tel: (307) 577-5774

ABOUT THE B&B

Built in 1917, Durbin Street Inn is a large two-story American foursquare located in Casper's historic district that prides itself on good food and a friendly atmosphere. Choose from four large non-smoking guest rooms with shared baths, including queen-size or double beds, robes, and one with a fireplace. Or, you can choose the non-smoking guest room with private bath, small sitting room, and fridge. Awake to a full country breakfast where scrambled eggs, bacon, sausage, hash browns, fruit juice, home-made jams, and such specialties as honey-wheat pancakes, biscuits and gravy, scones, brunch omelet torte, spicy sausage and potatoes, and roast beef hash are served family-style. After breakfast, gather in the common room with fireplace, or enjoy the deck, patio, and flower and vegetable gardens. Nearby are walking/hiking/cycling trails, river rafting and canoeing, covered wagon and horseback trips along Oregon Trail, golfing, skiing, museums, historic sites, Fort Casper, Independence Rock, Devil's Gate, Hell's Half Acre, boating, swimming, fishing, shopping, and craft shops.

SEASON

all year

ACCOMMODATIONS

four rooms with shared baths; one room with private bath

Cheddar-Dill Scones

2½ cups all-purpose flour
1 cup shredded cheddar cheese (preferably sharp cheddar)
¼ cup chopped fresh parsley
1 tablespoon baking powder
2 teaspoons dill weed
½ teaspoon salt
¾ cup butter (or margarine)
2 lightly beaten eggs
½ cup milk

Preheat oven to 400°F. In a medium bowl, combine all ingredients except butter, eggs, and milk. Cut in butter until crumbly. Stir in eggs and milk until just moistened. Turn dough onto a lightly floured surface and knead until smooth (1 minute). Divide dough in half, and roll each half into 8" pie-shaped wedges. Place 1" apart on cookie sheets. Bake for 15 – 20 minutes or until lightly browned. *Tip:* Dough can be made ahead, cut, and frozen for later use. To bake, place frozen dough on cookie sheet sprayed with cooking spray. Bake at 375°F for 15 minutes, then at 400°F for 5 – 10 minutes. *Makes 16 scones.*

Cherry Bars

"My guests rave about these bars, served warm and fresh for breakfast." — Lucille Kruse

1½ cups sugar
1 cup butter
4 eggs
1 teaspoon vanilla
1½ teaspoons baking powder
3 cups all-purpose flour
1 teaspoon salt
20-oz. can cherry pie filling

Frosting:
6 tablespoons sugar
4 tablespoons margarine
4 tablespoons milk
½ teaspoon vanilla

Preheat oven to 325°F. Cream the sugar and butter. Add eggs 1 at a time and beat well. Add vanilla, baking powder, flour, and salt. Spread half of batter into a 17 x 11" pan. Spread cherry pie filling on top of batter. Drop the balance of the batter on top of the cherries by teaspoon. Bake for 35 – 40 minutes. While bars are cooling, prepare frosting. Combine all ingredients and boil for 2 minutes, cool slightly, then drizzle on cake. *Makes 15 bars.*

Calmar Guesthouse Bed & Breakfast

Lucille B. Kruse
103 North Street
Calmar, Iowa 52132
Tel: (319) 562-3851

ABOUT THE B&B

*O*pen since 1986, the Calmar Guesthouse is a beautiful, remodeled Victorian home with warm hospitality, good food, and quiet elegance. The house features stained glass windows, refinished wood, handmade quilts, crafts, antiques, and queen-size beds. Breakfast is served in the formal dining room in elegant fashion, with candles and music. Nearby activities include a bike trail, golf, tennis, outdoor swimming, canoeing, trout fishing, and more. Local places of interest include Billy Brothers world famous wood-carved clocks, the Norwegian Museum, the Laura Ingalls Museum, the World's Smallest Church, the Little Brown Church in the Vale (the inspiration for the song), the two-mile underground Niagara Cave, Spook Cave, and many beautiful parks.

SEASON

all year

ACCOMMODATIONS

five rooms with shared baths

Bedford's Covered Bridge Inn

Martha and Greg Lau
R.D. 1, Box 196
Schellsburg, Pennsylvania, 15559
Tel: (814) 733-4093

ABOUT THE B&B

Situated near Exit 11 of I-76 (the Pennsylvania Turnpike), Bedford's Covered Bridge Inn borders 4000-acre Shawnee State Park, a lovely trout stream, and the Colvin covered bridge. From this idyllic location, guests can pursue hiking, biking, fishing, cross-country skiing, birding, and antique hunting right from the inn's door. Nearby swimming and boating on Shawnee Lake, visits to Old Bedford Village and Bedford's historic district, driving tours, downhill skiing at Blue Knob Resort, and tours of Bedford's 14 covered bridges round out the list of local activities. Inside the inn, the Lau's attention to detail creates an atmosphere that is comfortable and inviting. The historic farmhouse (circa 1823) boasts six guest rooms with private baths, traditional and country decor, and memorable breakfasts. "There's no doubt what everyone's favorite activity is," say Martha and Greg, "sitting on the inn's wraparound porch and wishing for a life in Bedford County, too!"

SEASON

all year

ACCOMMODATIONS

six rooms with private baths;
one cottage for couples
or families

Cranberry-Orange Rolls

2 sticks frozen bread dough
½ cup softened butter
⅔ lb. light-brown sugar
12-oz. container Ocean Spray Fruit Sauce

Thaw bread sticks for several hours at room temperature (covered). Roll each into a rectangle. Spread each rectangle with butter, brown sugar, and finally the fruit sauce. Roll rectangles lengthwise and slice at 1" intervals. Place in a large iron skillet or casserole dish. Let rise until doubled in size or store (covered) overnight in refrigerator (remove from fridge ¾ hour before baking). Bake in a preheated 350°F oven for approximately 30 minutes or until thoroughly browned. Serve warm. *Serves 8.*

Danish Apple Bars

"This recipe conjures up memories of my childhood when we'd tag along with parents to Aunt Catherine's card parties. After cards, a lunch including these Danish apple bars was served. I recall being bored waiting for the card games to end but the apple bars were worth waiting for." — Bonnie Maher

3 cups all-purpose flour
1 teaspoon salt
1 cup shortening
7 tablespoons milk
1 beaten egg yolk
1 cup crushed corn flakes
8 large pared and sliced apples (about 8 cups)
1 cup sugar
1 teaspoon ground cinnamon
1 stiffly beaten egg white
1 cup sifted confectioners' sugar
3 tablespoons water
1 teaspoon vanilla

Preheat oven to 375°F. Sift together flour and salt; cut in shortening until crumbly. Combine milk and egg yolk, stirring into crumb mixture until evenly moistened. Divide dough almost in half. Roll out larger half and place on a 15½ x 10½ x 1" jelly roll pan. Press dough up onto sides of pan. Sprinkle with corn flakes. Arrange apple slices over corn flakes. Combine sugar and cinnamon, and sprinkle over apples. Roll out other half of dough to fit top. Make vents in top. Moisten edges of dough with water to seal. Spread egg white over crust. Bake for 1 hour or until golden. Slice into bars. Combine confectioners' sugar, water, and vanilla for glaze to drizzle over bars while warm, and serve. *Serves 12.*

Dreams of Yesteryear Bed and Breakfast

Bonnie and Bill Maher
1100 Brawley Street
Stevens Point, Wisconsin 54481
Tel: (715) 341-4525

ABOUT THE B&B

This elegant, turn-of-the-century Victorian Queen Anne was home to three generations of the Jensen family before being purchased in 1987 and restored by current owners Bonnie and Bill Maher. An article Bonnie wrote about the restoration was featured in the Winter 1991 issue of Victorian Homes magazine. In 1990, after giving many tours, the Mahers opened their home as the Dreams of Yesteryear Bed and Breakfast. Listed on the National Register of Historic Places, Dreams of Yesteryear is located three blocks from historic downtown Stevens Point, two blocks from the Wisconsin River and Green Circle jogging/hiking/biking trails, a half mile from the University of Wisconsin, and near wonderful restaurants, theaters, and antique shops. Your visit includes a gourmet breakfast, warm hospitality, and wonderful memories.

SEASON

all year

ACCOMMODATIONS

two rooms with private baths; two rooms with shared bath

Idlewyld
Bed & Breakfast

Joan and Dan Barris
350 Walnut Avenue
Lakeside, Ohio 43440
(Mailing address:
13458 Parkway Drive
Lakewood, Ohio 44107)
Tel: (419) 798-4198

ABOUT THE B&B

*I*dlewyld has a homey atmosphere where guests can relax
and enjoy the tranquil beauty,
friendly atmosphere, and timeless
charm of 19th century Lakeside, on
the shores of Lake Erie. The century-
old home has both an upper porch
and a lower wraparound porch furnished with Amish hickory rockers.
There are 14 rooms at Idlewyld,
each distinctively decorated in a
country style. Hosts Joan and Dan
Barris take special pride in offering
both delicious and nutritious breakfast fare. Dan's specialty is popping
corn on Saturday nights in the
vintage popcorn popper on the
front porch. Joan's special interest
is nutrition, and Idlewyld is the site
of an annual wellness/spa weekend
held in late summer.

SEASON

May to October

ACCOMMODATIONS

five rooms with private baths;
nine rooms with shared baths

Date-Nut Pudding

*"This recipe goes a long way back to my days at a girls'
boarding school in Ohio. We all looked forward to enjoying
this pudding at Thanksgiving and Christmas. Although
called 'pudding,' this delicious treat is very thick and chewy.
On rainy days at Idlewyld, I often have impromptu tea
parties for our house-bound guests and this might be one of
my selections." — Joan Barris*

4 well-beaten eggs
2 cups sugar
2 tablespoons melted butter
2 tablespoons hot water
2 cups finely cut dates
1 cup chopped nuts of your choice
2 cups all-purpose flour
1 tablespoon baking power
1 teaspoon salt
Whipped cream

Preheat oven to 350°F. Combine ingredients (add sugar
gradually). Bake in a 13 x 9" pan for 35 – 40 minutes until
toothpick inserted in center comes out clean. Serve warm
with whipped cream. *Serves 18 – 24.*

Dunscroft's Yummy Pecan Buns

2 loaves frozen bread dough
2 cups halved pecans
1 cup melted butter (not margarine)
Brown sugar (enough to coat balls of dough)

Thaw bread dough. Cover the bottom of a 13 x 9" metal pan with pecan halves. Put brown sugar in a large bowl. Place in a row in front of you (from left to right) the dough, melted butter, brown sugar, and pan with pecans. Pinch off 1½ – 2" balls of dough. Roll in butter, then brown sugar, and place over the pecans. Repeat until all the dough is used. Cover with a light dishcloth and let rise for 2 hours or overnight in a warm place. Bake in a preheated 350°F oven for 20 – 25 minutes until nicely browned. Using an oblong-shaped tray or serving plate, hold tightly over buns and immediately invert. Serve warm with 2 forks for pulling apart. *Makes 16 – 18 buns.*

Dunscroft By-The-Sea

Alyce and Wally Cunningham
24 Pilgrim Road
Harwich Port
Cape Cod, Massachusetts 02646
Tel: (800) 432-4345 or
(508) 432-0810

ABOUT THE B&B

With its beautiful, private mile-long beach on the warmest-water side of Cape Cod, Dunscroft By-The-Sea offers the ultimate romantic splurge. Tastefully decorated in a love theme, Dunscroft has a delightful surprise for you 'round every corner: a puffed heart adorns a canopied bed, a diminutive cupid greets you by the front door, and richly bound verses of love on your bedside table inspire the senses by candlelight. Beautiful king and queen bed chambers (including canopies, fourposters, or sleighs), in-room private baths and fireplaces, two suites with a private entrance, and charming honeymoon cottage with fireplace await your indulgence. To complete the romantic setting, a select bottle of sparkling champagne, a heart-laden basket of luscious, red strawberries and hand-dipped chocolates, and one lovely long-stemmed rose en vase may be ordered for your room upon arrival. Bountiful, full breakfast included.

SEASON

all year

ACCOMMODATIONS

eight rooms with private baths;
one honeymoon cottage with
private bath

Roses and Lace Inn

Shirley and Mark Sparks
Highway 231 South,
PO Box 852
Ashville, Alabama 35953
Tel: (205) 594-4366

ABOUT THE B&B

Built in 1890, this spacious three-story bed and breakfast is located in the center of quaint Ashville, Alabama. Listed on the National Register of Historic Places, the house is resplendent with Victorian elegance. Features such as wraparound porches, balconies, stained glass windows, carved mantles, winding stairs, and period furniture make Roses and Lace an excellent example of the area's craftsmanship and architectural integrity. Roses and Lace is a family-owned business and innkeepers Shirley and Mark look forward to your visit. Come and relax, walk to town and shop for antiques, or shop at the famed Boaz outlet city, just 30 minutes away.

SEASON

all year

ACCOMMODATIONS

two rooms with private baths; two rooms with shared baths

Fresh Fruit Popovers

Fruit sauce:
1½ cups sour cream
2 tablespoons white sugar
2 tablespoons brown sugar
1 tablespoon rum
1 teaspoon orange or lemon rind
½ teaspoon ground cinnamon
¼ teaspoon ground nutmeg

Popovers:
6 tablespoons vegetable oil
2 eggs
1 cup milk
1 cup all-purpose flour
½ teaspoon salt
Orange segments, banana slices, and any other fresh fruit in
    season (e.g., peaches, strawberries, kiwis, and grapes)

Make fruit sauce the night before by combining and stirring all ingredients. Chill overnight.

To make popovers: Preheat oven to 425°F. Place 1 tablespoon oil in each of 6 custard cups. Place cups on a cookie sheet and place in the oven for 5 minutes. Meanwhile, beat eggs well. Stir in milk. Sift flour and salt, then add to eggs. Stir just enough to get the lumps out. Pour into sizzling hot custard cups. Cook 25 minutes, then serve at room temperature.

To assemble: Invert custard cup to drop popover out on a plate. Break popover apart, tearing down the sides but leaving it in 1 piece. Spoon fruit sauce over popover and onto the plate. Pile with fruit and serve. Repeat with the other popovers. *Serves 6.*

Fruit Cobbler

1½ cups orange juice
¼ cup sugar (if fruit is sweet, use less; for rhubarb or tart fruits, use more)
1 tablespoon cornstarch
4 cups fruit of your choice, cut into bite-size pieces
1 cup all-purpose flour
2 tablespoons sugar
½ tablespoon salt
¼ cup canola oil (or melted butter or margarine)
½ cup non-fat buttermilk
1 tablespoon sugar with dash of ground cinnamon mixed in

Preheat oven to 375°F. In a heavy saucepan, stir orange juice, sugar, and cornstarch together until blended. Heat until bubbly. Add fruit and simmer until just cooked (this can be done the night before, if wished). Remove from heat and set aside. Spray Corningware dish or other flat baking dish with non-stick cooking spray, and pour fruit mixture into it. In a mixing bowl, combine flour, sugar, and salt. Whisk until blended. Add oil and fold in with rubber spatula until mixture looks crumbly. Add buttermilk and stir in just until you have a light fluffy dough. Spoon dollops of dough onto fruit leaving some fruit to show through. Sprinkle with cinnamon sugar. Bake on low rack of oven for about 8 minutes or until fruit begins to bubble (don't overbake). If dough has not turned a bit golden on top, set on high rack of oven and brown top for about 30 seconds. Serve immediately. *Tip:* You can also serve this dish warm with ice cream on top as a dessert instead of breakfast fare. *Serves 4.*

The Summer House

Kay and David Merrell
158 Main Street
Sandwich, Massachusetts 02563
Tel: (508) 888-4991

ABOUT THE B&B

The Summer House is an elegant circa 1835 Greek Revival twice featured in Country Living magazine. It was owned by Hiram Dillaway, a prominent mold-maker and colorist at the Boston & Sandwich Glass Factory. Large, sunny bedchambers feature antiques, hand-stitched quilts, and working fireplaces. Stroll to dining, shops, museums, galleries, pond and gristmill, and boardwalk to beach. Bountiful breakfasts change daily and include freshly ground coffee, tea, fruit juice, and fresh fruit served in stemware. Entrées of frittata, stuffed French toast, quiche, or omelets are accompanied by scones, puff pastry, muffins, or fruit cobblers. Dishes are enhanced with vegetables, berries, and herbs from the inn's garden. English-style afternoon tea is served at an umbrella table in the garden. Boston, Newport, Providence, Martha's Vineyard, and Nantucket make pleasant day trips. Innkeepers Kay and David Merrell (former executive secretary and aerospace engineer respectively) enjoy wood-working, gardening, quilting, jogging, backpacking, and the tranquility of Cape Cod.

SEASON

all year

ACCOMMODATIONS

one room with private bath;
four rooms with shared baths

Buttonwood Inn

Liz Oehser
190 Georgia Road
Franklin, North Carolina 28734
Tel: (704) 369-8985

ABOUT THE B&B

This small mountain bed and breakfast with a cozy home atmosphere awaits your visit. Sleep in chenille- or quilt-covered antique beds surrounded by country furnishings, collectibles, and crafts. Two rooms on the first floor each have a double and twin bed with private bath, while the two rooms on the second floor each have a double bed and share a common bath. Breakfast delights include artichoke quiche, sausage apple ring filled with puffy scrambled egg, Dutch babies with raspberry sauce, stuffed French toast, blintz soufflé, muffins, and cinnamon scones with home-made lemon butter. After breakfast, enjoy gem mining, hiking, horseback riding, water rafting, golf, or tennis. Stay long enough to tour Biltmore Estate in nearby Asheville, drive through the Smokey Mountain Parkway to Cherokee Indian Reservation, or "shop till you drop" in Gatlinburg. Hospitality, comfort, and delightful breakfasts are this inn's priorities.

SEASON

April to December 15

ACCOMMODATIONS

two rooms with private baths; two rooms with shared bath

Glazed Raisin Scones

2 cups all-purpose flour
¼ cup sugar
2½ teaspoons baking powder
½ teaspoon salt
½ cup slightly softened butter or margarine
¾ cup raisins
2 eggs
¼ – ⅓ cup milk
Additional sugar (for glaze)

Preheat oven to 400°F. In a large bowl, mix flour, sugar, baking powder, and salt. Cut in butter until mixture resembles coarse crumbs. Mix in raisins. In a small bowl, mix 1 egg and 1 egg yolk; reserve remaining white in another bowl. Mix eggs into flour mixture. Mix in enough of the milk to make a dough that holds together. Turn onto a lightly floured surface and knead 5 – 6 times. Halve dough. Pat each half into a circle ½" thick. Cut each into 8 triangles. Place spaced apart on a lightly greased baking sheet. With a fork, beat reserved egg white until bubbly and brush on scones. Sprinkle generously with additional sugar. Bake 14 – 18 minutes until golden brown. Serve warm with butter and fruit preserves. To reheat scones, place on baking sheet in preheated 350°F oven and heat about 5 minutes until warm. *Makes 16 scones.*

Indian Pudding (Vermont-Style)

½ cup coarse ground yellow cornmeal
½ cup maple syrup
4 cups scalding hot milk
2 tablespoons melted unsalted butter
1½ teaspoons ground cinnamon
1 teaspoon ground ginger
½ teaspoon ground allspice
½ teaspoon salt
3 lightly beaten eggs
Heavy cream

Preheat oven to 350°F. Combine the cornmeal and maple syrup in the top of a double boiler. Stir in the hot milk. Put 2" of simmering water in the bottom of the double boiler, put upper part over it and cook, stirring constantly, for about 20 minutes (until thick and smooth). Remove from heat, take top part off the bottom part of the double boiler, and stir in the butter, spices, and salt. Add the eggs and beat well. Pour mixture into a generously buttered 1½-quart baking dish. Put the baking dish into a larger pan, and pour about 1" of boiling water into the larger pan. Bake for approximately 1½ hours or until pudding is set, stirring every 30 minutes. Serve warm with apple topping (see recipe on next page) and heavy cream poured over top. *Serves 6.*

(continued on next page)

West Hill House

Dotty Kyle and Eric Brattstrom
RR1, Box 292
Warren, Vermont 05674
Tel: (802) 496-7162

ABOUT THE B&B

Up a quiet country lane on nine peaceful acres, this 1860s farmhouse boasts stunning mountain views, gardens, pond, and apple orchard, and is just one mile from Sugarbush Ski Resort and adjacent golf course/cross-country ski trails. Besides having an outdoor sports paradise at its doorstep, West Hill House is also near fine restaurants, quaint villages, covered bridges, unique shops, antique hunting, arts, museums, theater, and concerts. After a busy day, guests enjoy the comfortable front porch or roaring fireplace, eclectic library of books and videos, Oriental rugs, art, antiques, and the interesting company of other guests. Bedrooms feature premium linens, down comforters, and good reading lights. There's also a common guest pantry with wet bar and fridge. Breakfast specialties include sticky buns, soufflés, baked apple pancakes, fresh fruits, and more. Dotty and Eric, veteran B&B vacationers themselves, work to create an atmosphere of warmth and hospitality in their lovely small inn. Dotty's the chef, artist, and decorator, while Eric's the creative builder, remodeler, and stained glass artisan.

SEASON

all year

ACCOMMODATIONS

six rooms with private baths

Apple topping:
3 – 4 tart apples (such as Granny Smith)
4 tablespoons butter
¼ cup sugar
1 teaspoon ground cinnamon
½ teaspoon ground nutmeg

Thinly slice apples. Melt butter in a pan (do not let it brown) and place apples inside. Mix together sugar, cinnamon, and nutmeg and sprinkle over apples in pan. Continue cooking over medium-low heat until apples are soft but not mushy, constantly stirring so they do not stick or brown (about 5 – 8 minutes).

Mary's Irish Raisin Scones

"This recipe was given to us by guest Mary Early. When she checked in, I thought she was right off the plane from Ireland — she had such a strong Irish accent. But she's actually lived in The Bronx for over 30 years! I made Mary's recipe on the day she checked out and her scones have been a hit ever since." — David Horan

4 cups all-purpose flour
¾ cup sugar
3 heaping teaspoons baking powder
¼ teaspoon baking soda
1 teaspoon salt
¼ cup butter
1 cup raisins
1 egg
2 tablespoons sour cream
2 cups buttermilk
Melted butter
Sprinkle of sugar

(continued on next page)

The Melville House

Vince De Rico and David Horan
39 Clarke Street
Newport, Rhode Island 02840
Tel: (401) 847-0640

ABOUT THE B&B

Built circa 1750 and on the National Register of Historic Places, The Melville House is located in the heart of Newport's historic Hill District on a quiet gas-lit street. One of the few inns in Newport dedicated to the Colonial style, it's just one block up from Thames Street with its Brick Market and the harborfront where many of the city's finest restaurants, luxurious sailboats, antique shops, and galleries can be found. The Melville House is also close to the Tennis Hall of Fame, lavish Vanderbilt, Astor, and Belmont family mansions, the Naval War College, and Newport's finest ocean beaches. The Melville House breakfast menu features home-made granola, muffins, breads, buttermilk biscuits, scones, Yankee cornbread, stuffed French toast, fresh fruit sourdough pancakes, and Rhode Island johnnycakes. An afternoon tea is served every day, featuring refreshments, home-made biscotti, and soup (on cold days), over which innkeepers Vince and David share their Newport experiences.

SEASON

all year

ACCOMMODATIONS

five rooms with private baths;
two rooms with shared bath;
winter fireplace suite

Preheat oven to 425°F. Mix flour, sugar, baking powder, baking soda, and salt together. Cut butter into small pieces. With a pastry cutter, cut butter into flour mixture until well blended. Add raisins to flour and mix well with your fingers. In a small bowl, beat together the egg, sour cream, and buttermilk. Pour this milk mixture slowly into the flour mixture while constantly stirring with a fork (you might not need all the milk mixture). Stir with a fork just until it all comes together. Roll the dough out onto a floured surface, knead for about 2 minutes, then form into a ball. Divide the dough in half and form each half into a flat disk. Cut each disk with a pastry cutter into 6 triangles and place on an ungreased baking sheet. Bake for about 20 minutes or until golden brown and firm. Brush with butter and sprinkle with sugar. *Makes 12 scones.*

Mary's Little Angels

"I like to use a heart-shaped cutter on these biscuits, which have a beautiful color and are really delicious."
— *Mary Shaw*

2 packages active dry yeast (2 tablespoons)
¼ cup lukewarm water
5 cups self-rising flour
1 teaspoon baking soda
2 tablespoons sugar
1 cup shortening (Crisco recommended)
2 cups V8 juice

Dissolve yeast in lukewarm water, and set aside. Mix flour, baking soda, and sugar. Add shortening and mix. Add in yeast and V8 juice and mix well. Roll onto floured board and cut out biscuits with a cookie cutter. Start baking in a cold oven at 450°F until lightly browned (approximately 10 – 12 minutes). *Makes 18 – 20 biscuits.*

The Shaw House Bed and Breakfast

Mary and Joe Shaw
613 Cypress Court
Georgetown, South Carolina
29440
Tel: (803) 546-9663

ABOUT THE B&B

The Shaw House Bed and Breakfast is a spacious two-story home in a serene, natural setting. From the glass-walled den, enjoy bird-watching and a beautiful view overlooking miles of marshland formed by four rivers, which converge and flow into the Intercoastal Waterway. Outlined by tall white columns, the wide front porch extends the width of the home and features old-fashioned rockers — ready and waiting for guests who are welcomed as family. All rooms are air conditioned, with private baths and a smattering of antiques. Enjoy a full southern breakfast come morning and bed turn-backs and chocolate come bedtime — plus some loving extras.

SEASON

all year

ACCOMMODATIONS

three rooms with private baths

The Babbling Brook Inn

Helen King
1025 Laurel Street
Santa Cruz, California 95060
Tel: (800) 866-1131 or
(408) 427-2437

ABOUT THE B&B

Cascading waterfalls, a meandering creek, and a romantic gazebo grace an acre of gardens, pines, and red-woods surrounding this secluded inn. Built in 1909 on the foundation of an 1870 tannery, a 1790 grist mill, and a 2000-year old Indian fishing village, the Babbling Brook features rooms in country French decor, all with private bath, telephone, and television, and most with cozy fireplace, private deck, and outside entrance. Included in your stay is a large, country breakfast and afternoon wine and cheese, where Helen's prize-winning cookies await you on the tea cart in front of a roaring fireplace. Two blocks off Highway 1, the Babbling Brook is within walking distance to the beach, wharf, boardwalk, shops, tennis, running paths, and historic homes. Three golf courses and 200 restaurants are within 15 minutes' drive. A world-record holding angler, Mrs. Pacific Palisades 1955, one-time international tour organizer, and mother of six, Helen King has happily found her niche as a gourmet cook and owner/inn-keeper of this award-winning B&B.

SEASON

all year

ACCOMMODATIONS

12 rooms with private baths

Mrs. King's Cookies

"Every afternoon, these prize-winning cookies make their way off the tea cart into guests' mouths. One guest even remarked that she could smell their wonderful aroma from the parking lot as she arrived." — Helen King

2 cups butter
2 cups brown sugar
2 cups white sugar
4 eggs
2 teaspoons vanilla
4 cups all-purpose flour
2 teaspoons baking powder
2 teaspoons baking soda
2 teaspoons salt
2 cups white chocolate chips
2 cups milk chocolate chips
3 cups raisins
3 cups walnuts
2 cups old-fashioned rolled oats
3 cups orange-almond granola mix (or add grated orange rind to granola)

Preheat oven to 375°F. Blend first 3 ingredients until creamy. Add eggs and vanilla. Sift flour, baking powder, baking soda, and salt, and add to egg mixture, beating well. Stir in remaining ingredients. When well mixed, shape into balls the size of golf balls and bake on an ungreased cookie sheet for 8 – 10 minutes or until barely golden. *Tips:* Cookies are best when slightly undercooked and served warm from the oven. Dough keeps well when refrigerated — simply bake as needed. ***Makes 9 dozen cookies.***

Oatmeal-Carrot Cookies

"The wonderful aroma of these cookies baking gets anyone's stay at Dreams of Yesteryear off to a wonderful start. You can make a batch of these and then freeze unbaked cookies on a baking sheet. When guests are about to arrive, just pop a dozen or so in the oven for the best potpourri smell around."
— Bonnie Maher

¾ cup margarine
1¾ cups all-purpose flour
¾ cup brown sugar
½ cup sugar
1 egg
1 teaspoon baking powder
¼ teaspoon baking soda
½ teaspoon ground cinnamon
¼ teaspoon ground cloves
1 teaspoon vanilla
2 cups rolled oats
1 cup finely shredded carrots
½ cup raisins (optional)

Preheat oven to 370°F. Mix all ingredients together and drop by teaspoonfuls 2" apart on a lightly greased cookie sheet. Bake for 10 – 12 minutes. *Makes 4 dozen cookies.*

Dreams of Yesteryear Bed and Breakfast

Bonnie and Bill Maher
1100 Brawley Street
Stevens Point, Wisconsin 54481
Tel: (715) 341-4525

ABOUT THE B&B

This elegant, turn-of-the-century Victorian Queen Anne was home to three generations of the Jensen family before being purchased in 1987 and restored by current owners Bonnie and Bill Maher. An article Bonnie wrote about the restoration was featured in the Winter 1991 issue of Victorian Homes magazine. In 1990, after giving many tours, the Mahers opened their home as the Dreams of Yesteryear Bed and Breakfast. Listed on the National Register of Historic Places, Dreams of Yesteryear is located three blocks from historic downtown Stevens Point, two blocks from the Wisconsin River and Green Circle jogging/hiking/biking trails, a half mile from the University of Wisconsin, and near wonderful restaurants, theaters, and antique shops. Your visit includes a gourmet breakfast, warm hospitality, and wonderful memories.

SEASON

all year

ACCOMMODATIONS

two rooms with private baths;
two rooms with shared bath

Rockinghorse
Bed & Breakfast

Sharleen and Jerry Bergum
RR1, Box 133
Whitewood, South Dakota 57793
Tel: (605) 269-2625

ABOUT THE B&B

A cedar clapboard-sided house built in 1914 to accommodate local timber teams, Rockinghorse was moved to its present location by Sharleen and Jerry, who have lovingly restored the interior. Handsome wood floors, columns, and trims, along with antiques, country charm decor, and the original stairway grace the home. Rockinghorse is situated in the rustic Black Hills, where you can watch deer graze nearby and wild turkeys strut across the valley. Listen to the sounds of coyotes in the evening while a rooster's crow awakens you in the morning. You can also pet a bunny, ride the horse-drawn wagon, or have wood/fiber artist Sharleen help you master the spinning wheel. A gift shop is also on the premises. The B&B is near historic Deadwood, the world renowned Passion Play, the scenic Spearfish Canyon route, and it's one-hour's drive from Mt. Rushmore. Full breakfast includes fresh fruits (in season), home-made breads, blueberry pancakes, and special egg-cheese dishes.

SEASON

all year

ACCOMMODATIONS

one room with private bath;
two rooms with shared bath

Overnight Cinnamon Rolls

"My grandma used to bake cinnamon rolls like this when I was a child. I've added the convenience of a blender and now use whole wheat grain — nonetheless they're just as good as ever." — Sharleen Bergum

4 cups whole wheat flour
5½ cups all-purpose flour
3 cups lukewarm water
1 package active dry yeast (1 tablespoon)
2 teaspoons salt
1 cup sugar
2 eggs
½ cup margarine
1 cup whipping cream
2 cups brown sugar
1 cup margarine
Margarine
Brown sugar
Ground cinnamon
Raisins (optional)

(continued on next page)

Around 3 p.m., combine whole wheat and all-purpose flour in a large bowl and set aside. In a blender, blend water, yeast, salt, sugar, eggs, and ½ cup margarine. Pour the blender ingredients into the flour mixture and mix well. Cover and set dough aside for several hours. At 10:00 p.m., mix together whipping cream, brown sugar, and 1 cup margarine. Place this mixture in 2 13 x 11" (or equivalent) baking pans. Roll dough out into a rectangle. Spread with margarine, brown sugar, cinnamon, and raisins. Roll dough into tube and cut into ¼" slices. Place slices cut side down into prepared baking pans. Cover with a towel and place in a draft-free area. Let rise until morning. Bake in a preheated 350°F oven for 25 minutes. Serve warm. *Makes approx. 40 rolls.*

Idlewyld
Bed & Breakfast

Joan and Dan Barris
350 Walnut Avenue
Lakeside, Ohio 43440
(Mailing address:
13458 Parkway Drive
Lakewood, Ohio 44107)
Tel: (419) 798-4198

ABOUT THE B&B

I dlewyld has a homey atmosphere where guests can relax
and enjoy the tranquil beauty,
friendly atmosphere, and timeless
charm of 19th century Lakeside, on
the shores of Lake Erie. The century-
old home has both an upper porch
and a lower wraparound porch furnished with Amish hickory rockers.
There are 14 rooms at Idlewyld,
each distinctively decorated in a
country style. Hosts Joan and Dan
Barris take special pride in offering
both delicious and nutritious breakfast fare. Dan's specialty is popping
corn on Saturday nights in the vintage popcorn popper on the front
porch. Joan's special interest is nutrition, and Idlewyld is the site of an
annual wellness/spa weekend held
in late summer.

SEASON

May to October

ACCOMMODATIONS

five rooms with private baths;
nine rooms with shared baths

Peach Cobbler

"This is a very old family recipe for the best peach cobbler I've
ever tasted. I use it as a breakfast dish because of the low
sugar content — I let the natural sweetness of the peaches do
the job (which my calorie-conscious guests appreciate!). The
batter alone makes a great shortcake." — Joan Barris

2 eggs
½ cup sugar
6 tablespoons melted butter or margarine
⅔ cup milk
2 cups all-purpose flour
4 teaspoons baking powder
½ teaspoon salt
12 large or 16 medium peaches, pared and sliced
⅔ cup sugar
1 teaspoon ground cinnamon

Preheat oven to 375°F. In a large mixing bowl, beat eggs
until light. Add sugar, melted butter, and milk. Sift flour,
baking powder, and salt into egg mixture. Mix thoroughly.
Butter a 13 x 9" baking pan and fill with peaches. Mix sugar
and cinnamon together and sprinkle over peaches. Pour batter
over peaches. Bake for 35 – 40 minutes. Serve warm with milk,
cream, whipped cream, or ice cream. *Serves 15 – 18.*

ecan Crescents

"One of Duff Green's favorite pecan recipes."
— *Stephen Kerr, chef of Duff Green Mansion*

5 tablespoons butter
¾ cup brown sugar
½ cup chopped pecans
¼ cup water
2 packages crescent roll dough
3 tablespoons butter (not oleo or margarine)
¼ cup sugar
2 teaspoons ground cinnamon

Preheat oven to 375°F. Melt 5 tablespoons butter in a 13 x 9 x 2"
pan. Sprinkle brown sugar over the butter. Add chopped
pecans. Sprinkle with water. Separate crescent roll dough into
rectangles. Mix 3 tablespoons butter, sugar, and cinnamon.
Spread on dough. Roll up each rectangle. Using a thread, slice
into 5 pieces. Place crescents in pan and bake for 20 minutes.
Flip out of pan onto wax paper. Let cool and serve. *Makes 20
rolls.*

The Duff Green Mansion

Mr. and Mrs. Harry Carter Sharp
1114 First East Street
Vicksburg, Mississippi 39188
Tel: (601) 636-6968

ABOUT THE B&B

T*he Duff Green Mansion
is located in Vicksburg's
historic district. Built in
1856, it's considered one of the
finest examples of Paladian architecture in the state of Mississippi. The
mansion was built by Duff Green, a
prosperous merchant, for his bride
Mary Lake Green (whose parents
gave the land property as a wedding
gift). Many parties were held here
during the antebellum days but it
was hastily converted to a hospital
for both Confederate and Union soldiers during the siege of Vicksburg
and the remainder of the Civil War.
Mary Green gave birth to a son
during the siege in one of the caves
next to the mansion and appropriately named him Siege Green. The
over 12,000 square foot mansion
has been restored and features seven
guest rooms, luxurious antiques,
private baths, room service, southern plantation breakfasts, cocktails,
and a swimming pool.*

SEASON

all year

ACCOMMODATIONS

seven rooms (including two
suites) with private baths

West Hill House

Dotty Kyle and Eric Brattstrom
RR1, Box 292
Warren, Vermont 05674
Tel: (802) 496-7162

ABOUT THE B&B

Up a quiet country lane on nine peaceful acres, this 1860s farmhouse boasts stunning mountain views, gardens, pond, and apple orchard, and is just one mile from Sugarbush Ski Resort and adjacent golf course/ cross-country ski trails. Besides having an outdoor sports paradise at its doorstep, West Hill House is also near fine restaurants, quaint villages, covered bridges, unique shops, antique hunting, arts, museums, theater, and concerts. After a busy day, guests enjoy the comfortable front porch or roaring fireplace, eclectic library of books and videos, Oriental rugs, art, antiques, and the interesting company of other guests. Bedrooms feature premium linens, down comforters, and good reading lights. There's also a common guest pantry with wet bar and fridge. Breakfast specialties include sticky buns, souf-flés, baked apple pancakes, fresh fruits, and more. Dotty and Eric, veteran B&B vacationers themselves, work to create an atmosphere of warmth and hospitality in their lovely small inn. Dotty's the chef, artist, and decorator, while Eric's the creative builder, remodeler, and stained glass artisan.

SEASON

all year

ACCOMMODATIONS

six rooms with private baths

Ranger Cookies

"I was first offered these ranger cookies by my friend, Vilma Smith, whose mother made them often. When I was 12 years old, I asked her for the recipe and have been making them ever since (and I'm a grandma several times over!)."
— Dotty Kyle

½ cup unsalted butter
½ cup white sugar
½ cup light-brown sugar
1 egg
½ teaspoon vanilla
1 cup all-purpose flour
¼ teaspoon baking powder
½ teaspoon baking soda
¼ teaspoon salt
1 cup oats
½ cup shredded unsweetened coconut

Preheat oven to 350°F. Cream butter and sugars together until fluffy. Add egg and vanilla, beating well. Add remaining dry ingredients together and mix well. Drop batter by rounded tablespoonfuls onto an ungreased baking sheet. Cook for 10 – 12 minutes. Cookies should be slightly soft and light brown on the bottom. Allow them to cool for 1 minute before removing from pan. *Makes 24 cookies.*

Spicy Lemon Scones

"A delightful breakfast treat best served as an accompaniment to eggs." — Dick Wall

2½ cups all-purpose flour
1 tablespoon baking powder
1 teaspoon ground cinnamon
¼ teaspoon ground allspice
¼ teaspoon ground cloves
½ teaspoon salt
8 tablespoons butter, cut into small pieces
½ cup currants or dark raisins
¼ cup sugar
2 tablespoons candied lemon peel, finely diced
⅔ cup milk

Icing:
⅓ cup confectioners' sugar
1½ teaspoons milk

Preheat oven to 375°F. Thoroughly stir all flour, baking powder, spices, and salt into a bowl. With fingers, rub pieces of cold butter into flour mixture until fine granules are formed. Add currants (or raisins), sugar, and lemon. Add milk and stir to form a soft dough. Lightly flour a board and turn out dough, kneading it lightly about 10 times. Separate dough into 8 or 10 balls and place on an ungreased cookie sheet. Bake 12 – 15 minutes or until golden brown. Cool on a wire rack. Mix confectioners' sugar and milk into a smooth icing. Drizzle icing over each scone and serve. *Serves 6 – 8.*

Golden Maple Inn

Jo and Dick Wall
Wolcott Village, Vermont
05680-0035
Tel: (800) 639-5234 or
(802) 888-6614

ABOUT THE B & B

Originally the home of prominent mill owner H.B. Bundy, this historic 1865 B&B is nestled alongside northern Vermont's Lamoille River — famous for excellent trout fishing and quiet canoeing. Guests can read or doze in the library, work a picture puzzle in the parlor, or listen to the gurgle of the river from the comfort of an Adirondack chair. Jo and Dick's delightful candlelit breakfasts include fresh-ground coffees, teas, juice, fresh fruit in season, home-made granolas, and a scrumptious daily specialty entrée, all prepared in their country kitchen from only the finest local ingredients. To complete the day, teas and sweets are served to guests each evening in the library and parlor. Country walks, trout fishing, canoeing, biking, and back-country skiing are all available right from the inn. Golden Maple is located near the historic Fisher Covered Railroad Bridge, Bread & Puppet Museum, Cabot Creamery, Ben & Jerry's Ice Cream Factory, and the shops of Stowe Village.

SEASON

all year

ACCOMMODATIONS

three rooms (including one suite) with private baths

Garth Woodside Mansion

Diane and Irv Feinberg
RR #1, Box 304
Hannibal, Missouri 63401
Tel: (314) 221-2789

ABOUT THE B&B

Experience affordable elegance in this 1871 Victorian country estate on 39 magnificent acres of meadows and woodlands. On the National Register of Historic Places, Garth Woodside Mansion has remained unchanged outside, while graceful arched doors, handsomely decorated rooms featuring original furnishings spanning over 150 years, and magnificent three-story spiral "Flying Staircase" await you inside. You'll enjoy marble fireplaces, canopy beds, your own nightshirt, an exceptional full breakfast, an afternoon beverage, and more. All rooms are air conditioned and have a private bath. The location is ideal for seeing Mark Twain Country. Come for a romantic and magical stay — your experience will be something out of the ordinary.

SEASON

all year

ACCOMMODATIONS

eight rooms with private baths

Sweet Cheese Rolls

(Recipe from Breakfast Inn Bed, Easy and Elegant Recipes from Garth Woodside Mansion.)

¾ cup sugar
¼ cup chopped pecans
1 tablespoon grated orange rind
6 ozs. softened cream cheese
2 10-oz. cans refrigerated flaky biscuits
½ cup melted margarine

Preheat oven to 350°F. Combine sugar, pecans, and rind. Cut cream cheese into 20 equal pieces. Separate each biscuit into 2 layers, and place 1 piece of cream cheese between layers. Seal edges. Dip each filled biscuit in melted margarine, then in sugar mixture. Place on a cookie sheet and bake for 15 – 20 minutes or until lightly browned. ***Makes 20 rolls.***

Sweet Potato Biscuits

2 cups mashed sweet potatoes, warm
¾ cup sugar
½ cup shortening
2 cups all-purpose flour
7 teaspoons baking powder
1 teaspoon salt

Preheat oven to 350°F. Mix first 3 ingredients. Sift remaining dry ingredients and add to potato mixture. Roll out and cut biscuits. Bake about 20 minutes. Serve with Virginia ham and/or fig preserves. *Serves 12.*

Pickett's Harbor

Sara and Cooke Goffigon
PO Box 97AA
Cape Charles, Virginia 23310
Tel: (804) 331-2212

ABOUT THE B&B

*C*hesapeake Bay on Virginia's historic Eastern Shore is home to seagulls, pelicans, sandpipers — and Pickett's Harbor Bed and Breakfast. Enjoy acres of private beach on the southernmost tip of the Delmarva Peninsula. Your hosts Sara and Cooke are descended from the original settlers of the area and, in 1976, built this traditional home by the seashore, complete with high ceilings, fireplaces, antiques, and wooden floorboards made from 200-year-old barns along the James River. Every morning, awake to Sara's full country breakfast where, on any given day, you can sample a fruit cup, juice, paper-thin cured ham, and home-made three-fruit and fig jams (which Sara now sells). Set off on a quiet country lane and surrounded by sea grasses and a pine forest, Pickett's Harbor is marvelously isolated yet close to most attractions on the Eastern Shore, as well as to Norfolk, Hampton, and Virginia Beach.*

SEASON

all year

ACCOMMODATIONS

three rooms with private baths;
three rooms with shared baths

"An Elegant Victorian Mansion" Bed & Breakfast Inn

Lily and Doug Vieyra
1406 'C' Street
Eureka, California 95501
Tel: (800) 386-1888 or
(707) 442-5594

ABOUT THE B&B

Featured in many newspapers and magazines — not to mention on television and radio — this restored national historic landmark offers Eureka's most prestigious and luxurious accommodations. Spirited and eclectic innkeepers provide lavish hospitality in the splendor of a meticulously restored 1888 Victorian masterpiece, complete with original family antique furnishings. The inviting guest rooms offer both graceful refinement and modern-day comfort, individually decorated with Victorian elegance. Guests enjoy gourmet breakfasts and a heavenly night's sleep on top-quality mattresses, as well as secured parking and laundry service. Located in a quiet, historic residential neighborhood overlooking the city and Humboldt Bay, the non-smoking inn is near carriage rides, bay cruises, restaurants, and the theater, and is just minutes from giant Redwood parks, coastal beaches, ocean charters, and horseback riding.

SEASON

all year

ACCOMMODATIONS

one suite with private bath; three rooms with shared baths

Swiss Scones

"A welcome change from the usual muffins, these scones have a very delicate taste and are wonderful with scrambled eggs or simply with a bowl of fresh fruit." — Lily Vieyra

1½ cups all-purpose flour
¼ cup sugar
¼ teaspoon baking soda
1¼ teaspoons baking powder
¼ teaspoon salt
⅓ cup cold butter, cut in small pieces
½ cup golden raisins
Grated rind of small orange
½ cup buttermilk (or ½ cup milk with 1 tablespoon lemon juice)
Enough milk or cream to brush top of scones
2 tablespoons sugar mixed with ¼ teaspoon ground cinnamon

Preheat oven to 425°F. Place first 5 ingredients in a medium bowl and mix well. Cut butter into flour mixture with pastry cutter, until it resembles course meal. Add raisins and orange rind. Add buttermilk and mix with fork until dough leaves sides of bowl. Place dough on floured board and pat into a circle or rectangle ½" thick. Cut in 2" circles or hearts with cookie cutter and place on lightly greased cookie sheet (parchment paper also works). Space about 1½" apart. Brush tops with cream or milk and sprinkle with sugar/cinnamon mixture (avoid getting sugar on cookie sheet as it will burn). Bake for 12 – 14 minutes, until tops are lightly brown. Serve fresh from the oven or let cool and place in an airtight container. Scones can be stored 1 – 2 days, but are best fresh. Variations: Substitute dates for raisins or try chocolate chips. *Makes 12 scones.*

Tiny Tasty Tipsy Buns

Dough (prepared in bulk):
2 packages active dry yeast (2 tablespoons)
4 tablespoons sugar
¼ cup lukewarm water
½ teaspoon salt
¾ cup sour cream
Grated rind of 1 lemon
2 egg yolks
1 cup melted butter
1 teaspoon vanilla
2 cups whole wheat flour
2 cups all-purpose flour

Bun filling:
½ cup currants
1 tablespoon brandy flavoring diluted with 2 tablespoons water
¾ cup brown sugar
2 tablespoons ground cinnamon
⅓ dough (see above)

(continued on next page)

Martin Oaks Bed & Breakfast

Marie and Frank Gery
PO Box 207, 107 First Street
Dundas, Minnesota 55019
Tel: (507) 645-4644

ABOUT THE B&B

In 1869, the Archibald Brothers had this home built as a wedding present for their sister, Sarah Etta Archibald. Now listed on the National Register of Historic Places, Martin Oaks, the Archibald-Martin House, and the Carriage House occupy half a city block. Located in historic Dundas Village, Martin Oaks transports guests to an era where elegant women and fine gentlemen enjoyed good conversation and classical music, and savored elegant foods served on fine china. Three charming bedrooms filled with antiques offer the opportunity for a memorable, quiet evening. Martin Oaks is less than five minutes away from Northfield, Carleton, and St. Olaf colleges, and is near superb shopping and bookstore browsing, fine antique hunting on and off Division Street, golf courses, hiking, and cross-country skiing. Minneapolis, St. Paul, and the Mall of America are within a 40-minute drive.

SEASON

all year

ACCOMMODATIONS

three rooms with shared baths

Pan filling:
3 tablespoons butter
3 tablespoons honey
3 tablespoons brown sugar
⅓ cup pecan pieces

Note: Don't let buns rise before baking or they won't be tiny.

To make dough: Stir together the yeast, sugar, water, and salt, and set aside to let yeast bubble. Combine sour cream, lemon rind, egg yolks, melted butter, and vanilla into a mixing bowl; mix well. Stir in yeast mixture, then add the whole wheat flour and 1½ cups of the all-purpose flour. Knead this dough on a floured bread board, adding the rest of the flour as needed, until dough is smooth and elastic (about 10 minutes). Turn dough into a greased bowl, cover, and refrigerate at least 4 hours. Divide dough into thirds, keeping ⅓ out to make buns and refrigerating the rest for up to 5 days.

To make bun filling: Put currants into a container with brandy-water, and heat in the microwave oven 30 seconds. Mix the brown sugar and cinnamon. Roll dough into a ⅛" thick rectangle on a floured board. Sprinkle brown sugar mixture onto dough, then sprinkle on currants. Roll up tightly, and cut into 1" slices.

To make pan filling: Preheat oven to 350°F. In a 10 x 8" or 9 x 9" glass baking pan, melt butter and mix in honey. Pour butter mixture into pan. Sprinkle first with brown sugar, then with pecans. Place roll slices on top of pecans and brown sugar. Bake for 20 – 25 minutes (keeping an eye on them for the last few minutes). After taking pan out of the oven, immediately invert it on a serving plate. Let cool before serving. *Serves 6 – 8.*

Victorian Cookies

3-oz. package cream cheese
½ cup butter or margarine
½ teaspoon grated lemon rind
1 cup all-purpose flour
2 tablespoons sugar
Apricot or strawberry preserves

Preheat oven to 375°F. Cream together cream cheese and butter until smooth and light. Beat in lemon rind. Combine flour and sugar. Stir in half of the flour mixture to creamed mixture, blending well. Stir in remaining flour. Roll dough onto a lightly floured board to ⅛" thickness (any thicker and cookies tend to unfold when baking). Cut into 2" rounds. Spoon ¼ – ½ teaspoon preserves in center of each round. Form into a triangle by folding in 3 edges. Pinch edges together gently and bake for 12 – 14 minutes. Cool cookies for a few minutes. Remove to a rack to complete cooling. Store in a tin. *Makes 3 – 4 dozen cookies.*

Garth Woodside Mansion

Diane and Irv Feinberg
RR #1, Box 304
Hannibal, Missouri 63401
Tel: (314) 221-2789

ABOUT THE B&B

Experience affordable elegance in this 1871 Victorian country estate on 39 magnificent acres of meadows and woodlands. On the National Register of Historic Places, Garth Woodside Mansion has remained unchanged outside, while graceful arched doors, handsomely decorated rooms featuring original furnishings spanning over 150 years, and magnificent three-story spiral "Flying Staircase" await you inside. You'll enjoy marble fireplaces, canopy beds, your own nightshirt, an exceptional full breakfast, an afternoon beverage, and more. All rooms are air conditioned and have a private bath. The location is ideal for seeing Mark Twain Country. Come for a romantic and magical stay — your experience will be something out of the ordinary.

SEASON

all year

ACCOMMODATIONS

eight rooms with private baths

Holden House — 1902 Bed & Breakfast Inn

Sallie and Welling Clark
1102 West Pikes Peak Avenue
Colorado Springs, Colorado
80904
Tel: (719) 471-3980

ABOUT THE B&B

Experience the romance of the past with the comforts of today at Holden House — 1902 Bed & Breakfast Inn. This storybook Victorian and carriage house filled with antiques and family heirlooms is located in a residential area near the historic district and central to the Pikes Peak region. Enjoy the front parlor, living room with a fireplace and wingback chairs, or the wide veranda with mountain views. Immaculate guest rooms boast queen-size beds, down pillows, and private baths, while honeymoon suites feature "tubs for two" and fireplaces. Enjoy complimentary refreshments, home-made cookies, and friendly resident cats "Mingtoy" and "Muffin."

SEASON

all year

ACCOMMODATIONS

six rooms with private baths

White/Milk Chocolate Chunk Cookies

"A favorite for afternoon tea, the Holden House's bottomless chocolate chip cookie jar is always a hit with our bed and breakfast guests." — Sallie Clark

¾ cup brown sugar
¾ cup butter or margarine
2 eggs
1 teaspoon vanilla
2½ cups all-purpose flour
1 teaspoon baking soda
½ package (6 ozs.) milk chocolate chunks
½ package (5 ozs.) Hershey vanilla chips
¼ cup chopped walnuts

Preheat oven to 375°F or 400°F. Soften brown sugar and butter in microwave oven for 1 minute on high. Add eggs and vanilla. Mix well. Add flour and baking soda to sugar-egg mixture. When well mixed, add chocolate chunks, vanilla chips, and walnuts. Place well-rounded teaspoonfuls on ungreased cookie sheet. Bake for 10 – 12 minutes or until slightly brown on top. *Makes approx. 2 dozen cookies.*

French Toast

Pancakes

Waffles

Aebleskiver (Danish Ball Pancakes)

4 separated eggs
2 tablespoons sugar
½ teaspoon salt
2 tablespoons vegetable oil
2 cups buttermilk
1 teaspoon baking soda
1 teaspoon baking powder
2 cups all-purpose flour
Oil or lard

Beat egg whites until stiff; set aside. Beat rest of ingredients until batter is very smooth. Fold in egg whites. Heat well-seasoned monk's pan (see tip below) with ⅛ teaspoon oil or lard in each of the 7 holes. Fill each hole with batter. When browned on one side (almost right away), turn with knitting needle and keep turning until needle comes out clean after piercing through the cake. Serve with flavored butters, such as maple or cinnamon honey (you can write or call Shirley for the recipes) syrup, jam, and brown or white sugar. *Tips:* You can purchase a cast-iron monk's pan at Scandinavian gift shops or at small town hardware stores in Danish communities. As for servings, plan on each person eating 7 – 10 cakes. *Makes approx. 48 pancakes (serves 6).*

Lindgren's Bed & Breakfast

Shirley Lindgren
County Road 35, PO Box 56
Lutsen, Minnesota 55612-0056
Tel: (218) 663-7450

ABOUT THE B&B

L*ess than two hours from Duluth, Minnesota, and Thunder Bay, Ontario, this 1920s rustic log home with manicured grounds and walkable shoreline resides on Lake Superior in Superior National Forest. The living room features an 18-foot beamed ceiling, massive stone fireplace, and hunting trophies. Guest rooms are cozily designed in either knotty cedar, pine, or rustic paneling. Scenic points of interest include Split Rock Lighthouse, Gooseberry Falls, and Tettegouche State Park. Depending on the season, you can choose from hiking trails, skyride and alpine slide, mountain biking, horseback riding, golf, tennis, fishing, snowmobiling, and cross-country and downhill skiing. Any number of fine restaurants are nearby, and you're within walking distance of Lutsen Resort, the oldest in the state. Your hosts are retired after 35 years of owning and operating a successful garden center, landscaping, nursery, and floral business in Minneapolis, and enjoy fishing, hunting and, most of all, people, which is why they opened their home as a bed and breakfast!*

SEASON

all year

ACCOMMODATIONS

four rooms with private baths

Ghent House Bed & Breakfast

Diane and Wayne Young
411 Main, PO Box 478 (US 42)
Ghent, Kentucky 41045
Tel: (502) 347-5807

ABOUT THE B&B

Halfway between Cincinnati and Louisville, Ghent House is a gracious reminder of the antebellum days of the old South. It was built in 1833 in the usual style of the day — a central hall with rooms on either side of the kitchen and a dining room in back. A beautiful fantail window and two English coach lights enhance the front entrance, while a rose garden and gazebo grace the rear of the home. There are crystal chandeliers, fireplaces, and Jacuzzis in the guest rooms. Ghent House has a spectacular view of the Ohio River, and one can almost imagine the time when steamboats regularly traveled up and down its waters. Awake mornings to the aroma of coffee or tea, then have your breakfast in either the formal dining room or the breakfast room overlooking the river. At Ghent House, you'll enjoy and appreciate the charming blend of yesteryear with modern convenience and relaxation.

SEASON

all year

ACCOMMODATIONS

three suites with private baths

Amish Cinnamon Raisin French Toast

2 eggs
½ cup milk
1 teaspoon vanilla
12 – 14 slices cinnamon raisin bread
2 teaspoons ground cinnamon

Combine eggs, milk, and vanilla, and beat. Dip bread slices into egg mixture. Place in a lightly greased skillet. Sprinkle with cinnamon, brown slightly, and flip over. Sprinkle with more cinnamon, and brown lightly. Serve with jam, jelly, confectioners' sugar, or syrup. *Serves 6 – 8.*

Apricot-Pecan French Toast

(Recipe from What's Cooking at Carrington's Bluff.)

½ cup finely chopped dried apricots
¼ cup orange juice
8 ozs. cream cheese
¼ cup coarsely chopped pecans
16 slices sourdough bread

2 cups milk
1 cup half-and-half cream
6 eggs
6 tablespoons sugar
4 teaspoons grated orange rind
1 teaspoon vanilla
1 teaspoon salt
½ cup butter (or as needed)

Apricot syrup:
18 ozs. apricot preserves
¾ cup orange juice

(continued on next page)

Carrington's Bluff B&B

Gwen and David Fullbrook
1900 David Street
Austin, Texas 78705
Tel: (512) 479-0638

ABOUT THE B&B

The setting is Shoal Creek Bluff and an 1877 Texas farmhouse nestled in the arms of a 500-year-old oak tree. Enter innkeepers Gwen (from Texas) and David (from Britain), who transformed it into an English country B&B. Today, Carrington's Bluff B&B combines Texas hospitality with English charm to make your stay both unique and delightful. Upon arrival, you'll find yourself surrounded by rooms filled with English and American antiques, handmade quilts, and the sweet smell of potpourri. The 35-foot front porch beckons you to sit among the plants and flowers and enjoy the gentle breezes with your morning coffee and afternoon tea. The smell of fresh brewed gourmet coffee invites you to a breakfast that begins with fresh fruit and home-made granola served on fine English china. Home-made muffins or breads and a house specialty ensure you won't go away hungry. Carrington's Bluff is near the University of Texas and the State Capital grounds, and just minutes from parks, hiking and biking trails, shopping, and wonderful restaurants.

SEASON

all year

ACCOMMODATIONS

six rooms with private baths;
two rooms with shared bath

In a saucepan, combine the apricots and ¼ cup orange juice and bring to a boil. Simmer for 10 minutes or until the apricots are tender, then cool to room temperature. In a small bowl, combine the cream cheese, pecans, and apricot mixture. Spread over 8 slices of bread, forming 8 sandwiches. In a bowl, combine milk, half-and half, eggs, sugar, orange rind, vanilla, and salt. Dip the sandwiches into the egg mixture to completely coat. In a skillet, melt 2 tablespoons of the butter. Add the sandwiches and cook until golden brown, adding more butter to the skillet as necessary. In a heavy saucepan, combine the preserves and ¾ cup orange juice. Bring to a boil, stirring occasionally. Serve apricot syrup hot with the French toast. *Serves 8.*

Baked French Toast

4 slices Texas toast (1" thick white bread)
6 large eggs
1½ cups milk
1 cup light cream
1 teaspoon vanilla
¼ teaspoon ground cinnamon
¼ teaspoon ground nutmeg
¼ cup softened butter or margarine
½ cup firmly packed brown sugar
1 tablespoon light corn syrup

Butter a 9" square baking pan. Overlap bread slices to completely fill pan. In a medium bowl, combine eggs, milk, cream, vanilla, cinnamon, and nutmeg, mixing well. Pour over bread slices, then cover and refrigerate overnight. Next day, remove from fridge ¾ hour before baking and preheat oven to 350°F. In a small bowl, combine butter, brown sugar, and corn syrup, mixing well. Spread this mixture evenly over the bread. Bake 45 – 60 minutes or until puffed and golden. Serve with warm maple syrup. *Serves 6 – 8.*

The Inn On Golden Pond

Bonnie and Bill Webb
PO Box 680, Route 3
Holderness, New Hampshire 03245
Tel: (603) 968-7269

ABOUT THE B&B

I n 1984, Bonnie and Bill Webb left their desk jobs in southern California to establish The Inn On Golden Pond, an 1879 colonial home located near Squam Lake, setting for the classic film On Golden Pond. Ideal in all seasons, this central area of beautiful New Hampshire offers hiking, bicycling, golfing, water activities, skiing, and skating. The inn is known for its refreshingly friendly yet professional atmosphere. Rooms are individually decorated in traditional country style, featuring hardwood floors, braided rugs, country curtains, and bedspreads. There are seven spacious guest rooms and one extra- large suite, all with private baths. Morning is a treat as Bonnie makes all the breads, muffins, coffee cakes, and her special rhubarb jam. A full breakfast is offered each day featuring regional favorites like baked French toast and apple pancakes.

SEASON

all year

ACCOMMODATIONS

eight rooms (including one suite) with private baths

Alexander Hamilton House

Barbara Notarius
49 Van Wyck Street
Croton-on-Hudson, NY 10520
Tel: (914) 271-6737

ABOUT THE B&B

The Alexander Hamilton House (circa 1889) is a sprawling Victorian home situated on a cliff overlooking the Hudson River. Grounds include a mini orchard and in-ground pool. The home has many period antiques and collections and offers: a queen-bedded suite with a fireplace in the living room; a double-bedded suite with fireplace and a small sitting room; two large rooms with queen beds (one with an additional day bed); and a bridal chamber with king-size bed, Jacuzzi, entertainment center, pink marble fireplace, and skylights. A one-bedroom apartment is also available with a double bed, living room/kitchen, private bath, and separate entrance. Nearby attractions include West Point, the Sleepy Hollow Restorations, Lyndhurst Mansion, Boscobel (a fabulous Federal period restoration), the Rockefeller mansion, hiking, biking, sailing, and New York City (under an hour away by train or car).

SEASON

all year

ACCOMMODATIONS

six rooms with private baths

Banana-Walnut Stuffed French Toast

16 slices cinnamon raisin bread
Softened cream cheese
4 large sliced bananas
Chopped walnuts
Ground cinnamon
4 eggs
½ cup milk
½ teaspoon vanilla
Butter

Spread cream cheese on all slices of bread. Place sliced bananas on half of bread slices and sprinkle with walnuts and cinnamon. Cover with remaining slices (to form a sandwich). Combine eggs, milk, and vanilla. Dip sandwiches into egg mixture. Melt butter in a skillet and sauté sandwiches on both sides. Serve with warm maple syrup. *Serves 4.*

Belgian Waffles

2 cups all-purpose flour
2 teaspoons baking powder
2 tablespoons confectioners' sugar
1 tablespoon vegetable oil
2 cups milk
3 separated eggs
2 teaspoons vanilla
Pinch of salt
Fruit
Whipped cream

Combine all ingredients except egg whites. Beat egg whites until stiff and fold into batter (do not overmix). Using a 4-oz. ladle, pour mixture in hot waffle iron and bake for approximately 2 minutes. Top with fruit and whipped cream and serve hot. *Makes 8 waffles.*

Glynn House Victorian Inn

Betsy and Karol Paterman
43 Highland Street, PO Box 719
Ashland, New Hampshire 03217
Tel: (603) 968-3775

ABOUT THE B&B

Come enjoy the gracious elegance of this beautifully restored 1890 Queen Anne home — from the cupola of the inn's tower and gingerbread wraparound veranda to the carved oak foyer and pocket doors. Each of the beautifully appointed bedrooms has its own distinctive mood, distinguished by unique interior design, period furniture, the fragrance of fresh flowers, and soft, fluffy robes. A memorable full breakfast is served in the dining room, consisting perhaps of eggs Benedict or eggs Neptune, Belgian waffles, thick French toast, ambrosia, juice, and the specialty of the house — strudel. After breakfast, take a walk or boat ride around famous Squam Lake (where the movie On Golden Pond was filmed) just a few minutes away, and enjoy all that the Lakes Region and White Mountains have to offer. Allow Betsy and Karol to provide hospitality with a warm smile and make you feel as though you're part of their family.

SEASON

all year

ACCOMMODATIONS

five rooms with private baths;
two rooms with shared bath

Blue Harbor House, A Village Inn

Jody Schmoll and
Dennis Hayden
67 Elm Street
Camden, Maine 04843
Tel: (800) 248-3196 or
(207) 236-3196

ABOUT THE B&B

A classic village inn on the Maine Coast, the Blue Harbor House welcomes guests to relax in a restored 1810 Cape where yesterday's charms blend perfectly with today's comforts. The beautiful town of Camden, renowned for its spectacular setting where the mountains meet the sea, is just outside the door. The inn's bright and inviting guest rooms surround you with country antiques and hand-fashioned quilts — several even have canopy beds and whirlpool tubs. Breakfasts feature such specialties as lobster quiche, cheese soufflé, and blueberry pancakes with blueberry butter. As for dinner, guests can arrange to have a romantic candle-lit affair or an old-fashioned down-east lobster feed.

SEASON

all year

ACCOMMODATIONS

eight rooms with private baths; two carriage-house suites with private baths

Blueberry Buttermilk Pancakes with Blueberry Butter

Pancake batter:
¾ teaspoon baking soda
1½ cups buttermilk
1½ cups all-purpose flour
¾ cup whole wheat flour
¾ cup rolled oats (optional)
¾ teaspoon baking powder
1 teaspoon salt (optional)
1½ teaspoons sugar
6 separated eggs (discarding ¼ of egg yolks)
4½ tablespoons melted butter
1½ cups milk

Blueberry butter:
¼ lb. softened butter
⅓ cup confectioners' sugar
1 teaspoon vanilla
10 ozs. well-drained ripe blueberries
¼ cup shredded unsweetened coconut

(continued on next page)

Dissolve baking soda in the buttermilk. Sift flours, oats, baking powder, salt, and sugar together. Beat egg yolks and melted butter into dry ingredients. Add buttermilk and milk, stirring to blend. Beat egg whites stiff and fold in. Drop by spoonfuls onto a hot griddle, add 6 – 10 blueberries, flipping once when evenly browned. To make butter: In a food processor, mix butter, sugar, and vanilla into a thick paste. Add berries and coconut. Smother blueberry butter over pancakes and garnish with a few extra berries. *Serves 8.*

The Blue Door

Anna Belle and Bob Schock
13707 Durango Drive
Del Mar, California 92014
Tel: (619) 755-3819

ABOUT THE B&B

*E*njoy New England charm in a quiet southern California setting overlooking Torrey Pines State Reserve. A garden level two-room suite, with wicker accessories, king-size or twin beds, and adjoining private bath, is yours. The sitting room with couch, desk, chairs, and color TV opens onto your private patio. Breakfast is served in the spacious country kitchen-dining room warmed by a fire on chilly days. Anna Belle prides herself on creative breakfast menus featuring home-baked goods. Breakfast specialties include blue-berry-banana muffins, Swedish oatmeal pancakes, and Blue Door orange French toast. Bob is a retired Navy Commander now designing and building custom furniture. Your hosts will gladly direct you to the nearby racetrack, beach, zoo, or University of California at San Diego.

SEASON

all year

ACCOMMODATIONS

two-room suite with private bath

Blue Door French Toast

"This is the specialty of the house. The distinctive orange sauce is made from navel oranges picked right off our tree."
— Anna Belle Schock

4 eggs
1 cup milk or half-and-half cream
¾ cup orange juice
8 slices French bread, cut diagonally 1½" thick
Orange sauce (see recipe below)
2 peeled and quartered bananas

Blend eggs, milk, and orange juice in blender. Arrange bread slices in shallow tray and pour egg mixture over it. Cover and refrigerate overnight. In the morning, let warm to room temperature. Fry on lightly buttered griddle until golden brown on both sides and heated through. Serve with warm orange sauce and garnish plate with banana quarters.

Orange sauce:
4 – 5 peeled and sectioned navel oranges, saving juice to make ¾ cup
5 teaspoons cornstarch
¼ cup sugar
Grated rind of 1 orange

In a small saucepan or microwave-safe bowl, mix cornstarch and sugar. Add orange juice and stir until smooth. Cook over medium heat (or in microwave oven on high), stirring often until thick and clear. Add rind and orange sections. Pour over French toast. *Serves 4.*

Breakfast Crepes

Spray olive oil
1 teaspoon light tamari sauce (or soya sauce)
¼ cup hot water
½ chopped yellow onion or 4 chopped scallions
2 large minced garlic cloves
½ large seeded and chopped green bell pepper
3 medium potatoes, cooked, peeled, and chopped
16 ozs. green chili sauce
6 beaten eggs
Salt and pepper
12 crepes
Fresh mint

Spray skillet with olive oil. Add tamari sauce and hot water. Cook the onion, garlic, green pepper, and potatoes until brown and tender (add hot water and tamari as needed). Meanwhile, heat green chili sauce in a separate pan. Add eggs to the potato mixture and scramble them in. Stir carefully until eggs are cooked. Salt and pepper to taste. Divide mixture among crepes. Fold up crepes and place them seam side down, 2 to a plate. Cover with heated green chili sauce and garnish with fresh mint if wished. Serve with fresh fruit and bran muffins. *Serves 6.*

The Red Violet Inn

Ruth and John Hanrahan
344 North 2nd Street
Raton, New Mexico 87740
Tel: (800) 624-9778 or
(505) 445-9778

ABOUT THE B&B

Follow the Sante Fe Trail and step back into the past at this appealing 1902 red brick Victorian home, three blocks from Raton's historic downtown. Guests have use of the parlor, dining room, porches, and flower-filled yard, and are invited to enjoy the classical music during the social hour from 5:30 – 6:30 p.m. Full breakfast is served in the formal dining room, accompanied by friendly conversation. A theater and gallery are within a few blocks, hiking and fishing facilities (at Surarite State Park) are just 10 miles away, and Capulin Volcano National Monument is less than 30 minutes away. Other area attractions include a golf course, several antique shops, and a museum. Red Violet is a non-smoking inn.

SEASON

all year

ACCOMMODATIONS

two rooms with private baths;
two rooms with shared bath

Beaver Creek House

Shirley and Donald Day
20432 Beaver Creek Road
Hagerstown, Maryland 21740
Tel: (301) 797-4764

ABOUT THE B&B

Comfort, relaxation, and hospitality await you at this turn-of-the-century country Victorian home, located in the historic area of Beaver Creek, Maryland. Step back to a quiet, gentler time and enjoy the family antiques and memorabilia that fill the inn. Choose from five centrally air-conditioned guest rooms, and enjoy a country breakfast served on the spacious wraparound screen porch or in the elegantly appointed dining room. Sit in the courtyard by the fountain, stroll through the country garden, or linger by the fish pond and gaze at the mountain. Nearby are the National Historic parks of Antietam, Harpers Ferry, the C&O Canal, and the Appalachian Trail. Guests may also hike, bike, golf, ski, shop at the many local antique shops, and dine at excellent restaurants in Hagerstown.

SEASON

all year

ACCOMMODATIONS

five rooms with private baths

Buttermilk-Pecan Pancakes

2 cups all-purpose flour
1 teaspoon baking soda
1 teaspoon salt
2 tablespoons sugar
½ cup coarsely chopped pecans
2 well-beaten eggs
2 cups buttermilk
2 tablespoons melted shortening

Sift dry ingredients together in a bowl. Combine well-beaten eggs and buttermilk to melted shortening. Add to dry ingredients, stirring until flour is barely moistened (do not overstir). Drop batter on hot, lightly greased griddle. Turn when golden brown. Serve with butter and warm maple syrup or honey. *Makes approx. 16 pancakes.*

Buttermilk-Pecan Waffles

2 cups all-purpose flour
1 tablespoon baking powder
1 teaspoon baking soda
½ teaspoon salt
4 eggs
2 cups buttermilk
½ cup melted butter or margarine
3 tablespoons chopped pecans

Combine flour, baking powder, baking soda, and salt; set aside. Beat eggs until light. Add buttermilk to eggs and mix well. Add dry ingredients to egg mixture and beat until smooth. Stir in melted butter. Pour about ¾ cup batter onto a greased preheated waffle iron. Sprinkle with a few pecans. Cook until done. Repeat with rest. Serve warm. *Makes 7 waffles (8").*

The Hen-Apple Bed and Breakfast

Flo and Harold Eckert
409 South Lingle Avenue
Palmyra, Pennsylvania 17078
Tel: (717) 838-8282

ABOUT THE B&B

Built around 1825, the Hen-Apple is an intimate and fully restored bed and breakfast filled to the brim with everything country and old-fashioned. It offers a relaxed atmosphere with six air-conditioned guest rooms (each with private bath), a porch filled with rockers, a screened porch for warm weather dining, a herb garden, lots of flowers, and a shady retreat in the orchard. The Hen-Apple's well-rounded breakfasts are something to remember — especially the cinnamon French toast — with tea served in the afternoon. Just two miles from Hershey, Pennsylvania, Palmyra is an antique lover's dream. In addition, wineries, shopping outlets, Hershey attractions, the riverboat, and horse racing are nearby. Your hosts, Flo and Harold Eckert, love going to flea markets and auctions, and enjoy reading, gardening, and music. Flo is also a Christmas enthusiast so, come the merry season, the B&B sports a tree in just about every room and an impressive Santa collection.

SEASON

all year

ACCOMMODATIONS

six rooms with private baths

The Country Caboose

Lisa Thompson
852 Willoughby Lane
Stevensville, Montana 59870
Tel: (406) 777-3145

ABOUT THE B&B

The Country Caboose is indeed that — an authentic caboose dating back to 1923, made of wood and painted red, of course. It is set on real rails in the middle of the countryside. The caboose sleeps two and offers a spectacular view of the Bitterroot Mountains right from your pillow. The Caboose breakfast menu features such goodies as huckleberry pancakes, strawberry waffles, French toast with fruit, and quiche. Local activities include touring St. Mary's Mission and the Marcus Daly Mansion, hiking mountain trails, fishing, and hunting.

SEASON

summer

ACCOMMODATIONS

room and private bath
in a 1923 wooden caboose

Caboose Babies

4 tablespoons unsalted butter, melted
2 eggs
½ cup milk
½ cup all-purpose flour
½ teaspoon almond extract
1 teaspoon grated lemon rind
Sliced bananas dipped in orange juice
Fresh ground nutmeg
¼ cup whipped topping

Preheat oven to 475°F. Beat eggs; add milk, flour, almond extract, and lemon rind. Pour hot, melted butter into a pie pan, pour batter into pan, then return it to the oven. Cook 12 minutes until pancake is puffed. Serve immediately with sliced bananas dipped in fresh orange juice, and top with freshly ground nutmeg and whipped topping. *Serves 2.*

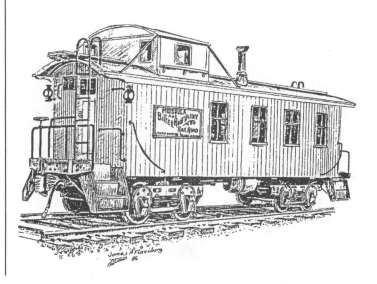

Cheese and Currant Pancakes

½ cup all-purpose flour
1 tablespoon sugar
1 teaspoon baking powder
¼ teaspoon ground cinnamon
2 eggs
½ cup creamed cottage cheese
2 tablespoons milk
1 tablespoon canola oil
1 teaspoon vanilla
2 tablespoons currants

Combine flour, sugar, baking powder, and cinnamon. In a separate bowl, beat together eggs, cottage cheese, milk, oil, and vanilla. Add to dry ingredients, stirring until blended but still slightly lumpy. Stir in currants. For each pancake, pour 1 rounded tablespoon of batter onto a hot, lightly greased griddle. Cook until golden, turning to cook other side when pancakes have a bubbly surface. Serve with butter or margarine and maple syrup. *Makes 1 dozen pancakes.*

The Summer House

Kay and David Merrell
158 Main Street
Sandwich, Massachusetts 02563
Tel: (508) 888-4991

ABOUT THE B&B

*T*he Summer House is an elegant circa 1835 Greek Revival twice featured in Country Living magazine. It was owned by Hiram Dillaway, a prominent mold-maker and colorist at the Boston & Sandwich Glass Factory. Large, sunny bedchambers feature antiques, hand-stitched quilts, and working fireplaces. Stroll to dining, shops, museums, galleries, pond and gristmill, and boardwalk to beach. Bountiful breakfasts change daily and include freshly ground coffee, tea, fruit juice, and fresh fruit served in stemware. Entrées of frittata, stuffed French toast, quiche, or omelets are accompanied by scones, puff pastry, muffins, or fruit cobblers. Dishes are enhanced with vegetables, berries, and herbs from the inn's garden. English-style afternoon tea is served at an umbrella table in the garden. Boston, Newport, Providence, Martha's Vineyard, and Nantucket make pleasant day trips. Innkeepers Kay and David Merrell (former executive secretary and aerospace engineer respectively) enjoy woodworking, gardening, quilting, jogging, backpacking, and the tranquility of Cape Cod.

SEASON

all year

ACCOMMODATIONS

one room with private bath;
four rooms with shared baths

Kerri and Stephen Wagner
110 Menefee Mountain Lane
Washington, Virginia 22747
Tel: (703) 675-3046

ABOUT THE B&B

Perched atop Menefee Mountain (elevation 1,043 feet) and situated on several hundred acres of pristine land, this large contemporary stone home has a round, glass-walled living room and 65-foot veranda to enhance the panoramic mountain vistas offered from every direction. The house has light hardwood floors and Oriental rugs throughout, not to mention Kerri's exotic plants and Stephen's original art. You may choose from three elegant and tasteful rooms, each with private bath, queen-size bed, mountain views, sitting/reading area, ceiling fan, and central heat and air conditioning. A full sumptuous breakfast is served daily, and there are home-baked treats in your room and mints by your bedside. A certified National Wildlife habitat, Sycamore's gardens are the perfect spot for a stroll — perhaps you'll see a white-tailed deer or wild turkey. Some of the finest dining in the east is just moments away. Also nearby is Skyline Drive, Luray Caverns, Old Rag Mountain, vineyards, antique and craft shops, golf, tennis, hot-air ballooning, canoeing, horseback riding, and berry picking.

SEASON

all year

ACCOMMODATIONS

three rooms with private baths

Cinnamon Apple Puff

Shortening or butter for greasing quiche dish
1 very large tart apple (like Granny Smith), peeled, seeded, and
    sliced very thin
3 tablespoons butter
3 eggs
½ cup all-purpose flour
½ cup whole milk
1 teaspoon sugar
Dash of salt
2 tablespoons cinnamon sugar
Juice of a whole lemon

Preheat oven to 475°F. Liberally grease a 9" fluted quiche dish. Sauté the apple in 1 tablespoon butter until slightly tender. Spread the apple slices evenly in the quiche dish. Mix together the eggs, flour, milk, sugar, and salt until blended well, and pour over apple slices. Bake for 10 minutes. Remove from oven, dot with remaining 2 tablespoons butter, and sprinkle with cinnamon sugar. Return to the oven for 5 minutes. Bring to the table puffed, and sprinkle the lemon juice over the puff. *Serves 4.*

Country Cottage Crepes

"My Polish mother-in-law served these as a dessert, but my B&B guests love them as a very special and unusual breakfast treat." — Edie Senalik

¼ lb. butter

Filling:
1 lb. cottage cheese
¼ cup raisins
½ cup sugar
2 eggs

Crepe batter:
1 egg
1 tablespoon sugar
1 cup all-purpose flour
¾ cup water
Pinch of salt

Preheat oven to 350°F. Melt ¼ lb. butter in a 13 x 9" baking dish and set aside. Mix filling ingredients and set aside. Mix batter ingredients until smooth (if batter is too thick, water may be added). Fry a small amount of batter in a crepe pan (or small skillet) in a small amount of butter. Turn when top of crepe seems to dry. Place cooked crepe in baking dish, fill with cottage cheese filling, and fold edges into the middle. When all crepes have been fried and filled, bake for 20 minutes. *Makes 4 – 5 crepes.*

Bed & Breakfast at Edie's

Edie Senalik
233 East Harpole
Williamsville, Illinois 62693
Tel: (217) 566-2538

ABOUT THE B&B

Step back in time to an era when life was more leisurely. *Bed & Breakfast at Edie's* is located in the peaceful and charming village of Williamsville, Illinois, just 10 minutes north of Springfield. The 1915 mission-style house is large and gracious. Edie serves a delicious and bountiful continental breakfast, with home-made bagels being her specialty. Sleep in queen-size beds with down pillows. Relax in the large living room, TV room, or enjoy the wide wraparound veranda or rear patio. The nearby state capitol offers plays, symphonies, Abraham Lincoln's tomb and home, and many other interesting attractions. Lincoln's New Salem village is just 20 minutes to the east.

SEASON

all year

ACCOMMODATIONS

four rooms with shared baths

Harbour Woods

Christine and Joe Titka
PO Box 121
Southwest Harbor, Maine 04679
Tel: (207) 244-5388

ABOUT THE B&B

Christine and Joe welcome you to their gracious 1800s Maine farmhouse across the street from the Great Harbor Marina. By having a small number of guest rooms, Harbour Woods offers an intimate social setting accented by family keepsakes, antiques, flowers, and softly glowing oil lamps. What's more, the warm tones and subtle designs of the wall coverings create an atmosphere of casual elegance. Each morning, a candlelight breakfast becomes a dining experience of the finest kind. Listen to soft music and enjoy a variety of coffees, teas, juices, in-season fruits, home-baked breads, muffins, and entrées of the day, which are imaginatively prepared and presented. A cookie jar and tea for the munches and a refrigerator stocked with complimentary soft drinks are always available. Guest rooms are distinctively decorated and feature queen-size beds, crackling fireplaces, evening mints and candy, telephones, and private baths with luxurious towels and a selection of rich soaps. And, of course, you may privately reserve the B&B's indoor spa, which awaits to refresh and relax you after a full day of activities in Acadia National Park.

SEASON

all year

ACCOMMODATIONS

three rooms with private baths;
private cottages with
private baths (seasonal)

Crème Caramel Apple French Toast

2 cups light-brown sugar
1 cup butter
4 tablespoons clear corn syrup
2 teaspoons vanilla
8 large Granny Smith apples, cored, peeled, and sliced
1 loaf French bread, sliced 1" thick
6 eggs
1 cup milk
½ cup heavy cream
1 teaspoon ground cinnamon
Whipped cream

In a saucepan, combine brown sugar, butter, corn syrup, and 1 teaspoon vanilla. Melt and stir until smooth and caramelized. Spread half of caramel in the bottom of a 13 x 9" non-stick baking pan (save other half for topping). Overlap sliced apples on top of caramel. Lay sliced French bread on top of apples. In a large bowl, blend eggs, milk, cream, cinnamon, and remaining 1 teaspoon vanilla. Pour mixture over bread. Cover and refrigerate overnight. Remove from fridge ¾ hour before baking. Bake uncovered in a preheated 350°F oven for approximately 35 – 45 minutes or until golden brown. Cut into 6 – 8 pieces and invert to serve. Drizzle remaining caramel over bread and top each piece with a dollop of whipped cream. *Serves 6 – 8.*

Dutch Babies

"When these delicacies bubble up all over, they look more like 'Moon Babies!' Serve them with a dab of strawberry, raspberry, or blueberry jam — and listen to the oohs and aahs." — Pat Cameron

3 eggs
½ cup all-purpose flour
½ cup milk
2 tablespoons melted butter
¼ teaspoon salt (or to taste)
Fruit jam of your choice

Preheat oven to 400°F. With a French whip, lightly beat the eggs. Add the flour in 4 parts, whipping the mixture smooth each time. Add milk in 2 parts, then add the melted butter and salt. Pour mixture into 2 well-greased or buttered 9" pie pans (glass only). Bake for 10 minutes and reduce oven to 350°F for 5 – 10 minutes more, until pancakes are puffed. Top each with a dollop of your favorite fruit jam and serve immediately. *Serves 2.*

Freeman House

Pat and Bob Cameron
1825 Lakeshore Drive
Branson, Missouri 65616
Tel: (800) 727-0723 or
(417) 334-8564

ABOUT THE B&B

A quiet, little resort town nestled in the beautiful Ozark mountains, Branson is home to a variety of music shows and to three of the finest fishing lakes in the country. It is also home to Freeman House, situated in a park-like setting along Lake Taneycomo (renowned nation-wide for some of the finest trout fishing anywhere). This B&B offers fishermen all the amenities you could want: Cast your line by the nearby dock or by boat, catch up to five trout, bring your bounty home, warm up in the spa after your brisk morning on the lake, then sit down to a fresh trout breakfast. Or, if you prefer, you can cook your own catch on the lakefront grill. For the non-fishermen, you can enjoy a relaxing day in one of Freeman House's three distinctive guest rooms or around the pool, or browse through the quaint shops in Branson. In the evening, you can treat your ears to one of the many music shows in town — just minutes away.

SEASON

all year

ACCOMMODATIONS

three rooms (including two suites) with private baths

Mulberry Bed and Breakfast

Frances A. Murphy
257 High Street
Wareham, Massachusetts 02571
Tel: (508) 295-0684

ABOUT THE B&B

Built in 1847 as a residence by blacksmith Aaron Sampson, Mulberry Bed and Breakfast was purchased in 1924 by the paternal grandfather of Mulberry's current owner, who turned it into a general store. In 1987, Frances (a retired elementary school teacher) transformed it into Mulberry Bed and Breakfast, which offers guests a colonial Victorian atmosphere with antique furnishings throughout. Three guest rooms with shared baths, a music room, two fireplaces, and a cozy kitchen enhance guests' visits. A hearty New England breakfast includes home-made jams, jellies, and breads along with French toast and other specialties. On pleasant mornings, breakfast may be served on the spacious deck in view of the impressive mulberry tree. Fran has lived in the area all her life and can direct guests to places of interest. She enjoys bicycling, gardening, cross-country skiing, and furniture restoration and she, along with Tootles and Tinsel (her cats), welcome your visit.

SEASON

all year

ACCOMMODATIONS

three rooms with shared baths

Elegant Autumn French Toast

1 small peeled and sliced apple
2 tablespoons cream cheese
2 slices cinnamon raisin or cinnamon apple bread
1 beaten egg
2 tablespoons milk
1 teaspoon sugar
¼ teaspoon salt
1 tablespoon butter

Microwave apple for 1 minute. Spread cream cheese on each slice of bread. Top 1 slice with baked apples and cover with second slice (like a sandwich). In a shallow bowl, combine egg, milk, sugar, and salt. Dip sandwich in French toast mixture and fry in melted butter until golden. Serve with bacon, sausage, or ham. *Serves 1.*

Erma's Special French Toast

3-oz. package softened cream cheese
1½ tablespoons lemon curd
6 slices white bread
3 tablespoons chopped pecans
3 eggs
2 tablespoons milk
Sprinkle of confectioners' sugar
Orange slices

Mix softened cream cheese and lemon curd together. Spread evenly on bread slices. Sprinkle 3 of the slices with the chopped nuts. Press the other 3 slices on top and press firmly. Cut "sandwiches" on the diagonal. Beat eggs lightly with a fork. Add milk and continue beating egg mixture with a fork. Dip sandwiches one at a time into egg mixture, then let drain a little, and fry as you would regular French toast. Just before serving, sift a little confectioners' sugar on top. Garnish with orange slices, and serve with syrup (if desired). *Tip:* Sandwiches can be made the night before. Simply wrap them in waxed paper and keep in the refrigerator. Remove from fridge ¾ hour before ready to dip in egg mixture and fry. *Serves 2.*

Rummel's Tree Haven Bed & Breakfast

Erma and Carl Rummel
41 North Beck Street (M-25)
Sebewaing, Michigan 48759
Tel: (517) 883-2450

ABOUT THE B&B

Located in the village of Sebewaing, Michigan, in the hollow of the thumb on Saginaw Bay, Rummel's Tree Haven was originally built as the farm home of Barbara and Frederick Beck in 1878. Today, Erma and Carl Rummel call it home and offer comfort and convenience to all travelers. The B&B is surrounded by many trees, which gives it an air of privacy — one tree even grows right through the porch roof! Saginaw Bay offers fine fishing, hunting, boating, bird-watching, or just relaxing. The Rummels love having company and will make you feel welcome.

SEASON

all year

ACCOMMODATIONS

two rooms with private baths

The Country Caboose

Lisa Thompson
852 Willoughby Lane
Stevensville, Montana 59870
Tel: (406) 777-3145

ABOUT THE B&B

The Country Caboose is indeed that — an authentic caboose dating back to 1923, made of wood and painted red, of course. It is set on real rails in the middle of the countryside. The caboose sleeps two and offers a spectacular view of the Bitterroot Mountains right from your pillow. The Caboose breakfast menu features such goodies as huckleberry pancakes, strawberry waffles, French toast with fruit, and quiche. Local activities include touring St. Mary's Mission and the Marcus Daly Mansion, hiking mountain trails, fishing, and hunting.

SEASON

summer

ACCOMMODATIONS

room and private bath
in a 1923 wooden caboose

French Toast with Orange and Pecans

4 eggs
⅔ cup orange juice
⅓ cup milk
¼ cup sugar
¼ teaspoon ground nutmeg
¼ teaspoon vanilla
½ loaf sliced French bread
⅓ cup melted butter
½ cup pecan halves
2 tablespoons grated orange rind

Beat together eggs, orange juice, milk, sugar, nutmeg, and vanilla. Place bread slices in a single layer on a large, flat dish. Pour milk mixture over bread. Cover and refrigerate overnight. In the morning, remove dish from fridge about ¾ hour before baking. Preheat oven to 400°F, pour melted butter onto a baking pan, then place bread on pan. Sprinkle with orange rind and pecans. Bake 20 – 25 minutes. Serve with maple syrup or fresh fruit. *Serves 4.*

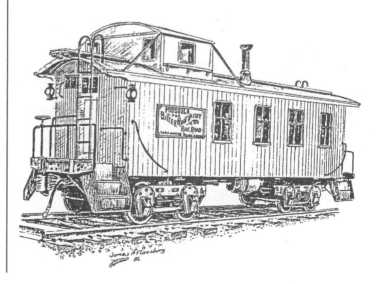

Fruit-Stuffed French Toast with Strawberry-Nut Sauce

6 ozs. softened cream cheese
12 slices raisin bread
6 teaspoons strawberry jam
3 eggs
¼ cup milk
1 teaspoon vanilla
2 teaspoons sugar

Spread cream cheese on 6 slices of raisin bread. Spread jam on remaining 6 slices of raisin bread. Put bread slices together (cream cheese side to jam side) and set aside. Mix eggs, milk, vanilla, and sugar. Dip sandwiches in egg mixture, then grill on both sides. Cut diagonally and spoon sauce (see below) over wedges before serving. *Serves 6.*

Strawberry nut sauce:
2 teaspoons cornstarch
⅔ cup cold water
1 cup strawberry jam
2 teaspoons lemon juice
¼ cup chopped walnuts

Mix cornstarch and water and set aside. Heat jam to a boil and add water-cornstarch mixture. Stir constantly and bring to boil, then simmer 3 minutes. Add lemon juice, then chopped walnuts. Spoon approximately 1 tablespoon over 2 wedges of French toast.

Bridgeford House

Denise and Michael McDonald
263 Spring Street
Eureka Springs, Arkansas 72632
Tel: (501) 253-7853

ABOUT THE B&B

In the heart of Eureka Springs's historic district, Bridgeford House is an 1884 Queen Anne/Eastlake-style Victorian delight. Outside, you'll find shady porches that invite you to pull up a wicker chair and enjoy the panorama of horse-drawn carriages and Victorian homes that is uniquely Spring Street. Yet Bridgeford House is far enough away from downtown that it affords you the luxury of a peaceful and quiet stay. Select from four distinct accommodations: a two-room suite or three large, comfortable bedrooms. From your private entrance, you'll step into rooms tastefully filled with antique furnishings. Your comfortable bedroom and large modern bathroom offer a variety of distinctive touches that let you know you are indeed a special guest — things like fresh hot coffee in your room, color TV, and air conditioning. The large gourmet breakfast is just the right send-off for a pleasant day in one of America's most charming and unusual cities. Denise and Michael are full-time innkeepers and can devote their full attention to all of your needs.

SEASON

all year

ACCOMMODATIONS

four rooms (including one suite) with private baths

Holden House — 1902 Bed & Breakfast Inn

Sallie and Welling Clark
1102 West Pikes Peak Avenue
Colorado Springs, Colorado
80904
Tel: (719) 471-3980

ABOUT THE B&B

Experience the romance of the past with the comforts of today at Holden House — 1902 Bed & Breakfast Inn. This storybook Victorian and carriage house filled with antiques and family heirlooms is located in a residential area near the historic district and central to the Pikes Peak region. Enjoy the front parlor, living room with a fireplace and wingback chairs, or the wide veranda with mountain views. Immaculate guest rooms boast queen-size beds, down pillows, and private baths, while honeymoon suites feature "tubs for two" and fireplaces. Enjoy complimentary refreshments, home-made cookies, and friendly resident cats "Mingtoy" and "Muffin."

SEASON

all year

ACCOMMODATIONS

six rooms with private baths

German Puff Pancakes with Spiced Apples

Egg mixture:
1 cup milk
1 cup all-purpose flour
6 eggs
2 teaspoons vanilla

Apple mixture:
5 medium apples (any variety)
½ cup water
4 tablespoons butter or margarine
½ teaspoon each ground cinnamon, nutmeg, and ginger
½ cup brown sugar
½ cup mincemeat

Extras:
8 pats butter or margarine
Whipped cream
Freshly grated nutmeg
8 sliced apple wedges

(continued on next page)

Whip milk, flour, eggs, and vanilla. Set aside. Place pat of butter in each of 8 12-oz. individual soufflé/serving bowls. Preheat bowls in 400°F oven for 10 – 15 minutes or until butter is popping hot. In the meantime, cut apples into chunks and place in a frying pan with water and butter. Cook for 15 minutes or until apples are moderately soft. Add a bit more water if apples become too dry while cooking.

When cooked, add cinnamon, nutmeg, ginger, brown sugar, and mincemeat to apples. Continue cooking another 5 – 10 minutes or until well mixed and hot. When butter in dishes in the oven is popping hot, add an even measurement of pancake batter to each dish. Turn up oven to 425°F for 10 minutes then back down to 400°F for another 5 minutes or until pancakes are puffed up and slightly brown on edges. Remove from oven, place an even measure of apples in the center of each pancake. Top with a dollop of whipped cream and sprinkle with freshly grated nutmeg. Place a wedge of apple on top as garnish and serve on a cloth doily on a plate (**this is necessary** as pancakes are extremely hot and may crack plates if doilies aren't used!). *Serves 8.*

Papaya Paradise

Jeanette and Bob Martz
395 Auwinala Road
Kailua, Oahu, Hawaii 96734
Tel: (808)
261-0316

ABOUT THE B&B

*I*f you're looking for privacy, quiet, and miles of beautiful, uncrowded white sandy beach, look no further than Papaya Paradise. Located 20 miles from Honolulu airport on the windward side of Oahu in Kailua, Papaya Paradise is removed from the hectic activity of Waikiki yet near all major attractions and Waikiki nightlife. Tropical rattan and wicker guest rooms have a private entrance, private bath, two comfortable beds and lounge chairs, ceiling fans, air conditioning, and cable TV, and open onto a 20 x 40 foot swimming pool and Jacuzzi surrounded by tropical plants, trees, and flowers. Breakfast is served on the lanai overlooking the pool and Jacuzzi. For your convenience, your hosts furnish beach towels, hats, mat, chairs, coolers, boogie boards, a refrigerator and microwave oven, and a small library with relaxing reading chairs.

SEASON

all year

ACCOMMODATIONS

two rooms with private baths

Hawaiian French Toast

4 eggs
1 teaspoon vanilla
1 tablespoon each maple syrup, sour cream, and sugar
8-oz. can crushed and drained pineapple
¼ cup milk
8 slices day-old bread, crusts trimmed if desired
6 tablespoons butter or margarine
Confectioners' sugar
Shredded unsweetened coconut

In a blender, whirl eggs, vanilla, syrup, sour cream, sugar, pineapple, and milk until smooth. Cut bread slices diagonally in half and arrange in a large shallow dish. Pour egg-pineapple mixture over bread and let soak in, then turn to coat other side. In a large frying pan over medium heat, melt about 2 tablespoons butter or margarine. Place a few pieces of soaked bread in pan and cook until browned on the bottom. Turn and brown other side. Use remaining butter as needed. Remove to a warm platter and keep warm in a 200°F oven until all bread has been cooked. Dust with confectioners' sugar and sprinkle with shredded coconut. *Serves 4.*

Lemon-Ricotta Pancakes

"One travel writer wrote that she still dreams about these pancakes." — Christopher Sellers

¾ cup all-purpose flour
½ teaspoon ground nutmeg
1 cup ricotta cheese
1 tablespoon sugar
1 teaspoon baking powder
2 eggs
⅔ cup milk
Juice and grated rind of 1 lemon
Confectioners' sugar

In a large bowl, combine and blend all ingredients. Pour ⅓ cup batter onto a hot greased griddle. Spread batter into a 5" circle. Cook until golden, turning once. Arrange on a platter and dust with confectioners' sugar. Serve with Vermont maple syrup. *Makes 10 – 12 pancakes.*

Grünberg Haus Bed & Breakfast
Waterbury, Vermont

Grünberg Haus Bed and Breakfast

Christopher Sellers and
Mark Frohman, RR2,
Box 1595RD, Route 100 South
Waterbury, Vermont 05676-9621
Tel: (800) 800-7760 (reservations)
or (802) 244-7726

ABOUT THE B&B

This picture-postcard Austrian-style B&B is tucked away on a secluded hillside in Vermont's Green Mountains, perfectly situated for visits to Stowe, Montpelier, Waterbury, and Burlington. Individually decorated guest rooms open onto the carved wood balcony, which offers wonderful views from the stucco and wood-trimmed chalet. The giant stone fireplace and wood stove in the BYOB pub are favorite gathering places. After hiking or cross-country skiing on the inn's trails, help Mark feed the chickens and enjoy a full, musical breakfast, with selections such as maple-poached pears, apple and cheddar muffins, and ricotta-stuffed French toast. The evening fire warms up the grand piano where you're likely to hear innkeeper Chris playing anything from Mozart to Phantom of the Opera. Nearby activities include spectacular autumn leaf-picking, world-class downhill skiing, golf, boating, bicycling, gliding, canoeing, antique hunting, outlet shopping, and touring Ben & Jerry's ice cream factory. And you can enjoy the Grünberg Haus's own Jacuzzi, sauna, tennis courts, cross-country ski center, and hiking trails.

SEASON

all year

ACCOMMODATIONS

six rooms with private baths; five rooms with shared baths; three cabins and one carriage house with private baths

Ferry Point House Bed & Breakfast on Lake Winnisquam

Diane and Joe Damato
100 Lower Bay Road
Sanbornton, New Hampshire
03269
Tel: (603) 524-0087

ABOUT THE B&B

This gracious, 175-year-old Country Victorian is located on picturesque Lake Winnisquam, in a spot commanding a panoramic view of lake and mountains. The gazebo on the point compliments the sandy beach and allows for quiet moments by the water. A 60-foot veranda and all of the rooms are blessed with breathtaking views. Return to the warm, friendly feeling of New England's past with antique furniture, collectibles, and fresh flowers in your room. The lake and surrounding area offer an endless variety of activities, including swimming, fishing, and boating at the inn. Horseback riding, golf, tennis, dinner cruises, scenic train and plain rides, antique shopping, and fine restaurants are all close by. Each morning, you'll be treated to a very special gourmet breakfast with delights such as stuffed French toast, cheese baked apples, poached pears, and select home-baked breads and muffins.

SEASON

Memorial Day through October

ACCOMMODATIONS

six rooms with private baths

Memère's French Breakfast Crepes

"In my family for generations, this very special and much requested recipe has taken me years of practice to even come close to the way my grandmother made them (my mother is still teaching me!). When done to perfection, these crepes should be thin, crisp, and 'melt in your mouth' delicious."
— Diane Damato

2 cups all-purpose flour
1 teaspoon baking soda
½ teaspoon salt
1¾ cups milk
3 eggs
Solid shortening
Fresh slices of strawberries or raspberries
Warm maple syrup

Note: These must be cooked in a cast-iron pan (Grandmother and Mother say there's no other way).

Combine flour, baking soda, and salt. In a separate bowl, beat eggs and milk with a wire whisk and add to flour mixture. Batter should be smooth and without lumps. Melt 1 tablespoon of shortening in a pan over moderately high heat. When shortening begins to smoke, it's time to add the batter. Carefully place 2 serving spoons of batter into the pan in a circular motion. Using the back of the spoon, quickly spread the batter to cover the bottom of the pan and fill in any holes. Flip when underside browns and sides begin to curl. Brown this side and serve immediately. Repeat with rest of batter. Garnish with fresh, sliced strawberries or raspberries and top with warm maple syrup. *Makes approx. 10 crepes.*

Oatmeal Waffles with Spiced Apples

1½ cups all-purpose flour
1 cup quick-cooking oats
1 tablespoon baking powder
½ teaspoon ground cinnamon
¼ teaspoon salt
2 slightly beaten eggs
1½ cups milk
6 tablespoons melted butter
2 tablespoons brown sugar

In a large mixing bowl, mix flour, oats, baking powder, cinnamon, and salt. In a small mixing bowl, stir together eggs, milk, butter, and brown sugar. Add to flour mixture all at once. Stir just until blended. Pour 1 – 1½ cups batter onto grid of a preheated, lightly greased waffle iron. When done, remove with a fork. Top with spiced apples (below). *Makes 4 waffles.*

Spiced apples:
2 cooking apples, peeled, cored, and thinly sliced
2 tablespoons melted unsalted butter
¼ cup toasted pecan halves
1 tablespoon brown sugar
⅛ teaspoon ground cinnamon
⅛ teaspoon ground nutmeg
1 teaspoon vanilla

Cook apples in butter in a large skillet over low heat, stirring occasionally until tender. Add pecans and remaining ingredients, tossing gently. *Serves 4.*

Thornrose House at Gypsy Hill

Suzanne and Otis Huston
531 Thornrose Avenue
Staunton, Virginia 24401
Tel: (800) 861-4338 or
(703) 885-7026

ABOUT THE B&B

Thornrose House is a turn-of-the-century Georgian Revival with a wraparound veranda and nearly one acre of gardens with Greek colonnades. It is adjacent to the 300-acre Gypsy Hill Park with facilities for tennis, golf, swimming, and summer band concerts. Breakfast begins with the house specialty of Bircher muesli, a Swiss concoction of oats, fruit, nuts, and whipped cream. This is followed by an ever changing menu of hot entrées and fresh baked muffins and breads. Fireplaces in the sitting room and dining room warm you on chilly mornings and winter evenings, while a baby grand piano invites you to share your musical talents. Thornrose House is conveniently located in the heart of the Shenandoah Valley, which offers hiking, biking, antique hunting, historical museums, summer theater, and numerous fine restaurants.

SEASON

all year

ACCOMMODATIONS

five rooms with private baths

Lakeside Farm
Bed and Breakfast

Joy and Glenn Hagen
RR 2, Box 52
Webster, South Dakota
57274-9633
Tel: (605) 486-4430

ABOUT THE B&B

More than a century ago, a Norwegian immigrant pioneer established a tree claim on the rugged, beautiful South Dakota prairie. He chose the spot for its fertile soil, gently rolling hills, and proximity to Waubay Lake. Today, this pioneer's grandson, Glenn Hagen, and Glenn's wife Joy own and operate Lakeside Farm. Feel free to explore the grove, barns, and pastures or just relax with a cup of tea in the farmhouse. Enjoy a long, leisurely morning in bed until you're awakened by the tantalizing smell of Joy's home-cooked breakfast. Or if you prefer to wake up with the chickens, you can come outdoors for morning chores. Lakeside Farm is the perfect overnight stop on your way to or from the Black Hills, only a day's drive away. Other things to see and do include Historic Fort Sisseton, Sica Hollow State Park, Waubay National Wildlife Refuge, Native American and pioneer museums, boating, hunting, fishing, rodeo, and bicycling.

SEASON

all year

ACCOMMODATIONS

one room with private bath;
two rooms with shared bath

Oat Pancakes

2 cups all-purpose flour
1 cup rolled oats
2 teaspoons baking soda
2 teaspoons baking powder
½ teaspoon salt
½ teaspoon ground cinnamon
¼ teaspoon ground nutmeg
4 eggs
¾ cup melted butter
2 cups buttermilk

Mix dry ingredients in a large bowl. Mix eggs, melted butter, and buttermilk in a small bowl, whisking to blend. Make a well in center of dry ingredients and stir in buttermilk mixture (do not overmix). Spray skillet or pancake grill with cooking oil spray. Using a ¼ cup measure for each pancake, pour batter onto hot grill. Cook until bubbles appear on top and underside is golden. Turn to brown other side. Keep pancakes warm in a 200°F oven. Serve with chunky applesauce, if desired. *Serves 6.*

Palisades Fruit Puffs

6 large eggs
1 tablespoon sugar
1 cup all-purpose flour
1 cup milk
¼ teaspoon salt
½ teaspoon vanilla
4 tablespoons butter
Confectioners' sugar

Preheat oven to 450°F. In a medium bowl, beat eggs and sugar with electric mixer on high speed until frothy (approximately 1 minute). Slowly add flour, beating on medium speed until blended. Stir in milk, salt, and vanilla. Melt butter in 4 oven-proof skillets (8"). Pour egg mixture into hot skillets. Bake 12 –15 minutes or until brown and puffed. Remove from oven and sprinkle with confectioners' sugar. Serve with your favorite filling (see below for suggestions).

Filling options *(serves 4):*
1) Bananas Amaretto
2 tablespoons butter
1 tablespoon light-brown sugar
4 firm sliced bananas
¼ cup Amaretto liqueur
Whipped or sour cream
Ground nutmeg

(continued on next page)

Palisades Paradise
B&B

Gail Goetz
1200 Palisades Avenue
Redding, California 96003
Tel: (916) 223-5305

ABOUT THE B&B

Y*ou'll feel you're in paradise when you enjoy the magnificent sunsets over the Sacramento River and breathtaking views of the city and surrounding mountains from this beautiful contemporary home. Housing two lovely rooms with queen beds, garden spa, fireplace, wide-screen TV/VCR, and homelike atmosphere, Palisades Paradise is a serene setting for a quiet hideaway, yet conveniently located one mile from shopping and Interstate 5. Visiting Mt. Shasta and Mt. Lassen are a must, while water skiing, mountain climbing, and river rafting are nearby for the adventurous at heart. The B&B was established in 1986 and is still owned and operated by Gail Goetz, an early childhood resource specialist.*

SEASON

all year

ACCOMMODATIONS

two rooms with shared bath

Melt butter in a skillet. Add brown sugar and sauté bananas until slightly soft, but not mushy. Gently stir in liqueur. Fill puffs with mixture and top with whipped or sour cream, and a sprinkling of nutmeg.

2) Assorted Fruit
Fill puffs with strawberries and sliced kiwi (nice for Christmas!), sliced peaches and blueberries, or canned apples with brown sugar and ground cinnamon. Top with whipped cream or yogurt.

3) Mandarin Orange Sauce
2 tablespoons sugar
1 tablespoon cornstarch
¾ cup water
2 tablespoons frozen orange juice concentrate
11-oz. can mandarin oranges
Whipped cream
Sliced almonds

Combine sugar and cornstarch in a medium saucepan. Stir in water and frozen orange juice concentrate. Cook on medium heat, stirring until thick and bubbly. Cook and stir 2 more minutes. Pour into puffs, top with whipped cream, sprinkle with sliced almonds, and serve. *Tip:* This sauce is also very good over French toast.

Peach French Toast à la Garth

(Recipe from Breakfast Inn Bed, Easy and Elegant Recipes from Garth Woodside Mansion.)

29-oz. can sliced peaches
1 cup brown sugar
½ cup butter or margarine
2 tablespoons water
1 loaf French bread (12 – 14 slices)
5 eggs
1½ cups milk
1 tablespoon vanilla

Drain peaches and reserve syrup. Heat sugar and butter on medium-low until melted. Add water and continue cooking until sauce becomes thick and foamy. Pour into a 13 x 9" baking dish and cool 10 minutes. Place peaches on cooled caramel sauce and cover with slices of bread placed close together. In a blender, add eggs, milk, and vanilla until mixed. Pour over bread, cover, and refrigerate overnight. Remove from fridge ¾ hour before baking. Bake in a preheated 350°F oven for 40 minutes. If browning too fast, loosely cover with foil for the last 10 – 15 minutes. Serve with warmed peach syrup. *Serves 12 – 14.*

Garth Woodside Mansion

Diane and Irv Feinberg
RR #1, Box 304
Hannibal, Missouri 63401
Tel: (314) 221-2789

ABOUT THE B&B

Experience affordable elegance in this 1871 Victorian country estate on 39 magnificent acres of meadows and woodlands. On the National Register of Historic Places, Garth Woodside Mansion has remained unchanged outside, while graceful arched doors, handsomely decorated rooms featuring original furnishings spanning over 150 years, and magnificent three-story spiral "Flying Staircase" await you inside. You'll enjoy marble fireplaces, canopy beds, your own nightshirt, an exceptional full breakfast, an afternoon beverage, and more. All rooms are air conditioned and have a private bath. The location is ideal for seeing Mark Twain Country. Come for a romantic and magical stay — your experience will be something out of the ordinary.

SEASON

all year

ACCOMMODATIONS

eight rooms with private baths

Snug Harbor Inn

Laurine "Sis" and Kenneth Hill
1226 West 10th Avenue
Anchorage, Alaska 99501
Tel: (907) 272-6249

ABOUT THE B&B

*S*nug Harbor Inn offers you *cheerful comfort in a relaxed "home away from home" atmosphere, where absolute privacy is yours. Relax while surrounded by antiques, art, Alaskan artifacts, and period furnishings. Accommodations feature handmade quilts and some have their own private entrance. Fully equipped kitchen, complimentary coffee, tea, and hot chocolate available 24 hours a day, color TV, and complimentary bicycles are at your disposal. The friendly, efficient staff has your every comfort in mind, making Snug Harbor the first choice for the business and pleasure traveler. Located in the heart of Anchorage, Snug Harbor is just four blocks from the central business district, and close to shopping, entertainment, fine dining, and sightseeing. The trail head for Anchorage's extensive bicycle and jogging paths is also nearby.*

SEASON

all year

ACCOMMODATIONS

four rooms with private baths;
two rooms with shared bath

Pineapple Upside-Down French Toast

2 tablespoons butter
¼ cup brown sugar
½ cup crushed pineapple
¾ teaspoon ground cinnamon
1 egg
⅔ cup milk
½ teaspoon vanilla
Dash of salt
6 slices raisin bread, cut in half diagonally

Preheat oven to 400°F. Melt butter in a 9" cake or pie pan, being careful not to burn it. Spread the brown sugar and pineapple evenly over the bottom of the pan. Sprinkle with cinnamon. Beat egg with milk, vanilla, and salt. Dip the bread into the liquid mixture and arrange the cut slices in the pan, overlapping them neatly. Cook uncovered for 20 – 25 minutes. Serve with heavy cream, maple syrup, or yogurt. *Serves 4 – 6.*

Pumpkin Pancakes

2 cups biscuit mix
1 tablespoon brown sugar
2 teaspoons ground cinnamon
1 teaspoon ground allspice
1½ cups soy milk
2 tablespoons canola oil
2 eggs
½ cup pumpkin, pureed fresh or canned
1 teaspoon vanilla

Combine dry ingredients in a large bowl and mix. Add remaining ingredients and beat until smooth. Cook on a griddle. *Tip:* Also great with 1 cup fresh blueberries added to batter. *Makes 12 – 16 pancakes.*

Chatsworth Bed & Breakfast

Donna and Earl Gustafson
984 Ashland Avenue
St. Paul, Minnesota 55104
Tel: (612) 227-4288

ABOUT THE B&B

Whether an international traveler or a visitor from Minnesota, you can consider this spacious 1902 Victorian home on a large corner lot with maple and basswood trees as your home. Choose a room with a four-poster bed and private double whirlpool bath, one with African-Asian decor and an adjoining porch, or one with Victorian, Oriental, or antique Scandinavian decor. Enjoy a leisurely breakfast in a beautifully paneled dining room and take time to read or relax by the fireplace in the lace-curtained living room. Chatsworth B&B is just two blocks from the Governor's Mansion on historic Summit Avenue and three blocks from the many excellent restaurants and unique shops on Grand Avenue. Also in the near vicinity are numerous colleges and churches. Only minutes away from this quiet family neighborhood is the Twin Cities International Airport, the Mall of America, and the downtown areas of both Saint Paul and Minneapolis.

SEASON

all year

ACCOMMODATIONS

three rooms with private baths;
two rooms with shared bath

Brambly Hedge Cottage

Jacquelyn Smyers
HCR 31, Box 39
Jasper, Arkansas 72641
Tel: 1-800-BRAMBLY or
(501) 446-5849

ABOUT THE B&B

"*A*bsolutely charming," wrote National Geographic Traveler *of this old Ozark mountaintop farmhouse on scenic Highway 7, four miles south of Jasper, Arkansas. A Tennessee guest commented, "The place is uniquely beautiful, the food delicious, and the view inspiring." Three guest rooms with private baths reflect country French elegance in a homestead log cabin. A full breakfast is served on the deck overlooking Buffalo River Valley or behind the screened porch in rocking chairs. You're only minutes from the "Grand Canyon of the Ozarks," challenging-to-easy hiking trails, and canoeing on Buffalo National River. If art is more your style, you'll be happy to know that discriminating collectors still find the work of true artisans in the Jasper area. For those who wish to sample a night out on the town, Eureka Springs and Branson (Missouri) are nearby. Small group special-interest tours and relaxing massages can be arranged. Hostess Jacquelyn Smyers includes her handmade tatted lace and samovar collection in the decor. She's also a designer, commercial artist, and author of* Come For Tea *and the children's book* The Cloud That Came Into The Cabin *(inspired by the clouds on Sloan Mountain where Brambly Hedge is located).*

SEASON

all year

ACCOMMODATIONS

three rooms with private baths

Rib-Stickin' Pancakes

"No telling where this recipe came from but it's wonderful. The cakes have taste and delightful texture, fill you up, but rest easy in your stomach." — Jacquelyn Smyers

Dry ingredients:
1 cup all-purpose flour
¼ cup white or yellow cornmeal
2 tablespoons wheat germ
2 tablespoons bran
1 scant teaspoon salt
1 tablespoon baking powder

Wet ingredients:
2 eggs
1 cup milk
1 tablespoon vegetable oil
Water as needed to thin batter

Mix dry ingredients. Add wet ingredients and stir, pressing out big lumps. Add a slosh of water to thin batter so it will pour well. When water drops dance on a hot greased griddle, pour ladles of batter on it and cook until the cake tops bubble. Turn them over for a short spell. With a fork, lift a bit of crust in the middle of each one to be sure it's done (nobody likes gooey pancakes!). *Makes 7 pancakes.*

Ricotta-Stuffed French Toast

"Our friend Walter used to treat us to this breakfast treat on hiking trips in the mountains." — Christopher Sellers

1 loaf Italian bread, unsliced
8 ozs. ricotta cheese
4 eggs
½ cup cream
1 tablespoon vanilla
½ teaspoon ground nutmeg
½ teaspoon ground cinnamon
Confectioners' sugar

Thinly slice bread into 24 slices. Spread 12 slices with fresh ricotta cheese, then top with remaining 12 slices. Beat together fresh eggs, cream, vanilla, nutmeg, and cinnamon. Dip bread and cheese sandwiches into egg mixture. Grill slowly until browned. Dust with confectioners' sugar and serve with Vermont maple syrup. *Serves 8.*

Grünberg Haus Bed & Breakfast
Waterbury, Vermont

Grünberg Haus Bed and Breakfast

Christopher Sellers and Mark Frohman, RR2, Box 1595RD, Route 100 South Waterbury, Vermont 05676-9621
Tel: (800) 800-7760 (reservations) or (802) 244-7726

ABOUT THE B&B

This picture-postcard Austrian-style B&B is tucked away on a secluded hillside in Vermont's Green Mountains, perfectly situated for visits to Stowe, Montpelier, Waterbury, and Burlington. Individually decorated guest rooms open onto the carved wood balcony, which offers wonderful views from the stucco and wood-trimmed chalet. The giant stone fireplace and wood stove in the BYOB pub are favorite gathering places. After hiking or cross-country skiing on the inn's trails, help Mark feed the chickens and enjoy a full, musical breakfast, with selections such as maple-poached pears, apple and cheddar muffins, and ricotta-stuffed French toast. The evening fire warms up the grand piano where you're likely to hear innkeeper Chris playing anything from Mozart to Phantom of the Opera. Nearby activities include spectacular autumn leaf-picking, world-class downhill skiing, golf, boating, bicycling, gliding, canoeing, antique hunting, outlet shopping, and touring Ben & Jerry's ice cream factory. And you can enjoy the Grünberg Haus's own Jacuzzi, sauna, tennis courts, cross-country ski center, and hiking trails.

SEASON

all year

ACCOMMODATIONS

six rooms with private baths; five rooms with shared baths; three cabins and one carriage house with private baths

Down the Shore B&B

Annette and Al Bergins
201 Seventh Avenue
Belmar, New Jersey 07719
Tel: (908) 681-9023

ABOUT THE B&B

Down the Shore Bed & Breakfast is unique. The house was built specifically to be used as a residence and as a bed and breakfast. There are two guest rooms with a shared guest parlor and a shaded 40-foot front porch. Down the Shore Bed & Breakfast is located one block from the beach and boardwalk. The house may be new but the proprietors are not new to innkeeping. Before moving to Belmar, they operated another bed and breakfast in their lakeside home in Denville, New Jersey. As you can see from the recipe, healthful food is the mainstay of the breakfasts here.

SEASON

summer

ACCOMMODATIONS

two rooms with private baths

Serious Waffles

"These waffles are hearty, but don't have the off-taste you sometimes find with whole grain batters."
— Annette Bergins

Waffle mix (prepared in bulk):
2 lbs. store-bought pancake/waffle mix
1 cup stone-ground cornmeal
1 cup soy flour
½ cup powdered milk
½ cup wheat germ
½ cup whole wheat flour
3 tablespoons baking powder

Batter:
1 cup waffle mix (recipe above)
1 cup skim milk
1 egg or ¼ cup egg substitute

Combine all waffle mix ingredients and store for immediate and future use (keep about 2 lbs. in the pantry and the balance in the freezer). To cook, combine all batter ingredients well. Spray waffle iron with non-stick cooking spray and proceed as you would with any other mix. *Serves 1.*

Snug Harbor French Toast

10 slices aged white bread, cut into 1" squares
1 tablespoon ground cinnamon
Raisins to taste
12 ozs. sliced cream cheese
1 mashed or blended banana (or peach or pineapple)
⅓ cup maple syrup
½ tablespoon vanilla
½ teaspoon ground nutmeg
6 large eggs
2 cups whole milk

In an 13 x 8" shallow glass baking dish sprayed with non-stick cooking spray, spread half of the bread squares. Dust with a cover of cinnamon and sprinkle raisins to taste. Distribute the sliced cream cheese to cover the bread completely. Cover the cheese with the remainder of the bread squares, then repeat the distribution of raisins and sprinkle with the remaining cinnamon. Set aside while you blend the liquid portion of this dish.

Combine the fruit, syrup, vanilla, nutmeg, and purée them. Add the eggs; blend. Add the milk and blend the complete mixture until it becomes as frothy as a thick eggnog. Pour this liquid over the bread and cheese mixture, completely saturating it. Press down with your hands and set aside for at least 30 minutes, or cover and keep overnight in your refrigerator (remove from fridge ¾ hour before baking). Preheat oven to 375°F. Set your baking dish into a pan of water about ½" deep. Cook for 45 – 60 minutes or until a knife inserted into the center comes out clean. Slice and serve hot with maple syrup or rum raisin ice cream. *Serves 6 – 8.*

Snug Harbor Inn

Laurine "Sis" and Kenneth Hill
1226 West 10th Avenue
Anchorage, Alaska 99501
Tel: (907) 272-6249

ABOUT THE B&B

Snug Harbor Inn offers you cheerful comfort in a relaxed "home away from home" atmosphere, where absolute privacy is yours. Relax while surrounded by antiques, art, Alaskan artifacts, and period furnishings. Accommodations feature handmade quilts and some have their own private entrance. Fully equipped kitchen, complimentary coffee, tea, and hot chocolate available 24 hours a day, color TV, and complimentary bicycles are at your disposal. The friendly, efficient staff has your every comfort in mind, making Snug Harbor the first choice for the business and pleasure traveler. Located in the heart of Anchorage, Snug Harbor is just four blocks from the central business district, and close to shopping, entertainment, fine dining, and sightseeing. The trail head for Anchorage's extensive bicycle and jogging paths is also nearby.

SEASON

all year

ACCOMMODATIONS

four rooms with private baths; two rooms with shared bath

Turtleback Farm Inn

Susan and William Fletcher
Route 1, Box 650
Eastsound (Orcas Island)
Washington 98245
Tel: (206) 376-4914

ABOUT THE B&B

Located on the loveliest of the San Juan Islands, Turtleback Farm Inn is noted for its detail-perfect restoration, elegantly comfortable and spotless rooms, glorious setting, and award-winning breakfasts. A perfect spot for a memorable getaway, you'll feel welcome and pampered by the warm hospitality of Susan and Bill Fletcher and their staff. A short ferry ride from Anacortes, Washington, Orcas Island is a haven for anyone who covets spectacular scenery, varied outdoor activities, unique shopping, and superb food. As spring turns into summer, the warm days encourage you to enjoy nature and island life at their best: Flowers are in full bloom, birds flutter, and whales, seals, and porpoise lazily coast through the shimmering waters of the Sound. After a day of hiking, fishing, bicycling, kayaking, sailing, windsurfing or just reading by the inn's pond, enjoy a relaxing soak in your private bath or a sherry on the deck overlooking the valley below. After a tasty dinner at one of the Island's many fine restaurants, snuggle down under one of the inn's custom-made woolen comforters and peacefully doze off — with visions of the delicious breakfast awaiting you in the morning.

SEASON

all year

ACCOMMODATIONS

seven rooms with private baths

Spiced Oat Waffles

2 cups buttermilk
3 separated eggs, whites beaten until they hold a stiff
    but not dry peak
3 tablespoons honey
½ cup melted and cooled butter
½ cup all-purpose flour
½ cup rolled oats (not quick cooking)
1 cup whole wheat flour
1 tablespoon baking powder
1½ teaspoons baking soda
¾ teaspoon salt
¼ teaspoon freshly grated nutmeg
½ cup toasted and chopped pecans

Blend buttermilk, egg yolks, honey, and melted butter together in a blender, then transfer to a large bowl. Mix together the dry ingredients, then add to the buttermilk mixture. Fold in the chopped nuts and egg whites. Bake on a hot waffle iron according to the manufacturer's directions. Serve with pure maple syrup and butter. Or, serve with a fruit butter made by blending 1 tablespoon of concentrated orange juice and ½ teaspoon grated orange rind into ¼ lb. butter, adding honey to taste. *Makes 4 – 6 waffles.*

Spicy Apple-Nut Pancakes

1 cup all-purpose flour
¾ cup sugar
1 teaspoon baking powder
¾ teaspoon baking soda
¼ teaspoon salt
½ teaspoon ground cinnamon
¼ teaspoon ground nutmeg
½ teaspoon ground cloves
¼ teaspoon mace
1 large egg
1¼ cups buttermilk
4 teaspoons vegetable oil
1 large tart apple (such as Granny Smith)
¾ cup walnuts

Combine dry ingredients, then set aside. In a large bowl, beat egg. Stir in buttermilk and oil. Wash and core apple, then cut into large pieces and place in a food processor fitted with a steel blade. Add walnuts to the processor bowl. Pulse several times, leaving apples and nuts as coarse as possible. Stir apples and nuts into egg mixture. Stir dry ingredients into egg mixture. Cook pancakes on heated, oiled griddle. When brown on bottom, turn and cook on other side. Serve with butter or sour cream. *Serves 4.*

Durham House Bed & Breakfast Inn

Marguerite and Dean Swanson
921 Heights Boulevard
Houston, Texas 77008
Tel: (713) 868-4654

ABOUT THE B&B

Located just five minutes from downtown Houston, Durham House Bed & Breakfast Inn is a fully restored Queen Anne Victorian home listed on the National Register of Historic Places. The present owners, Marguerite and Dean Swanson, acquired the home in 1985 with full intention of restoring it to its original elegance and opening it to the public as an authentic Victorian bed and breakfast inn. Today, guests are invited to experience the genuine Victorian ambiance of the inn, and can select from gracious accommodations that include upstairs bedrooms and the privacy of a spacious carriage house. Perhaps the best reason for choosing Durham House is to experience Marguerite's special brand of southern hospitality, not to mention her fantastic full breakfast. For a change of pace, this unique bed and breakfast hosts murder mystery dinner parties using original mysteries written exclusively for Durham House.

SEASON

all year

ACCOMMODATIONS

five rooms with private baths; one room with shared bath

Sycamore Hill House & Gardens

Kerri and Stephen Wagner
110 Menefee Mountain Lane
Washington, Virginia 22747
Tel: (703) 675-3046

ABOUT THE B&B

Perched atop Menefee Mountain (elevation 1,043 feet) and situated on several hundred acres of pristine land, this large contemporary stone home has a round, glass-walled living room and 65-foot veranda to enhance the panoramic mountain vistas offered from every direction. The house has light hardwood floors and Oriental rugs throughout, not to mention Kerri's exotic plants and Stephen's original art. You may choose from three elegant and tasteful rooms, each with private bath, queen-size bed, mountain views, sitting/reading area, ceiling fan, and central heat and air conditioning. A full sumptuous breakfast is served daily, and there are home-baked treats in your room and mints by your bedside. A certified National Wildlife habitat, Sycamore's gardens are the perfect spot for a stroll — perhaps you'll see a white-tailed deer or wild turkey. Some of the finest dining in the east is just moments away. Also nearby is Skyline Drive, Luray Caverns, Old Rag Mountain, vineyards, antique and craft shops, golf, tennis, hot-air ballooning, canoeing, horseback riding, and berry picking.

SEASON

all year

ACCOMMODATIONS

three rooms with private baths

Thick French Toast with Sautéed Apples

8 medium eggs
1 teaspoon grated nutmeg
½ – ¾ cup half-and-half cream
12 slices firm Italian bread, 1½" thick
Vegetable oil for frying
4 – 5 tablespoons butter
6 Granny Smith apples, cored, peeled, and thinly sliced
2 tablespoons cinnamon sugar

Whisk together the eggs, nutmeg, and half-and-half until well mixed. Dip bread slices into mixture, coat thoroughly, and fry in oil until browned evenly on both sides. Place in oven to hold on warm while preparing apples. In a large frying pan, melt the butter on medium heat. Add apples and raise heat to medium-high. Gently sauté apples for about 5 minutes, sprinkle cinnamon sugar over, and continue to sauté until apples are just tender (don't overcook). Spoon apples over the French toast and serve. *Serves 6.*

Whole Grain No-Cholesterol Pancakes

1 cup whole wheat flour
2 tablespoons baking powder
2 tablespoons sugar
½ teaspoon ground allspice
¼ teaspoon ground nutmeg
2 lightly beaten egg whites
1 cup skim milk
2 tablespoons canola or vegetable oil
Vegetable oil cooking spray
Fresh strawberries (optional)
Thinly sliced ham (optional)

Combine first 5 ingredients, then make a well in center of the mixture. Combine egg whites, skim milk, and oil. Add to dry ingredients, stirring just until moistened. Let stand 20 minutes. For each pancake, spoon about 2 tablespoons batter onto a moderately hot griddle coated with cooking spray. Turn pancakes when tops are covered with bubbles and edges look cooked. Garnish, if desired, with strawberries and ham. *Makes 8 – 10 pancakes.*

The Manor at Taylor's Store B&B Country Inn

Mary Lynn and Lee Tucker
Route 1, Box 533
Smith Mountain Lake, Virginia 24184
Tel: (800) 248-6267 or
(703) 721-3951

ABOUT THE B&B

The Manor at Taylor's Store is an enchanting, historic 120-acre estate in the picturesque foothills of the Blue Ridge Mountains. Guests enjoy luxurious accommodations in the elegant plantation home replete with antiques. Special amenities include a hot tub, exercise room, billiard room, large-screen TV with movies, guest kitchen, and porches and fireplaces throughout. There are six private, spring-fed ponds on the property for swimming, fishing, and canoeing. Nearby, Smith Mountain Lake offers additional recreational opportunities. All guests are treated to a heart-healthy gourmet breakfast in the formal dining room with panoramic views of the countryside. Warm, southern hospitality has made The Manor at Taylor's Store one of the best-known B&B inns in Virginia.

SEASON

all year

ACCOMMODATIONS

six suites with private baths; one cottage for families/groups with private bath

THE MANOR AT
TAYLOR'S
STORE

Quiches

Omelets

Frittatas

Stratas

Apple and Brie Omelet Marlborough

The Marlborough

Diana Smith
320 Woods Hole Road
Woods Hole, Massachusetts
02543
Tel: (508) 548-6218

"This surprisingly wonderful blend of flavors lends itself to the inn's well-known gourmet breakfast menus. Guests always love it and are happy to add the recipe to their own collections." — Diana Smith

1½ tablespoons butter
¼ medium-size Granny Smith apple, peeled and thinly sliced
⅛ teaspoon ground nutmeg
1 teaspoon sugar
1 tablespoon brown sugar
1 tablespoon chopped walnuts
3 eggs
6 cubes brie cheese (½")

In a heavy skillet, melt ½ tablespoon butter. Sauté apple slices in melted butter until glassy, but not mushy. Sprinkle apples with nutmeg and sugar. Remove apples to a side dish to stop the cooking; set aside. Mix together brown sugar and walnuts; set aside. In an omelet pan or heavy 6 – 8" skillet, melt 1 tablespoon butter, heating until bubbly. Break eggs into a bowl and whisk until foamy. Pour egg gently into bubbling butter. As eggs set, lift edges to let uncooked liquid flood under. When the eggs are almost set, turn the heat off. Put brie on one half of the omelet. Top with sautéed apple slices and fold the omelet in half. Let sit for 3 – 4 minutes to allow brie to melt. Remove to a warmed plate and sprinkle with brown sugar and nut topping. *Serves 1.*

ABOUT THE B&B

The Marlborough is a romantic Cape Cod cottage complete with picket fence, trellis, and garden set up on a hill among the trees. Rooms have private baths and are individually decorated with quilts, coordinated scented linens, and collectibles. Gather for conversation, read, or watch television in the large comfortable parlor. Full gourmet breakfast, including wonderfully brewed coffee and teas, is served outside by the kidney-shaped pool or inside by the fireplace, depending on the season. Informal afternoon tea is served in season, while high tea is served on Sundays in the off-season. Excellent restaurants are nearby, as is Woods Hole Oceanographic Institute, beaches, shopping, bike paths, and ferries to Martha's Vineyard. Great starting point for day trips to locations all over Cape Cod and the islands, Plymouth, Boston, and Providence. Innkeeper Diana Smith enjoys helping guests get the most out of their visit. A computer consultant before purchasing the inn, Diana enjoys bicycle touring, hand needlework (including quilting, cross-stitch, and crewel) and cooking.

SEASON

all year

ACCOMMODATIONS

five rooms with private baths

The Babbling Brook Inn

Helen King
1025 Laurel Street
Santa Cruz, California 95060
Tel: (800) 866-1131 or
(408) 427-2437

ABOUT THE B&B

Cascading waterfalls, a meandering creek, and a romantic gazebo grace an acre of gardens, pines, and redwoods surrounding this secluded inn. Built in 1909 on the foundation of an 1870 tannery, a 1790 grist mill, and a 2000-year old Indian fishing village, the Babbling Brook features rooms in country French decor, all with private bath, telephone, and television, and most with cozy fireplace, private deck, and outside entrance. Included in your stay is a large, country breakfast and afternoon wine and cheese, where Helen's prize-winning cookies await you on the tea cart in front of a roaring fireplace. Two blocks off Highway 1, the Babbling Brook is within walking distance to the beach, wharf, boardwalk, shops, tennis, running paths, and historic homes. Three golf courses and 200 restaurants are within 15 minutes' drive. A world-record holding angler, Mrs. Pacific Palisades 1955, one-time international tour organizer, and mother of six, Helen King has happily found her niche as a gourmet cook and owner/innkeeper of this award-winning B&B.

SEASON

all year

ACCOMMODATIONS

12 rooms with private baths

Artichoke Frittata

32-oz. box frozen artichoke hearts
1 large chopped onion
2½ cups half-and-half cream
12 eggs
1 tablespoon Worcestershire sauce
1 tablespoon mustard (Coleman's dry recommended)
2 teaspoons seasoning salt
3 broken-up sourdough English muffins
1 lb. grated Monterey Jack cheese
½ cup Italian-seasoned bread crumbs
½ cup grated Parmesan cheese
Paprika or chopped parsley

Preheat oven to 350°F. Defrost artichoke hearts. Chop in a blender or Cuisinart. Coat a 13 x 9" pan with spray shortening and spread with the artichoke hearts. Top with onions. Blend cream with eggs and seasonings. Pour half over the artichokes in the pan. Blend the English muffins into the rest of the egg mixture until smooth. Pour the muffin-egg mixture over ingredients in the pan and add Monterey Jack cheese. Stir to blend. Top with Italian bread crumbs and Parmesan cheese. Sprinkle with paprika or chopped parsley as desired. Bake 1 hour and 15 minutes (or until center is set) on center rack of oven. Cool slightly, then cut into squares. *Makes 30 squares.*

Asparagus Quiche

10 stalks fresh asparagus, cooked and drained
5 well-beaten eggs
1 cup milk
1 teaspoon salt
2 tablespoons fresh basil
1 cup grated Swiss cheese

Preheat oven to 350°F. Spray the bottom of a 10" pie plate with non-stick cooking spray. Place asparagus in pie plate. Mix eggs with 1 cup milk. Add salt and basil and pour mixture over asparagus. Cover with cheese. Bake for 30 minutes or until set. Allow to cool slightly before cutting. *Serves 6.*

Pickett's Harbor

Sara and Cooke Goffigon
PO Box 97AA
Cape Charles, Virginia 23310
Tel: (804) 331-2212

ABOUT THE B&B

Chesapeake Bay on Virginia's historic Eastern Shore is home to seagulls, pelicans, sandpipers — and Pickett's Harbor Bed and Breakfast. Enjoy acres of private beach on the southernmost tip of the Delmarva Peninsula. Your hosts Sara and Cooke are descended from the original settlers of the area and, in 1976, built this traditional home by the seashore, complete with high ceilings, fireplaces, antiques, and wooden floorboards made from 200-year-old barns along the James River. Every morning, awake to Sara's full country breakfast where, on any given day, you can sample a fruit cup, juice, paper-thin cured ham, and home-made three-fruit and fig jams (which Sara now sells). Set off on a quiet country lane and surrounded by sea grasses and a pine forest, Pickett's Harbor is marvelously isolated yet close to most attractions on the Eastern Shore, as well as to Norfolk, Hampton, and Virginia Beach.

SEASON

all year

ACCOMMODATIONS

three rooms with private baths;
three rooms with shared baths

Hidden Pond
Bed & Breakfast

Priscilla and Larry Fuerst
PO Box 461
Fennville, Michigan 49408
Tel: (616) 561-2491

ABOUT THE B&B

Hidden Pond Bed & Breakfast is set on 28 acres of woods, perfect for bird-watching, hiking, cross-country skiing, or just relaxing in a rowboat on the pond. Guests can enjoy seven entry-level rooms, including bedrooms and baths, living room with fireplace, dining room, library, kitchen, and breakfast porch. Priscilla and Larry, who work for rival airlines, understand the importance of a soothing, calm, and slow-paced overnight stay. They enjoy pleasing guests and creating an atmosphere of quiet elegance. Unwind and take in the sun on the outdoor deck or patio. Turndown service, complimentary soft drinks, tea, hot chocolate, or an evening sherry is offered. Full hot breakfast is served in the sunwashed garden room at your leisure, and features fresh fruits, breads, muffins, and a hot entrée. This lovely retreat is near the beaches of Lake Michigan, the boutiques of Saugatuck, and the winery and cider mill in Fennville.

SEASON

all year

ACCOMMODATIONS

two rooms with private baths

Asparagus Strata

"This is our staple during the June asparagus season. Many copies of this recipe go home with our guests."
— Larry Fuerst

9 eggs
2 cups milk
1½ cups seasoned bread cubes
1 cup grated low-fat cheddar cheese
1 lb. cooked and drained pork breakfast sausage
2 cups asparagus, cut into 1" pieces and steamed just until tender
4 ozs. sliced mushrooms
Salt and pepper

Mix ingredients all together. Cover and refrigerate overnight. Remove from fridge ¾ hour before baking. Bake in a preheated 375°F oven for 45 minutes in a 13 x 9" pan. *Serves 8.*

Avocado, Bacon, and Potato Frittata

1 tablespoon olive oil
1 small chopped onion
1 small boiled potato, peeled and sliced
"Mrs. Dash" mixed seasoning or salt and pepper to taste
2 strips bacon, fried crisp and crumbled
1 ripe avocado, peeled and sliced
1 chopped scallion
2 large eggs, lightly beaten with 1 tablespoon water
¼ cup grated cheese of your choice

In a 10" oven-proof Teflon skillet, swirl olive oil over medium heat. Add onion, potato, and seasoning. Stir occasionally until vegetables are browned. Sprinkle bacon, avocado, and scallion evenly in pan. Pour in egg mixture and sprinkle cheese over top. Cook until lightly set. Sit skillet under broiler on top rack of oven about 1 minute or until top is set. Remove from broiler, cut in 2 with a wooden knife, and slide onto plates. *Tip:* To speed morning preparation, cook potato and bacon the night before and refrigerate. *Serves 2.*

The Summer House

Kay and David Merrell
158 Main Street
Sandwich, Massachusetts 02563
Tel: (508) 888-4991

ABOUT THE B&B

The Summer House is an elegant circa 1835 Greek Revival twice featured in Country Living magazine. It was owned by Hiram Dillaway, a prominent mold-maker and colorist at the Boston & Sandwich Glass Factory. Large, sunny bedchambers feature antiques, hand-stitched quilts, and working fireplaces. Stroll to dining, shops, museums, galleries, pond and gristmill, and boardwalk to beach. Bountiful breakfasts change daily and include freshly ground coffee, tea, fruit juice, and fresh fruit served in stemware. Entrées of frittata, stuffed French toast, quiche, or omelets are accompanied by scones, puff pastry, muffins, or fruit cobblers. Dishes are enhanced with vegetables, berries, and herbs from the inn's garden. English-style afternoon tea is served at an umbrella table in the garden. Boston, Newport, Providence, Martha's Vineyard, and Nantucket make pleasant day trips. Innkeepers Kay and David Merrell (former executive secretary and aerospace engineer respectively) enjoy woodworking, gardening, quilting, jogging, backpacking, and the tranquility of Cape Cod.

SEASON

all year

ACCOMMODATIONS

one room with private bath; four rooms with shared baths

Durbin Street Inn B&B

Sherry and Don Frigon
843 South Durbin Street
Casper, Wyoming 82601
Tel: (307) 577-5774

ABOUT THE B&B

Built in 1917, Durbin Street Inn is a large two-story American foursquare located in Casper's historic district that prides itself on good food and a friendly atmosphere. Choose from four large non-smoking guest rooms with shared baths, including queen-size or double beds, robes, and one with a fireplace. Or, you can choose the non-smoking guest room with private bath, small sitting room, and fridge. Awake to a full country breakfast where scrambled eggs, bacon, sausage, hash browns, fruit juice, home-made jams, and such specialties as honey-wheat pancakes, biscuits and gravy, scones, brunch omelet torte, spicy sausage and potatoes, and roast beef hash are served family-style. After breakfast, gather in the common room with fireplace, or enjoy the deck, patio, and flower and vegetable gardens. Nearby are walking/hiking/cycling trails, river rafting and canoeing, covered wagon and horseback trips along Oregon Trail, golfing, skiing, museums, historic sites, Fort Casper, Independence Rock, Devil's Gate, Hell's Half Acre, boating, swimming, fishing, shopping, and craft shops.

SEASON

all year

ACCOMMODATIONS

four rooms with shared baths;
one room with private bath

Brunch Omelet Torte

"This do-ahead recipe requires some time to prepare, but is sensational for a special breakfast or brunch."
— Sherry Frigon

17¼-oz. package (2 sheets) frozen pre-rolled sheets of puff pastry, thawed

Potatoes:
¼ cup butter or margarine
3 cups (6 medium) new red potatoes, sliced ⅛" thick
1 cup onions, sliced ⅛" thick and separated into rings
¼ teaspoon salt
¼ teaspoon pepper

Omelet:
2 tablespoons butter or margarine
6 eggs
¼ cup chopped fresh parsley
⅛ tablespoon salt
⅛ teaspoon pepper
2 tablespoons water

(continued on next page)

Filling:
½ lb. thinly sliced cooked ham
2 cups shredded cheddar cheese
1 slightly beaten egg
1 tablespoon water

On a lightly floured surface, roll each sheet of puff pastry into a 12" square Lay 1 sheet into a 10" pie pan, and set aside.

To make potatoes: In a 10" skillet, melt butter until sizzling. Add potatoes, onions, salt, and pepper. Cover and cook over medium-high heat, turning occasionally until potatoes are lightly browned and crisply tender (approximately 12 – 15 minutes). Set aside.

To make omelet: In cleaned skillet, melt 1 tablespoon butter until sizzling. Meanwhile, in a small bowl, stir together all omelet ingredients except remaining 1 tablespoon butter. Pour half of omelet mixture (¾ cup) into skillet with sizzling butter. Cook over medium heat. As omelet sets, lift slightly with spatula to allow uncooked portion to flow underneath. Continue cooking until set (2 – 3 minutes). Slide omelet onto cookie sheet. Repeat with remaining butter and omelet mixture.

To make filling: Layer ingredients into pie pan with puff pastry in the following order: 1 omelet, ¼ lb. ham, half of fried potatoes, 1 cup shredded cheese, remaining potatoes, ham, cheese, and omelet. Top with remaining sheet of puff pastry. Press together edges of both sheets of puff pastry to form a rim. Trim off excess puff pastry. Crimp or flute edges of puff pastry. Cover and refrigerate overnight or preheat oven to 375°F. In a small bowl, stir together 1 egg and 1 tablespoon water and brush over puff pastry. Bake for 30 – 35 minutes or until golden brown. Let stand 5 minutes; cut into wedges. If torte is refrigerated overnight, let stand at room temperature 30 minutes before baking as directed above. *Tip:* Your favorite deli meats can be substituted for the ham. *Serves 8.*

Bed & Breakfast at Sills Inn

Tony Sills
270 Montgomery Avenue
Versailles, Kentucky 40383
Tel (800) 526-9801

ABOUT THE B&B

Guests are treated to true southern hospitality as soon as they step into this restored 1911, three-story Victorian inn in downtown Versailles — the center of bluegrass horse country and just seven minutes west of Lexington Airport/Keeneland Racetrack and 10 minutes from the Lexington area. Each of the 11 accommodations is distinctively decorated and has its own private bath, including six suites with double Jacuzzis. A full gourmet breakfast is served on the sun porch on china, crystal, and linen. Guests are also treated to freshly baked chocolate chip cookies, a refrigerator stocked with soft drinks, hot drinks, and popcorn anytime they're in need of a snack. The pampering continues as guests choose from the inn's restaurant menu book, have dinner reservations made for them, and are given a map highlighting their way to the restaurant. Guests fall asleep reading previous comments from the guest diary and dream about those wonderful blueberry muffins and eggs Benedict waiting for them in the morning.

SEASON

all year

ACCOMMODATIONS

11 rooms (including six suites) with private baths

Chicken Quiche

Rice crust:
1 cube chicken bouillon
1 cup boiling hot water
1 cup Minute rice
1 beaten egg
1 cup Parmesan cheese

Filling:
2 cubes chicken bouillon
2 cups boiling hot water
3 cups of diced cooked chicken
1 cup+ chopped green bell peppers
¾ cup chopped onions
3 cups shredded cheddar cheese

Egg mixture:
9 extra-large eggs
1 tablespoon Tabasco sauce
1 teaspoon garlic salt
1 teaspoon black pepper

(continued on next page)

Preheat oven to 325°F.

To prepare rice crust: Mix bouillon with hot water until dissolved. Mix with rice and set aside until set. Once set, add egg and cheese and mix together well. Pat down in a deep-dish pie pan sprayed well with non-stick cooking spray. Set aside.

To prepare filling: Mix bouillon with hot water until dissolved. Combine chicken, green peppers, and onions, then add bouillon mixture. Microwave on high for 6 minutes. Drain and cool (so cheese won't melt when added). Mix in cheese and place on rice crust.

To prepare egg mixture: Beat all ingredients together well. Mix into filling. Push filling away from sides of pie pan, creating space for egg mixture to pool (this will help reduce overflow during cooking). Place pie pan on a foil-covered cookie sheet, and cover and tent entire cookie sheet (including pie pan) with foil.

Bake for 1 hour and 45 minutes or until egg mixture sets. Let cool before cutting. *Tip:* Individual slices reheat well in the microwave oven. *Serves 8.*

Martin Oaks
Bed & Breakfast

Marie and Frank Gery
PO Box 207, 107 First Street
Dundas, Minnesota 55019
Tel: (507) 645-4644

ABOUT THE B&B

In 1869, the Archibald Brothers had this home built as a wedding present for their sister, Sarah Etta Archibald. Now listed on the National Register of Historic Places, Martin Oaks, the Archibald-Martin House, and the Carriage House occupy half a city block. Located in historic Dundas Village, Martin Oaks transports guests to an era where elegant women and fine gentlemen enjoyed good conversation and classical music, and savored elegant foods served on fine china. Three charming bedrooms filled with antiques offer the opportunity for a memorable, quiet evening. Martin Oaks is less than five minutes away from Northfield, Carleton, and St. Olaf colleges, and is near superb shopping and bookstore browsing, fine antique hunting on and off Division Street, golf courses, hiking, and cross-country skiing. Minneapolis, St. Paul, and the Mall of America are within a 40-minute drive.

SEASON

all year

ACCOMMODATIONS

three rooms with shared baths

Coach's Quiche

"Several years ago, the folks in the school where I taught decided we'd put together a cookbook, and that's where this recipe is from. By now, the cookbook is well worn and more than a bit stained, but I still keep it around as a memory of good friends." — Marie Gery

9" unbaked pie shell
10-oz. package frozen chopped spinach
1 medium minced onion
5 separated eggs
1 cup milk or half-and-half cream
8-oz. package cream cheese at room temperature
¾ cup bread crumbs
1 cup grated Parmesan cheese
¼ cup butter
1 large can mushroom pieces and stems
1 teaspoon tarragon leaves
Salt and pepper to taste

Preheat oven to 400°F. Have unbaked pie shell ready before beginning to prepare quiche batter. Cook spinach according to package directions; drain well. Sauté onion in butter until translucent. Beat egg yolks until light. Add milk, cream cheese, bread crumbs, and Parmesan cheese, and beat well. Add cooked spinach, onion, mushrooms, tarragon leaves, salt, and pepper. Wash beaters, then beat egg whites until firm. Fold egg whites into above mixture and pour into pie shell. Bake until top is brown (about 15 – 20 minutes). Reduce heat to 350°F and bake until a knife blade inserted in center comes out clean (about 45 minutes – 1 hour). *Serves 6 – 8.*

Corn Quiche

(Recipe from Breakfast at Nine, Tea at Four: Favorite Recipes From The Mainstay Inn.)

9" unbaked pie shell
3 eggs
¼" slice of onion
1 tablespoon all-purpose flour
1 tablespoon sugar
1 teaspoon salt
3 tablespoons melted butter
1⅓ cups scalded light cream
2 cups corn, fresh or frozen (defrosted)
Fresh parsley
Peach half
Fresh strawberries

Preheat oven to 375°F. In a blender, combine eggs, onion, flour, sugar, and salt. Add butter and cream, and blend. Add corn and blend only slightly. Pour into unbaked pie shell and bake for 45 minutes. Garnish with fresh parsley, peach half, and fresh strawberries. *Serves 6 – 8.*

The Mainstay Inn

Sue and Tom Carroll
635 Columbia Avenue
Cape May, New Jersey 08204
Tel: (609) 884-8690

ABOUT THE B&B

According to the Washington Post, "The jewel of them all has got to be the Mainstay." Built by a pair of wealthy gamblers in 1872, this elegant, exclusive clubhouse is now among the premier B&B inns in the country. The Mainstay now comprises three historic buildings on one of the most beautiful streets of the historic Cape May district. Guests enjoy 16 antique-filled rooms and suites (some with fireplaces and whirlpool baths), three parlors, spacious gardens, and rocker-filled verandas. Breakfast and afternoon tea served daily. Beautiful beaches, historic attractions, biking, birding, golf, and tennis are all available in Cape May, a National Historic Landmark community.

SEASON

all year

ACCOMMODATIONS

16 rooms (including seven suites) with private baths

Dreams of Yesteryear
Bed and Breakfast

Bonnie and Bill Maher
1100 Brawley Street
Stevens Point, Wisconsin 54481
Tel: (715) 341-4525

ABOUT THE B&B

This elegant, turn-of-the-century Victorian Queen Anne was home to three generations of the Jensen family before being purchased in 1987 and restored by current owners Bonnie and Bill Maher. An article Bonnie wrote about the restoration was featured in the Winter 1991 issue of Victorian Homes magazine. In 1990, after giving many tours, the Mahers opened their home as the Dreams of Yesteryear Bed and Breakfast. Listed on the National Register of Historic Places, Dreams of Yesteryear is located three blocks from historic downtown Stevens Point, two blocks from the Wisconsin River and Green Circle jogging/hiking/biking trails, a half mile from the University of Wisconsin, and near wonderful restaurants, theaters, and antique shops. Your visit includes a gourmet breakfast, warm hospitality, and wonderful memories.

SEASON

all year

ACCOMMODATIONS

two rooms with private baths;
two rooms with shared bath

Crustless Quiche

¼ lb. butter
½ cup all-purpose flour
6 large beaten eggs
1 cup milk
1 lb. cubed Monterey Jack cheese
3-oz. package softened cream cheese
2 cups cottage cheese
1 teaspoon baking powder
1 teaspoon salt
1 teaspoon sugar

Preheat oven to 350°F. Melt butter in a small saucepan. Add flour and cook until smooth. Add eggs and beat. Add remaining ingredients and stir until well blended. Pour in well-greased 13 x 9" pan. Bake uncovered for 45 minutes. *Tip:* This recipe can be used as a breakfast dish or cut into small pieces as an hors d'oeuvre. *Serves 12.*

Famous Guesthouse Quiche

"This basic quiche can be used with other ingredients or vegetables of your choice. I get the best results by leaving it simple and tasty." — Lucille Kruse

White bread slices
1 cup cheddar cheese
¾ cup cubed ham
6 eggs
1 cup milk
¼ cup chopped green and red bell peppers
Chives

Preheat oven to 350°F. Spray or oil a standard quiche pan. Line the bottom with bread slices. Cover with cheese. Sprinkle ham over cheese. Beat eggs and add milk, then pour this over the bread, cheese, and ham in the pan. Sprinkle with chopped peppers and chives. Bake for 30 – 35 minutes. Serve hot. *Serves 6.*

Calmar Guesthouse Bed & Breakfast

Lucille B. Kruse
103 North Street
Calmar, Iowa 52132
Tel: (319) 562-3851

ABOUT THE B&B

Open since 1986, the Calmar Guesthouse is a beautiful, remodeled Victorian home with warm hospitality, good food, and quiet elegance. The house features stained glass windows, refinished wood, handmade quilts, crafts, antiques, and queen-size beds. Breakfast is served in the formal dining room in elegant fashion, with candles and music. Nearby activities include a bike trail, golf, tennis, outdoor swimming, canoeing, trout fishing, and more. Local places of interest include Billy Brothers world famous wood-carved clocks, the Norwegian Museum, the Laura Ingalls Museum, the World's Smallest Church, the Little Brown Church in the Vale (the inspiration for the song), the two-mile underground Niagara Cave, Spook Cave, and many beautiful parks.

SEASON

all year

ACCOMMODATIONS

five rooms with shared baths

La Corsette Maison Inn

Kay Owen
629 1st Avenue East
Newton, Iowa 50208
Tel: (515) 792-6833

ABOUT THE B&B

To spend the night at the Maison Inn is to be the personal house guest of Kay Owen, and to enjoy charming French bed chambers, down-filled pillows, and beckoning hearths. Kay lives in this opulent, mission-style mansion built in 1909 by early Iowa state senator August Bergman. Here amid the charm of the original mission oak woodwork, art nouveau stained glass windows, brass light fixtures, and even some of the original furnishings, Kay operates the highly acclaimed La Corsette restaurant, considered a unique dining experience by gourmets nationwide. The Maison Inn is a delightful extension of that experience. Choose from seven distinctive accommodations (some with double whirlpools and fireplaces), including the penthouse, where you'll be nudged awake in the morning by a rainbow of sunlight coming through the mass of beveled glass windows. In the morning, be prepared for a delectable breakfast served in the gracious tradition of La Corsette.

SEASON

all year

ACCOMMODATIONS

seven rooms (including two suites) with private baths

Farmer's Frittata

10 slices chopped bacon
4 ozs. diced onions
3 medium potatoes, cooked with skins on and diced
11 eggs
1¼ cups milk
1 teaspoon salt
¼ teaspoon pepper
4 ozs. shredded cheddar cheese
4 ozs. shredded Swiss cheese

Preheat oven to 350°F. Sauté bacon and onions. Drain fat. Put bacon mixture in the bottom of a greased 10" quiche pan. Sprinkle diced potatoes over. Beat eggs and milk, then add salt and pepper. Pour over potato mixture. Sprinkle the cheeses over the top. Bake 1 hour and 15 minutes. *Serves 6.*

Gables Frittata

½ lb. pork breakfast sausage
2 cups shredded zucchini
2 chopped green onions
½ teaspoon oregano
½ teaspoon basil
1 tablespoon (packaged) powdered Italian salad dressing mix
6 eggs
½ cup whipping cream
4 ozs. softened cream cheese
1 cup shredded mozzarella cheese
1 cup shredded cheddar cheese

Preheat oven to 325°F. Brown sausage and drain on a paper towel. Place the sausage in an 8" quiche pan or pie plate. Spread the zucchini and onions over the sausage, and sprinkle with oregano, basil, and powdered Italian salad dressing mix. Beat the eggs with the whipping cream and pour over zucchini and sausage. Cut the cream cheese into cubes and sprinkle evenly over the top. Cover with mozzarella and cheddar cheese. Bake for 45 minutes or until set. *Serves 6.*

7 Gables Inn

Leicha and Paul Welton
PO Box 80488
Fairbanks, Alaska 99708
Tel: (907) 479-0751

ABOUT THE B&B

*T*his 10,000 square foot Tudor-style house is located within walking distance of the University of Alaska Fairbanks campus, which is probably why 7 Gables began as a fraternity house. Its convenient location (between the airport and train station) is further enhanced by being right in the middle of a number of major attractions in the area: Riverboat Discovery, Pump House Restaurant, Cripple Creek Resort, University Museum, and Alaskaland. You enter the B&B through a floral solarium into a foyer with antique stained glass and indoor waterfall. Other features include cathedral ceilings, wine cellar, and wedding chapel. Some additional amenities include laundry facilities, Jacuzzis, cable TV and in-room phones, canoes, bikes, gourmet breakfasts, luggage or game storage, and library collection. Leicha enjoys cooking, music, hosting parties, and learning foreign languages, while Paul collects books and manages the inn's marketing and maintenance.

SEASON

all year

ACCOMMODATIONS

eight rooms with private baths; one room with shared bath

Bedford's Covered Bridge Inn

Martha and Greg Lau
R.D. 1, Box 196
Schellsburg, Pennsylvania 15559
Tel: (814) 733-4093

ABOUT THE B&B

Situated near Exit 11 of I-76 (the Pennsylvania Turnpike), Bedford's Covered Bridge Inn borders 4000-acre Shawnee State Park, a lovely trout stream, and the Colvin covered bridge. From this idyllic location, guests can pursue hiking, biking, fishing, cross-country skiing, birding, and antique hunting right from the inn's door. Nearby swimming and boating on Shawnee Lake, visits to Old Bedford Village and Bedford's historic district, driving tours, downhill skiing at Blue Knob Resort, and tours of Bedford's 14 covered bridges round out the list of local activities. Inside the inn, the Lau's attention to detail creates an atmosphere that is comfortable and inviting. The historic farmhouse (circa 1823) boasts six guest rooms with private baths, traditional and country decor, and memorable breakfasts. "There's no doubt what everyone's favorite activity is," say Martha and Greg, "sitting on the inn's wraparound porch and wishing for a life in Bedford County, too!"

SEASON

all year

ACCOMMODATIONS

six rooms with private baths; one cottage for couples or families

Garden Frittata

4 slices bacon
1 large chopped onion
1½ cups lightly steamed vegetable in season (asparagus, zucchini, broccoli, etc.)
6 beaten eggs
1½ cups grated Swiss cheese

In an 11" iron skillet, brown bacon and reserve, removing most of the drippings. In remaining drippings, sauté onion. Add crumbled bacon, vegetables, and eggs. Top with Swiss cheese. Place a lid on skillet and allow to cook on low heat until nearly set. Finish under broiler in oven until top is brown. *Serves 6.*

He-Man Omelet

6 ozs. hash brown potatoes
4 eggs
⅓ cup water
¼ teaspoon salt
Dash of onion powder and garlic powder
4 – 8 drops hot sauce (such as Tabasco)
1 cup chopped ham
½ cup shredded sharp cheddar cheese
Chopped chives or green onion or parsley

Fry hash brown potatoes until crisp and browned. Combine remaining ingredients (except ham) and pour over potatoes. Add chopped ham. Cover and cook until firm. Lift potatoes once or twice and tilt pan so liquid egg mixture can run under to cook. Add shredded cheese and let melt. Serve garnished with chopped chives, green onion, or parsley. *Serves 2.*

The Parson's House

Sandy and Harold Richardson
638 Forest Avenue
Crete, Nebraska 68333
Tel: (402) 826-2634

ABOUT THE B&B

L aze on the porch swing of this 11-room, foursquare-style house built at the turn of the century. The inside of the Parson's House is equally relaxing, and has been refinished and furnished mostly in antiques. Doane College and its beautiful campus is located just one block away. Lincoln, the state capital and home of the University of Nebraska and the Lied Center for the Performing Arts, is 25 miles away. Host Harold, a Baptist minister with a local UCC church, also runs a remodeling business, while hostess Sandy manages real estate rentals as well as the bed and breakfast. Together, they'll make your stay as comfortable and relaxing as possible, and make you feel like the Parson's House is your "home away from home." A full breakfast is served in the formal dining room.

SEASON

all year

ACCOMMODATIONS

two rooms with shared bath

Rockinghorse Bed & Breakfast

Sharleen and Jerry Bergum
RR1, Box 133, Whitewood
South Dakota 57793
Tel: (605) 269-2625

ABOUT THE B&B

A cedar clapboard-sided house built in 1914 to accommodate local timber teams, Rockinghorse was moved to its present location by Sharleen and Jerry, who have lovingly restored the interior. Handsome wood floors, columns, and trims, along with antiques, country charm decor, and the original stairway grace the home. Rockinghorse is situated in the rustic Black Hills, where you can watch deer graze nearby and wild turkeys strut across the valley. Listen to the sounds of coyotes in the evening while a rooster's crow awakens you in the morning. You can also pet a bunny, ride the horse-drawn wagon, or have wood/fiber artist Sharleen help you master the spinning wheel. A gift shop is also on the premises. The B&B is near historic Deadwood, the world renowned Passion Play, the scenic Spearfish Canyon route, and it's one-hour's drive from Mt. Rushmore. Full breakfast includes fresh fruits (in season), home-made breads, blueberry pancakes, and special egg-cheese dishes.

SEASON

all year

ACCOMMODATIONS

one room with private bath;
two rooms with shared bath

Kountry Keish

"At our B&B, we have fresh eggs from our chicken flock and also raise a large garden, so this quiche recipe is really home-made." — Sharleen Bergum

9" pie crust mix
12 bacon slices
4 beaten eggs
2 cups half-and-half cream
1½ cups grated Swiss cheese
⅓ cup diced sautéed onions
½ cup chopped broccoli or spinach

Bake pie crust according to directions. Fry bacon crisp and cut into bite-size pieces. Mix eggs and cream together. Line pie crust with cheese, then add bacon, vegetables, and finally egg mixture over cheese. Bake in a preheated 425°F oven for 15 minutes, then reduce to 300°F for 30 minutes. Test with a knife inserted in center. Let stand 10 minutes, then serve. *Serves 6.*

Oven Omelet

¼ cup butter
18 eggs
1 cup sour cream
1 cup milk
2 teaspoons salt
¼ teaspoon pepper
¼ cup chopped green onions

Preheat oven to 325°F. Melt butter in 12 x 9" pan in oven —
watching closely so as not to burn it. Beat eggs, sour cream,
milk, salt, and pepper in a bowl. Add green onions, including
stems, and pour into pan with butter. Bake for 35 minutes until
set but still moist. *Serves 8 – 10.*

The Hen-Apple
Bed and Breakfast

Flo and Harold Eckert
409 South Lingle Avenue
Palmyra, Pennsylvania 17078
Tel: (717) 838-8282

ABOUT THE B&B

Built around 1825, the Hen-Apple is an intimate and
fully restored bed and
breakfast filled to the brim with
everything country and old-fashioned. It offers a relaxed atmosphere
with six air-conditioned guest
rooms (each with private bath), a
porch filled with rockers, a screened
porch for warm weather dining, a
herb garden, lots of flowers, and a
shady retreat in the orchard. The
Hen-Apple's well-rounded breakfasts are something to remember
— especially the cinnamon French
toast — with tea served in the
afternoon. Just two miles from
Hershey, Pennsylvania, Palmyra
is an antique lover's dream. In
addition, wineries, shopping outlets,
Hershey attractions, the riverboat,
and horse racing are nearby. Your
hosts, Flo and Harold Eckert, love
going to flea markets and auctions,
and enjoy reading, gardening, and
music. Flo is also a Christmas
enthusiast so, come the merry
season, the B&B sports a tree in
just about every room and an
impressive Santa collection.

SEASON

all year

ACCOMMODATIONS

six rooms with private baths

Harbour Woods

Christine and Joe Titka
PO Box 1214
Southwest Harbor, Maine 04679
Tel: (207) 244-5388

ABOUT THE B&B

*C*hristine and Joe welcome you to their gracious 1800s Maine farmhouse across the street from the Great Harbor Marina. By having a small number of guest rooms, Harbour Woods offers an intimate social setting accented by family keepsakes, antiques, flowers, and softly glowing oil lamps. What's more, the warm tones and subtle designs of the wall coverings create an atmosphere of casual elegance. Each morning, a candlelight breakfast becomes a dining experience of the finest kind. Listen to soft music and enjoy a variety of coffees, teas, juices, in-season fruits, home-baked breads, muffins, and entrées of the day, which are imaginatively prepared and presented. A cookie jar and tea for the munches and a refrigerator stocked with complimentary soft drinks are always available. Guest rooms are distinctively decorated and feature queen-size beds, crackling fireplaces, evening mints and candy, telephones, and private baths with luxurious towels and a selection of rich soaps. And, of course, you may privately reserve the B&B's indoor spa, which awaits to refresh and relax you after a full day of activities in Acadia National Park.

SEASON

all year

ACCOMMODATIONS

three rooms with private baths; private cottages with private baths (seasonal)

Puffy Cheesy Strata

Crustless white bread slices (enough to make 2 layers covering bottom of 13 x 9" pan)
½ lb. grated white sharp cheddar cheese
¾ lb. grated Monterey Jack cheese
8 eggs
2½ cups milk
Sprinkle of grated Monterey Jack cheese
Fresh parsley

Place 1 layer of bread in a 13 x 9" non-stick baking pan. Grate together both cheeses, then sprinkle ⅓ cheese mixture evenly on top of bread. Add a second layer of bread. Blend together eggs and milk. Pour evenly over bread slices. Top with remaining ⅔ of cheese mixture. Cover and refrigerate overnight, allowing bread slices to soak up liquid. Remove from fridge ¾ hour before baking. Bake, covered, in a preheated 350°F oven approximately 35 – 40 minutes, taking cover off halfway through. When done, cheese should be puffy and just starting to turn light brown. Cut into 6 – 8 pieces and garnish with a sprinkle of cheese and fresh parsley. *Serves 6 – 8.*

Spinach Soufflé Quiche

9" pastry shell
½ of 10 oz. package of Stouffer's frozen spinach soufflé
3 strips cooked bacon
3 ozs. grated Swiss or cheddar cheese (or a mixture of both)
5 tablespoons grated Parmesan cheese
4 large eggs
1½ cups half-and-half cream
Dash of salt
⅛ teaspoon cayenne pepper
¼ teaspoon ground nutmeg or to taste
Paprika (optional)

Preheat oven to 375°F. Arrange uncooked pastry shell in 10" quiche dish. Cut frozen spinach in 1" cubes and place on top of crust. Crumble bacon and sprinkle over spinach. Sprinkle grated cheeses over bacon. In a separate bowl, beat eggs, then add half-and-half, salt, pepper, and nutmeg. Pour this mixture over cheese in quiche dish. Sprinkle with paprika (optional) and bake for 40 minutes or until center is well set. Cool 5 minutes before cutting into serving pieces. *Serves 6 – 8.*

"An Elegant Victorian Mansion" Bed & Breakfast Inn

Lily and Doug Vieyra
1406 'C' Street
Eureka, California 95501
Tel: (800) 386-1888 or
(707) 442-5594

ABOUT THE B&B

*F*eatured in many newspapers and magazines — not to mention on television and radio — this restored national historic landmark offers Eureka's most prestigious and luxurious accommodations. Spirited and eclectic innkeepers provide lavish hospitality in the splendor of a meticulously restored 1888 Victorian masterpiece, complete with original family antique furnishings. The inviting guest rooms offer both graceful refinement and modern-day comfort, individually decorated with Victorian elegance. Guests enjoy gourmet breakfasts and a heavenly night's sleep on top-quality mattresses, as well as secured parking and laundry service. Located in a quiet, historic residential neighborhood overlooking the city and Humboldt Bay, the non-smoking inn is near carriage rides, bay cruises, restaurants, and the theater, and is just minutes from giant Redwood parks, coastal beaches, ocean charters, and horseback riding.

SEASON

all year

ACCOMMODATIONS

one suite with private bath;
three rooms with shared baths

Buttonwood Inn

Liz Oehser
190 Georgia Road
Franklin, North Carolina 28734
Tel: (704) 369-8985

ABOUT THE B&B

*T*his small mountain bed and breakfast with a cozy home atmosphere awaits your visit. Sleep in chenille- or quilt-covered antique beds surrounded by country furnishings, collectibles, and crafts. Two rooms on the first floor each have a double and twin bed with private bath, while the two rooms on the second floor each have a double bed and share a common bath. Breakfast delights include artichoke quiche, sausage apple ring filled with puffy scrambled egg, Dutch babies with raspberry sauce, stuffed French toast, blintz soufflé, muffins, and cinnamon scones with home-made lemon butter. After breakfast, enjoy gem mining, hiking, horseback riding, water rafting, golf, or tennis. Stay long enough to tour Biltmore Estate in nearby Asheville, drive through the Smokey Mountain Parkway to Cherokee Indian Reservation, or "shop till you drop" in Gatlinburg. Hospitality, comfort, and delightful breakfasts are this inn's priorities.

SEASON

April to December 15

ACCOMMODATIONS

two rooms with private baths;
two rooms with shared bath

Strawberry Omelet

Omelet:
3 large separated eggs with whites at room temperature
3 tablespoons sugar
1 tablespoon rum
Pinch of salt

Preheat oven to 350°F. Butter a 10" oven-proof skillet or omelet pan. Beat yolks with 1 tablespoon sugar and rum. Add a pinch of salt to egg whites and beat until frothy. Gradually add remaining 2 tablespoons sugar to the egg whites and beat until peaks form. Fold this mixture into the yolk mixture. Pour into skillet or omelet pan and bake 20 minutes. Next, follow recipe for strawberry butter and topping. *Serves 2+.*

Strawberry butter:
½ cup unsalted butter
½ cup strawberry jam
2 teaspoons lemon juice

Topping:
2 tablespoons sour cream
2 sliced strawberries

Whip butter, then add jam and lemon juice. Whip until smooth; refrigerate. To finish omelet, spread strawberry butter on half of omelet and fold over. Top with 2 tablespoons strawberry butter, sour cream, and sliced strawberries.

Summer House Strata

1 loaf "day-old" Italian bread
⅔ cup chopped ham
⅔ cup chopped cheese of your choice (Swiss recommended)
3 eggs
2½ cups milk
3 tablespoons olive oil
2 tablespoons prepared mustard

Spray 10" quiche or pie dish with non-stick cooking spray. Cut enough ½" bread cubes to generously fill quiche dish — mound high in the center. Sprinkle ham and cheese on top. In a medium bowl, beat remaining ingredients until well mixed. Pour over bread cubes, cover with plastic wrap, and refrigerate overnight. In the morning, remove dish from fridge about ¾ hour before baking. Bake in a preheated 350 – 375°F oven about 15 minutes or until set and top is golden (if top browns too much, cover loosely with aluminum foil to complete baking). Serve immediately (dish tends to deflate like a soufflé as it cools). *Tip:* An 8" dish serves about 5. *Serves 7 – 8.*

The Summer House

Kay and David Merrell
158 Main Street
Sandwich, Massachusetts 02563
Tel: (508) 888-4991

ABOUT THE B&B

The Summer House is an elegant circa 1835 Greek Revival twice featured in *Country Living* magazine. It was owned by Hiram Dillaway, a prominent mold-maker and colorist at the Boston & Sandwich Glass Factory. Large, sunny bedchambers feature antiques, hand-stitched quilts, and working fireplaces. Stroll to dining, shops, museums, galleries, pond and gristmill, and boardwalk to beach. Bountiful breakfasts change daily and include freshly ground coffee, tea, fruit juice, and fresh fruit served in stemware. Entrées of frittata, stuffed French toast, quiche, or omelets are accompanied by scones, puff pastry, muffins, or fruit cobblers. Dishes are enhanced with vegetables, berries, and herbs from the inn's garden. English-style afternoon tea is served at an umbrella table in the garden. Boston, Newport, Providence, Martha's Vineyard, and Nantucket make pleasant day trips. Innkeepers Kay and David Merrell (former executive secretary and aerospace engineer respectively) enjoy woodworking, gardening, quilting, jogging, backpacking, and the tranquility of Cape Cod.

SEASON

all year

ACCOMMODATIONS

one room with private bath;
four rooms with shared baths

Hutton House

Loretta Murray and
Dean Ahren
PO Box 88, Route 250/219
Huttonsville, West Virginia
26273
Tel: (304) 335-6701

ABOUT THE B&B

Majestically situated above the tiny town of Huttonsville, this meticulously restored turn-of-the-century Queen Anne Victorian commands a broad view of the Tygart River Valley and the Laurel Mountains. Hutton House, which is listed in the National Register of Historic Places, features original oak woodwork, ornate windows, a three-story turret, arched pocket doors, wraparound porch, and a winding staircase. Antiques abound, and each of the guest rooms is furnished in its own individual style. Breakfast is a time to get to know your hosts and the other guests, while enjoying a variety of pancakes, French toast, and egg dishes along with fresh fruit, crème brulée, sorbet, or even porridge. Guests can then relax on the porch, play games on the lawn, or take a leisurely hike on the trail behind the house. Nearby attractions include Cass Railroad, National Radio Observatory, underground caverns, and rock climbing.

SEASON

all year

ACCOMMODATIONS

six rooms with private baths

Zucchini Frittata

½ tablespoon olive oil
1 teaspoon butter
3 – 4 ozs. grated zucchini
Sprinkle of salt
House of Tsang Mongolian Fire Oil
4 lightly beaten eggs
½ cup grated Monterey Jack cheese
2 tablespoons mild or hot salsa

Heat olive oil and butter in an 8" iron skillet until butter is melted. Cover the bottom of the pan with grated zucchini. Sprinkle with salt and 5 – 6 shakes of Fire Oil. Add eggs to the pan; don't stir. Cook the mixture on low heat until ¾ set. Sprinkle cheese on eggs and place under a preheated broiler until eggs puff and cheese is golden. Cut in half and put on individual plates with a tablespoon of salsa on each half.
Tip: The Mongolian Fire Oil is more flavorful than hot so don't let the name scare you — this dish won't be the same without it so try not to omit it. You'll also find yourself using it to perk up lots of other dishes. *Serves 2.*

Egg Dishes

Cheese Dishes

Meat Dishes

Alpen Rose Baked Eggs

10 beaten eggs
⅓ cup all-purpose flour
¾ teaspoon baking powder
10 ozs. pork breakfast sausage, fried and crumbled
1 lb. Monterey Jack cheese
1½ cups cottage cheese
¾ cup fresh mushrooms, sliced and fried

Preheat oven to 375°F. Mix eggs, flour, and baking powder together well. Add sausage, cheeses, and mushrooms to egg mixture, and beat well. Pour into a greased 13 x 9" glass baking pan. Bake for 35 – 40 minutes. *Serves 10.*

Alpen Rose Bed & Breakfast

Robin and Rupert Sommerauer
PO Box 769, 244 Forest Trail
Winter Park, Colorado 80482
Tel: (303) 726-5039

ABOUT THE B&B

Hidden in the forest just minutes from downtown Winter Park, the Alpen Rose is a bed and breakfast with Austrian warmth and hospitality. Share Robin and Rupert's love of the mountains by taking in the breathtaking view from the "common room," enhanced by aspens, wildflowers, and lofty pines. At Alpen Rose, you'll feel right at home whatever the season — from the spare cozy slippers and lushly quilted beds with down pillows to the steaming outdoor hot tub. What's more, each of the five bedrooms is decorated with treasures brought over from Austria, including traditional featherbeds. A full breakfast featuring homemade yogurt, granola, fresh fruit, freshly baked coffee cake or bread, an egg dish, and a meat dish awaits guests each morning in the sunny common room. Rupert was born in Salzburg, Austria. His wife, an American, met him in Germany after a stint there with Outward Bound. The superb natural beauty of Winter Park makes a great place to visit year-round.

SEASON

all year

ACCOMMODATIONS

five rooms with private baths

Carol and David Doelling
4817 Towne South
St. Louis, Missouri 63128
Tel: (314) 894-6796

ABOUT THE B&B

*R*ediscover Old World hospitality at Doelling Haus, where you'll delight in beautiful rooms reminiscent of a European country home decorated with German antiques and collectibles, handed down from the hosts' families and gathered during their travels. Hearty full breakfasts include German and Austrian delicacies, and home-made truffles await beside your bed. Many points of interest are nearby, including the famous Arch monument, Grant's Farm, the historic settlement of Kimmswick, recreational areas, malls, and fine restaurants. Carol will direct you to wonderful shops for antique-hunting and David, who owns a sports memorabilia store, will gladly show off his old baseball card collection. Come experience "Gemutlichkeit" (a sense of well-being) at Doelling Haus.

SEASON

all year

ACCOMMODATIONS

one suite with private bath;
one room with shared bath

Austrian Skillet Florentine

Note: This recipe is a variation of the Farmer's Breakfast (see recipe in this section). Omit the chicken and add spinach and hollandaise sauce.

4 – 6 large potatoes, scrubbed, peeled, and diced
6 slices thick bacon
Small package frozen chopped spinach
Hollandaise sauce mix
6 eggs

Prepare the bacon and potatoes same as for Farmer's Breakfast. Place in warm oven, then prepare the frozen spinach according to package directions, drain off excess liquid, and keep warm. Prepare the hollandaise sauce according to the package directions and keep warm while preparing the poached (or over easy or sunny side up) eggs. To serve, place a generous portion of the potato mixture on each plate, top with a few spoonfuls of spinach, place an egg on top, and drizzle with hollandaise sauce. *Serves 6.*

Bacon and Cheese Breakfast Pizza

Pastry for 1 single-crust pie (9")
½ lb. cooked and crumbled bacon
2 cups shredded mozzarella or cheddar cheese
4 eggs
1½ cups sour cream
2 tablespoons chopped fresh parsley

Preheat oven to 425°F. Roll pastry to fit into a 12" pizza pan, then bake for 5 minutes. Sprinkle bacon and cheese evenly over crust. Beat eggs, sour cream, and parsley in a bowl until smooth. Pour over pizza. Bake for 20 – 25 minutes or until pizza is puffy and lightly browned. *Serves 6 (main dish) or makes 18 appetizers.*

The Hen-Apple Bed and Breakfast

Flo and Harold Eckert
409 South Lingle Avenue
Palmyra, Pennsylvania 17078
Tel: (717) 838-8282

ABOUT THE B&B

Built around 1825, the Hen-Apple is an intimate and fully restored bed and breakfast filled to the brim with everything country and old-fashioned. It offers a relaxed atmosphere with six air-conditioned guest rooms (each with private bath), a porch filled with rockers, a screened porch for warm weather dining, a herb garden, lots of flowers, and a shady retreat in the orchard. The Hen-Apple's well-rounded breakfasts are something to remember — especially the cinnamon French toast — with tea served in the afternoon. Just two miles from Hershey, Pennsylvania, Palmyra is an antique lover's dream. In addition, wineries, shopping outlets, Hershey attractions, the riverboat, and horse racing are nearby. Your hosts, Flo and Harold Eckert, love going to flea markets and auctions, and enjoy reading, gardening, and music. Flo is also a Christmas enthusiast so, come the merry season, the B&B sports a tree in just about every room and an impressive Santa collection.

SEASON

all year

ACCOMMODATIONS

six rooms with private baths

The Shaw House
Bed and Breakfast

Mary and Joe Shaw
613 Cypress Court
Georgetown, South Carolina
29440
Tel: (803) 546-9663

ABOUT THE B&B

The Shaw House Bed and Breakfast is a spacious two-story home in a serene, natural setting. From the glass-walled den, enjoy bird-watching and a beautiful view overlooking miles of marshland formed by four rivers, which converge and flow into the Intercoastal Waterway. Outlined by tall white columns, the wide front porch extends the width of the home and features old-fashioned rockers — ready and waiting for guests who are welcomed as family. All rooms are air conditioned, with private baths and a smattering of antiques. Enjoy a full southern breakfast come morning and bed turn-backs and chocolate come bedtime — plus some loving extras.

SEASON

all year

ACCOMMODATIONS

three rooms with private baths

Baked Cheese Grits Casserole

"This is great for brunch with fruit and biscuits."
— Mary Shaw

1 cup grits, cooked in 4 cups water
3 eggs beaten in 1 cup milk
6-oz. box Jiffy corn muffin mix
¼ cup butter
1 lb. sautéed pork breakfast sausage
½ lb. shredded cheese
Paprika

Preheat oven to 325°F. Mix cooked grits, egg mixture, Jiffy mix, and butter in a casserole 15 x 12". Add sausage. Sprinkle top with cheese and paprika. Bake for about 30 minutes.
Serves 8 – 10.

Baked Eggs with Spinach

4 large bunches fresh trimmed spinach, or 2 10-oz. packages
frozen spinach
1 grated baked potato
3 ozs. softened cream cheese
½ teaspoon salt
Fresh ground pepper
4 eggs
2 cups grated cheddar cheese

Preheat oven to 375°F. Wash and cook spinach until tender.
Drain well and squeeze out excess water. Chop spinach, then
add potatoes, cream cheese, salt, and pepper. Mix well. Divide
into 4 individual buttered ramekins. Make a slight indentation
in center of each and break 1 egg in each dish. Cover top with
cheddar cheese. Bake uncovered until whites set (about 20
minutes). *Serves 4.*

Farewell Bend
Bed & Breakfast

Lorene Bateman
29 NW Greeley
Bend, Oregon 97701
Tel: (503) 382-4374

ABOUT THE B&B

*This recently remodeled
1920s Dutch Colonial-style
house is located just four
blocks from the unique shops and
abundant restaurants of downtown
Bend, on the picturesque banks of
the Deschutes River that meanders
through Drake and Mirror Pond
parks. During the summer, wild
geese, ducks, and a pair of swans
glide serenely on the water as a
variety of activities take place
nearby. Bend also offers white water
rafting, hiking, fishing, and windsurfing. In the winter months,
downhill skiing is just 22 miles
away at magnificent Mt. Bachelor,
not to mention the endless miles of
nearby cross-country skiing and
snowmobile trails. Each guest room
at Farewell Bend offers warm and
friendly decor, colorful handmade
bed quilts, and private baths with
terry bath robes. Relax in the living
room with one of the many books
or watch TV or a movie on the
VCR. Each morning, enjoy a full
breakfast including home-made
jams, muffins, and breads, served
in the family dining room or on the
summer deck.*

SEASON

summer and winter

ACCOMMODATIONS

two rooms with private baths

Doelling Haus

Carol and David Doelling
4817 Towne South
St. Louis, Missouri 63128
Tel: (314) 894-6796

Bauernfrühstuck — Farmer's Breakfast

"This Bavarian dish is traditionally served at supper, which is considered the small meal of the day. You'll discover that this dish makes a hearty breakfast and that it's not just for farmers anymore!" — Carol Doelling

4 – 6 large boiling potatoes, scrubbed, peeled, and diced
6 slices thick bacon
3 pre-cooked chicken breasts
Salt and pepper to taste
6 eggs
¼ teaspoon paprika

Preheat oven to 200°F. In a large frying pan, fry bacon until crisp; drain and reserve bacon drippings for the potatoes. Fry potatoes in bacon drippings. While potatoes are cooking, dice the chicken breasts into small pieces. Add chicken to potatoes and finish cooking until potatoes test done. Crumble bacon and add to the potato mixture. Season mixture with salt and pepper to taste. Sprinkle with approximately ¼ teaspoon of paprika and toss. Place potato mixture in the oven to keep warm. Poach eggs or prepare over easy or sunny side up. To serve, place a generous portion of potato mixture on each plate and top with an egg. Sprinkle with a dash of paprika. *Tip:* Prepare baked chicken breasts the night before to save time in morning preparation. *Serves 6.*

Bedford County Breakfast Casserole

2 cups milk
7 eggs
7 slices trimmed and cubed bread
1 cup diced ham
⅓ cup finely chopped onions
2 cups grated medium cheddar cheese
1 teaspoon dry mustard
Thinly sliced tomatoes
Chives

Combine milk and eggs and mix well. Fold in remaining ingredients and top with tomatoes and chives. Pour into a greased 13 x 9" pan. Refrigerate overnight. Remove from fridge ¾ hour before baking. Bake in a preheated 325°F oven for 1 hour in top of oven. *Serves 6.*

Bedford's Covered Bridge Inn

Martha and Greg Lau
R.D. 1, Box 196
Schellsburg, Pennsylvania 15559
Tel: (814) 733-4093

ABOUT THE B&B

Situated near Exit 11 of I-76 (the Pennsylvania Turnpike), Bedford's Covered Bridge Inn borders 4000-acre Shawnee State Park, a lovely trout stream, and the Colvin covered bridge. From this idyllic location, guests can pursue hiking, biking, fishing, cross-country skiing, birding, and antique hunting right from the inn's door. Nearby swimming and boating on Shawnee Lake, visits to Old Bedford Village and Bedford's historic district, driving tours, downhill skiing at Blue Knob Resort, and tours of Bedford's 14 covered bridges round out the list of local activities. Inside the inn, the Lau's attention to detail creates an atmosphere that is comfortable and inviting. The historic farmhouse (circa 1823) boasts six guest rooms with private baths, traditional and country decor, and memorable breakfasts. "There's no doubt what everyone's favorite activity is," say Martha and Greg, "sitting on the inn's wraparound porch and wishing for a life in Bedford County, too!"

SEASON

all year

ACCOMMODATIONS

six rooms with private baths; one cottage for couples or families

1880 House

Elsie Collins
2 Seafield Lane, PO Box 648
Westhampton Beach, New York
11978
Tel: (800) 346-3290 or
(516) 288-1559

ABOUT THE B&B

Tucked away in the village of Westhampton Beach stands 1880 House, a bed and breakfast country retreat that's the perfect place for a romantic hideaway, a weekend of privacy, or just a change of pace from city life. Only 90 minutes from Manhattan, 1880 House is ideally situated on Westhampton Beach's exclusive Seafield Lane. Amenities include a swimming pool and tennis court and you're only a short, brisk walk to the ocean beach. Long a popular summer resort area, the Hamptons will more than satisfy your penchant for antique-hunting, and also offer many outstanding restaurants and shops. Indoor tennis facilities are available locally and Guerney's International Health Spa and scenic area of Montauk Point are nearby. 1880 House is not just a rural retreat but a home lovingly preserved by Mrs. Elsie Collins and filled with her antiques and personal touches.

SEASON

all year

ACCOMMODATIONS

three suites with private baths

Breakfast Casserole

1 lb. pork breakfast sausage
½ lb. grated sharp cheese
½ teaspoon dry mustard
½ teaspoon paprika
1 teaspoon salt
1 cup sour cream
10 – 16 eggs (depending on desired number of servings)
Vegetable oil spray

Preheat oven to 325°F. Cook sausage in a large skillet, then drain. Spray a 2 or 3 quart dish with vegetable spray. Put half of the grated cheese on the bottom of the dish. Mix spices with sour cream, add in the sausage, then spread sausage-sour cream mixture over grated cheese in dish. Beat eggs and pour over sausage mixture. Sprinkle remaining grated cheese on top. Bake for 25 – 30 minutes and serve. *Serves 6 – 14.*

Bridgeford Eggs

10¾-oz. can cream of chicken soup
10¾-oz. can cream of mushroom soup
1 cup mayonnaise
2 teaspoons juice
¼ cup golden sherry
¼ cup milk
12 hard-boiled eggs

Preheat oven to 350°F. Mix the first 6 ingredients together. Cover bottom of a 13 x 9" glass casserole dish with ⅓ of the sauce. Chop up the eggs and place in the dish. Cover with rest of the sauce. Bake for 20 minutes. Serve over rice or a split English muffin. *Tip:* Dish can be prepared the night before and baked in the morning. *Serves 10.*

Bridgeford House

Denise and Michael McDonald
263 Spring Street
Eureka Springs, Arkansas 72632
Tel: (501) 253-7853

ABOUT THE B&B

In the heart of Eureka Springs's historic district, Bridgeford House is an 1884 Queen Anne/Eastlake-style Victorian delight. Outside, you'll find shady porches that invite you to pull up a wicker chair and enjoy the panorama of horse-drawn carriages and Victorian homes that is uniquely Spring Street. Yet Bridgeford House is far enough away from downtown that it affords you the luxury of a peaceful and quiet stay. Select from four distinct accommodations: a two-room suite or three large, comfortable bedrooms. From your private entrance, you'll step into rooms tastefully filled with antique furnishings. Your comfortable bedroom and large modern bathroom offer a variety of distinctive touches that let you know you are indeed a special guest — things like fresh hot coffee in your room, color TV, and air conditioning. The large gourmet breakfast is just the right send-off for a pleasant day in one of America's most charming and unusual cities. Denise and Michael are full-time innkeepers and can devote their full attention to all of your needs.

SEASON

all year

ACCOMMODATIONS

four rooms (including one suite) with private baths

Blue Spruce Inn

Pat and Tom O'Brien
2815 Main Street
Soquel, California 95073
Tel: (800) 559-1137 or
(408) 464-1137

ABOUT THE B&B

The Blue Spruce Inn welcomes you with the distinct Pacific breeze that freshens the Central Coast hillsides that are golden with poppies, tempers the heat of the summer sun, and warms the sands during afternoon strolls on winter beaches. The inn is four miles south of Santa Cruz and one mile from Capitola Beach at the northern curve of Monterey Bay. Gracious personal service is the hallmark of this 1875 B&B inn, where beds are graced with Amish quilts and walls hung with original local art that blends the flavor of yesteryear with the luxury of today. There are quiet gardens in which to enjoy the sunshine of Soquel Village, delightful antique shops at the corner of the street and, a little farther, wineries, gift shops, and regional art displays. Bountiful breakfasts feature fresh fruits, home-made breads, and exceptional entrées. At the end of the day, the hot tub offers welcome respite and, when guests return to their rooms, pillows are fluffed and a special treat awaits — assuring the perfect ending to a wonderful day.

SEASON

all year

ACCOMMODATIONS

five rooms with private baths

Brunch Enchiladas

"My mother gave me this recipe many years ago — it's now my most asked-for recipe. I don't know where she got it, but it's definitely a part of our family history. My mother's family were early settlers in Santa Barbara, California, and my great-grandfather is even buried in Santa Barbara Mission." — Pat O'Brien

2 cups ground fully cooked ham
½ cup sliced green onions
½ cup finely chopped green bell peppers
2½ cups shredded cheddar cheese
8 flour tortillas (7" diameter)
4 beaten eggs
2 cups light cream or milk
1 tablespoon all-purpose flour
¼ teaspoon salt (optional)
¼ teaspoon garlic powder
Few drops of hot pepper sauce (such as Tabasco)
Avocado slices
Fresh salsa
Sour cream

(continued on next page)

In a bowl, combine ground ham, onions, and green peppers. Place ⅓ cup of this mixture and 3 tablespoons cheese at one end of tortilla. Roll up. Repeat with rest. Arrange tortillas seam-side down in a greased 12 x 7½ x 2" oven-proof casserole. Combine eggs, cream, flour, salt, garlic powder, and hot pepper sauce. Pour over tortillas.

Cover and refrigerate several hours or overnight. Remove from fridge ¾ hour before baking. Preheat oven to 350°F and bake for 45 – 60 minutes or until set. Sprinkle with remaining cheese. Bake 3 minutes more until cheese melts, then let stand 10 minutes. Garnish with last 3 ingredients. *Tip:* For a wonderful mix of textures and temperatures, serve this entrée with spicy Mexican corn muffins (see recipe in Muffins section) and chilled shrimp gazpacho soup (see recipe in Fruits, Vegetables, Soups section). *Serves 8.*

Variations: Try whole wheat flour tortillas and use fully cooked ground turkey or chicken in place of ham.

The Quail's Nest Bed and Breakfast

Nancy and Gregory Diaz
PO Box 221, Main Street
Danby, Vermont 05739
Tel: (802) 293-5099

ABOUT THE B&B

A circa 1835 country inn, The Quail's Nest is located just off Route 7 in Danby, Vermont — a quiet and picturesque town reminiscent of the last century. The inn's six rooms are wrapped in the warmth of hand-made quilts, and a delightful home-cooked breakfast will tempt you out of those quilts each morning! To the east of the inn is the magnificent Green Mountains National Forest, which boasts some of the finest swimming, hiking, fishing, hunting, and skiing in Vermont. Located 13 miles to the south, Manchester, Vermont, features factory outlet shopping, while crafts and antiques can be purchased right in the heart of Danby. A wide variety of restaurants to satisfy every palate are either a short drive or walk away.

SEASON

all year

ACCOMMODATIONS

four rooms with private baths; two rooms with shared bath

Cheddar Cheese Pie

"This recipe was given to me by my cousin and very special friend, Diana M. Spiller. It is rich in flavor and a favorite of all who try it." — Nancy Diaz

1 unbaked 9" pastry shell, chilled
4 eggs
1 cup heavy cream
1 cup milk
½ teaspoon salt
⅛ teaspoon Tabasco sauce
1 cup shredded Vermont cheddar cheese

Preheat oven to 450°F. Prick pastry shell with fork, then bake 10 minutes or until lightly browned. Reduce oven to 325°F. In a medium bowl, beat eggs, cream, milk, salt, and Tabasco sauce together. Spread cheese over bottom of pastry shell. Pour in egg mixture and bake 45 minutes. Check if ready by inserting a knife in the center — if it comes out clean, it's done. **Serves 6.**

Cheddar Creamed Eggs on Toast

4 slices bacon
1 medium chopped onion
1½ cups sharp cheddar cheese
3+ tablespoons all-purpose flour
1½ cups milk
6 sliced hard-cooked eggs

Brown bacon, crumble, and reserve. Drain most of drippings from skillet. Sauté onion in remaining drippings. Combine cheese and flour and add to onion in skillet. Add milk and stir on medium heat until mixture thickens. Fold in eggs and crumbled bacon. Serve over toast. *Serves 4.*

Millikan

Bedford's Covered Bridge Inn

Martha and Greg Lau
R.D. 1, Box 196
Schellsburg, Pennsylvania, 15559
Tel: (814) 733-4093

ABOUT THE B&B

Situated near Exit 11 of I-76 (the Pennsylvania Turnpike), Bedford's Covered Bridge Inn borders 4000-acre Shawnee State Park, a lovely trout stream, and the Colvin covered bridge. From this idyllic location, guests can pursue hiking, biking, fishing, cross-country skiing, birding, and antique hunting right from the inn's door. Nearby swimming and boating on Shawnee Lake, visits to Old Bedford Village and Bedford's historic district, driving tours, downhill skiing at Blue Knob Resort, and tours of Bedford's 14 covered bridges round out the list of local activities. Inside the inn, the Lau's attention to detail creates an atmosphere that is comfortable and inviting. The historic farmhouse (circa 1823) boasts six guest rooms with private baths, traditional and country decor, and memorable breakfasts. "There's no doubt what everyone's favorite activity is," say Martha and Greg, "sitting on the inn's wraparound porch and wishing for a life in Bedford County, too!"

SEASON

all year

ACCOMMODATIONS

six rooms with private baths;
one cottage for couples
or families

Anchuca

May Burns
1010 First East Street
Vicksburg, Mississippi 39180
Tel: (800) 469-2597 or
(601) 631-6800

ABOUT THE B&B

"*Anchuca*," *which means "my happy home" in the Amerindian language of Choctaw, is an opulent, gas-lighted Greek Revival mansion that has been lovingly restored to its original elegance. Listed on the National Register of Historic Places, Anchuca houses magnificent period antiques and artifacts and recreates the grandeur of yesterday in all its splendor. Beautifully landscaped gardens and brick courtyards surround the mansion, swimming pool, and covered Jacuzzi hot tub. All six rooms and suites have private baths, cable TV with HBO, and private telephones. Children of all ages and small pets are welcome. Anchuca is located in historic Vicksburg, Mississippi — site of one of the most important battles of the Civil War and home of the Vicksburg National Military Park. The mansion is close to the Military Park, Mississippi River boating, and new gambling casinos.*

SEASON

all year

ACCOMMODATIONS

six rooms (including one suite)
with private baths

Cheese Grits

3 cups water
1 teaspoon salt
1 cup old-fashioned grits
½ cup margarine
6 ozs. Cheese Whiz

Bring 3 cups of water to a brisk boil, adding salt and grits. Reduce heat to low, cover, and cook for 15 – 20 minutes, stirring occasionally. Stir in margarine and Cheese Whiz. Remove from heat and serve. *Serves 6.*

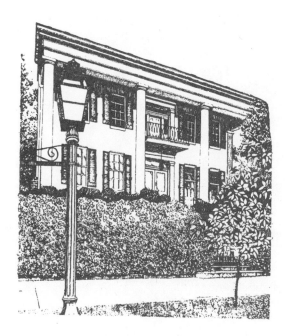

Chicken Crepes

"These are sure to warm you up on a cold winter's morning!" — Shirley Sparks

Crepe batter:
1 cup all-purpose flour
¼ teaspoon baking powder
¼ teaspoon salt
1¼ cups milk
1 egg
1 tablespoon melted oleo (or margarine)

Chicken filling:
3 tablespoons oleo (or margarine)
3 tablespoons all-purpose flour
½ teaspoon salt
2 cups chicken broth
1½ cups chopped cooked chicken
⅔ cup chopped apple
½ cup chopped celery
2 tablespoons chopped or grated onions

(continued on next page)

Roses and Lace Inn

Shirley and Mark Sparks
Highway 231 South, PO Box 852
Ashville, Alabama 35953
Tel: (205) 594-4366

ABOUT THE B&B

Built in 1890, this spacious three-story bed and breakfast is located in the center of quaint Ashville, Alabama. Listed on the National Register of Historic Places, the house is resplendent with Victorian elegance. Features such as wraparound porches, balconies, stained glass windows, carved mantles, winding stairs, and period furniture make Roses and Lace an excellent example of the area's craftsmanship and architectural integrity. Roses and Lace is a family-owned business and innkeepers Shirley and Mark look forward to your visit. Come and relax, walk to town and shop for antiques, or shop at the famed Boaz outlet city, just 30 minutes away.

SEASON

all year

ACCOMMODATIONS

two rooms with private baths;
two rooms with shared baths

To make batter: Sift together flour, baking powder, and salt. Stir in remaining ingredients and beat until smooth. Lightly butter a 7 – 8" skillet and heat until bubbly. For each crepe, pour ¼ cup batter into the skillet. Immediately rotate skillet until the thin batter covers the bottom like a film. Cook until light brown. Using a wide spatula, run it around the edges and flip. Cook other side. Cool crepes and stack with waxed paper between each crepe. *Tip:* These can be made in advance and warmed up the next day.

To make filling: Preheat oven to 350°F. Heat oleo (or margarine) over low heat until melted. Blend in flour and salt. Cook low, stirring constantly, until it's smooth and bubbly. Remove from heat. Stir in broth. Heat to boiling, stirring constantly. Continue boiling and stirring for 1 minute. In a separate bowl, mix chicken, apple, celery, onions, and ¾ cup chicken broth mixture. Place scant ½ cup chicken mixture in center of each crepe; roll up. Place crepes seam side down in an ungreased baking dish. Pour remaining chicken broth mixture over crepes. Bake uncovered until hot (about 20 minutes). *Serves 4.*

Coddled Eggs

1 egg
2 tablespoons shredded cheddar cheese
2 tablespoons shredded Mozzarella cheese
1 slice cooked and crumbled bacon

Spray inside of a medium coddler with non-stick cooking spray. Sprinkle crumbled bacon in bottom. Add 1 tablespoon of each cheese; break in egg, add remaining cheese. Screw on top and drop gently into boiling water to cover. Boil for 10 minutes and serve with fresh bread. *Serves 1.*

Alexander Hamilton House

Barbara Notarius
49 Van Wyck Street
Croton-on-Hudson, NY 10520
Tel: (914) 271-6737

ABOUT THE B&B

The Alexander Hamilton House (circa 1889) is a sprawling Victorian home situated on a cliff overlooking the Hudson River. Grounds include a mini orchard and in-ground pool. The home has many period antiques and collections and offers: a queen-bedded suite with a fireplace in the living room; a double-bedded suite with fireplace and a small sitting room; two large rooms with queen beds (one with an additional day bed); and a bridal chamber with king-size bed, Jacuzzi, entertainment center, pink marble fireplace, and skylights. A one-bedroom apartment is also available with a double bed, living room/kitchen, private bath, and separate entrance. Nearby attractions include West Point, the Sleepy Hollow Restorations, Lyndhurst Mansion, Boscobel (a fabulous Federal period restoration), the Rockefeller mansion, hiking, biking, sailing, and New York City (under an hour away by train or car).

SEASON

all year

ACCOMMODATIONS

six rooms with private baths

The Heirloom

Melisande Hubbs and
Patricia Cross
214 Shakeley Lane
Ione, California 95640
Tel: (209) 274-4468

ABOUT THE B&B

*D*own a country lane to an *expansive English romantic garden is a touch of the old south. The Heirloom is a brick, two-story southern antebellum home, circa 1863, located in the heart of California gold country. It was built by Virginians who came to California during the Gold Rush to be merchants in Ione, the supply center to the mining camps of Amador County. Sweet magnolias, wisteria, hammocks, croquet, verandas, cozy fireplaces, and heirloom antiques (including a historic piano) await you, not to mention a royal breakfast and gracious hospitality. Near the inn are over 20 wineries, Gold Rush historical points, museums, and nature walks, and opportunities for gourmet dining, gold panning, gliding, and hiking.*

SEASON

all year

ACCOMMODATIONS

four rooms with private baths;
two rooms with shared bath

Cornmeal Soufflé

"This corn recipe reflects the combined influence of the south, the gold miners, and the American Indians on our county."
— Melisande Hubbs

3 tablespoons butter
2 tablespoons chopped green onions
¼ cup yellow cornmeal
½ teaspoon oregano
1¼ cups milk
¾ cup grated Monterey Jack cheese
4 separated eggs

Preheat oven to 350°F. Melt butter in a medium saucepan. Sauté onions. Add cornmeal and oregano. Add milk to make a sauce. Add cheese, then egg yolks. Stir to blend. Whip egg whites to soft peaks. Fold into cornmeal mixture. Pour into 2 pint-size (2-cup) soufflé dishes. Set in a pan of water. Bake for 45 minutes. *Serves 4.*

Cornucopia's Croissants à l'Orange

(Recipe from Breakfast at Nine, Tea at Four: Favorite Recipes From The Mainstay Inn.)

6 croissants
9-oz. jar orange marmalade
3 ozs. orange juice
5 eggs
1 cup heavy cream
1 teaspoon almond extract
Strawberries
Mandarin orange sections

Cut croissants in half lengthwise and place bottom halves in buttered 12 x 9" oven-proof dish. Thin marmalade with orange juice and spoon over each bottom half, saving a little to be used as a glaze. Replace croissant tops. Beat eggs, cream, and almond extract. Pour over top of the croissants. Spoon some thinned marmalade over top. Soak overnight. Remove from fridge ¾ hour before baking. Bake in a preheated 350°F oven for about 25 minutes. Serve hot, and garnish with strawberries and mandarin orange sections. *Serves 6.*

The Mainstay Inn

Sue and Tom Carroll
635 Columbia Avenue
Cape May, New Jersey 08204
Tel: (609) 884-8690

ABOUT THE B&B

According to the Washington Post, "The jewel of them all has got to be the Mainstay." Built by a pair of wealthy gamblers in 1872, this elegant, exclusive clubhouse is now among the premier B&B inns in the country. The Mainstay now comprises three historic buildings on one of the most beautiful streets of the historic Cape May district. Guests enjoy 16 antique-filled rooms and suites (some with fireplaces and whirlpool baths), three parlors, spacious gardens, and rocker-filled verandas. Breakfast and afternoon tea served daily. Beautiful beaches, historic attractions, biking, birding, golf, and tennis are all available in Cape May, a National Historic Landmark community.

SEASON

all year

ACCOMMODATIONS

16 rooms (including seven suites) with private baths

The Babbling Brook Inn

Helen King
1025 Laurel Street
Santa Cruz, California 95060
Tel: (800) 866-1131 or
(408) 427-2437

ABOUT THE B&B

Cascading waterfalls, a meandering creek, and a romantic gazebo grace an acre of gardens, pines, and redwoods surrounding this secluded inn. Built in 1909 on the foundation of an 1870 tannery, a 1790 grist mill, and a 2000-year old Indian fishing village, the Babbling Brook features rooms in country French decor, all with private bath, telephone, and television, and most with cozy fireplace, private deck, and outside entrance. Included in your stay is a large, country breakfast and afternoon wine and cheese, where Helen's prize-winning cookies await you on the tea cart in front of a roaring fireplace. Two blocks off Highway 1, the Babbling Brook is within walking distance to the beach, wharf, boardwalk, shops, tennis, running paths, and historic homes. Three golf courses and 200 restaurants are within 15 minutes' drive. A world record-holding angler, Mrs. Pacific Palisades 1955, one-time international tour organizer, and mother of six, Helen King has happily found her niche as a gourmet cook and owner/innkeeper of this award-winning B&B.

SEASON

all year

ACCOMMODATIONS

12 rooms with private baths

Cottage Cheese Delight

"We receive many requests for this recipe. Leftovers make great fillings for crepes — simply roll slices over about 1 x 3" and you've got yourself a blintz!" — Helen King

1 cup milk
1 cup flour
1 pint low-fat cottage cheese
6 eggs
½ cup melted butter
1 lb. grated Monterey Jack cheese
Croissant or bread crumbs
Sour cream
Fruit conserve or fresh fruit of your choice

Preheat oven to 350°F. Blend milk, flour, cottage cheese, eggs, and butter. Grease an 8 x 8" or 9 x 9" pan and sprinkle with grated cheese. Pour egg mixture over and dust with crumbs. Bake 45 minutes. Cut into squares and top with sour cream and fruit conserve or fresh fruit. *Tip:* If doubling recipe, bake in a 13 x 9" pan for 1 hour and 20 minutes. You can bake it a day ahead, then reheat individual slices in the microwave oven (1 minute on high per square). *Serves 12 – 16.*

Country Breakfast Pie

4 slices bacon, cut in half
2 cups frozen hash brown potatoes
¼ cup minced green bell peppers
¼ cup minced onions
6 large lightly beaten eggs
¼ cup milk
½ teaspoon salt
⅛ teaspoon pepper
1 cup shredded cheddar cheese

Place bacon in a 9" glass Pyrex pie plate; cover with paper towels. Microwave on high 3 – 4 minutes or until crisp. Remove bacon, reserving drippings in pie plate. Crumble bacon and set aside. Spread potatoes, green peppers, and onions in pie plate. Microwave uncovered on high for 6 – 7 minutes. Combine eggs, milk, salt, and pepper. Pour over potato mixture. Cover with heavy-duty plastic wrap and microwave on high 6 – 7 minutes, giving dish a quarter turn after 3 minutes. Sprinkle with cheddar cheese and bacon; cover and microwave on high 1 – 2 minutes. Let stand 5 minutes, then cut into wedges.
Serves 6.

Historic Oakwood Bed and Breakfast

Naomi and Al Kline
715 East North Street
Talladega, Alabama 35160
Tel: (205) 362-0662

ABOUT THE B&B

Built in 1847, this antebellum home is listed on the National Register of Historic Places and furnished with many heirloom antiques. The house was commissioned by Andrew Bowie, the first mayor of Talladega. Enjoy browsing through the antique stores in the area, visiting the International Motorsports Hall of Fame, or exploring the lovely DeSoto Caverns. A public golf course and tennis courts and beautiful Cheaha Mountain State Park are nearby. The hearty breakfast your hosts serve features home-made biscuits and southern grits. Al and Naomi are musicians; Al is a retired operatic tenor and Naomi a pianist and organist. Traveling businesspeople and vacationers alike will enjoy this retreat into the quiet elegance of a bygone era.

SEASON

all year

ACCOMMODATIONS

one room with private bath;
two rooms with shared bath

Papaya Paradise

Jeanette and Bob Martz
395 Auwinala Road
Kailua, Oahu, Hawaii 96734
Tel: (808) 261-0316

ABOUT THE B&B

If you're looking for privacy, quiet, and miles of beautiful, uncrowded white sandy beach, look no further than Papaya Paradise. Located 20 miles from Honolulu airport on the windward side of Oahu in Kailua, Papaya Paradise is removed from the hectic activity of Waikiki yet near all major attractions and Waikiki nightlife. Tropical rattan and wicker guest rooms have a private entrance, private bath, two comfortable beds and lounge chairs, ceiling fans, air conditioning, and cable TV, and open onto a 20 x 40 foot swimming pool and Jacuzzi surrounded by tropical plants, trees, and flowers. Breakfast is served on the lanai overlooking the pool and Jacuzzi. For your convenience, your hosts furnish beach towels, hats, mat, chairs, coolers, boogie boards, a refrigerator and microwave oven, and a small library with relaxing reading chairs.

SEASON

all year

ACCOMMODATIONS

two rooms with private baths

Creamed Beef on Toast

"When I was in the military service, my favorite breakfast was what they called S-O-S. I've worked with the basic recipe over the years and came up with this winner." — Bob Martz

1 lb. ground round beef
1 teaspoon each dried basil, oregano, and thyme
Salt and pepper to taste
4 tablespoons chopped onions
5 tablespoons margarine
3 tablespoons all-purpose flour
2 cups hot milk (heated in microwave oven)
1 tablespoon sherry or cognac

In a heavy 10 or 12" skillet, cook ground round with basil, salt, and pepper. Remove meat mixture from skillet. In the same skillet, sauté onions in margarine until transparent (about 8 minutes). Add the flour, stirring with a wooden spoon approximately 1 minute. Add hot milk all at once, stirring constantly with a wire whisk until thickened. Remove from heat, stir in the sherry or cognac, and add meat mixture. Serve over toast or biscuits. Mixture will keep warm in the oven covered for 2 hours. *Tip:* For a healthier meal, use non-fat milk and no-cholesterol margarine. *Serves 4.*

Creamed Eggs with Smoked Salmon in Puff Pastry

4 puff pastry shells
8 large eggs
2 tablespoons butter
4 – 6 tablespoons chopped smoked salmon (or diced ham)
2 tablespoons each chopped red and green bell peppers
2 tablespoons sour cream
Hollandaise sauce mix
Parsley or paprika (optional)

Bake puff pastry shells according to package directions. Cool and prepare for serving.

Beat eggs until light and fluffy. In a frying pan, melt butter, then add salmon and peppers. Sauté until just barely limp. Add eggs, cooking and stirring until almost done, Add sour cream, and stir. Do not let eggs get too dry but remove from heat while still creamy. Spoon mixture into each pastry shell, allowing some of the egg mixture to overflow onto the plate. Cover with 2 – 3 tablespoons of hollandaise sauce, then sprinkle with parsley or paprika. Serve with fresh fruit in season (melon is excellent). *Serves 4.*

"An Elegant Victorian Mansion" Bed & Breakfast Inn

Lily and Doug Vieyra
1406 'C' Street
Eureka, California 95501
Tel: (800) 386-1888 or
(707) 442-5594

ABOUT THE B&B

Featured in many newspapers and magazines — not to mention on television and radio — this restored national historic landmark offers Eureka's most prestigious and luxurious accommodations. Spirited and eclectic innkeepers provide lavish hospitality in the splendor of a meticulously restored 1888 Victorian masterpiece, complete with original family antique furnishings. The inviting guest rooms offer both graceful refinement and modern-day comfort, individually decorated with Victorian elegance. Guests enjoy gourmet breakfasts and a heavenly night's sleep on top-quality mattresses, as well as secured parking and laundry service. Located in a quiet, historic residential neighborhood overlooking the city and Humboldt Bay, the non-smoking inn is near carriage rides, bay cruises, restaurants, and the theater, and is just minutes from giant Redwood parks, coastal beaches, ocean charters, and horseback riding.

SEASON

all year

ACCOMMODATIONS

one suite with private bath;
three rooms with shared baths

Dunscroft By-The-Sea

Alyce and Wally Cunningham
24 Pilgrim Road
Harwich Port, Cape Cod,
Massachusetts 02646
Tel: (800) 432-4345 or
(508) 432-0810

ABOUT THE B&B

With its beautiful, private mile-long beach on the warmest-water side of Cape Cod, Dunscroft By-The-Sea offers the ultimate romantic splurge. Tastefully decorated in a love theme, Dunscroft has a delightful surprise for you 'round every corner: a puffed heart adorns a canopied bed, a diminutive cupid greets you by the front door, and richly bound verses of love on your bedside table inspire the senses by candlelight. Beautiful king and queen bed chambers (including canopies, four-posters, or sleighs), in-room private baths and fireplaces, two suites with a private entrance, and charming honeymoon cottage with fireplace await your indulgence. To complete the romantic setting, a select bottle of sparkling champagne, a heart-laden basket of luscious, red strawberries and hand-dipped chocolates, and one lovely long-stemmed rose en vase may be ordered for your room upon arrival. Bountiful, full breakfast included.

SEASON

all year

ACCOMMODATIONS

eight rooms with private baths;
one honeymoon cottage with
private bath

Dunscroft's Baked Eggs with Pineapple

Butter (not margarine)
24 – 30 slices crisped and drained bacon
¾ cup sour cream
12 eggs
Dill weed
12 pineapple rings

Butter a 12-cup muffin pan. Place 2 – 2½" slices of bacon in bottom of each muffin cup. Place 1 dollop of sour cream over bacon in muffin cups. Break 1 egg over sour cream, and sprinkle dill weed over top of eggs. Bake 10 – 15 minutes in a preheated 350°F oven. Heat pineapple rings in the microwave oven until hot. Use a spatula to remove eggs from muffin pan and place each on a hot pineapple ring. Serve with buttered, toasted English muffins. *Tips:* To adjust recipe, figure 2 eggs per person and 1 pineapple ring per egg. Try chili sauce instead of sour cream. *Serves 6 (makes 12 baked eggs).*

Easiest Turkey and Ham Timbales

(Recipe from The Best of High Meadows — A Selected Recipe Collection.)

2 ozs. cubed turkey, ham, or chicken
2 ozs. shredded sharp cheddar cheese
2 – 3 eggs
½ cup milk
2 tablespoons chopped scallions
½ teaspoon paprika
½ teaspoon white pepper
1 teaspoon grated Parmesan cheese

Preheat oven to 375°F. Lightly grease 2 6-oz. custard cups and place cubed meat and shredded cheese on the bottom of each cup. Mix eggs, milk, scallions, paprika, and pepper, and pour half into each custard cup (on top of meat and cheese). Top with Parmesan cheese and bake for 30 minutes. Serve hot. *Serves 2.*

High Meadows Inn

Peter Sushka and Jae Abbitt
High Meadows Lane,
Route 4, Box 6
Scottsville, Virginia
24590
Tel: (804) 286-2218

ABOUT THE B&B

As Virginia's only inn that is on the National Register of Historic Homes and has a renaissance farm vineyard, High Meadows offers a rare opportunity to experience 170 years of architectural history and 10 years of new viticultural growth. High Meadows is a grand, unique house, where guests are welcomed with champagne and stay in rooms furnished with period antiques and art, each with private bath. The innkeepers' many special touches and attention to detail make your visit one to be remembered. Enjoy the simplicity of nature on the 50 surrounding acres of gardens, footpaths, forests, and ponds. Owner/chef Peter Sushka ensures that dining at High Meadows is just as pleasurable as lodging there. Start with a breakfast of fresh orange juice, a variety of home-made breads, muffins, and scones, fresh fruit, gourmet egg dishes, and coffee or tea. End your day with a multi-course dinner, offering distinctive northern European and Mediterranean dishes.

SEASON

all year

ACCOMMODATIONS

11 rooms (including four suites) with private baths; two-room cottage with private bath

Caledonia Farm — 1812

Phil Irwin
47 Dearing Road
Flint Hill, Virginia 22627
Tel: (800) BNB-1812 or
(703) 675-3693

ABOUT THE B&B

With Virginia's Blue Ridge Mountains as a backdrop, Caledonia Farm offers its guests a beautiful setting amid scenic pasturelands surrounded by stone fences. The farm's federal-style house and companion summer kitchen were completed in 1812. Restoration was completed in 1965, with the original two-foot-thick stone walls and 32-foot-long beams remaining intact along with the original mantels, paneled windows, and wide pine floors. The winter kitchen's huge fireplace provides a delightful atmosphere during cool seasons while three porches offer a variety of views in the warmer months. Guest rooms are air conditioned, and have working fireplaces, individual heat control, and fine double beds. The B&B is called Caledonia (the mythological name for Scotland) to honor the original immigrants to this magnificent area.

SEASON

all year

ACCOMMODATIONS

two suites with private baths;
two rooms with shared bath

Eggs Benedict Caledonia

2 English muffins, cut in half
Butter or margarine
4 slices Canadian bacon or ham
4 poached eggs (whites set with yolks liquid)
Hollandaise sauce mix
3 tablespoons lemon juice

Toast or broil muffin halves and spread with butter. Top with slices of Canadian bacon or ham, then keep warm in 160°F oven. Place poached eggs on muffins. Prepare hollandaise sauce using 3 tablespoons lemon juice instead of water. Cover eggs with sauce. Garnish as desired. *Serves 2.*

Eggs in a Nest

1 tablespoon butter
2 (preferably thick) slices white or whole wheat bread
2 eggs

With a round cookie cutter, cut out center of each bread slice. Set aside centers. In a buttered frying pan, fry one side of bread slices. Flip slices over. Drop 1 egg in the middle of each slice. Leave for 1 minute, then flip back to first side for a few seconds. Remove from pan. Fry bread centers on both sides and place over eggs as a garnish. *Serves 1.*

Chalet Kilauea —
The Inn at Volcano

Lisha and Brian Crawford
PO Box 998
Volcano Village, Hawaii 96785
Tel: (808) 967-7786

ABOUT THE B&B

Explore treasures from around the world at Chalet Kilauea, a lush Hawaiian haven nestled in Volcano Village. Owners Lisha and Brian Crawford are international travelers who know the art of hospitality. At the inn, choose from superior rooms inspired by Oriental, African, or European themes, or the Treehouse Suite, with most featuring marble Jacuzzi tubs. Tempt your appetite with a candlelit, two-course gourmet breakfast featuring local and international cuisine. Luxuriate in the Jacuzzi, relax by the fireplace, peruse the library, or wander in the garden. The vacation homes are spacious, graced with charming decor, and are the ultimate in Volcano comfort. They are particularly suited for families, larger parties, and those seeking complete privacy. All offer a full kitchen and include afternoon tea and use of the Jacuzzi. Near the inn, you'll find Hawaii Volcanoes National Park, Black Sand Beach, and the city of Hilo with all its splendors. Opportunities abound for lava viewing, hiking, biking, golfing, swimming, bird watching, exploring, and just plain unwinding!

SEASON

all year

ACCOMMODATIONS

five rooms with private baths;
six vacation homes

Betsy and Karol Paterman
43 Highland Street
PO Box 719
Ashland, New Hampshire 03217
Tel: (603) 968-3775

ABOUT THE B&B

Come enjoy the gracious elegance of this beautifully restored 1890 Queen Anne home — from the cupola of the inn's tower and gingerbread wraparound veranda to the carved oak foyer and pocket doors. Each of the beautifully appointed bedrooms has its own distinctive mood, distinguished by unique interior design, period furniture, the fragrance of fresh flowers, and soft, fluffy robes. A memorable full breakfast is served in the dining room, consisting perhaps of eggs Benedict or eggs Neptune, Belgian waffles, thick French toast, ambrosia, juice, and the specialty of the house — strudel. After breakfast, take a walk or boat ride around famous Squam Lake (where the movie On Golden Pond was filmed) just a few minutes away, and enjoy all that the Lakes Region and White Mountains have to offer. Allow Betsy and Karol to provide hospitality with a warm smile and make you feel as though you're part of their family.

SEASON

all year

ACCOMMODATIONS

five rooms with private baths; two rooms with shared bath

Eggs Neptune

4 English muffins
4 ozs. crab meat (snow, king, or lobster meat)
8 eggs
Fresh dill

Poach eggs, then put in a bowl with ice water (they will keep overnight in the refrigerator). Toast muffins. Warm crab meat in the microwave oven or by placing in hot water for a few minutes, then squeezing out excess water. Place crab meat on muffins. Top with eggs heated in hot water for 2 minutes, and garnish with hollandaise sauce (see below) and fresh dill. *Serves 4.*

Hollandaise sauce:
2 egg yolks
1 tablespoon warm water
Juice of ¼ lemon
¼ lb. butter
Dash of cayenne pepper

Mix egg yolks, water, and lemon juice and whip for 2 minutes with wire whisk. In a double boiler, melt butter. Put aside and keep warm, but not hot. Put egg mixture in a bowl and set on top of double boiler. Whip constantly with wire whisk and add butter in a steady, very slow stream (otherwise egg mixture will break). Sauce is ready when it reaches the consistency of thick molasses. Add cayenne pepper.

Eggs St. Moritz

½ lb. shredded Swiss (or Jarlsberg or Havarti or Edam) cheese
2 tablespoons white Worcestershire sauce
½ cup heavy cream
12 well-beaten eggs
Sprinkle of fresh dill

Preheat oven to 350°F. Spread shredded cheese in the bottom of a buttered or sprayed 13 x 9" pan. Whip Worcestershire sauce into the cream, then divide into 2 equal portions of ¼ cup each. Pour one ¼ cup of cream immediately into pan and reserve the rest. Beat eggs and pour over the cheese and cream in the pan. Pour the second ¼ cup of cream over the top of the eggs. Sprinkle with dill and bake for 35 – 45 minutes until eggs are set and top is golden and puffy. Garnish with fresh dill.
Tip: This dish can be served right from the pan on a buffet or cut into squares and served on individual plates. *Serves 9 – 12.*

Ashling Cottage

Goodi and Jack Stewart
106 Sussex Avenue
Spring Lake, New Jersey 07762
Tel: (800) 237-1877 or
(908) 449-3553

ABOUT THE B&B

For generations, rambling Victorian homes have fronted the spring-fed lakes from which Spring Lake, New Jersey, gets its name. Tree-lined walkways surround the lakes, and wooden foot bridges connect grassy areas of park. Sun, sand, surf, and serenity in equal measure — Spring Lake offers all this and Ashling Cottage, too. Since 1877, the visiting gentry have enjoyed sumptuous breakfasts on the porches of this lovely and intimate seaside inn, overlooking both ocean and lake. Today, the tradition continues with casual hospitality and personal attention offered for your vacationing pleasure. While leisure activities abound (such as golf, tennis, biking, horseback riding, and sightseeing in nearby New York and Philadelphia), the most delightful feature of this inn and this town is the guilt-free ability to do absolutely nothing!

SEASON

May to October

ACCOMMODATIONS

eight rooms with private baths;
two rooms with shared bath

The Voss Inn

Frankee and Bruce Muller
319 South Willson
Bozeman, Montana 59715
Tel: (406) 587-0982

ABOUT THE B&B

Built in 1883 by a prominent journalist and mining engineer named Mat Alderson, The Voss Inn is an elegant brick Victorian with a spacious front porch overlooking an English cottage perennial garden. The six guest rooms (each with private bath) and the guest parlor are furnished in Victorian antiques. Guests eat a full gourmet breakfast in the privacy of their rooms. The antique radiator bun warmer is a star attraction of the upstairs buffet area where guests help themselves to an elegant fruit plate, freshly baked muffins or cinnamon rolls, and their choice of an egg/meat dish served in individual ramekins or hot or cold cereal. Owners Frankee and Bruce Muller previously operated a photographic safari camp in the African country of Botswana. Bruce now guides customized trips into Yellowstone National Park and the surrounding areas. Their special interests include wildlife, fly fishing, skiing, golf, and, of course, gourmet cooking — all of which can be enjoyed to the utmost in Bozeman.

SEASON

all year

ACCOMMODATIONS

six rooms with private baths

Eggs with Potatoes and Cheese Sauce

Potatoes:
3 large russet potatoes, scrubbed and washed
1 small chopped onion
4 chopped parsley sprigs
½ cup melted butter
Salt and pepper to taste

Cheese sauce:
½ cup butter
½ cup all-purpose flour
¾ teaspoon salt
¼ teaspoon pepper
¾ teaspoon mustard powder
3 cups milk
1 lb. grated medium cheddar cheese

8 eggs
8 strips thickly cut bacon, cooked crisp and crumbled

(continued on next page)

To prepare potatoes: Grate potatoes directly into a bowl of cold salted water. Let stand 5 minutes. Drain, rinse, and pat dry with paper towels. Mix with chopped onion, parsley, and melted butter. Bake in a 13 x 8" glass baking dish at 400°F until brown and crispy (about 1 hour).

To prepare cheese sauce: Melt the butter in a large saucepan over medium heat. Add the flour and stir vigorously, then add the salt, pepper, and mustard powder while still stirring. Stir for 2 minutes. Add 1 cup of the milk slowly while stirring constantly (adding more milk as necessary to keep mixture from thickening too much). Add cheese to mixture and reduce heat to medium-low. Let cheese melt completely, stirring constantly, and add as much of the remaining milk to thin sauce slightly.

To assemble: Preheat oven to 350°F. Spray 8 8-oz. ramekins with cooking spray. Place a handful (approximately ½ cup) of potatoes in the bottom of each ramekin. Top potatoes with ⅓ cup of cheese sauce, making a well in the center with the back of a spoon. Break an egg in the center. Top with crumbled bacon. Bake for 25 minutes or until egg white is fully cooked and yolk is still soft. *Serves 8.*

Golden Maple Inn

Jo and Dick Wall
Wolcott Village, Vermont
05680-0035
Tel: (800) 639-5234 or
(802) 888-6614

ABOUT THE B&B

Originally the home of prominent mill owner H.B. Bundy, this historic 1865 B&B is nestled alongside northern Vermont's Lamoille River — famous for excellent trout fishing and quiet canoeing. Guests can read or doze in the library, work a picture puzzle in the parlor, or listen to the gurgle of the river from the comfort of an Adirondack chair. Jo and Dick's delightful candlelit breakfasts include fresh-ground coffees, teas, juice, fresh fruit in season, home-made granolas, and a scrumptious daily specialty entrée, all prepared in their country kitchen from only the finest local ingredients. To complete the day, teas and sweets are served to guests each evening in the library and parlor. Country walks, trout fishing, canoeing, biking, and back-country skiing are all available right from the inn. Golden Maple is located near the historic Fisher Covered Railroad Bridge, Bread & Puppet Museum, Cabot Creamery, Ben & Jerry's Ice Cream Factory, and the shops of Stowe Village.

SEASON

all year

ACCOMMODATIONS

three rooms (including one suite) with private baths

Festive Holiday Eggs

"A very old Wall family recipe traditionally served on Christmas morning." — Dick Wall

1 dozen eggs
8 strips maple-smoked bacon
Garlic salt
Seasoned pepper
Crushed red pepper flakes
Parsley

Preheat oven to 325°F. Grease a 12-cup shallow muffin pan. Cut bacon crosswise into 1" squares and place 5 squares evenly around edge of each muffin cup, keeping half the bacon inside and half outside each cup. Break 1 egg into each cup. Add a dash of seasonings (to taste) onto each egg. Bake for 25 minutes. Carefully loosen baked eggs from cups with a sharp knife and lift with tablespoon onto paper towels to blot. Serve hot. *Serves 6 – 8.*

Feta, Phyllo, and Spinach Croustade

"This elegant-looking recipe is actually quite simple to do and never fails to impress our guests. Even those who generally don't care for spinach seem to love this dish." — Kay Merrell

8 sheets frozen phyllo dough (17 x 12" rectangles), thawed
½ cup finely chopped onions
3 tablespoons margarine or butter
10-oz. package frozen chopped spinach, thawed and
    squeezed dry
3 tablespoons all-purpose flour
¼ teaspoon dried crushed tarragon
⅛ teaspoon pepper
1 cup milk
2 eggs
1 cup creamed cottage cheese
½ cup crumbled feta cheese
2 tablespoons melted butter or margarine

(continued on next page)

The Summer House

Kay and David Merrell
158 Main Street
Sandwich, Massachusetts 02563
Tel: (508) 888-4991

ABOUT THE B&B

The Summer House is an elegant circa 1835 Greek Revival twice featured in Country Living magazine. It was owned by Hiram Dillaway, a prominent mold-maker and colorist at the Boston & Sandwich Glass Factory. Large, sunny bedchambers feature antiques, hand-stitched quilts, and working fireplaces. Stroll to dining, shops, museums, galleries, pond and gristmill, and boardwalk to beach. Bountiful breakfasts change daily and include freshly ground coffee, tea, fruit juice, and fresh fruit served in stemware. Entrées of frittata, stuffed French toast, quiche, or omelets are accompanied by scones, puff pastry, muffins, or fruit cobblers. Dishes are enhanced with vegetables, berries, and herbs from the inn's garden. English-style afternoon tea is served at an umbrella table in the garden. Boston, Newport, Providence, Martha's Vineyard, and Nantucket make pleasant day trips. Innkeepers Kay and David Merrell (former executive secretary and aerospace engineer respectively) enjoy woodworking, gardening, quilting, jogging, backpacking, and the tranquility of Cape Cod.

SEASON

all year

ACCOMMODATIONS

one room with private bath;
four rooms with shared baths

Remove phyllo dough from freezer the night before and place in refrigerator to thaw.

Preheat oven to 350°F. In a large non-stick skillet, sauté onions in margarine or butter until tender. Add squeezed spinach, breaking up with a fork. Stir in flour, tarragon, and pepper; add milk. Cook and stir on low heat until thick and bubbly. Lightly beat 2 eggs and add to skillet in a folding motion. When eggs have set, fold in cottage and feta cheese. Turn to lowest heat and assemble phyllo as follows.

Place a large non-stick pizza pan in the middle of your counter. Carefully remove phyllo dough from carton and unfold. Take 1 sheet and fold in thirds lengthwise. Place one end of folded sheet in center of pizza pan, extending the other end out over the side of the pan. Repeat with 7 more sheets, arranging them in spoke fashion evenly around pan. (The inner ends of each sheet should overlap in center of pan and should be about 3" apart at the outer ends of each spoke.)

Spread the filling in an 8" circle in the center of the phyllo dough. Lift the end of 1 phyllo strip and gently "bunch together" and place on top of filling. Repeat with the other 7 strips, leaving a 3" circle of filling in center exposed in center. Drizzle with 2 tablespoons melted butter and bake on middle shelf for about 15 minutes or until dough is golden brown. Cut into 8 wedges and serve immediately. *Serves 8.*

Grandma's Saucy Eggs on Toast

10-oz. can cream of mushroom soup, undiluted
1 cup half-and-half cream
1 tablespoon chopped pimiento
¼ teaspoon ground nutmeg
6 hard-cooked eggs, chopped
8 slices toast

Combine soup, half-and-half, pimiento, and nutmeg. Stir well, and cook over low heat until heated thoroughly. Stir in eggs. Heat until warm, stirring constantly. Spoon over toast. **Serves 4.**

Grandma's House Bed & Breakfast

Hilda and Charlie Hickman
734 Pollard Road
Kodak, Tennessee 37764
Tel: (800) 676-3512 or
(615) 933-3512

ABOUT THE B&B

Grandma's House is located at the base of the Great Smoky Mountains National Park, minutes away from the resort cities of Pigeon Forge and Gatlinburg. On a quiet country lane that leads to the French Broad River, Grandma's House is in the center of all East Tennessee attractions, including Knoxville (site of the 1982 World's Fair), Oak Ridge (Atomic City), Norris (site of Tennessee's first dam), and Dandridge (second oldest city in Tennessee). The large colonial style, two-story house is decorated with antiques, crafts, and many interesting heirlooms. Three spotless guest rooms, each with a private bath, are on the second floor. A country "loosen your belt" breakfast is served around the big oak table each morning. Your hosts are both native East Tennesseans with lots of southern hospitality to share with their guests. The motto at Grandma's House is, "guests at first, friends that last."

SEASON

all year

ACCOMMODATIONS

three rooms with private baths

Chalet Kilauea — The Inn at Volcano

Lisha and Brian Crawford
PO Box 998
Volcano Village, Hawaii 96785
Tel: (808) 967-7786

ABOUT THE B&B

Explore treasures from around the world at Chalet Kilauea, a lush Hawaiian haven nestled in Volcano Village. Owners Lisha and Brian Crawford are international travelers who know the art of hospitality. At the inn, choose from superior rooms inspired by Oriental, African, or European themes, or the Treehouse Suite, with most featuring marble Jacuzzi tubs. Tempt your appetite with a candlelit, two-course gourmet breakfast featuring local and international cuisine. Luxuriate in the Jacuzzi, relax by the fireplace, peruse the library, or wander in the garden. The vacation homes are spacious, graced with charming decor, and are the ultimate in Volcano comfort. They are particularly suited for families, larger parties, and those seeking complete privacy. All offer a full kitchen and include afternoon tea and use of the Jacuzzi. Near the inn, you'll find Hawaii Volcanoes National Park, Black Sand Beach, and the city of Hilo with all its splendors. Opportunities abound for lava viewing, hiking, biking, golfing, swimming, bird watching, exploring, and just plain unwinding!

SEASON

all year

ACCOMMODATIONS

five rooms with private baths; six vacation homes

Gujarati Indian Eggs with Broiled Tomato

2 beaten eggs
1 tablespoon water
1 teaspoon masala mix*
1 tablespoon butter
1 tomato, cut into ½" slices
Sprinkle of grated Parmesan cheese
Sprinkle of lemon pepper
Parsley
Asian chili sauce

* masala mix = equal parts ground coriander, cumin, turmeric, mild chili powder, and 3 parts mild curry powder

Combine eggs, water, and masala mix, and cook in a buttered frying pan as scrambled eggs or an omelet. Cover tomatoes with cheese and broil in the oven for a few minutes until done. Sprinkle cooked tomatoes with lemon pepper, and serve with eggs. Garnish with parsley and some chili sauce. *Serves 1.*

Ham and Swiss Stuffed Puff Pastry

(Recipe from What's Cooking at Carrington's Bluff.)

1 package (2 sheets) frozen puff pastry, thawed
1 tablespoon Dijon mustard
8 – 10 slices deli-sliced ham
8 – 10 slices deli-sliced Swiss cheese
1 beaten egg
1 tablespoon light cream

Preheat oven to 400°F. Unfold puff pastry. Spread mustard over 1 sheet of puff pastry. Cover with a layer of ham then a layer of cheese, alternating until all is used. Cover with other sheet of puff pastry. Whip together eggs and cream. Brush edges of pastry with egg mixture. Seal with fork. Cut slits in top with a sharp knife. Bake for 15 – 20 minutes or until golden brown and puffed. *Serves 8.*

Carrington's Bluff B&B

Gwen and David Fullbrook
1900 David Street
Austin, Texas 78705
Tel: (512) 479-0638

ABOUT THE B&B

The setting is Shoal Creek Bluff and an 1877 Texas farmhouse nestled in the arms of a 500-year-old oak tree. Enter innkeepers Gwen (from Texas) and David (from Britain), who transformed it into an English country B&B. Today, Carrington's Bluff B&B combines Texas hospitality with English charm to make your stay both unique and delightful. Upon arrival, you'll find yourself surrounded by rooms filled with English and American antiques, handmade quilts, and the sweet smell of potpourri. The 35-foot front porch beckons you to sit among the plants and flowers and enjoy the gentle breezes with your morning coffee and afternoon tea. The smell of fresh brewed gourmet coffee invites you to a breakfast that begins with fresh fruit and home-made granola served on fine English china. Home-made muffins or breads and a house specialty ensure you won't go away hungry. Carrington's Bluff is near the University of Texas and the State Capital grounds, and just minutes from parks, hiking and biking trails, shopping, and wonderful restaurants.

SEASON

all year

ACCOMMODATIONS

six rooms with private baths; two rooms with shared bath

Joyce and Bob Guerrera
2720 Colonial Drive
Pigeon Forge, Tennessee 37863
Tel: (615) 428-0370

ABOUT THE B&B

*D*elight in the true country charm of this antique-filled, two-story log home with its six uniquely decorated bedrooms. Enjoy an evening by the cozy fireplace or day dream on the front porch to the soothing sound of Mill Creek dancing by. Take a leisurely stroll around the three acres and enjoy the innumerable willows, hemlocks, and redbuds, or any of the beautiful gardens. Treat your taste buds to Day Dreams's bountiful country breakfast each morning. Perfect for family reunions and retreats, the inn is situated within minutes of the Pigeon Forge trolley and many action-packed attractions, including Dollywood, factory outlet shopping, horseback riding, golf, evening shows, and dinner theater.

SEASON

all year

ACCOMMODATIONS

six rooms with private baths

Hash Brown Casserole

2½ cups frozen hash brown potatoes, skillet-cooked
½ cup chopped broccoli
½ cup chopped tomatoes (or mild salsa)
2 tablespoons chopped (or dried) onions
Salt and pepper to taste
6 beaten eggs (or enough to cover casserole)
Milk
1 cup each grated cheddar and mozzarella cheese

Preheat oven to 350°F. Spray 13 x 9" pan with vegetable spray. Layer potatoes, broccoli, tomatoes, onions, and salt and pepper. Beat eggs and add a small amount of milk. Pour just enough to cover the layered ingredients in the pan. Cook for 30 minutes or until eggs are done. Remove from oven. Add grated cheeses and return to oven long enough for cheese to melt. Cut into squares and serve hot. *Tip:* For variety, try adding 2 slices chopped ham or 2 cooked, ground sausages to the layered ingredients. *Serves 6.*

Heart-Healthy Spinach Soufflé

The Heirloom

Melisande Hubbs and
Patricia Cross
214 Shakeley Lane
Ione, California 95640
Tel: (209) 274-4468

4 tablespoons butter or margarine
2 chopped green onions
2 cubes chicken bouillon
2 tablespoons all-purpose flour
½ teaspoon salt
½ teaspoon pepper
Dash of ground nutmeg
2 cups milk
1 cup Swiss cheese
2 10-oz. packages frozen spinach, cooked and squeezed dry
8 egg whites

Preheat oven to 350°F. Melt butter in a large saucepan. Sauté green onions. Add dry bouillon. Add flour and seasonings, and mix well. Add milk to make a sauce. When slightly thickened, add cheese. Heat until cheese is melted and mixed in well. Add spinach. Beat egg whites just until peaks are formed. Fold into spinach mixture. Pour into an ungreased soufflé dish or individual dishes. Place in a water bath. Bake for 40 – 50 minutes. *Serves 6.*

ABOUT THE B&B

Down a country lane to an expansive English romantic garden is a touch of the old south. The Heirloom is a brick, two-story southern antebellum home, circa 1863, located in the heart of California gold country. It was built by Virginians who came to California during the Gold Rush to be merchants in Ione, the supply center to the mining camps of Amador County. Sweet magnolias, wisteria, hammocks, croquet, verandas, cozy fireplaces, and heirloom antiques (including a historic piano) await you, not to mention a royal breakfast and gracious hospitality. Near the inn are over 20 wineries, Gold Rush historical points, museums, and nature walks, and opportunities for gourmet dining, gold panning, gliding, and hiking.

SEASON

all year

ACCOMMODATIONS

four rooms with private baths;
two rooms with shared bath

Hillside House Bed & Breakfast

Jo Ann, Bud, and Sue
1729 East 18th Street
Spokane, Washington 99203
Tel: (509) 534-1426 during the
day or (509) 535-1893 during
nights and weekends

ABOUT THE B&B

Situated on the South Hill of Spokane, Hillside House offers exquisite hospitality in a country setting that's only three miles from downtown. Overlooking city and mountains, this cozy and tastefully decorated house features antiques, including linens and dishes, and rooms with views. Your hosts Bud, Jo Ann, and Sue are third generation B&B innkeepers — Jo Ann's mother helped her mother host guests in 1916 in Rush City, Minnesota. Bud owns an engineering firm and lectures nationally to the construction/engineering industry, while Jo Ann operates a marketing firm. They enjoy cooking (having published a cookbook of their own), entertaining, and guiding guests to the area's most exciting places and events. Bud and Jo Ann also operate the Lazy Bee, a remote getaway near the Canadian border where they lead jeep safaris in the mountains.

SEASON

all year

ACCOMMODATIONS

two rooms with shared bath

Huevos Rancheros

(Recipe from Favorites from the Lazy Bee.)

"My husband Bud orders huevos rancheros at restaurants all around the country just to see what they come up with (some of the strangest concoctions have been found in the South!). Here's our hands-down favorite — an adaptation of a recipe from Bud's brother Gino, a charter yacht captain in the Virgin Islands." — Jo Ann Bender

6 corn tortillas (6" diameter)
½ cup vegetable oil
1 can refried beans
2 cups grated cheese (in order of preference: Longhorn, Monterey Jack, cheddar, or mozzarella)
6 eggs
2 cups chopped lettuce
Salsa or hot sauce
Sour cream
Cut-up tomatoes

Fry tortillas until crisp in hot oil. Drain on paper towels and keep warm in oven. Heat beans with 2 tablespoons of oil left over from frying tortillas. Spread beans in a thin or thick layer on tortillas. Cover tortilla shell with grated cheese. Fry eggs to taste. Plop an egg on each tortilla and serve with lettuce, salsa, sour cream, and tomatoes in bowls so each guest can serve him or herself as wished. *Serves 6.*

Impossible Pie

"We serve this dish on Sunday mornings alongside baked tomatoes, a variety of home-made muffins, fruit compotes, and blackberry cherry cobbler. Folks leave the table very happy and satisfied." — Dorsey Allison Comer

1 lb. mild sausage, browned, crumbled, and drained
⅓ cup chopped onions
½ cup fresh sliced mushrooms
1 cup mixture of fresh French sorrel, basil, and parsley, chopped
12-oz. package shredded mozzarella cheese
1 cup biscuit mix
4 eggs
2 cups milk
Paprika to taste

Preheat oven to 400°F. Layer sausage, onions, mushrooms, and herbs in a deep glass pie dish. Top with mozzarella cheese. Beat the remaining ingredients with a hand beater until smooth. Pour over layered ingredients, then sprinkle with paprika. Bake for about 45 minutes or until set. Let stand about 5 minutes before serving. *Serves 6.*

Sleepy Hollow Farm Bed & Breakfast

Beverley Allison and
Dorsey Allison Comer
16280 Blue Ridge Turnpike
Gordonsville, Virginia 22942
Tel: (800) 215-4804 or
(703) 832-5555

ABOUT THE B&B

Along the scenic and historic byway of Virginia Route 231, a red mailbox signals your arrival to Sleepy Hollow Farm. If you miss the mailbox, look for a green barn with a very red roof, a gazebo, a pond, and a brick house snoozing under trees in a sleepy hollow. Generations of farm families have lived here since the late 1700s, and today Sleepy Hollow Farm attracts a wide spectrum of guests, including many international sojourners. Memories to take home with you include the "Dolley Madison hospitality" of innkeepers Beverley Allison and Dorsey Allison Comer, the farm's pure spring water, and the commanding landscapes of surrounding horse, cattle, and sheep farms. And, unlike many B&Bs, this one is equipped to handle children.

SEASON

all year

ACCOMMODATIONS

four rooms (including one suite) with private baths; guest cottage with two suites and private baths

Glynn House
Victorian Inn

Betsy and Karol Paterman
43 Highland Street
PO Box 719
Ashland, New Hampshire 03217
Tel: (603) 968-3775

ABOUT THE B&B

Come enjoy the gracious elegance of this beautifully restored 1890 Queen Anne home — from the cupola of the inn's tower and gingerbread wrap-around veranda to the carved oak foyer and pocket doors. Each of the beautifully appointed bedrooms has its own distinctive mood, distinguished by unique interior design, period furniture, the fragrance of fresh flowers, and soft, fluffy robes. A memorable full breakfast is served in the dining room, consisting perhaps of eggs Benedict or eggs Neptune, Belgian waffles, thick French toast, ambrosia, juice, and the specialty of the house — strudel. After breakfast, take a walk or boat ride around famous Squam Lake (where the movie On Golden Pond was filmed) just a few minutes away, and enjoy all that the Lakes Region and White Mountains have to offer. Allow Betsy and Karol to provide hospitality with a warm smile and make you feel as though you're part of their family.

SEASON

all year

ACCOMMODATIONS

five rooms with private baths;
two rooms with shared bath

Italian Eggs with Asparagus and Smoked Ham

¼ cup butter
1 cup sliced mushrooms
¼ lb. premium smoked ham
1 clove chopped garlic
⅓ medium green bell pepper
½ lb. cut asparagus
8 eggs
1 tablespoon minced fresh basil
½ teaspoon dried oregano
Pinch of salt and pepper
⅓ teaspoon crushed red pepper (optional)
4 ozs. cream cheese
4 ozs. shredded mozzarella cheese
¼ cup grated Parmesan cheese

In a large skillet, heat ½ the butter. Add mushrooms, ham, garlic, and green pepper. Sauté over medium heat until vegetables are tender. Remove with slotted spoon and set aside. Blanch asparagus until crisp tender. Whisk together eggs, herbs, and seasonings. Add cream cheese in small pieces. Just before serving, heat remaining butter in skillet and add egg mixture, folding with spatula to blend cream cheese. When eggs are half set, add vegetable-ham mixture, mozzarella, parmesan, and drained asparagus. Continue to cook gently, folding with spatula until eggs are just done. Serve immediately. *Serves 8.*

Japanese Eggs

2 beaten eggs
1 tablespoon water
1 teaspoon Oriental sesame oil*
1 teaspoon black mustard seed
1 tablespoon butter

Combine ingredients and cook in a buttered frying pan as scrambled eggs. Serve with rice and garnish with fresh fruit. **Serves 1.**

*available at Oriental grocery stores.

Chalet Kilauea — The Inn at Volcano

Lisha and Brian Crawford
PO Box 998
Volcano Village, Hawaii 96785
Tel: (808) 967-7786

ABOUT THE B&B

Explore treasures from around the world at Chalet Kilauea, a lush Hawaiian haven nestled in Volcano Village. Owners Lisha and Brian Crawford are international travelers who know the art of hospitality. At the inn, choose from superior rooms inspired by Oriental, African, or European themes, or the Treehouse Suite, with most featuring marble Jacuzzi tubs. Tempt your appetite with a candlelit, two-course gourmet breakfast featuring local and international cuisine. Luxuriate in the Jacuzzi, relax by the fireplace, peruse the library, or wander in the garden. The vacation homes are spacious, graced with charming decor, and are the ultimate in Volcano comfort. They are particularly suited for families, larger parties, and those seeking complete privacy. All offer a full kitchen and include afternoon tea and use of the Jacuzzi. Near the inn, you'll find Hawaii Volcanoes National Park, Black Sand Beach, and the city of Hilo with all its splendors. Opportunities abound for lava viewing, hiking, biking, golfing, swimming, bird watching, exploring, and just plain unwinding!

SEASON

all year

ACCOMMODATIONS

five rooms with private baths;
six vacation homes

The Marlborough

Diana Smith
320 Woods Hole Road
Woods Hole, Massachusetts
02543
Tel: (508) 548-6218

ABOUT THE B&B

Threomantic Cape Cod cottage
complete with picket fence,
trellis, and garden set up on a hill
among the trees. Rooms have
private baths and are individually
decorated with quilts, coordinated
scented linens, and collectibles.
Gather for conversation, read, or
watch television in the large
comfortable parlor. Full gourmet
breakfast, including wonderfully
brewed coffee and teas, is served
outside by the kidney-shaped pool or
inside by the fireplace, depending on
the season. Informal afternoon tea is
served in season, while high tea is
served on Sundays in the off-season.
Excellent restaurants are nearby, as
is Woods Hole Oceanographic
Institute, beaches, shopping, bike
paths, and ferries to Martha's
Vineyard. Great starting point for
day trips to locations all over Cape
Cod and the islands, Plymouth,
Boston, and Providence. Innkeeper
Diana Smith enjoys helping guests
get the most out of their visit. A
computer consultant before
purchasing the inn, Diana enjoys
bicycle touring, hand needlework
(including quilting, cross-stitch,
and crewel) and cooking.

SEASON

all year

ACCOMMODATIONS

five rooms with private baths

Marlborough Egg-Stuffed Bakers

"This wonderful breakfast entrée is not only popular with my guests, it's easy to make and healthy, too." — Diana Smith

6 large scrubbed baking potatoes
½ cup melted butter
12 fork-beaten eggs
2 cups chopped broccoli, cooked and drained
2 tablespoons diced green onions or chives
1½ cups shredded Monterey Jack cheese

Bake potatoes in a preheated 400°F oven for 45 – 60 minutes. Test with a fork for doneness. Potatoes should be cooked, but firm. Cool slightly. Melt butter in a saucepan. Cut potatoes in half lengthwise. Run a knife around the inside edge of each potato, about ¼" inside the skin to loosen pulp and then scoop out pulp with a spoon, leaving a potato shell (save potato pulp for home fries or hash). Using a pastry brush, brush melted butter inside and outside of potato shells. Put shells back into the oven on a cookie sheet for 15 minutes to brown slightly.

(continued on next page)

Meanwhile, put remaining butter into a heavy skillet and heat until bubbly. Add eggs and stir until firm but not dry. Turn off the heat. Add broccoli and green onions. When potato shells have browned, remove from oven and fill with egg and broccoli mixture, dividing it equally between the 12 potato halves. Top with shredded cheese and place under a broiler until cheese is bubbly. Serve hot with warm corn muffins spread with green pepper jelly.

Tips: Egg substitute can be used in place of whole egg, margarine in place of butter, and low-sodium/low-fat cheese instead of regular cheese for a very heart-healthy entrée. Potatoes can be prepared a day ahead and kept covered with foil and refrigerated. They need only to be browned and stuffed before serving. *Serves 6.*

7 Gables Inn

Leicha and Paul Welton
PO Box 80488
Fairbanks, Alaska 99708
Tel: (907) 479-0751

ABOUT THE B&B

This 10,000 square foot Tudor-style house is located within walking distance of the University of Alaska Fairbanks campus, which is probably why 7 Gables began as a fraternity house. Its convenient location (between the airport and train station) is further enhanced by being right in the middle of a number of major attractions in the area: Riverboat Discovery, Pump House Restaurant, Cripple Creek Resort, University Museum, and Alaskaland. You enter the B&B through a floral solarium into a foyer with antique stained glass and indoor waterfall. Other features include cathedral ceilings, wine cellar, and wedding chapel. Some additional amenities include laundry facilities, Jacuzzis, cable TV and in-room phones, canoes, bikes, gourmet breakfasts, luggage or game storage, and library collection. Leicha enjoys cooking, music, hosting parties, and learning foreign languages, while Paul collects books and manages the inn's marketing and maintenance.

SEASON

all year

ACCOMMODATIONS

eight rooms with private baths; one room with shared bath

McKinley Breakfast

"This recipe is jokingly called the 'McKinley Breakfast' (after the mountain), which is derived from the peaks of the sandwich. It's an easy dish to fix and an interesting twist on the traditional ham and egg breakfast." — Leicha Welton

1 cup chopped ham
1 cup grated cheddar cheese
1 tablespoon Dijon mustard
¼ cup mayonnaise
6 slices whole wheat bread
3 eggs
1½ cups milk

In a medium bowl, combine the ham, cheese, mustard, and mayonnaise. Make 3 sandwiches with this ham mixture. Cut each sandwich diagonally into 4 triangular pieces. Place the sandwich pieces with their points sticking up (like mountain peaks) into a glass baking dish sprayed with non-stick cooking spray. In another bowl, combine the eggs and milk. Pour over the sandwich pieces, making sure that the bread has been soaked in the mixture. Refrigerate overnight. Remove from fridge ¾ hour before baking. Bake in a preheated 325°F oven for 40 minutes. *Serves 6.*

Michigan Week Eggs

"This recipe goes back 35 years, originating from a family friend who gave it to my parents, who gave it to me."
— *Larry Fuerst*

2 cans cream of chicken soup
¼ cup sherry
½ lb. sliced mushrooms
5 – 6 tablespoons butter
12 eggs
¾ lb. grated Romano cheese

Preheat oven to 350°F. Add sherry to chicken soup. Sauté mushrooms in butter. Soft scramble eggs and set aside. Put ¾ of soup mixture on bottom of a 13 x 9" pan. Add half the cheese, all the eggs, then the mushrooms. Cover with remaining soup and finish with the rest of the cheese. Bake for 40 – 45 minutes.
Serves 4 – 6.

Hidden Pond Bed & Breakfast

Priscilla and Larry Fuerst
PO Box 461
Fennville, Michigan 49408
Tel: (616) 561-2491

ABOUT THE B&B

Hidden Pond Bed & Breakfast is set on 28 acres of woods, perfect for bird-watching, hiking, cross-country skiing, or just relaxing in a rowboat on the pond. Guests can enjoy seven entry-level rooms, including bedrooms and baths, living room with fireplace, dining room, library, kitchen, and breakfast porch. Priscilla and Larry, who work for rival airlines, understand the importance of a soothing, calm, and slow-paced overnight stay. They enjoy pleasing guests and creating an atmosphere of quiet elegance. Unwind and take in the sun on the outdoor deck or patio. Turndown service, complimentary soft drinks, tea, hot chocolate, or an evening sherry is offered. Full hot breakfast is served in the sunwashed garden room at your leisure, and features fresh fruits, breads, muffins, and a hot entrée. This lovely retreat is near the beaches of Lake Michigan, the boutiques of Saugatuck, and the winery and cider mill in Fennville.

SEASON

all year

ACCOMMODATIONS

two rooms with private baths

Brambly Hedge Cottage

Jacquelyn Smyers
HCR 31, Box 39
Jasper, Arkansas 72641
Tel: 1-800-BRAMBLY or
(501) 446-5849

ABOUT THE B&B

"*A*bsolutely charming," wrote *National Geographic Traveler* of this old Ozark mountaintop farmhouse on scenic Highway 7, four miles south of Jasper, Arkansas. A Tennessee guest commented, "The place is uniquely beautiful, the food delicious, and the view inspiring." Three guest rooms with private baths reflect country French elegance in a homestead log cabin. A full breakfast is served on the deck overlooking Buffalo River Valley or behind the screened porch in rocking chairs. You're only minutes from the "Grand Canyon of the Ozarks," challenging-to-easy hiking trails, and canoeing on Buffalo National River. If art is more your style, you'll be happy to know that discriminating collectors still find the work of true artisans in the Jasper area. For those who wish to sample a night out on the town, Eureka Springs and Branson (Missouri) are nearby. Small group special-interest tours and relaxing massages can be arranged. Hostess Jacquelyn Smyers includes her handmade tatted lace and samovar collection in the decor. She's also a designer, commercial artist, and author of *Come For Tea* and the children's book *The Cloud That Came Into The Cabin* (inspired by the clouds on Sloan Mountain where Brambly Hedge is located).

SEASON

all year

ACCOMMODATIONS

three rooms with private baths

Ozarks Eggs Benedict

"This long-time holiday breakfast favorite of my mom's family looks beautiful, tastes great, and warmly satisfies. It's also the easiest breakfast I know how to make!"
— *Jacquelyn Smyers*

2 hard-boiled eggs
2 tablespoons butter
2 tablespoons all-purpose flour
¼ teaspoon salt (to taste)
¼ teaspoon pepper (to taste)
1 cup milk
¼ – ½ cup of ham pieces, crumbled crisp bacon, or cooked
    pork breakfast sausage bits (optional)
4 slices toasted bread
Mint sprigs

After hard-boiling eggs, peel, half, and separate yolks from whites. Grate the yolks into a dish and cut the whites into medium chunks in another dish. Melt butter over low heat. Add flour, stir to blend, then add salt and pepper. Add milk all at once, stirring well. Continue to stir over medium heat until sauce bubbles and gets thick. Add meat bits if you wish. Remove from heat; add egg white chunks. To serve: Toast 4 slices of bread. Place 2 on each of 2 plates. Spoon sauce across both slices and top with grated egg yolk. Garnish with mint sprigs. *Tip:* If sauce needs to be warmed in the microwave oven, be careful not to overdo it or the egg whites become terribly tough. *Serves 2+.*

Picture-Perfect Breakfast Pizza

1 each red, yellow, and green bell pepper, thinly sliced
1 medium onion, thinly sliced
1 cup diced ham
1½ tablespoons butter

Sauté the above ingredients in a skillet until the peppers and the onion become soft. Set aside.

Biscuit/pizza dough:
2 cups all-purpose flour
½ cup cold butter, cut into bits
1 tablespoon baking powder
Pinch of salt
1 cup light cream (half-and-half)

Topping:
6 medium eggs
2 cups shredded cheese (raw milk cheddar or any medium to
   sharp cheese)

(continued on next page)

Turtleback Farm Inn

Susan and William Fletcher
Route 1, Box 650
Eastsound (Orcas Island)
Washington 98245
Tel: (206) 376-4914

ABOUT THE B&B

Located on the loveliest of the San Juan Islands, Turtleback Farm Inn is noted for its detail-perfect restoration, elegantly comfortable and spotless rooms, glorious setting, and award-winning breakfasts. A perfect spot for a memorable getaway, you'll feel welcome and pampered by the warm hospitality of Susan and Bill Fletcher and their staff. A short ferry ride from Anacortes, Washington, Orcas Island is a haven for anyone who covets spectacular scenery, varied outdoor activities, unique shopping, and superb food. As spring turns into summer, the warm days encourage you to enjoy nature and island life at their best: Flowers are in full bloom, birds flutter, and whales, seals, and porpoise lazily coast through the shimmering waters of the Sound. After a day of hiking, fishing, bicycling, kayaking, sailing, windsurfing or just reading by the inn's pond, enjoy a relaxing soak in your private bath or a sherry on the deck overlooking the valley below. After a tasty dinner at one of the Island's many fine restaurants, snuggle down under one of the inn's custom-made woolen comforters and peacefully doze off — with visions of the delicious breakfast awaiting you in the morning.

SEASON

all year

ACCOMMODATIONS

seven rooms with private baths

Preheat oven to 425°F. In the work bowl of a food processor (using the steel blade), blend the dough's dry ingredients with the butter until the mixture resembles coarse meal. Add the cream through the feed tube and blend briefly until the dough begins to gather into a ball. Remove the dough and pat into a round on a floured board. Let rest a few minutes, then divide into 6 equal pieces. Roll each piece on the floured board into an 8" round. Pinch the outside edge up into a ½" rim around each circle. The diameter of each round will now be a little over 5". Transfer each round to a buttered cookie sheet, top with the pepper mixture, leaving a well in the center. Break a medium egg into each center and top with about ⅓ cup shredded cheese. Bake 15 minutes or until the eggs are set, then serve immediately. *Serves 6.*

Popeye's Morning

2 cans cream of potato soup
2 cups sour cream
4 10-oz. packages chopped spinach
1 cup grated Monterey Jack cheese
8 eggs

Preheat oven to 325°F. Mix soup and sour cream. Defrost spinach in the microwave oven; squeeze well. Add to soup mixture, mixing well. Divide equally into individual au gratin dishes. Make an indentation in the middle of the dish and break egg into space. Sprinkle with grated cheese. Bake until egg is set and spinach is bubbly (approximately 25 – 30 minutes). *Serves 8.*

The Oval Door

Judith McLane and
Dianne Feist
988 Lawrence Street
Eugene, Oregon 97401
Tel: (503) 683-3160

ABOUT THE B&B

This early 20th-century farmhouse-style home with a two-sided wraparound porch is actually newly built, yet its vintage 1920s design fits into the neighborhood so well that people are surprised to learn it was built circa 1990! Each of the four spacious guest rooms feature a private bath. In addition, guests can enjoy the Tub Room — a whirlpool bath for two, with bubbles, candles, and music. Newly decorated and inviting, the common living room has a fireplace and the library offers comfortable chairs to watch TV or VCR or browse through the travel books. Located just two blocks from the city's center, it's an easy walk to the Hult Center for the Performing Arts, many of Eugene's fine restaurants and shops, and a short drive to the University of Oregon. Guests enjoy a full breakfast served in the dining room. Extra touches include a terry robe, Perrier, and candies.

SEASON

all year

ACCOMMODATIONS

four rooms with private baths

Grandma's House
Bed & Breakfast

Hilda and Charlie Hickman
734 Pollard Road
Kodak, Tennessee 37764
Tel: (800) 676-3512 or
(615) 933-3512

ABOUT THE B&B

Grandma's House is located at the base of the Great Smoky Mountains National Park, minutes away from the resort cities of Pigeon Forge and Gatlinburg. On a quiet country lane that leads to the French Broad River, Grandma's House is in the center of all East Tennessee attractions, including Knoxville (site of the 1982 World's Fair), Oak Ridge (Atomic City), Norris (site of Tennessee's first dam), and Dandridge (second oldest city in Tennessee). The large colonial style, two-story house is decorated with antiques, crafts, and many interesting heirlooms. Three spotless guest rooms, each with a private bath, are on the second floor. A country "loosen your belt" breakfast is served around the big oak table each morning. Your hosts are both native East Tennesseans with lots of southern hospitality to share with their guests. The motto at Grandma's House is, "guests at first, friends that last."

SEASON

all year

ACCOMMODATIONS

three rooms with private baths

Pork in Milk Gravy

2 lb. pork tenderloin, cut ¾" thick
All-purpose flour for dredging
Salt and pepper to taste
2 tablespoons butter
2 cups milk

Trim excess fat from tenderloin. Dredge tenderloin with flour. Season with salt and pepper. Brown in butter at 350°F in electric skillet (or over medium to medium-high heat on stove). Reduce temperature to 225°F (or low to medium-low heat on stove); cover skillet. Cook for 30 minutes to 1 hour or until pork is tender. Add milk. Heat, uncovered, until bubbling hot and milk gravy is slightly thickened. Serve immediately. *Serves 6 – 8.*

Sausage Delights

1 cup biscuit mix
⅓ cup milk
2 tablespoons mayonnaise
1 lb. bulk pork breakfast sausage
1 large chopped onion
1 egg
4 ozs. chopped green chilies, drained
2 cups grated cojack cheese or medium cheddar cheese

Preheat oven to 350°F. Combine the biscuit mix, milk, and mayonnaise and spread evenly over the bottom of a greased and floured 13 x 9" pan. Brown the sausage and onion and drain well. Spread mixture evenly over the dough mixture. Combine the remaining ingredients well and spread over the top. Bake for 25 – 35 minutes. Let cool for 10 minutes and serve warm. *Serves 6 – 8.*

Snug Harbor Inn

Laurine "Sis" and Kenneth Hill
1226 West 10th Avenue
Anchorage, Alaska 99501
Tel: (907) 272-6249

ABOUT THE B&B

Snug Harbor Inn offers you cheerful comfort in a relaxed "home away from home" atmosphere, where absolute privacy is yours. Relax while surrounded by antiques, art, Alaskan artifacts, and period furnishings. Accommodations feature handmade quilts and some have their own private entrance. Fully equipped kitchen, complimentary coffee, tea, and hot chocolate available 24 hours a day, color TV, and complimentary bicycles are at your disposal. The friendly, efficient staff has your every comfort in mind, making Snug Harbor the first choice for the business and pleasure traveler. Located in the heart of Anchorage, Snug Harbor is just four blocks from the central business district, and close to shopping, entertainment, fine dining, and sightseeing. The trail head for Anchorage's extensive bicycle and jogging paths is also nearby.

SEASON

all year

ACCOMMODATIONS

four rooms with private baths; two rooms with shared bath

Hutton House

Loretta Murray and
Dean Ahren
PO Box 88, Route 250/219
Huttonsville, West Virginia
26273
Tel: (304) 335-6701

ABOUT THE B&B

Majestically situated above the tiny town of Huttonsville, this meticulously restored turn-of-the-century Queen Anne Victorian commands a broad view of the Tygart River Valley and the Laurel Mountains. Hutton House, which is listed in the National Register of Historic Places, features original oak woodwork, ornate windows, a three-story turret, arched pocket doors, wraparound porch, and a winding staircase. Antiques abound, and each of the guest rooms is furnished in its own individual style. Breakfast is a time to get to know your hosts and the other guests, while enjoying a variety of pancakes, French toast, and egg dishes along with fresh fruit, crème brulée, sorbet, or even porridge. Guests can then relax on the porch, play games on the lawn, or take a leisurely hike on the trail behind the house. Nearby attractions include Cass Railroad, National Radio Observatory, underground caverns, and rock climbing.

SEASON

all year

ACCOMMODATIONS

six rooms with private baths

Sausage Madeira

10 – 12" hot Italian sausage
¼ cup Madeira wine
2 tablespoons butter
1 – 2 carrots
½ medium onion (preferably sweet)

Fry the sausage thoroughly and let brown on all sides (this can be done the night before); set aside. Pour the sausage oil off of the pan. Deglaze the pan with the wine and butter, and cook until bubbly. Thinly slice the carrot and onion. Add to the pan and cook until carrots are soft but crisp and onion is getting clear. Slice sausage and add to pan, and heat all together. Serve immediately. *Serves 2.*

Sausage Soufflé

1 lb. pork breakfast sausage, cooked, drained, and crumbled
8-oz. can sliced mushrooms
2 large sliced onions
16 slices whole wheat bread, crusts removed
1 lb. grated sharp cheese
5 eggs
2 cups milk
¼ teaspoon ground nutmeg
1 teaspoon dry mustard

Cook sausage in a large skillet. When cooked, drain, crumble, and set aside. Sauté mushrooms and onions together, then add to sausage. Butter a 13 x 9" soufflé baking dish. Line it with bread. Layer half of sausage mixture over top bread, then layer half of grated cheese over sausage mixture. Again, layer bread, rest of sausage mixture, and rest of cheese, ending with a last layer of bread. Beat together the eggs, milk, nutmeg, and mustard together, then pour over bread in dish. Refrigerate for 24 hours. Remove from fridge ¾ hour before baking. Bake in a preheated 350°F oven for 1 hour or until a knife inserted in the center comes out clean. *Serves 12 – 16.*

1880 House

Elsie Collins
2 Seafield Lane, PO Box 648
Westhampton Beach, New York
11978
Tel: (800) 346-3290 or
(516) 288-1559

ABOUT THE B&B

Tucked away in the village of Westhampton Beach stands 1880 House, a bed and breakfast country retreat that's the perfect place for a romantic hideaway, a weekend of privacy, or just a change of pace from city life. Only 90 minutes from Manhattan, 1880 House is ideally situated on Westhampton Beach's exclusive Seafield Lane. Amenities include a swimming pool and tennis court and you're only a short, brisk walk to the ocean beach. Long a popular summer resort area, the Hamptons will more than satisfy your penchant for antique-hunting, and also offer many outstanding restaurants and shops. Indoor tennis facilities are available locally and Guerney's International Health Spa and scenic area of Montauk Point are nearby. 1880 House is not just a rural retreat but a home lovingly preserved by Mrs. Elsie Collins and filled with her antiques and personal touches.

SEASON

all year

ACCOMMODATIONS

three suites with private baths

The Rosewood Mansion Inn

Lynn and David Hausner
54 North Hood Street
Peru, Indiana 46970
Tel: (317) 472-7051

ABOUT THE B&B

Built by Elbert Shirk in 1872, *The Rosewood Mansion Inn is a lovely Victorian home situated near the downtown area of Peru, Indiana. The mansion has 19 rooms, including eight bedrooms, each with private bath. As a welcome change from impersonal hotel or motel accommodations, the inn offers the warmth and friendliness of home, coupled with the privacy and elegance of a fine hotel — a combination that makes for a truly unique experience. Enjoy the warmth of the oak panel library, the splendor of the three-story staircase with stained glass windows, the elegance of the Victorian parlor, or the comfort and charm of your room. Consider Rosewood Mansion for your next romantic getaway, anniversary, party, business meeting, or corporate retreat. Nearby points of interest include Mississinewa Reservoir (featuring boating, fishing, hiking, picnicking, and water skiing), Miami County Museum, International Circus Hall of Fame, Cole Porter's home and burial site, tennis, golf, and antique shops.*

SEASON

all year

ACCOMMODATIONS

eight rooms with private baths

Sausage Strudel

3 lbs. bulk sage sausage
2 chopped onions
3 lbs. mushrooms
1½ cups cream cheese
20 leaves phyllo dough (5 per strudel)
½ cup butter

Preheat oven to 400°F. Fry sausage and put in a large bowl. Fry onions and mushrooms until just dry. Add to bowl. Mix in cream cheese. Layer 5 phyllo leaves with butter and roll with ¼ of sausage mixture. Repeat with remaining phyllo leaves. Bake for 25 minutes. Brush with butter before baking. Makes 4 strudels. *Serves 20.*

Scalloped Turkey

(Recipe from Favorites from the Lazy Bee.)

"As a young Air Force wife, I wrote articles for a Texas newspaper. Even then, as a budding cook, I was beginning my recipe collection of American basics. This was the result of one of my features for the Denison Herald and a fine recipe to make with leftover turkey." — Jo Ann Bender

2 cups cooked turkey, cubed
2 cups turkey broth
2 tablespoons all-purpose flour
2 tablespoons shortening
3 cups bread crumbs
⅓ cup melted butter
1 teaspoon powdered sage
¼ cup milk
¼ teaspoon salt
1 tablespoon chopped onions
Parsley

Preheat oven to 350°F. Place turkey chunks in a buttered 12 x 9" baking dish. Make gravy from broth, flour, and shortening (or use leftover gravy). Mix remaining ingredients together lightly and spread evenly over the turkey chunks. Pour gravy over the top. Bake for about 30 minutes until cooked through and lightly browned. Cut in squares and garnish with parsley, if desired. Serve with mashed potatoes. *Serves 12.*

Hillside House Bed & Breakfast

Jo Ann, Bud, and Sue
1729 East 18th Street
Spokane, Washington 99203
Tel: (509) 534-1426 during the day or (509) 535-1893 during nights and weekends

ABOUT THE B&B

*S*ituated on the South Hill of Spokane, Hillside House offers exquisite hospitality in a country setting that's only three miles from downtown. Overlooking city and mountains, this cozy and tastefully decorated house features antiques, including linens and dishes, and rooms with views. Your hosts Bud, Jo Ann, and Sue are third generation B&B innkeepers — Jo Ann's mother helped her mother host guests in 1916 in Rush City, Minnesota. Bud owns an engineering firm and lectures nationally to the construction/ engineering industry, while Jo Ann operates a marketing firm. They enjoy cooking (having published a cookbook of their own), entertaining, and guiding guests to the area's most exciting places and events. Bud and Jo Ann also operate the Lazy Bee, a remote getaway near the Canadian border where they lead jeep safaris in the mountains.

SEASON

all year

ACCOMMODATIONS

two rooms with shared bath

The Ancient Pines B&B

Genevieve Simmens
2015 Parley Street
Nauvoo, Illinois 62354
Tel: (217) 453-2767

ABOUT THE B&B

Surrounded by 140-year-old evergreens, this turn-of-the century home features exquisite exterior brick detailing, stained glass windows, and etched glass front door — all part of the original construction. Pressed tin ceilings, carved woodwork, an open staircase, claw-foot tubs, and lovingly decorated bedrooms grace the interior. You can relax on the front veranda and watch the workers at the nearby winery or find seclusion on the side porch. There are herb and flower gardens to wander in, a lawn for croquet, and a library for playing chess or music. When day is done, you'll drift off in clean, comfortable beds, lulled to sleep by the whispering pines, then awake to the smell of baking bread. A heart-healthy menu can be provided upon request.

SEASON

all year

ACCOMMODATIONS

three rooms with shared baths

Scrambled Eggs with Ham and Onions

1 tablespoon butter
1 medium onion, sliced thin
8-oz. cubed ham (not canned variety)
8 beaten eggs
¼ cup milk

Brush skillet with butter. Add onion and sauté covered for 5 minutes. Add ham and cook 5 minutes, stirring constantly. Combine beaten eggs with milk, then add to skillet. Cook, stirring, until done but still soft (do not brown). *Serves 6.*

The Ancient Pines

Southern Sausage Grits Casserole

1 lb. bulk pork breakfast sausage
3 cups hot cooked grits
2½ cups shredded cheddar cheese
3 tablespoons butter or margarine
3 beaten eggs
1½ cups milk
Pimiento strips (optional)
Parsley (optional)

Preheat oven to 350°F. In a heavy skillet, cook sausage until browned; drain well. Spoon sausage into a lightly greased 13 x 9 x 2" baking dish. Combine hot grits, cheese, and butter. Stir until cheese and butter melt. Combine eggs and milk; stir into grits. Pour over sausage. Bake for 1 hour. Garnish with pimiento strips and parsley, if desired. *Tip:* This can be made and refrigerated overnight. Remove from fridge ¾ hour before baking and follow above directions. *Serves 15.*

Historic Oakwood Bed and Breakfast

Naomi and Al Kline
715 East North Street
Talladega, Alabama 35160
Tel: (205) 362-0662

ABOUT THE B&B

Built in 1847, this antebellum home is listed on the National Register of Historic Places and furnished with many heirloom antiques. The house was commissioned by Andrew Bowie, the first mayor of Talladega. Enjoy browsing through the antique stores in the area, visiting the International Motorsports Hall of Fame, or exploring the lovely DeSoto Caverns. A public golf course and tennis courts and beautiful Cheaha Mountain State Park are nearby. The hearty breakfast your hosts serve features home-made biscuits and southern grits. Al and Naomi are musicians; Al is a retired operatic tenor and Naomi a pianist and organist. Traveling businesspeople and vacationers alike will enjoy this retreat into the quiet elegance of a bygone era.

SEASON

all year

ACCOMMODATIONS

one room with private bath;
two rooms with shared bath

Holden House — 1902 Bed & Breakfast Inn

Sallie and Welling Clark
1102 West Pikes Peak Avenue
Colorado Springs, Colorado
80904
Tel: (719) 471-3980

ABOUT THE B&B

*E*xperience the romance of the past with the comforts of today at Holden House — 1902 Bed & Breakfast Inn. This storybook Victorian and carriage house filled with antiques and family heirlooms is located in a residential area near the historic district and central to the Pikes Peak region. Enjoy the front parlor, living room with a fireplace and wingback chairs, or the wide veranda with mountain views. Immaculate guest rooms boast queen-size beds, down pillows, and private baths, while honeymoon suites feature "tubs for two" and fireplaces. Enjoy complimentary refreshments, home-made cookies, and friendly resident cats "Mingtoy" and "Muffin."

SEASON

all year

ACCOMMODATIONS

six rooms with private baths

Southwestern Eggs Fiesta

12 eggs
3 snack-size flour tortillas (6" diameter)
6 ozs. cheddar cheese slices
Crumbled cooked turkey bacon or bacon bits
Cilantro (also known as coriander)
Sour cream
Mild picante sauce
Parsley

Preheat oven to 375°F. Well grease 6 individual soufflé dishes (5 – 8 oz. size) with non-stick cooking spray and break 2 eggs into each dish. Slice tortillas in half and place around the insides of the soufflé dishes (a half tortilla per dish). Top with 1-oz. slice of cheddar cheese and crumbled bacon or bacon bits, then sprinkle with a dash of cilantro. Bake for 30 minutes or until eggs are done, cheese is melted, and tortilla is slightly brown. Top with a dab of sour cream and teaspoon of mild picante sauce. Sprinkle a dash of cilantro on top and serve on a plate. Garnish with parsley if desired. *Tip:* Recipe can be easily adapted to make additional servings by following a ratio of 2 eggs and 1-oz. slice cheese per person, and 1 tortilla for 2 persons. *Serves 6.*

Spiced Bacon

1 cup brown sugar
1 teaspoon ground cinnamon
3 tablespoons water
1 lb. bacon

Mix brown sugar, cinnamon, and water into a thick syrup. Layer bacon with paper towels in a microwave-safe dish. Cook half the normal time, according to your microwave oven's instructions. Remove and blot on a clean paper towel. Wash and dry dish. Arrange half-cooked bacon in a single layer in dish (without paper towels). Brush with cinnamon mixture. Return to microwave oven and finish cooking. Drain on pastry rack set in baking sheet. Hold in warm oven until ready to serve. *Serves 4 – 6.*

New Berne House Inn

Marcia Drum and
Howard Bronson
709 Broad Street
New Bern, North Carolina
28560
Tel: (800) 842-7688 or
(919) 636-2250

ABOUT THE B&B

New Berne House Inn is centrally located in the Colonial town of New Bern and within comfortable walking distance of numerous historic sights, highlighted by Tryon Palace and its formal gardens, only one block away. Quaint shops, fine restaurants, and historic buildings are all in the neighborhood. New Berne House's seven guest rooms feature queen- and king-size beds, antiques and collectibles, private baths, and telephones and clock radios, along with other amenities to pamper guests. A full breakfast is served in the dining room from 8:00 to 9:00 a.m., but coffee is available as early as 6:30 a.m. Throughout the day, guests are invited to join the innkeepers in the library or parlor for light refreshments, television, and good conversation. Two weekends each month are reserved for a "juicy" who-done-it Mystery Package, which blends in nicely with the Inn's two haunted rooms (where "odd occurrences" have been reported over the years!).

SEASON

all year

ACCOMMODATIONS

seven rooms with private baths

Durbin Street Inn B&B

Sherry and Don Frigon
843 South Durbin Street
Casper, Wyoming 82601
Tel: (307) 577-5774

ABOUT THE B&B

Built in 1917, *Durbin Street Inn is a large two-story American foursquare* located in Casper's historic district that prides itself on good food and a friendly atmosphere. Choose from four large non-smoking guest rooms with shared baths, including queen-size or double beds, robes, and one with a fireplace. Or, you can choose the non-smoking guest room with private bath, small sitting room, and fridge. Awake to a full country breakfast where scrambled eggs, bacon, sausage, hash browns, fruit juice, home-made jams, and such specialties as honey-wheat pancakes, biscuits and gravy, scones, brunch omelet torte, spicy sausage and potatoes, and roast beef hash are served family-style. After breakfast, gather in the common room with fireplace, or enjoy the deck, patio, and flower and vegetable gardens. Nearby are walking/hiking/cycling trails, river rafting and canoeing, covered wagon and horseback trips along Oregon Trail, golfing, skiing, museums, historic sites, Fort Casper, Independence Rock, Devil's Gate, Hell's Half Acre, boating, swimming, fishing, shopping, and craft shops.

SEASON

all year

ACCOMMODATIONS

four rooms with shared baths;
one room with private bath

Spicy Sausage and Potatoes

1½ lb. (about 6 links) mild Italian sausage, cut into 1" pieces and marinated overnight in ½ cup Chianti wine (or Johnsonville Italianti Sausage, which is already marinated with Chianti wine)
10 small new red potatoes, quartered
½ teaspoon pepper
½ teaspoon dried thyme leaves
1 clove minced garlic
1 cup red onions, sliced ⅛" thick
¼ cup chopped fresh parsley
1 green bell pepper, cut into 1" pieces

In a 10" skillet, combine sausage, potatoes, pepper, thyme, and garlic. Cook over medium-high heat, stirring occasionally until potatoes are browned (10 – 12 minutes). Reduce heat to medium-low. Cover and cook until potatoes are tender (8 – 10 minutes). Stir in remaining ingredients. Continue cooking, uncovered, until vegetables are crisply tender (4 – 5 minutes). Serve with scrambled eggs, fresh garden tomatoes in season, and wheat scones or corn bread. *Tip:* Use a cast-iron skillet and serve from it. *Serves 6.*

Sunday Soufflé

5 – 6 slices French bread, cubed
2 cups grated cheddar cheese
½ cup cubed ham or bulk pork breakfast sausage (optional)
4 eggs
1 teaspoon Worcestershire sauce
2 cups milk

Cover the bottom of a buttered 1½-quart baking dish with half
of the bread cubes. Alternate layers of bread and cheese (and
ham or sausage if you wish), ending with a top layer of cheese.
Combine the remaining ingredients until well blended and pour
over the dry mixture. Refrigerate overnight. Bring the dish to
room temperature and bake in a preheated 350°F oven for
1 hour or until golden brown. *Serves 6 – 8.*

Snug Harbor Inn

Laurine "Sis" and Kenneth Hill
1226 West 10th Avenue
Anchorage, Alaska 99501
Tel: (907) 272-6249

ABOUT THE B&B

Snug Harbor Inn offers you
cheerful comfort in a relaxed
"home away from home"
atmosphere, where absolute privacy
is yours. Relax while surrounded by
antiques, art, Alaskan artifacts, and
period furnishings. Accommodations feature handmade quilts and
some have their own private
entrance. Fully equipped kitchen,
complimentary coffee, tea, and hot
chocolate available 24 hours a day,
color TV, and complimentary
bicycles are at your disposal. The
friendly, efficient staff has your
every comfort in mind, making
Snug Harbor the first choice for the
business and pleasure traveler.
Located in the heart of Anchorage,
Snug Harbor is just four blocks
from the central business district,
and close to shopping, entertainment, fine dining, and sightseeing.
The trail head for Anchorage's
extensive bicycle and jogging paths
is also nearby.

SEASON

all year

ACCOMMODATIONS

four rooms with private baths;
two rooms with shared bath

Carole and Mill Seaman
35 Centennial Drive
Custer, South Dakota 57730
Tel: (605) 673-3333

ABOUT THE B&B

This unusual 1891 Victorian Gothic home, which has quite a historic past in Custer, is now on the National Register of Historic Places. Antique light fixtures, ceiling fans, door transoms, stained glass windows, and "gingerbread" accents help preserve Custer Mansion's turn-of-the-century mood. Six lovely bedrooms are individually decorated in country and Victorian flavor and are named for songs. Delicious home-cooked breakfasts are served in the spacious dining room, with adjacent butler pantry used for serving juice, coffee, and tea. The one-acre yard offers plenty of room for outdoor relaxing and features a shaded patio near a natural rocky hillside. Custer Mansion is located near Mt. Rushmore, town of Crazy Horse, Custer State Park, and many other attractions. Nearby activities include swimming, hiking, fishing, golfing, and hiking in the beautiful Black Hills. Mill, a retired school administrator, and Carole, mother of six and grandmother of twelve, specialize in western hospitality and delicious food.

SEASON

all year

ACCOMMODATIONS

two rooms with private baths; four rooms with shared baths

Tex-Mex Eggs

"Light, delicious, and different, this recipe originates from a southwestern B&B." — Carole Seaman

6 large eggs
½ cup cream
¼ teaspoon salt
⅛ teaspoon pepper
4-oz. can chopped green chilies, drained
1 cup shredded cheddar cheese

Preheat oven to 325°F. Lightly oil a 9" square pan or baking dish. Beat eggs well. Add cream, salt, pepper, and chilies. Put cheese in the bottom of the pan and pour egg mixture over it. Bake for 25 minutes or until set. *Serves 6.*

Vegetable Cheese Soufflé

¼ cup butter or margarine
¼ cup all-purpose flour
½ teaspoon salt
Dash of cayenne pepper
1 cup milk
8 ozs. grated sharp cheddar cheese
3 egg yolks
6 – 8 sliced mushrooms
2 tablespoons diced red bell peppers
½ cup diced broccoli or asparagus tips
2 teaspoons olive oil
6 egg whites
Confectioners' sugar

Preheat oven to 400°F. To make roux: Melt butter, then blend in flour, salt, and cayenne pepper. Add milk all at once. Cook over medium heat until mixture thickens and bubbles. Remove from heat. Add cheese, and stir until melted. Beat egg yolks in a separate bowl until thick and lemon colored. Slowly add to cheese mixture, stirring constantly. Reserve, cover, and keep warm. Sauté mushrooms, red peppers, and broccoli or asparagus tips in olive oil, and reserve.

Beat egg whites to stiff peaks. In a mixing bowl, add 2 cups roux to vegetables and fold in egg whites. Pour into an ungreased soufflé dish or individual ramekins. Bake in a hot water bath for 15 – 20 minutes or until "top hat" is lightly browned. Sprinkle with confectioners' sugar and serve immediately. *Serves 6.*

Blue Harbor House, A Village Inn

Jody Schmoll and
Dennis Hayden
67 Elm Street
Camden, Maine 04843
Tel: (800) 248-3196 or
(207) 236-3196

ABOUT THE B&B

A classic village inn on the Maine Coast, the Blue Harbor House welcomes guests to relax in a restored 1810 Cape where yesterday's charms blend perfectly with today's comforts. The beautiful town of Camden, renowned for its spectacular setting where the mountains meet the sea, is just outside the door. The inn's bright and inviting guest rooms surround you with country antiques and hand-fashioned quilts — several even have canopy beds and whirlpool tubs. Breakfasts feature such specialties as lobster quiche, cheese soufflé, and blueberry pancakes with blueberry butter. As for dinner, guests can arrange to have a romantic candle-lit affair or an old-fashioned down-east lobster feed.

SEASON

all year

ACCOMMODATIONS

eight rooms with private baths; two carriage-house suites with private baths

The Red Violet Inn

Ruth and John Hanrahan
344 North 2nd Street
Raton, New Mexico 87740
Tel: (800) 624-9778 or
(505) 445-9778

ABOUT THE B&B

Follow the Sante Fe Trail and step back into the past at this appealing 1902 red brick Victorian home, three blocks from Raton's historic downtown. Guests have use of the parlor, dining room, porches, and flower-filled yard, and are invited to enjoy the classical music during the social hour from 5:30 – 6:30 p.m. Full breakfast is served in the formal dining room, accompanied by friendly conversation. A theater and gallery are within a few blocks, hiking and fishing facilities (at Surarite State Park) are just 10 miles away, and Capulin Volcano National Monument is less than 30 minutes away. Other area attractions include a golf course, several antique shops, and a museum. Red Violet is a non-smoking inn.

SEASON

all year

ACCOMMODATIONS

two rooms with private baths; two rooms with shared bath

Veggie Eggs Benedict

1 chopped red bell pepper
1 chopped green bell pepper
1 chopped yellow bell pepper
1 chopped red onion
2 tablespoons olive oil

Sauce:
2 tablespoons butter
2 tablespoons all-purpose flour
⅛ teaspoon white pepper
½ teaspoon salt
1 cup milk
2 large egg yolks
⅓ cup shredded Swiss cheese
2 teaspoons lemon juice
1 teaspoon Dijon mustard

3 English muffins
6 large poached eggs
¼ cup grated Parmesan cheese
Paprika

Sauté peppers and onion in olive oil until crisp and tender. Keep warm. In a saucepan, melt butter using a whisk. Blend in flour, pepper, and salt. Cook over medium heat until smooth (about 1 minute). Add milk and bring mixture to a boil, stirring constantly. When it thickens, remove from heat. In a separate bowl, blend a bit of the hot mixture into the egg yolks, then add egg mixture to the saucepan. Blend well, cooking about 1 minute. Add Swiss cheese and cook until cheese melts. Remove from heat. Stir in lemon juice and mustard. Spoon cooked pepper mixture onto toasted English muffin half. Top with poached egg and sauce. Sprinkle with Parmesan cheese and paprika. *Serves 6.*

Vermont Cheddar Pie

"Eggs gathered each morning from Mark's chickens make this a special dish at the Grünberg Haus."
— Christopher Sellers

2½ cups diced parboiled potatoes
½ cup chopped onions
1 teaspoon salt-free lemon-herb seasoning
½ teaspoon garlic powder
⅓ cup chopped steamed spinach
⅓ cup crumbled feta cheese
¼ cup freshly grated Romano cheese
1 cup grated white cheddar cheese
2 eggs
½ cup low-fat milk
Parsley flakes
Paprika

Preheat oven to 350°F. Grease a glass pie plate. Combine potatoes and ¼ cup onions, and press into pie plate as a crust. Sprinkle with seasoning and garlic powder. Carefully put a layer of spinach and crumbled feta cheese into the crust, then top with Romano, then cheddar cheese. Combine eggs and milk, and pour carefully over cheeses. To garnish the pie, make a small circle of ¼ cup onions in center of pie, sprinkle parsley flakes in a larger circle around the onions, and sprinkle paprika in a larger circle around parsley flake circle. Bake for 1 hour. *Serves 6.*

Grünberg Haus Bed & Breakfast
Waterbury, Vermont

Grünberg Haus Bed and Breakfast

Christopher Sellers and
Mark Frohman, RR2,
Box 1595RD, Route 100 South
Waterbury, Vermont 05676-9621
Tel: (800) 800-7760 (reservations)
or (802) 244-7726

ABOUT THE B&B

This picture-postcard Austrian-style B&B is tucked away on a secluded hillside in Vermont's Green Mountains, perfectly situated for visits to Stowe, Montpelier, Waterbury, and Burlington. Individually decorated guest rooms open onto the carved wood balcony, which offers wonderful views from the stucco and wood-trimmed chalet. The giant stone fireplace and wood stove in the BYOB pub are favorite gathering places. After hiking or cross-country skiing on the inn's trails, help Mark feed the chickens and enjoy a full, musical breakfast, with selections such as maple-poached pears, apple and cheddar muffins, and ricotta-stuffed French toast. The evening fire warms up the grand piano where you're likely to hear innkeeper Chris playing anything from Mozart to Phantom of the Opera. Nearby activities include spectacular autumn leaf-picking, world-class downhill skiing, golf, boating, bicycling, gliding, canoeing, antique hunting, outlet shopping, and touring Ben & Jerry's ice cream factory. And you can enjoy the Grünberg Haus's own Jacuzzi, sauna, tennis courts, cross-country ski center, and hiking trails.

SEASON

all year

ACCOMMODATIONS

six rooms with private baths;
five rooms with shared baths;
three cabins and one carriage
house with private baths

The Manor at Taylor's Store B&B Country Inn

Mary Lynn and Lee Tucker
Route 1, Box 533
Smith Mountain Lake, Virginia
24184
Tel: (800) 248-6267 or
(703) 721-3951

ABOUT THE B&B

The Manor at Taylor's Store is an enchanting, historic 120-acre estate in the picturesque foothills of the Blue Ridge Mountains. Guests enjoy luxurious accommodations in the elegant plantation home replete with antiques. Special amenities include a hot tub, exercise room, billiard room, large-screen TV with movies, guest kitchen, and porches and fireplaces throughout. There are six private, spring-fed ponds on the property for swimming, fishing, and canoeing. Nearby, Smith Mountain Lake offers additional recreational opportunities. All guests are treated to a heart-healthy gourmet breakfast in the formal dining room with panoramic views of the countryside. Warm, southern hospitality has made The Manor at Taylor's Store one of the best-known B&B inns in Virginia.

SEASON

all year

ACCOMMODATIONS

six suites with private baths;
one cottage for families/groups
with private bath

Virginia Ham Breakfast Soufflé

1 lb. Virginia ham sausage or turkey sausage
4 chopped green onions
1 – 2 cloves minced garlic
2 8-oz cartons egg substitute
1 cup skim milk
¼ teaspoon salt
¼ teaspoon ground red pepper (cayenne)
¾ teaspoon powdered mustard
½ cup grated sharp cheddar cheese
6 slices whole wheat bread, cubed
Vegetable oil cooking spray

Cook first 3 ingredients in a large skillet until sausage is browned, stirring until sausage crumbles. Drain. Rinse sausage with hot water, drain well, and press between layers of paper towels. Set aside. Combine egg substitute and next 4 ingredients in a large bowl. Stir in sausage mixture, cheese, and bread cubes. Spoon into 10 6-oz. ramekins or custard cups coated with cooking spray, then cover and chill 8 hours. Remove from refrigerator 30 minutes before baking. Preheat oven to 350°F. Bake uncovered for 30 minutes or until set. Serve immediately. *Makes 10 servings.*

THE MANOR AT TAYLOR'S STORE

Zucchini-Turkey Sausage Split

"Serve this tasty recipe for brunch, with soup or salad for lunch, or cut into quarters as hors d'oeuvres." — Helen King

1 lb. finely chopped zucchini squash
1 chopped onion
14-oz. carton fresh salsa
1 lb. grated cheddar cheese
1 cup mayonnaise
½ cup Parmesan cheese
1 lb. cooked and crumbled turkey sausage
2 beaten eggs
¼ cup fresh chopped parsley
2 cups bread or cracker crumbs
Seasonings: salt, pepper, 1 teaspoon oregano, or chopped fresh
    herbs to taste
English muffin halves or corn biscuits (Orowheat Australian
    biscuits recommended)

Mix all ingredients together and spoon over split English muffins or corn biscuits. Broil until golden and serve hot.
Serves 12 – 24 (more as hors d'oeuvres).

The Babbling Brook Inn

Helen King
1025 Laurel Street
Santa Cruz, California 95060
Tel: (800) 866-1131 or
(408) 427-2437

ABOUT THE B & B

Cascading waterfalls, a meandering creek, and a romantic gazebo grace an acre of gardens, pines, and redwoods surrounding this secluded inn. Built in 1909 on the foundation of an 1870 tannery, a 1790 grist mill, and a 2000-year old Indian fishing village, the Babbling Brook features rooms in country French decor, all with private bath, telephone, and television, and most with cozy fireplace, private deck, and outside entrance. Included in your stay is a large, country breakfast and afternoon wine and cheese, where Helen's prize-winning cookies await you on the tea cart in front of a roaring fireplace. Two blocks off Highway 1, the Babbling Brook is within walking distance to the beach, wharf, boardwalk, shops, tennis, running paths, and historic homes. Three golf courses and 200 restaurants are within 15 minutes' drive. A world record-holding angler, Mrs. Pacific Palisades 1955, one-time international tour organizer, and mother of six, Helen King has happily found her niche as a gourmet cook and owner/ innkeeper of this award-winning B&B.

SEASON

all year

ACCOMMODATIONS

12 rooms with private baths

Index

Index

*M*akes a unique gift!

Purchase through your local bookstore or send form along with check or money order to:

Callawind Publications Inc.
3383 Sources Boulevard, Suite 205
Dollard-des-Ormeaux, Quebec, Canada
H9B 1Z8

OR

Callawind Publications Inc.
2083 Hempstead Turnpike, Suite 355
East Meadow, New York 11554-1730
USA

You may return books *in original condition* **at any time for a full refund on the purchase price.**

Qty	Description	Total
	Rise & Dine: Savory Secrets from America's Bed & Breakfast Inns @ US$14.95 / C$19.95 **each.**	
	Shipping: Surface mail @ US$3.95 / C$4.95 **for 1 book. US$0.80 / C$1.00 for each additional book** (allow 2 – 4 weeks for delivery).	
	7% GST sales tax (Canadian orders only).	
	Resellers: Please call (514) 685-9109 for more information. *Important: Prices subject to change without notice.*	_____

Name _____   Tel. _____

Address _____

City _____ State/Prov. _____ Zip/Postal code_____

Payment enclosed: ❑ **Check (payable to Callawind Publications)**   ❑ **Money order**

To help us better understand our readers, kindly provide the following information:

Where did you first see this book? _____

Are you buying it for yourself or as a gift? _____

Comments about the book _____

_____

Questions? Call (514) 685-9109 or send e-mail to callawind@accent.net